Jewish FAQs

Jewish FAQs

---

*An Internet Rabbi's Answers
to Frequently Asked Questions
about Judaism*

Rabbi Daniel Kohn

To order additional copies of this book, contact:
Xlibris Corporation
1-888-795-4274
www.Xlibris.com
Orders@Xlibris.com
39497

Contents

This book is dedicated to all of the students that I have ever taught, adults and youth, whether in person or via e-mail over the past twenty-five years. Just remember, the questions are always more important than the answers!

Acknowledgments

I'd like to thank everyone at Xlibris who helped in the production of this book, especially Katy Anne Rosell and Charisse Desabelle who meticulously checked the manuscript and made excellent suggestions for improving it. I'd also like to thank Rhea Villacarlos, Charliz Elle, Jo Arciaga, Liz Actub and many others who helped shepard my manuscript through the publishing process.

Thanks to Victoria Remler (www.victoriaremeler.com) for the author's photo.

I would like to also thank Lauren Hawley who read an early manuscript and made some invaluable suggestions.

All quotes and translations from traditional Hebrew texts—such as the Hebrew Bible, the Talmud, and various works of Midrashic literature—are entirely my own. While my command of Hebrew and Aramaic is by no means perfect, I may have possibly made some mistakes or mistranslations, and they are also my own.

Although there are many different spelling conventions for representing the Hebrew guttural sound that is similar to the last sound as in the name of the composer Bach, I have chosen to represent this sound in all English transliterations of Hebrew words as "ch." The only exception is the word "Chanukkah," which for idiosyncratic reasons I consistently spelled as "Hanukkah."

Usually in works of Judaic, Hebrew words are presented in italics the first time they are used to indicate that they are from a foreign language. However, there may be no "first" time a reader encounters such a Hebrew word due to the question-and-answer format of the book. Therefore, *no* Hebrew words are in italics rather all appear with capital letters. Most are translated and explained in context. However, for a complete listing of such terms, please refer to the "Glossary of Hebrew Words and Concepts" in the back.

Official disclaimer: I have no official or even informal connection with America Online or any of its affiliates online or elsewhere, nor do I even continue to serve as a volunteer answering "Ask a Rabbi" questions anymore either for AOL or any online entity. I don't even use AOL as my Internet service provider! This book is not an official product of America Online, nor do any of the questions or answers represent the views or opinions of AOL. This book is solely a personal venture and represents no one except my own idiosyncratic opinions and individual scholarship as a rabbi. In addition, the e-mail questions that appear in this book have been highly edited and rewritten so as to protect the privacy of the questioners and obscure all identifying information. The answers have also been updated and revised. So if you sent an e-mail to AOL's "Ask a Rabbi" service years ago and think that I might have been the one who answered your question and you suspect that maybe that e-mail correspondence is now part of this book and for some reason you are unhappy about that despite the fact that no one else will know that it was you, I want to apologize in advance and reassure you that I don't even have any identifying or contact information for any of the original e-mail questioners anymore to share with anyone else. So rest assured your identity is safe forever!

Introduction

Around 1995, I received a fairly innocuous e-mail asking if I wanted to volunteer some of my time each week and help kick off a new online service for America Online called "Ask a Rabbi." At that time, AOL was aggressively expanding its customer base as the Internet was becoming more popular, and AOL was exploring new and different content areas to attract niche markets. Being fairly new to the Internet and e-mail myself, I was intrigued and responded favorably. Little did I anticipate the incredible experience that lay in store for me.

Debuting as a feature of AOL's "Jewish Community Online," approximately twenty rabbis—covering the spectrum of American denominations of Judaism—answered the call and became the initial, original volunteer staff of "Ask a Rabbi." After several weeks, however, I had almost forgotten that I had signed up to answer questions because I did not receive a single e-mail question from "Ask a Rabbi." However, word of this new service began to slowly spread all over the growing AOL online community; for little by little, my online mailbox began to fill up with e-mail questions sent to me via this new service. Over time, I ended up devoting several hours a day to answering the many questions I received. I was later told by one of the coordinators of this service that for several years I actually was answering the lion's share of the e-mail questions that began to pour in because, apparently, people liked my style and began to send questions addressed specifically to me. I was developing a fan base!

I loved the challenge of answering questions that covered a wide range of Jewish subjects. I was able to answer many of the questions I received fairly quickly based on my years of education and training as a rabbi with experience in both Jewish education and congregational work. However, other questions sent me meandering through the shelves of my professional library, pouring through the myriad volumes of traditional texts in Hebrew and Aramaic, searching for the answer to a particularly intriguing question. The questions I received constituted my personal curriculum for ongoing Jewish professional development—and I never knew what I would end up learning next! I received an amazing and valuable Jewish education in my role as a volunteer staff member of "Ask a Rabbi," not just in the Jewish content but also especially in *how* to answer questions.

What I found particularly enjoyable and challenging was trying to answer e-mail questions in a format that would take advantage of this still-emerging e-mail culture and decorum of communication. E-mail exchanges are typically—or least, should be—fairly short, direct, and to the point. The questions I received were from people who wanted straight, succinct, simple answers. They did not want or need long-winded explanations, nor did I assume that they would have the patience to scroll through several computer screens' worth of background information. Therefore, I tried to oblige by being as direct as possible in response. You have a question? Fine, I have an answer. It was not always possible for me to condense a complicated question down to a screen or two of information, but I always tried to adhere to the "KISS" principle—*Keep it simple, stupid!*

While the topics people asked about were broad and fascinating, I discovered that I learned a great deal more about the questioners and their lives than they might have ever learned from my answers. Their questions—as you will soon read—sometimes unintentionally revealed fascinating and complicated lives and challenging social situations. Some people were struggling with interfaith relationships, others with how to cope with the loss of a family member or how to mourn someone's death in a traditional Jewish manner. Others wondered about the afterlife or how to negotiate the emotional challenge of how to include estranged family members in an upcoming life cycle celebration. And in a number of cases, young people wanted advice about how to negotiate delicate personal matters of rather shocking romantic intimacy!

In most cases, it seemed to me that people wanted personal advice and subjective spiritual guidance rather than straight, dry academic information about the Jewish tradition; they were seeking human contact and a personal touch. Often, they did not know any rabbis or had no connections to the organized Jewish community, and many were not even Jewish. The Internet was their only contact with other Jews, much less Jewish spiritual leaders. How ironic and even sad that our society has evolved into a place where people seek out companionship and spiritual guidance via one of the most physically and socially distancing forms of communication invented. Even so, given the anonymity and constraints of e-mail communication, I tried to provide as much of a human touch as possible and express my personal interest in them and their lives. While some of the questions may seem simplistic and the answers easily accessible, remember that this was largely before the Google Web search engine became so popular and before Wikipedia, the user-generated online encyclopedia of everything, even existed. For many people, writing to a rabbi on the Internet was the fastest, most direct method of getting an answer to their question.

As a rabbi ordained in the Conservative movement, one among the various major denominations of American Judaism, I answered a fair number of questions that were directed explicitly to a Conservative rabbi. However, the vast majority of questions that I received were not that specifically directed. As a result, the answers to many of the questions I received should be of interest to Jews from *all* denominations, whether formally affiliated with a particular Jewish denomination or not, and especially non-Jews who may be interested in learning more about a wide variety of Jewish topics.

Although I answered over 1,300 questions over the course of eight years—approximately two questions a day for eight years straight—I selected what I thought were the most representative, unusual, and touching questions and their answers. I ended up choosing nearly 300—barely 3 percent—of all the questions I received. These 300 questions and answers represent my professional Jewish FAQ. For those unfamiliar with the terminology of the World Wide Web, this means "frequently asked questions." Web sites and services often create FAQ areas in order to present the bare bones of what they offer and how to access it. This book, therefore, is a FAQ about the Jewish religion—nearly all of it! As you will see simply from the table of contents, the questions I answered cover the gamut of practically all topics of Jewish life, whatever people asked me about over the course of eight years. The questions have been highly edited and rewritten so as to protect the privacy of the questioners and to emend their idiosyncratic grammar and creative spelling. However, I tried to adhere as much as possible to the original spirit and unique situations described because the language and context of the questions were often quite valuable in helping me craft a response. My answers are essentially the same as when I sent them out, save for the numerous spelling and typographical errors that I inadvertently missed when I originally responded to these questions. However, I also significantly rewrote some answers to make them more readable in contrast to a more choppy and sloppy prose that is tolerable in an e-mail format but not for publication in a book. In some cases, I also updated the information to better mesh with contemporary political and social events. You may also notice that some of the material in the answers I wrote may appear familiar in other wording in different answers throughout the book. This is due to the fact that many individual questions necessitated the inclusion of some of the same information. While I have removed much of the identical repetitions, I hope that the few remaining partly parallel passages will not be too repetitious or tedious to bear. Instead, I would like to think that certain facts and points are so crucial that they bear subtle reminding throughout the entire book so as to establish a basic curriculum of the most important ideas and values in the Jewish tradition.

The "Ask a Rabbi" service is no longer limited to the AOL community. As with all initial proprietary Internet services, the "Jewish Community

Online" of AOL was transferred to the World Wide Web some years ago and spun off into its own independent site. It can be reached at www. Jewish.com and still even has an "Ask a Rabbi" service. Most of the questions and answers in this book no longer appear online in any place. I also have no formal or official connection with America Online or the www.Jewish.com Web site, nor do I continue to serve as a volunteer answering these types of questions anymore for any online entity. Therefore, the vast majority of the questions in this book are appearing in a publicly accessible format for the first time in nearly a decade.

The questions that I received over the years were not organized in any particular or obvious order. Therefore, when compiling this book, I needed to assemble the questions and answers into some coherent arrangement and sequence. First of all, I focused on the basic groupings of questions into chapters. The topics of individual questions ranged quite widely. But a number of general topics emerged, but there were so many that I continually consolidated and regrouped until I was able to narrow it down to seventeen basic chapters with some combinations of subjects. I admit that 17 is not a neat or even number, and there is no particular significance to this number. But I was constrained by two self-imposed goals.

The first goal was that I wanted to ensure that there were a sufficient number of questions all pertaining to a specific subject to constitute a chapter. Therefore, I chose the number 10 as the minimum number of questions to make up a chapter because the number 10 is a significant number in the Jewish tradition (for example, there are the Ten Commandments, the Ten Plagues sent by God on the Egyptians, ten Israelite spies that spread an unfavorable report about the land of Israel prior to the Israelite conquest, ten adult Jews that are required to constitute a prayer quorum, or Minyon, and so on). While many chapters contain significantly more than ten questions, this was my minimum number.

The second goal was to arrange the various and disparate chapters into a coherent order that flowed naturally from one topic to the next. Unfortunately, this was far more challenging, but a number of subject groupings did emerge as well as a unique flow to the topics. The first chapter and the next few were obvious choices. Beginning from outside of the Jewish community looking in, unfortunately, one of the first historical realities that many people associate with Jews is anti-Semitism even though it happens to be one of the most peripheral aspects of Jewish life.

Moving slowly from the outside of the Jewish community to the center, it only seemed logical to first present issues related to Jewish identity, religious conversion, and interfaith relationships. This last topic of Jewish identity blended into the next chapter dealing with life cycle events and family issues. Because of the emotional intensity associated with this last topic regarding family affairs, it was natural to include the following chapter about ethical issues, or trying to figure out the right way to act in certain situations. I then noticed that many questions asking about doing the right thing tended to be from younger people, so I then inserted the chapter of questions from kids and teens. It also became obvious that a recurring theme in the questions I received from young people tended to focus on their romantic lives, so this led to the chapter on sex.

Although as a rabbi I was free to apply the wisdom of the Jewish tradition as idiosyncratically as I chose, I elected to utilize and interpret traditional Jewish texts whenever possible. This then led to the chapter on the Hebrew Bible and Torah study that naturally led to the topic of Jewish history and the various denominations of American Jewish life today. And one of the primary elements that differentiate the various branches of Judaism is their interpretation of Jewish law and how to deal with the Jewish mystical tradition, hence the placement of this chapter on that topic. The three areas of Jewish practice where the modern denominations of Judaism differ the most are how to celebrate Shabbat and the Jewish holidays, the system of dietary practices called Kashrut, and expressions of Jewish prayer; this determined the order of the next three chapters. However, I should point out that due to the number and complexity of questions that I received about the festival of Passover, this topic warranted its own treatment in a separate chapter. After dealing with prayer, it only made sense that the final chapters should focus on the predominate concerns of all liturgical systems, namely, death and mourning, spirituality, and finally Jewish beliefs and understanding of God. So if you were keeping track of all of the topics I just mentioned, you would now know the subjects and order of all of the seventeen chapters in this book!

However, I couldn't end it there. As is true in so many areas of Jewish life and learning, one good question leads to another. There were so many good questions that deserved more detailed answers and explanations that I included a series of indices to provide a little more material for additional study. At the end of the book are two short articles I wrote about the Jewish dietary laws of Kashrut and the Passover Seder rituals so as to present these complex subjects in a more orderly and comprehensive fashion. I also included a short list of suggested readings and Web sites that I have found helpful and informative in my own research.

Question-and-answer books can be frustrating and confusing because maybe a particular question that you have about Judaism appears in this book—but how would you ever know unless you read the whole book cover to cover? To address this concern, I included a short explanation about the internal content and order of the questions in the introduction to most chapters. However, to spare readers from searching a chapter in vain to determine if a particular question—or answer—appears, I have included what I hope will be a very helpful index of *all* of the questions in every chapter at the end of the book. While I hope that readers will want to read this book from front to back cover, for anyone who wishes to pick and choose and locate a particular topic, I urge you to consult "Appendix D: Index of Questions." The last and final section is a glossary of recurring Hebrew words and concepts that I used throughout the book. So this explains not only what is in this book but also why it appears where it does.

In earlier times of Jewish history, people used to write to distant rabbis asking questions about all aspects of Jewish life and would have to wait weeks, if not months or even years, to receive their answers. Over the centuries, rabbis published these compendia of questions and answers, creating a new class of Jewish legal literature called responsa literature. In fact, much of what modern Jewish scholars and historians now know about the scattered Jewish communities throughout Europe, the Middle East, and North Africa in the Middle Ages is revealed in the descriptions and questions of these medieval Jewish letter writers. Thanks to the Internet and e-mail, this genre of literature continues to thrive and grow.

I would never dream of comparing myself to the giants of the Jewish tradition who received and answered hundreds and even thousands of letters from pious Jews through the centuries as they were the scholars and rabbis who helped guide the path of the Jewish people throughout history offering their guidance and insights into Jewish life and law. The many volumes of traditional Jewish responsa literature remain a significant and important archive of the growth and development of Jewish law and literature. With the advent of the Internet and e-mail, every Jew and rabbi with an Internet connection can now contribute to the vast and continually growing shelves and gigabytes of Jewish wisdom. It is in this light that I am proud to be able to offer my own humble contribution to this ancient and venerable Jewish genre of literature and to the Jewish people.

Chapter 1

Anti-Semitism (Ten Questions)

"Anti-Semitism" is a word of relatively modern origin that refers exclusively to the hatred of Jews. It was actually coined in 1879 by an Austrian-Hungarian politician named Wilhelm Marr in his political tract *The Victory of Judaism over Germanicism* in which he warned about the dangers that Jews and Judaism posed to German culture. His writings were influential in the development of the Nazi party years later. This politician, Wilhelm Marr, invented the term "anti-Semitism" as a euphemism to replace the older, more common expression of "Jew hater" and actually won public office based on his efforts to mobilize political support from his fellow Jew haters. While a technical definition of the word "anti-Semitism" would seem to imply that this expression refers to discriminatory feelings toward both Jews and Arabs, as both are Semitic peoples native to the Middle East, such a definition ignores the contextual and historical origins of this word and the fact that it was created to describe only the hatred of Jews.

Many books have been devoted to the subject of what has been called humanity's longest and oldest hatred. Some people claim that anti-Semitism is based on religious reasons from Christian and Muslim exasperation with the Jewish people's refusal to convert en masse to either of these latter faiths, or even premonotheistic anger over the biblical dismissal of polytheistic deities. Others claim that it is based on economic and social reasons, painting the Jews as scapegoats in depressed and struggling societies. Frustratingly, there is no one single answer as to the reasons for anti-Semitism or why it has endured for so long and proved to be endemic to so many countries and cultures. Not surprisingly, many people, both Jews and non-Jews, were also curious and puzzled by this phenomenon; and many directed their questions about anti-Semitism to an easily accessible online source of information—me!

Question number 1: If the Hebrew Bible says that Jews are the people chosen by God, why are they persecuted so much? And where does that leave other religions such as Catholicism, Islam, etc.? Thank you for your time.

Answer: I have no idea why the rest of the world has hated Jews—and has for so long! It is one of the most ancient of human hatreds. It is a terrible thing, and many people have come up with different reasons for the origins of anti-Semitism. Here are some of the reasons some scholars have come up with for why different people in various historical eras have hated Jews.

In pagan times, some people claim that because the Hebrew Bible says that it is wrong and stupid to worship idols made of wood and stone, this angered the pagan peoples at that time. This is why the ancient nations hated the Jews.

According to the early history of the Christian church, Jews were blamed for the death of Jesus. Therefore, if Jews could kill Jesus, the Son of God, then they must be the devil and capable of all sorts of other evils. Jews were also accused of poisoning wells, killing Christian children for their blood, and worshipping the devil. Therefore, Christian Jew hatred was based on religion too.

Some people claim that Jew hatred is the result of Jews being different from everyone else. Because Jews were scattered and forced into exile long ago, Jews have—until recent times—lived as strangers among other peoples and were rarely accepted as native citizens of a country or a land. Therefore, these people claim that people hated Jews because they were always "illegal aliens."

Other people claim that Jews were hated because they had no choice but to take jobs and engage in occupations that other people didn't want to take, such as serving as moneylenders and rent collectors. Since no one liked such people, Jews were hated because they were perceived as being richer than other people although this was not true.

Some people claim that Jews were hated because they were thought of as smarter than other people. And someone who is smarter is sneakier, more clever, and therefore dangerous and not to be trusted.

The point is no one knows why non-Jews have hated or continued to hate Jews. You mentioned the idea that Jews are hated because they claim to be God's chosen people. But *every people* on earth claims to be God's chosen people, yet it is only the Jewish claim of uniqueness that seems to upset everyone!

And by the way, the Jewish claim to be God's chosen people does not mean that Jews themselves have believed that they are better than any other people. Rather, according to the Jewish religious tradition, Jews believe that they have been chosen by God to receive the Torah and observe the religious commandments of the Hebrew Bible. This is the only meaning of what being chosen means in the Jewish religion. I hope this answers your question even though it is not a really satisfying answer. I wish I knew the answer as to why people have hated the Jews for so long because if I knew, I could go about trying to solve it!

Question number 2: *I have heard that in biblical times the Orthodox rabbis practiced a secret form of medicine using herbs and mysterious healing arts, and because of this, it is rumored that these rabbis had a much longer life expectancy than their contemporaries. I hope you can* *help shed some light on what these traditions were and inform me as to where I may be able to find more information.*

Answer: Sorry to disappoint you, but there never was any ancient or secret form of medicine practiced by Jews of any kind. Sorry, never existed. Just to let you know, there were no such things as rabbis in biblical times either, around three thousand years ago. And if there were rabbis, they certainly were not Orthodox rabbis! The Orthodox movement only came into existence less than two hundred years ago.

Also, the idea that any Jews whatsoever had some sort of secret healing or medicinal powers is actually an anti-Semitic canard even though it seems to put the Jews in a positive light. This is because for thousands of years, anti-Semites accused Jews of having secret knowledge to either harm others or benefit only other Jews. Jews were actually accused of poisoning wells in the Middle Ages and causing the Black Death or the Plague that killed so many. And in more modern times, Joseph Stalin accused literally thousands of Jewish doctors in the Soviet Union of using their medical knowledge to poison top Soviet leaders, and only Stalin's death prevented their execution. So not only is this information false, but to persist and believe that it is true is actually a form of Jew hatred. Sorry to shatter your myth. However, I hope you will be interested in learning about some of the true and real contributions of Jews to modern world science and culture.

Question number 3: What is the Protocols of the Elders of Zion?

Answer: The *Protocols of the Elders of Zion* is a short booklet that claims to be the notes taken at a secret meeting of powerful Jews from all over the world back in the 1800s. In these so-called notes of this meeting, the Jews reveal their plans to take over and control the whole world as a long-term goal for all Jews everywhere.

The booklet is a fake and so is this goal. No Jew or Jews ever wrote it. However, it is still used as evidence by Jew haters everywhere as so-called proof that Jews are evil and are trying to take over the world. The booklet is actually very old, nearly 150 years old! Scholars of anti-Semitism claim that it was written first in France and had nothing to do with Jews! It was used to attack one of the French leaders at that time, called Napoleon III, in an effort to prove that he and his inner circle were out to control the world and reestablish the Napoleonic Empire throughout all of Europe. However, it was taken and adapted by Jew haters in czarist Russia and rewritten so as to attack Jews. It then became a very popular book in Russia over one hundred years ago and was used to deflect the frustration that many Russians had with the autocratic czarist government on the Jews.

In modern times, this booklet has become popular in many Arab countries and is still used to stir up hatred and anger toward the State of Israel. However, because it is such a phony, fake document whose only purpose is to attack Jews, many countries in Europe and North America have passed laws making it illegal to even print this book. So it is very hard to find a copy in the United States today.

It would be nice if this booklet were a relic from history and could be studied freely as a ridiculous piece of propaganda. Unfortunately, there are still people in the United States and around the world who are willing to believe the lies in this booklet. That is why it is often hard to find and why many people, including yourself probably, have a lot of questions about it.

Question number 4: Why do Christians fear or even hate Jews?

Answer: I'm not sure it is possible to claim that *all* Christians are afraid of Jews or hate them. I'm sure there are plenty of Christians who feel very comfortable and friendly with Jews. However, there are two basic reasons why many Christians may feel *challenged* by the presence of Jews.

1. A long time ago, after Jesus lived and died, many Christian leaders hoped and expected that all Jews would convert to

Christianity and abandon Judaism. Because this did not happen, many Christians felt long ago—and perhaps still feel—that the continuing presence of Jews throughout the last two thousand years of history somehow threatens the validity or truth of their own religion. Therefore, many Christians still want to try and convert Jews to be Christians.

2. The second reason some Christians may be uncomfortable or challenged by the presence of Jews is that many Christians believe that Jews are responsible for killing Jesus two thousand years ago. Even though this is not really true and many official modern Church pronouncements have specifically rescinded this doctrine, many Christians still feel that Jews are to blame. So perhaps this is why you may feel that some Christians are afraid or hate Jews.

Question number 5: What is the difference between modern and medieval anti-Semitism?

Answer: This is a complicated question, but to give you a very simple answer, medieval Jew hatred was based primarily on religion. Christians hated Jews because they believed that they were all responsible for killing Jesus. Also, in that time, they did not call it anti-Semitism but simply Jew hatred. They expressed it by attacking and murdering Jews and expelling them from different countries. Muslims in medieval times did not hate Jews but rather treated them—as well as Christians—as second-class citizens in Muslim society because they were fellow monotheists but still were not Muslims.

Modern anti-Semitism, which dates from barely 150 years ago, is a political form of Jew hatred. People have hated—and continued to hate—Jews for many different reasons and accuse Jews of being too rich and controlling banks, or for being too influential and controlling all of the newspapers and television, or for being too powerful and being in control of the government. Rather than express it directly, modern anti-Semites hide their real hatred and call it anti-Semitism, which is a nicer-sounding word than Jew hating; but it is still the same thing. Modern anti-Semitism is expressed in more subtle ways, such as not wanting to hire Jews for a job, or not accepting Jews into colleges or universities, or not wanting to sell homes to Jews in certain neighborhoods, or passing over someone who is Jewish in the workplace for a promotion. However, modern anti-Semitism can also be just as violent and deadly as the old kind.

Hating Jews—hating anyone for that matter—simply because of their religion or their race or their skin color or sexual preference is wrong. Whether it is ancient or modern, hating other people for such superficial and ridiculous reasons is always wrong and immoral.

Question number 6: *Why do you people insist on taking Palestinian land and murdering the Palestinians? What is happening in Gaza and the West Bank reminds me of what the Nazis used to do to Resistance fighters. What is wrong with you people?*

Answer: Why have you sent a question about Israeli governmental and military policies to an Internet service comprised exclusively of rabbis who do not live in Israel? This is not the appropriate address or forum for your question.

However, you should know that the substance of your question is less important to me than the fact that you are somehow holding Jews—all Jews, no matter where they may live—responsible for the actions of the Israeli government. Do you really expect me, a rabbi living in California, to somehow be responsible for or even able to answer and explain the official governmental positions of the Israeli government? That is absurd.

What it does indicate to me is that you are subtly blurring the lines between your legitimate political opposition to the governmental actions of the sovereign State of Israel with that of anti-Semitism. When you ask in your question, "Why do *you people* insist on taking Palestinian land," it leads me to believe that you are expressing your hatred of Jews, all Jews, and not merely asking a question about Israeli governmental policies and military tactics.

I must confess that your question frightens me. You scare me because you are using the excuse of events in another country to express your hatred of all Jews wherever they live around the world. You make the world an unsafe place, not only for Jews but also for everyone who is the target of bigots, racists, and xenophobes. I'm afraid (in more ways than one) that I am unable to answer your question.

Question number 7: *I am from Switzerland and I have great respect for Jews and Judaism, that is why I am concerned about the situation in the Middle East. I hope I do not offend you with my question, but I see many similarities between current Israeli governmental policies and the Nazis. The Nazis forcibly settled German colonists in different areas of Europe, saying they needed more "living room." It seems to me that the Israelis are doing the same thing with respect to the Palestinians. Another similarity is with European ghettos and the Palestinian towns and villages that are being blockaded by Israel. I look forward to hearing from you, and I hope that I have not offended you in any way.*

Answer: It is indeed unfortunate that you found no other parallels or ways to express yourself other than through a comparison of Israeli military tactics to those of the Nazis. Even if the points you make have some validity to them, it is offensive to Jews to ever be compared to their persecutors and executioners, and it also indicates your willingness to accept and pass along inflammatory comparisons, basically propaganda, issued by Jew-hating opponents of Israel and the Jewish people. I hope you understand that even seemingly valid points about Israeli governmental policies and military tactics, when compared to Nazis, are an unfortunate breach of tact, sensitivity, and erosion of historical memory. There is a *vast* difference between the crimes against humanity perpetrated by the Nazis and the present-day policies of the State of Israel, however flawed and unjust they may be.

I wish I could more specifically address your questions and concerns, but I am hesitant to do so because as a Jew who is not an Israeli citizen and as a rabbi whose expertise is in Jewish religious practice, I don't want to appear as if I have any official connection to the government of Israel or role as a spokesperson for the Israeli government or its military forces. Why do you think that I, as a rabbi, would have any such knowledge or authority to explain or perhaps even justify the actions of a foreign sovereign state? By assuming that I am able to play such a role is to mistakenly conflate the actions and responsibility for the State of Israel's government with all Jews who live outside of Israel around the world and who are citizens of other countries. I certainly don't mean to accuse you of anything as your e-mail is exceedingly polite and sensitive. But the idea that all Jews anywhere in the world are somehow responsible for the actions of the State of Israel is actually a component of modern-day anti-Semitism, and I just wanted you to be aware of that.

To provide you with an example of why this makes no sense logically, I have no idea what religion you may be if you adhere to or profess any particular faith. But if, for the sake of example, you were Catholic, would it be reasonable for me to ask you to explain Vatican policies or defend the actions or words of the pope? You may simply happen to be a knowledgeable Catholic and perhaps even more familiar than most Catholics with the history of the Vatican and policies and theological positions of the current pope. But that does not make you an official representative of the Vatican or the pope! The same is true regarding Jews around the world and the State of Israel.

There is one point you raise that I can address, and that concerns the so-called ghettoization of some Palestinian population centers in the West Bank and Gaza. I believe that these policies and practices are truly unfortunate and may indeed constitute international crimes. It is truly a shame and terrible that Palestinians are suffering as a result of Israeli policies restricting their movements through numerous roadblocks and the building of a vast security fence. But the current situation for Palestinians is quite different than the Jewish ghettos of Europe. The ghettos of medieval Europe were purposely designed to be small, cramped enclaves that Jews were forced to live in as a result of systematic *religious* discrimination, not due to any political or military threat that they posed to the Christian population of Europe that surrounded them. In contrast, the ghettos of the Nazis were intentionally created to serve as civilian prison-enclaves in which to temporarily incarcerate large populations of Jews as a stage in the systematic murder and genocide of the Jewish people of Europe.

In short, there is quite a bit of difference between the Nazis and the Israelis. And please recognize that even in your polite question, you unwittingly legitimize these horrific propagandistic distortions of historical reality and blur the line between fact and fiction. In other words, you unintentionally create the groundwork for future violence against Jews—whether in Israel or outside—by explicitly comparing Israelis to Nazis. Mark your words well, especially as a Swiss citizen, given the growing revelations as to how the Swiss government collaborated with and abetted the Nazi regime in the confiscation and exploitation of Jewish property and financial resources during World War II.

Question number 8: I recently got in a fight with a friend, and he ended up calling me a Jew. We eventually made up, but I had to ask him if he really was a racist. He apologized and claimed that he does not really hate me because I am Jewish, but I am not sure what to feel or believe anymore. I am still hurt, but am I overreacting?

Answer: It must have been very painful for you when your friend called you a Jew as if it were some kind of a curse word and suddenly made you feel like an outsider when he perhaps unintentionally revealed a dark part of his upbringing or environment. Your friend may not be a dyed-in-the-wool, complete racist, it is just that religious epithets can sometimes bubble up when they are least expected or even intended.

I think you handled the situation perfectly. You confronted him afterward and asked about his true feelings when you were both calmer. I think that whenever something hurtful and painful like this happens, it is crucial to speak to the person afterward after the pain and anger has subsided. But most important is tell them how you feel! Your friend will never truly know how painful and unacceptable it is to label anyone or call someone by his or her religion as a negative curse unless you tell them.

Maybe now, hopefully, your friend will begin to understand that it is not okay to harbor such feelings or use the word "Jew" as a pejorative term—which it is not, nor should it be used as a cuss word. It is merely a description of someone's religious identity, not a curse word. But sadly, it can and has been used as a dirty word by some people.

We can only begin to eliminate racism, hatred, and bigotry one person at a time through direct personal interaction. Mazal Tov, you have helped make the world a better place and helped influence a person to be more sensitive to pain and prejudice in the world!

Question number 9: Why aren't the Jewish people considered to be a race? Some friends have claimed that all Jews share certain physical features like big noses and dark hair. I have tried to explain that this is not true and that Judaism is more a culture than a race, and I have pointed to the existence of Ethiopian Jews, Asian Jews, and converts to the faith to prove my point that Jews are not a race, but to no avail. And they continue to tease me that I'm part of the Jewish race. Do you have any suggestions as to how to convince them?

Answer: Who cares what your friends think? You have already answered them exactly the way that I would have. If your friends can't accept the truth, what do you care? Why is it your job to convince them of anything, especially after you have already given them all of the appropriate information they might need to actually understand the reality of the Jewish people?

I don't mean to be offensive to your friends, but their stubbornness and inability, or choice not to understand, sound like some inherent, subtle anti-Semitism on their part or a deliberate attempt to goad and annoy you.

I'm sure they would vigorously deny such a charge, but what else can you call someone when they refuse to believe the reality that Jews are not a race and deliberately enjoy taunting you with their false accusations that clearly make you squirm? In addition, the examples that you quote them as claiming illustrated proof that Jews are a race sound awfully similar to the stereotypical images propagated by the Nazis.

As you indeed noted, anyone can convert to Judaism and become part of the Jewish people—African-American, White, Latino, and Asian. How can we be a race if anyone can join it? Race is something that cannot be changed or altered. If you weren't born Black, you can't just wake up one day and decide to be an African-American. The same applies to being Asian or Hispanic. For your friends to insist that this same model applies to the Jewish people is willful and deliberate ignorance, or prejudice.

The fact that there are some shared genetic traits among Jews of Eastern European origin simply means that these traits are shared among only Jews of Eastern European origin—not Jews from Morocco or Ethiopia or Italy or Israel. And given the tremendous amount of marrying within the same genetic pool, which is called intramarriage, it is not surprising that some Jews—or any people for that matter—will share some of the same common genetic traits. Also, clearly your friends have never been to California where there are plenty of Jews who have blond hair and blue eyes and look more Aryan than Hitler ever did!

It seems to me that your question is not about any answer I might provide but rather how should you deal with close-minded people who are unable to recognize the fact that their persistence in insisting that Jews are a race is actually a telltale characteristic of anti-Semitism. By sadistically insisting on their incorrect perception of reality, they are actually insulting you and dismissing your attempts to enlighten them. It also makes me wonder, and actually frightens me a little, that if their minds are so tightly closed on this relatively minor matter, what other areas of their minds are also closed off? What other culturally popular racist views do they also subscribe to? And keep in mind that modern anti-Semitism is characterized today by the absolute insistence by such people that they are not anti-Semitic—and they may even believe it! But what do you call someone who holds the same racist views of the Jewish people that Hitler did? Apparently in this case, you continue to call them your friends.

Therefore, what you need to explain to your friends is that you have already given them all the information they need to understand their mistake and that their persistent ignorant perception of the Jewish people is hurtful and insulting to you. You need to let them know that they would be better friends to you by not putting you on the spot about this all the time by constantly bringing up a subject that you are sensitive about and have already told them that you feel insulted that they cannot see the truth of the matter.

You don't need to reject them and stop being friendly with them. But hopefully, perhaps through your own personal relationship with them, you can encourage them to drop these views on their own. Maybe they will change their minds—and behavior—as they begin to understand how deeply you are hurt and offended by their words. Hopefully, their friendship with you will prove to be more attractive and powerful to them than their insistence on maintaining anti-Semitic distortions of reality.

Your *logic* will never convince these people about the truth of your answers because they are already close-minded about this subject and perhaps others. The only way to wean them of these prejudicial ideas is to have them recognize your humanity and make them realize that their insistence on these ideas is hurtful and painful to you, their friend. Maintaining anti-Semitic ideas has consequences in the real world. The least of which should be the loss of your friendship.

Question number 10: *I read a Web page the other day that claimed that the Holocaust never happened. At first, I thought this person was an anti-Semite; but then I began to think that if six million Jews died, where is the evidence? Maybe this guy is right! How come I've never seen any* *ashes, and how come that Anne Frank book got locked away in Israel? Is it a fake?*

Answer: If the anti-Semitic Holocaust deniers have already gotten you to question the reality of a well-established historical event to which there are still eyewitnesses, survivors, and massive amounts of physical evidence, then they have already won. If you want to learn about the evidence of the Holocaust, then do your own homework and don't ask questions based on pure ignorance of historical fact.

The book *The Diary of Anne Frank* is available in public libraries and bookstores all over the world (except in truly Jew-hating, anti-Semitic countries) and not locked away in Israel as you seem to believe. The original manuscript is part of Otto Frank's estate, Anne's father who survived the war and discovered his daughter's diary years later and had it published in her memory. Go read a copy yourself. There are also entire bookshelves devoted to the Holocaust. Go read them. There are probably thousands of Holocaust survivors still alive. Go find them and talk to them. There are thousands of American soldiers who liberated the concentration camps from the Nazis who saw with their own eyes the evidence of the Holocaust. Go talk to them before they all pass away of old age. There is evidence in Europe—the camps filled with the ashes and other horrifying evidence. Go take a trip and see with your own eyes. You can actually touch the ashes of human bodies, murdered Jews, and feel the gristle of their bones with your own fingers. Or if you don't want to travel that far, go visit the U.S. Holocaust Memorial Museum in Washington, D.C., or the Museum of Tolerance in Los Angeles. Seems a mighty waste of money to build those museums dedicated to an event that you believe just might never have happened.

And if you still believe the Holocaust never happened—then there are lots of other people who would love to talk to you about their racist, bigoted, prejudicial views of the world. You are exactly what they are looking for—someone who will not question the idiocy and ignorance of their views. Watch out—you are exactly whom Jews, African-Americans, Hispanics, and Asians fear most: a future racist.

Chapter 2

Interfaith Relations (Thirteen Questions)

Despite God's promise to Abraham that his descendants would be more numerous than the stars in the sky or the grains of sand on a beach (Genesis 22:17), the Jewish people has always remained rather small and a minority of the world's population. As a result, there has been an emphasis in the broader Jewish tradition on maintaining sufficient numbers of Jews through intramarriage, that is, Jews marrying other Jews.

Biblical, Talmudic, and medieval Jewish law all stress the importance of Jews marrying other Jews due to the fear that intermarriage—that is, Jews marrying members of other faith communities—would harm the long-term survival and uniqueness of the Jewish people, both demographically and spiritually, leading to greater assimilation of Jews and Judaism into the wider stream of humanity and possibly the dissolution of the Jewish people.

Despite a famous biblical lapse in policing this policy of endogamy (marrying in the faith) as described in the book of Ezra and Nehemiah in the Hebrew Bible (Ezra chapter 10), the Jewish people have remained profoundly cohesive in their marriage practices throughout the centuries of the Diaspora, or the dispersion of the Jews throughout the world. Despite the obvious intermixing of Jewish communities with the populations where they lived, even far-flung Jewish communities remained surprisingly vital and enduring. For example, in spite of the fact that the Jews of Cochin, India, look exactly like their Hindu neighbors, attesting to years of intermarriage, they still remained a discrete, identifiable Jewish community for centuries. The same applies to the Jews of Russia, Morocco, Yemen, Ethiopia, China, and other communities of the Jewish Diaspora.

It is only in modern times in the United States and other Western countries that pluralistic, tolerant social conditions have led to what some people feel is an overemphasis on Jewish intramarriage. Because of the overall reduction of widespread virulent anti-Semitism and the general attitude of greater tolerance, pluralism, and social and economic intermixing of classes and ethnic groups, all religious and cultural groups in the United States have experienced a rising incidence of interfaith marriage.

In 1990, a highly flawed but sensational National Jewish Population Survey estimated that 52 percent of the Jewish community in the United States was intermarried. This statistic, when publicized, led to an air of crisis in the Jewish community because sociological studies indicated that the experience of intermarriage tends to weaken one's communal ties and sense of identity as a Jew in succeeding generations. Whether the prevalence of interfaith relationships and marriage in the Jewish community is a crisis or an opportunity remains to be seen. What is clear is that many people involved in such relationships are still interested in exploring, maintaining, or creating a connection to the Jewish tradition sufficiently to send an e-mail to an anonymous rabbi sharing intimate details of their family life and asking for religious, spiritual advice about the challenges of interfaith dating, relationships, and marriages.

Question number 1: Where in the Torah does it talk about interfaith marriages?

Answer: There are a number of passages that deal with the concept of intermarriage in the Hebrew Bible. Here are some of them:

1. Deuteronomy 7:3-4—"Neither shall you make marriages with them: you shall not give your daughter to his son, nor his daughter shall you take for your son. For she will turn away your son from following Me, and they will serve other gods; thus the anger of the Lord will be kindled against you, and God will destroy you quickly." This is a pretty scary but clear quote because this quote by God in the Torah is essentially saying don't marry your children off to people from other religions because they will lead your Jewish sons and daughters away from Judaism. And God doesn't seem to like that prospect very much in this passage!

2. Exodus 34:16—"And if you take of their daughters to your sons, their daughters will go astray after their gods, and make your sons go astray after their gods." This quote is pretty much like the one above, and in fact, it comes earlier in the Torah since Exodus comes before Deuteronomy. I just thought that the quote from Deuteronomy was a lot clearer than this one, but you should see that this same law is quoted twice in the Torah to emphasize it.

3. 1 Kings 11:1-6—"Now king Solomon loved many foreign women, besides the daughter of Pharaoh, women of the Moabites, Ammonites, Edomites, Zidonians, and Hittites; of the nations concerning which the Lord said to the children of Israel: 'You shall not go among them, neither shall they come among you; for surely they will turn away your heart after their gods.' Still Solomon did cling to these women in love . . . And it came to pass, when Solomon was old, that his wives turned away his heart after other gods; and his heart was not whole with the Lord his God . . . for Solomon went after Ashtoreth the goddess of the Zidonians, and after Milcom the abomination of the Ammonites. And Solomon did that which was evil in the sight of the Lord." Now this is a pretty interesting endnote to the life of King Solomon who was considered the wisest of all Israelite kings. Apparently, due to his numerous foreign non-Jewish wives, he eventually ended up violating biblical laws and worshipping foreign gods. Pretty damning evidence against one of the most famous kings of the Hebrew Bible!

4. Nehemiah 10:31—"(The Israelites swore to God and said) 'We will not give our daughters to the peoples of the land, nor take

their daughters for our sons.'" This last quote is from a long story toward the end of the Hebrew Bible where after many years of living without religious guidance, many Jewish men had married non-Jewish women, but they ended up recognizing their sin and promised not to allow their children to intermarry.

The Talmud and other later rabbinic religious texts have lots of other laws and comments about interfaith marriages, but these quotes from the Hebrew Bible spell it out pretty clearly.

Question number 2: What are the differences between the Jewish and Christian religions? I am dating a young Jewish man, and I have been growing more interested in the Jewish religion. Can our relationship work out? Is it possible to bring together Judaism and Christianity?

Answer: An excellent book to read about Judaism and Christianity is *Judaism and Christianity: The Differences* by Trude Weiss-Rosmarin (Jonathan David Publishing, 1981). It is simply impossible to go into details about the differences between the two religions in the short space of an e-mail, plus you can read the book I just recommended. However, just so that you understand the profound chasm between the two religions, both theologically and ritually, here are some of the major differences:

1. Jewish monotheism versus Christian concept of Trinity. However it is understood, the concept that God is somehow mystically a unity of God the Father, Jesus the Son, and the Holy Spirit is utterly alien to the uncompromising Jewish idea that God is one.
2. Jewish understanding of the Messiah. According to the Jewish tradition, Jesus was not the Messiah, nor was he divine in any respect, nor did he absolve people of their sins. And he can never be accepted as a focus of worship or acknowledged as an intermediary in the direct, individual human-divine relationship. Jews do not need any intermediary in their relationship with God.
3. Free will versus original sin. The Jewish tradition holds that everyone has free will to do as they wish and that good and evil

stem from our own individual actions. Jews reject the concept that all humans are somehow tainted with something known as the original sin of Eve. The concept is utterly alien to Judaism.

4. Eschatology. This is a Greek word meaning "the end of days." Although there are vague Jewish concepts of an afterlife, the main focus of Judaism is on ethical, moral actions in this world. This is in contrast to the theological emphasis on heaven, hell, and spiritual salvation in Christianity. Judaism is more focused on this life than any potential afterlife.

5. Actions versus faith. Whereas most Christians acknowledge the importance of good acts, they will ultimately concede that a person's faith is more critical than their actions. Jews, however, hold that a person's faith is ultimately irrelevant; what is more important is acting appropriately, i.e., fulfilling God's commands as enumerated in the Hebrew Bible and interpreted and expanded upon by the Talmudic rabbis. Good deeds are more important than faith in the Jewish tradition.

6. Only one Bible. Whereas Christians believe that a new relationship with God was possible with the advent of Jesus, Jews continue to adhere to the original relationship with God as defined in the Hebrew Bible. Christianity is not an extension or development of Judaism; it is a completely separate religious offshoot of Judaism. There is only one Bible to Jews—the Hebrew Bible. The Christian Bible, no matter how dependent upon the Hebrew Bible it may be, is a holy book for Christians—not Jews.

To answer your question as to whether your relationship can work out and can you bridge the gap between your two religions, I have no idea. Not only are interfaith marriages forbidden in the Jewish religion, I hope that it has become patently obvious reading everything above that it is utterly impossible to synthesize two completely contrasting religions together. To try to do so makes a mockery of both of them. I recommend that you read another book called *Mixed Blessings: Marriage between Jews and Christians* by Paul and Rachel Cowan (Doubleday Publishing, 1987). I believe it will give you an insight into the challenges of interfaith marriages. You should also visit the Web site on an online magazine called InterFaithFamily.com that can provide you with more information on your situation. Good luck!

Question number 3: *I do not understand how intermarriage is causing the Jewish population to decrease. If all non-Jews have to convert to Judaism before they are allowed to marry Jews, then how can the Jewish population be decreasing? Is this not a requirement of all non-Jews who want to marry Jews?*

Answer: No, there is no such requirement forcing non-Jews to convert to Judaism before marrying a Jewish partner. While it is strongly encouraged in some Jewish denominations that non-Jewish spouses should convert to Judaism before a Jewish wedding, vast numbers of people simply do not know about nor do they care about this. While some traditional rabbis will refuse to officiate at interfaith weddings, many other more liberal or progressive rabbis are willing to perform interfaith weddings with no conversion.

Many people claim that interfaith marriages threaten the demographic future of Judaism based on sociological studies that indicate that when one partner retains their non-Jewish identity in an interfaith family, there is only a one in ten chance that their children will grow up with any sense of Jewish identity themselves. And among the Conservative and Orthodox Jewish communities, a child who has a Jewish father but not a Jewish mother is not even considered Jewish. Only a child with a Jewish mother is considered a Jew in the traditional Jewish community. This is how intermarriage is potentially decreasing the Jewish community.

Question number 4: *How can I convince a young person of how important it is to marry a person from the same faith?*

Answer: You can't. It is very difficult to convince anyone of anything if they themselves do not find the subject of personal value or significance. However, it is always valuable and important to share your thoughts and personal principles with someone with whom you have a close personal relationship. Keeping that in mind, here is a list of various arguments and points that you may wish to consider and discuss with the young person you have in mind. Be forewarned that nothing is ever guaranteed and that the most that anyone can ever hope for is to at least persuade someone else to consider the issue in greater depth. Also, please note that the following points are arguments that I have made in similar situations as yours. And I wish I could tell you I was always successful in convincing a young person to value dating partners within the Jewish community, but unfortunately I can't. But here are some points that I have tried in the past. I hope you have better luck than I have had!

1. Tell your young friend to find out more about Judaism and Jewish life. You might tell him or her that before venturing beyond your own religious community, it is only fair to see why Judaism is so important to other Jews. So do some homework and discover what a spiritually inspiring and intellectually engaging religion Judaism is or could be.

2. If Judaism and Jewish life are in any way important to him or her, then it makes sense to date and perhaps marry someone who is Jewish because you will at least share the same religion. Relationships are hard enough without adding in the complicating factor of different religions. If you date and perhaps marry someone else who is Jewish, you will at least have that much more in common between you to strengthen your relationship.

3. If Judaism and Jewish life are important to this person, be aware of who you date because dating is a dangerous habit that leads to marriage. We lie to ourselves if we claim that we can date for fun but then suddenly, at some point in our lives, switch gears and decide to marry only someone who is Jewish when we are ready to get serious. No one can control his or her own heart. Date people whom you are sincerely interested in possibly making a life with. After all, dating is a form of preparation for marriage by discovering the qualities in people that you want more of and those that you could live without!

4. If Judaism and Jewish life *are* important to you, then it makes sense to marry someone who is Jewish so that you will share the same values in life. Look, marriage is challenging enough without throwing in different religions and different values. To help ensure a successful marriage (but there are never any guarantees), at least make sure that you and your dating partner, and maybe your future spouse, share the same principles, standards, morals, and ethics in life; then the small differences between you won't be so important or threatening.

5. If Judaism and Jewish life are important to you, it makes sense to share the same spiritual path in life. If you truly want to grow with someone, develop and mature with another person and be true spiritual companions for life, it makes sense that you would want to engage in the same ritual, spiritual acts of faith together throughout your lives. It is kind of difficult to do that if one person is attending Yom Kippur services and the other one stays at home but eventually goes to Mass for Christmas. Get on the same religious page at least!

6. If Judaism and Jewish life are important to this person, then they may want to raise any children they have in the religion that is important to them. You may want to ensure that your children will share the same spiritual values and childhood experiences as you and that you can grow together as a family spiritually through your shared life cycle celebrations.

7. Even if Judaism and Jewish life are not especially important to this person now, people often change as they grow older and often become more religious—not less. When children are born, parents die, and we experience the ups and downs of normal life, our religion of origin often becomes more important to us as we age. Anticipate your entire life and future—not just what may be important to you this minute.

There are probably many other arguments and points to add, but I hope this serves as a beginning of an honest dialogue and discussion. The most important thing to do with trying to talk to anyone about the importance of Judaism is share why it is important to *you*. Judaism might not be important to this person right now, but they might be willing to give it some more thought if you communicate clearly how essential it is in your own life.

Question number 5: *I am Christian, and I am deeply in love with a Jewish woman. But she is scared to tell her parents about me and doesn't know what to do because she knows they will strongly disapprove. I don't want to destroy her family, but I don't want to give her up. I didn't realize that Jews think that Christians are so terrible. If we did marry, would her parents cut her off from their family? Would they ever acknowledge our children in any way?*

Answer: First of all, all Christians are not considered "terrible" in the Jewish tradition. No doubt, you are aware that every religious tradition prefers its adherents to marry within their own spiritual faith. The same is true for Judaism. And due to the relatively small number of Jews throughout the world, only around twelve or thirteen million and of them only around five million in the United States, we Jews tend to think of ourselves as an endangered species. Therefore, while your girlfriend's parents' potential reaction to an interfaith relationship may be extreme, it may be understandable given this context. I have no idea whether your girlfriend's parents would truly cut off their daughter from their family. It would indeed be sad if they did so and probably counterproductive. Unfortunately, we cannot always influence how other people choose to conduct their lives.

Therefore, given the emotional high stakes that you conveyed in your e-mail, you have several options to consider:

1. Convert to Judaism. If you become a Jew yourself, then there is no issue of intermarriage. However, I would never encourage someone to convert just for the sake of his partner. If you choose to become a Jew, you should make this decision for yourself and your own love of Judaism, not because you feel pressured into it for external reasons.

2. Break off the relationship. If you are truly concerned about your girlfriend's parents' negative reactions, then you may want to spare her this grief and anguish by terminating your relationship right now.
3. Ignore the potential reactions and continue with your relationship. After all, maybe her parents won't cut off their daughter from their family. Maybe it is a bluff or maybe not. You may decide that your relationship together is more important than the consequences.
4. Sit down and talk about the situation all together. The fact that your girlfriend has been keeping your relationship a secret from her parents cannot be a healthy thing for her, you, or her parents. Therefore, it might be beneficial to deal with the situation directly as adults and discuss ways to alleviate any tension and pain. The choice is up to you and your girlfriend. I wish you luck and strength in your decisions.

Question number 6: I am dating a young man who is not Jewish. We have decided that if we marry and have children, they will be raised Jewish. However, my boyfriend still wants them to be baptized in some way for his mother's sake. I have told him that this essentially would nullify their Jewish identity and they would have to convert back to being Jews! He claims that there are nonreligious ways of performing a Christian baptism. What should we do? Is there any way to rectify this situation?

Answer: Yes, there is a way to rectify the situation—don't get married and don't have children with this man! Just kidding, sort of. Seriously though, I agree with you. Performing a baptism does indeed communicate a mixed message about the religious identity of the children although it would not necessitate having to convert your children back to Judaism as they would continue to remain Jewish as a result of you, their mother, being Jewish and your raising them as Jews.

But having a baptism is only a symptom of the deeper question, which is the ultimate religious identity of your children-to-be and your family as a whole. From long experience, when someone raises this kind of issue—baptism, confirmation, or a Christmas tree or anything else—it usually indicates a deeper, more profound discomfort with the so-called mutual decision to raise children as Jews. Your boyfriend might only claim to want to baptize a child for his mother. But where will it end? Perhaps church attendance and Bible school are also around the corner? And even if your boyfriend might claim otherwise, we all change over time and frequently become more religious as we get older. Maybe he is more conflicted about raising his children as Jews than he has been able to articulate at this point in your relationship.

My advice to you is to talk about your relationship and your individual, personal religious and spiritual identities together. Don't foist off any discussion about religion on your potential future children after you get married. Have a serious discussion about this now. The issue isn't about baptism at all; it is about your relationship with a non-Jewish man. Work that out first and stop using hypothetical discussions about children as a substitute topic.

Question number 7: In our multicultural society, it seems that everyone is tolerant and accepting of everyone else. If the values that I choose to raise my children with are the same as someone else who is outside my religion, what is the problem? If I raise my children as Jews and incorporate my values into my family, why should my partner have to be Jewish?

Answer: Gosh, I wish that were true—that everyone in our multicultural society was tolerant and accepting of everyone else. Unfortunately, I still think we have a long way to go before we get there; but I definitely believe that overall, and in some places more than others, there has been a growing trend toward greater tolerance of our differences. Now, regarding your question, if you wish to date non-Jews or raise your children with someone outside of your religion, it is beyond my ability—or interest—to try and persuade you to do something you see no value in. So rest assured, what you do is your own business.

However, not everything related to religion simply has to do with values. Judaism is a unique way of understanding the presence of God in the world and has developed a special and precious set of spiritual practices for trying to elicit godliness in our world. Other religions have their own unique rituals too. But they are different from ours.

Just because you may share the same values as your non-Jewish partner does not necessarily mean that you are going to understand God or holiness in the same way. Making a Shabbat dinner with candles, Kiddush (blessing over the wine), HaMotzi (blessing over the Challot), singing Zemirot (Shabbat songs), and Birkat HaMazon (grace after meals) is an experience that is unique to our religion. A non-Jew may participate, appreciate, and value such rituals; but they are uniquely Jewish ways to experience God.

In other words, to use a metaphor, the mutual appreciation of classical music is not a sufficient basis to create a solid, healthy marital relationship. You might enjoy this particular genre of the music, but ultimately, you may end up preferring different composers and styles and even attending different concerts. True music is humming the same score together. It is great that you share the same values—but enjoying a traditional Shabbat dinner may have a profoundly more powerful spiritual resonance for you than burning incense to a statue of the Hindu god Ganesh or sitting in silence for an hour at a Quaker Friends meeting. Your partner does not have to be Jewish if being Jewish is not a value that either of you share.

Question number 8: My Jewish nephew married a non-Jew, and they have invited me to their son's christening ceremony. And I don't know whether I should attend. You see, my son who is Jewish is also married to a non-Jewish woman; and while they have not yet planned any Christian baby rituals for their young daughter, I am worried that I might communicate the message that it is okay for them to have their baby christened as well. I want my granddaughter to be raised as a Jew, but I also don't want to offend the rest of my family by not attending. What should I do?

Answer: Go to your nephew's baby's christening. Major family life cycle events are not the time or place to communicate personal policy statements or take stands on religious issues. These are the times to establish a sense of family cohesiveness and unity. You don't have to pretend to enjoy it or make small talk—but go. Your presence is important.

And if you think that by not going you are sending a message to your son who is intermarried, then indeed you are—and that message is that you are vindictive, emotionally manipulative, and hard-hearted. But by going, you will demonstrate in a powerful way your willingness to be flexible, open, loving, and accepting.

If you are concerned about how your son will raise his daughter, then speak to him and his wife about your concerns. Be direct and communicate candidly. From your question, I couldn't tell whether you have ever shared your feelings and aspirations about the religious identity of your granddaughter with your son and daughter-in-law. Talk to them! Be open and honest, but recognize that this is *your* concern and they may not share it. I recommend that you also share your feelings of hurt and pain if your grandchild is not going to be raised as a Jew and how difficult and painful it would be for you to attend the christening of your granddaughter. Tell them of your hopes and desires that perhaps your daughter-in-law may decide to raise their child as a Jew and perhaps even become a Jew herself one day. And by the way, I'm sure you are familiar with the fact that since your daughter-in-law is not Jewish, traditional Jewish communities will not accept her as a Jew even if she is raised with that identity unless she officially converts or is converted as a child by her parents.

And don't leave it at that; do some homework for them. Check out local synagogues and rabbis. Find one that is welcoming of interfaith couples; find a rabbi that you think they might be able to establish a rapport with. Find a synagogue with a good Jewish prekindergarten program and religious school. And then give them the phone numbers and addresses and then butt out. As difficult as this may be to accept, the less anxious and upset you are about this, the more effective you can be in encouraging your son and daughter-in-law to deal with these issues of religion. The more you make it your problem, the more it will indeed be your problem and your problem alone. You will alienate your son, and by overfunctioning for him, never allowing him the space and emotional room to grapple with the issue of his child's religious identity on his own.

And finally, get more involved in Jewish life yourself. If your son is already married to a non-Jewish woman, while you may have done your best to express the value of Judaism in your own life while raising him, it is never too late to continue to have an effect on your family through your own actions. By joining a synagogue, attending services regularly, going to Jewish adult education classes, celebrating Shabbat and holidays regularly, joining a Jewish book group, and taking Hebrew classes, planning a visit to Israel, you will make it abundantly clear to your son that you value Judaism in your life. And even if you ultimately fail to influence your son, at least you will have found and created a community to fulfill your own Jewish needs so that you may find some consolation in the fact that even if your daughter is not raised as a Jew, you yourself—in your own life—are still living a fulfilling Jewish life. You do not need to foist on to your son and his family your own personal unfulfilled needs for living a more Jewish lifestyle.

In conclusion, communicate with your family. Be open, honest, and direct. But be compassionate and accepting. If you want to continue to be an active influence in the life of your son and grandchild, this is your only hope of being a positive and appreciated presence.

Question number 9: I am Jewish and love Judaism, but I am seriously dating a Christian man. I feel like we are soul mates. We have talked about getting married and having kids, and he is more than willing to raise our children as Jews and keep Shabbat and everything. I have heard arguments from both sides about whether an interfaith marriage can work, but no one has given me a clear reason that really makes sense to me. I guess my question is what will I face in the future if our relationship works, and why should I even consider not marrying him.

Answer: If this man is your soul mate, then by all means you should continue to pursue your relationship with him. And if Judaism is indeed a high priority in your life and is the spiritual path that you intend to follow throughout your life, then it makes sense to ask your partner to consider converting to Judaism. It is that simple.

Interfaith relationships can work—but usually it is because one of the partners is willing to support the religious lifestyle choices of their spouse. Sociological studies confirm that two spouses who are actively involved in two separate religions is a very important factor in predicting future divorce! Does it mean it could happen to you? Who knows, but you should be aware of the experience of the majority of other interfaith couples. I believe that it is in your interest and your non-Jewish partner's interest for him to convert to Judaism for the following reasons:

1. You will be able to share the same spiritual values. It ultimately makes no difference if you guys argue about leaving the toilet seat down or who does the dishes. It is far more important that you share the same principles and religious goals that you both agree on the same path to achieve holiness in your lives.
2. You will be able to build a Jewish home together and observe Jewish rituals and customs together. If Judaism is a priority in your life, then I can only hope and assume that at some point you will begin—or continue—to observe Shabbat, Kashrut and go to synagogue and give Tzedakah (charity) and continue learning about Judaism. It is awfully difficult to build and maintain a Jewish home if one partner is not involved or even Jewish. Believe me, I deal with interfaith couples all of the time and hear the tension, pain, and complaints as they tell me of their frustrations with their non-Jewish spouses who are not supportive of creating a Jewish home.
3. I believe your partner should convert to Judaism, but not for you! Rather, he should convert because Judaism is a profound

and deeply spiritual, fulfilling tradition that he should want to be part of for his own spiritual benefit and enrichment. If your partner converts to Judaism only for you, it will probably be a superficial action that at some level is disrespectful to you and at a deeper level ignores and dishonors the vastness and wisdom of the Jewish tradition. If your partner converts, let it be because he is interested in Judaism. The really difficult question I often ask converts who are about to marry a Jewish partner is, "If, God forbid, you should get divorced—would you still remain a Jew?" Would your partner be able to answer this question in the affirmative?

4. I believe your partner should convert so that you can raise your children as Jews. Even if your partner is supportive of raising his kids as Jews, if he himself never converts to Judaism, he is sending a subtle but corrosive message that Judaism is not worthwhile enough for him to become a Jew. It's good enough for other people and little kids, but not him. It is difficult enough as it is to raise children who will want to continue to be Jews as adults, why complicate it with a non-Jewish spouse?

5. It is difficult enough to create and maintain a lifelong loving marriage; adding in the additional factor of a different religion further complicates the situation. You may be setting yourself up for many difficult arguments in the future remaining in an interfaith relationship. Even if Judaism doesn't mean much to you now, people tend to become more religious as they get older, as they have children, as their parents die, when it is time for their children's Bar/Bat Mitzvah celebrations and marriages and so on. Even if whatever church your boyfriend grew up in isn't important to him now, perhaps he will have stronger feelings for his own religion as he grows older.

Do both of yourselves a favor—do your relationship a favor—and decide what you want to do about Judaism in your lives right now. If he wants to convert, well and good! If not, then recognize that you may not be among the few and truly unique people who can make it work. But make a wise, informed, and conscious decision. I do not want to try and make you feel guilty and pressured to do anything or make your partner do anything—that is beyond my ability and interest. I don't mean to be aloof or callous, but this is your life—decide how you want to live it. Figure out exactly what role Judaism will play in your life—and your partner's life—alone or together.

Question number 10: I'm Christian, but my serious boyfriend is Jewish and pretty religious. I have wanted to break off our relationship because of our different religions, but he claims that God would not have enabled us to meet or fall in love if He didn't have a plan for us together. But we both understand that if we had children one day, our different religions would be a problem. So should we get married and simply not have kids? And if we do get married, should we have a Jewish wedding or a Christian ceremony?

Answer: It must be very frustrating to be in a serious relationship with someone yet to have such deep-seated religious issues dividing you. Marriage is difficult enough without complicating it with different religious values. I encourage you as a couple to choose one religion to follow together, whether Jewish or Christian. Choose one and join each other in that spiritual path. After all, how can you pledge to live your lives together and intertwine them if you can't even agree on how to relate and worship God together?

Since you wrote to me, a rabbi, I encourage *you* to convert to Judaism. You may not have shared all of the details of your religious commitment to whatever Christian denomination you happen to belong to, but I can only interpret this omission to perhaps an absence of deep-seated commitment to your own religious faith of origin. Judaism has a clearly articulated and profoundly spiritual path for helping non-Jews study and go through the conversion process. Once you find the right rabbi and synagogue community, I think that you will be surprised and pleased with the support and positive reinforcement you will find in the Jewish community. The Jewish community welcomes Jews by choice, and maybe you will find a spiritual home there.

Also, since you mention that your boyfriend is pretty religious, I must express some surprise that he has allowed himself to become so seriously involved in a relationship with a non-Jewish woman. While I don't know you, I'm sure you must indeed be a very special and loving woman for your religious Jewish boyfriend to go against some pretty deep traditional barriers to engage in interfaith relationships. And if Judaism is so important to your boyfriend, perhaps he should be the one asking you and trying to persuade you to convert to Judaism and join him as part of the Jewish people. Has he ever even brought it up?

Either way, I don't think you or your boyfriend should avoid this issue. And please don't make the mistake and assume that you would be able to live a happily married life without children. Although there are plenty of couples that do indeed choose not to have children or are unable to, you need to know that having children is a significant and important part of married life in Judaism. In fact, it is considered a violation of God's plan for human beings to refrain from having or adopting and raising children. But please don't enter into your marriage hoping that it will succeed only because of this decision to not have children. What if one of you changes your mind eventually? Choose one religion for both of you. That is my advice—which you are free to accept or ignore. I wish you luck and courage to make these difficult decisions.

Question number 11: My sister is engaged to a Jewish man, but we are both very religious Roman Catholics. And we are not sure if his family will have a problem with their different religions. Will our families clash, and will his parents forbid the marriage because she is Catholic? Should I urge my sister to convert to Judaism? I would hate for some disagreement to come because of our faiths; and besides, if we all love God, what is the problem?

Answer: You asked lots of excellent questions, and I'll do my best to address them all. But first, I have to begin by telling you that as much as you may be genuinely interested and concerned about all of these issues (which is why I will answer them), they are ultimately none of your business. This is about your sister's life and her relationship with her fiancé and future husband and his family. Of course, your sister's life affects you, and you should indeed want to be supportive. But be careful about getting overinvolved in her life. For instance, why are *you* writing to me? Does your sister share your concerns, or are these only your concerns? And if she does have questions, I would encourage her to write directly or seek advice from her own spiritual advisor. So I must—with a gentle smile—encourage you to butt out of your sister's business.

But because it sounds like your concern is genuine and that you would benefit from learning the answers as well, I will do my best to answer your questions. But this information is for you. Obviously, feel free to share whatever I write with your sister; but once again, if she has concerns, let her deal with her own life—not you. That is a recipe for disaster for both of you.

If your sister is concerned about her fiancé's parents having a problem because she is not Jewish, why is she idly wondering about this now? Why hasn't your sister already discussed this with her fiancé or his family directly? And why wait until now after they are already engaged? Didn't they talk about these issues before this point? It seems a little late to suddenly begin worrying about something that should have been addressed a while ago. And why are you asking me if religion is a problem between them? Go ask them!

And for your second question, once again, I have no idea if your families will clash due to different religions. Isn't that your sister's problem and her fiancé's? Once again, I must caution you against overinvolvement in your sister's life. If your family is indeed devout and you and your sister are committed Roman Catholics, why on earth would you want to persuade your sister to abandon her religion for the sake of her fiancé? That is a pretty weak reason to change one's spiritual path in life. If your sister wants to convert, that is her business. Of course, I would encourage her to explore conversion to Judaism if that is what she really wants to do, but I am utterly opposed to people converting for the sake of a marriage. It is insulting to your sister—and your faith—and it is insulting to Judaism. As a rabbi, I would not easily welcome someone converting to Judaism just because they are getting married to a Jew.

You are obviously very concerned about your sister's well-being and her future marriage; but remember, as close as you may be, this is your sister's life, not yours. Let her work out her life without your interference. Instead, give her the support and love that she wants and needs as she embarks on establishing a new family with her fiancé.

Question number 12: My Christian friend has told me that I will go to hell because I do not believe in Jesus. When I tell her that there is no proof of Jesus's miracles, am I right? I also tell her that it would not be just for God to punish people by going to hell just because they were raised to believe in a different religion. I have asked her to stop talking about this subject with me, but she refuses and accuses me of being afraid. What could I say to make her understand my point of view?

Answer: Your so-called friend is being quite rude to you. In my opinion, she is being very insensitive to your feelings and requests. Although it does seem she is indeed filled with zeal and enthusiasm for her religion, she is violating your friendship by not respecting your Jewish identity or your requests to not discuss the subject.

In dealing with zealous religious fanatics and missionary Christians, I have found that it is impossible, and even irrelevant, to try to debate the logic of their arguments. Their beliefs are based on nonrational emotional grounds; therefore, logic is irrelevant to their faith. Because of this, I cannot provide any proofs or arguments that your friend may find persuasive. I encourage you though to read up on the differences between Judaism and Christianity for your own knowledge. You also might consider checking out the Web site of the organization Jews for Judaism (jewsforjudaism.org) that is a Jewish organization dedicated to combating the efforts of Jews for Jesus and other Christian missionaries.

Ultimately, I don't think your friend is being very friendly to you with her cruel insistence that you will go to hell. She may tell you and even be convinced that she is doing this for your own spiritual welfare, but it seems to me that there is more than a little hostility in her arguments and refusal to respect your requests. My advice is that you politely and gently lay down the ground rules of your relationship, particularly that both of you should avoid the subject of trying to convince one another that he or she is wrong in their religious beliefs and practices. And if she cannot respect that, then you have to ask yourself, how badly do you want to remain friends with this person? It is a tough choice, but from my limited perspective, your friend is anything but!

Question number 13: I'm not Jewish, but I have attended numerous Jewish ceremonies and services for years. At these, I usually try to say as many of the prayers as I know, but I end up mumbling through the rest. Is this disrespectful? Also, some very traditional religious Jewish friends recently invited me to stay with them over the Sabbath. What should I do? Should I try to observe certain Jewish rules and customs? Can I go with them to their synagogue for worship services? I'm not sure what to do.

Answer: No one expects you to know more than you do about Judaism. Just as if I were to attend a Shinto religious ceremony in Japan, no one would expect me to know more about Shintoism than I do (which isn't very much) or expect me to participate. Judaism is not your religion, and you should feel under no obligation to recite any of the Hebrew or English prayers. The fact that you make such an effort is a wonderful statement about your interest and respect of the Jewish religion. Therefore, if you choose to be silent, that is also perfectly acceptable and respectful. If you choose to recite the Hebrew prayers but end up mumbling the prayers, that is also okay. Not being Jewish, no one expects you to either try reciting these prayers or even to recite them correctly or even at all. So relax and enjoy the aesthetic aspects of the religious services.

As a guest of a traditional religious Shabbat-observant family, once again, no one expects you to know more than you do. Therefore, ask your hosts what is appropriate and respectful. They will probably welcome your interest and will be only too happy to explain anything that you do not understand. Don't be embarrassed; ask them before you try to do something that you are not sure about.

As for going to synagogue with your friends, why not? Go and have a good time. But if they are Orthodox, please know that you may not be able to sit next to them during the services depending upon your own gender. In Orthodox religious services, men and women sit in different seating areas. Other than that, have a good time. You will probably learn a lot and maybe even have fun!

Chapter 3

Conversion and Jewish Identity
(Twenty Questions)

Converting to Judaism can be an arduous process. After all, the Jewish tradition is over three thousand years old, filled with a rich history of significant past events, great religious literature, sophisticated theology, a full calendar of holidays, and chock-full of home rituals, spiritual practices, prayers, customs, and commandments. It is a comprehensive way of life, and this wealth of knowledge can be an exhausting obstacle to a potential convert. It is no wonder that many formal courses for conversion to Judaism can take over a year—there is a lot to learn!

And would-be converts to Judaism have many choices to make at the outset of their religious conversion process; for instance, which Jewish denomination should they choose to oversee their conversion? Which rabbi should they choose for a tutor and mentor? And which synagogue should they begin attending? It can be quite daunting and complicated for many potential Jews by choice to consider.

Even for people who are born Jewish, there are many diverse ways to express one's Jewish identity. Some people express their Jewish identity through spiritual rituals such as prayer and synagogue activities. Other Jews identify more with cultural aspects of Jewish life such as enjoying traditional Jewish foods or Jewish dance, theater, film, and music. Others connect to the intellectual, academic history of Jewish life and spend time learning sacred Jewish texts, reading books of Judaica (like this one), and attending Jewish classes for adults; and still for others, their Jewish identity might consist solely of working out at a local Jewish community center equipped with a gym or indoor pool. There is no single correct way to be a Jew.

The issue of Jewish identity becomes even more complicated when Jews are involved in interfaith relationships and marriages and especially when they have children. Jewish and non-Jewish partners—and children—often feel torn and conflicted as to their spiritual identity. How should people in these complex situations express their Jewish identity? There are no easy answers about how to negotiate the challenges of living life as both a Jew and a member of another faith community.

Many Jews sent me questions as to how to practice their own religion while still more sent in questions seeking to clarify some of the confusing aspects of the formal process of conversion to Judaism. Others also asked about how to express their Jewish identity while involved in an interfaith relationship or marriage. All of these questions reveal a sincere desire to find a way to express an authentic connection to the Jewish tradition. However, there is no one way to be a Jew—and the following questions reveal a great deal of interest and confusion about just how to go about becoming or being a Jew in the modern world. I can only hope that my answers helped shed a light on these topics.

Question number 1: *I would like to convert to Judaism, but my husband does not want me to and I can understand his position. When we had our children, I insisted on baptizing them although my husband was not religious at all. Now that I am interested in becoming a Jew, he is angry that I spent so much time and effort convincing him to raise our children as Catholic and that I will just be confusing our kids. However, I feel very strongly about becoming a Jew now. What should I do?*

Answer: I encourage you and maybe your husband as well to see a marriage counselor. Whatever else is happening in your spiritual life, you need to ensure that your marriage is strong and that your extended family is understanding and supportive of your decision to convert to Judaism.

In terms of converting, that is a decision that you and you alone can make. But you should also take into serious consideration your husband's concerns and what impact your decision to become a Jew might have on your children whom you have already invested significant effort to raise as religious Catholics. Please know that you would be welcomed into the Jewish people after a conversion, but before you do so, I encourage you first to seek some spiritual and marriage counseling and then, after that, speak to a local rabbi and ask what it would involve so you can better understand the decision you are considering.

To give you an idea of what you might be getting into, here is a general outline of the steps for formal conversion to Judaism. The idea that someone could choose to become a Jew is an ancient idea going back even as far as the Hebrew Bible. In the book of Ruth, Ruth herself joins the Jewish people in her moving declaration of love and commitment to her mother-in-law Naomi when she says, "Your people shall be my people, and your God my God" (Ruth 1:16). Since that time, the rabbis and subsequent generations of Jews have formalized this process of becoming Jewish. To become a Jew today involves the following steps:

1. A Jew by choice must learn about the Jewish people and how to live a Jewish life. They must learn a little about Jewish history, theology, the Hebrew Bible, and other classical Jewish texts. They must also begin to learn how to at least read a little Hebrew (not necessarily speak it fluently), how to pray in Hebrew, the traditions of keeping Shabbat, the holidays, and Kashrut (Jewish dietary laws). Of course, no one can learn everything there is to know about all of these subjects; however, it is certainly expected that Jews by choice, and indeed all born Jews as well, should

learn how to be lifelong learners and observers of the Jewish tradition.

2. After approximately a year of study, a candidate for conversion is invited to appear before a Beit Din (a rabbinic court) consisting of three rabbis who will ask the candidate about themselves, their reasons for wanting to join the Jewish people and determine their level of knowledge, commitment, and sincerity. This is not a test but rather an interview to determine whether a candidate is sufficiently knowledgeable and emotionally ready to formally join the Jewish people.

3. If the Beit Din accepts them, a male will be circumcised or, since it is common practice to circumcise most baby boys in the hospital shortly after birth, they will undergo a quick, painless ritual ceremony called Hatafat Dam Brit (the drawing of a drop of covenantal blood). There is no equivalent ceremony for a woman.

4. At this point, both male and female candidates will immerse in a Mikvah (ritual bath) whose waters come from purely natural sources, such as rain, spring water, ice, or snowmelt. Anyone who enters a Mikvah must shower and be completely hygienically clean before they enter the waters to ensure that nothing whatsoever prevents the waters from coming into contact with all parts of their body. The candidate immerses himself or herself once fully then recites the blessing, "Praised are You, Adonai our God, who has sanctified us with Your commandments and commanded us concerning immersion." After a second immersion, that person emerges from the waters of the Mikvah as a complete and fully accepted Jew in the Jewish people.

A wonderful Midrash, or rabbinic folktale, claims that when Sarah, who was the wife of Abraham, finally gave birth to her son, Isaac, her breast milk was so abundant and nourishing even in her old age that the non-Jewish mothers from the surrounding peoples brought their newborn infants to suckle at Sarah's breast. The Midrash goes on to state that all Jews by choice are descendants of those non-Jewish babies and are returning to the source of their original ancestral nourishment.

Our community is truly blessed by the presence and participation of so many Jews by choice. May our community continue to be so enriched and nourished in the future.

Question number 2: *If Jews are truly God's chosen people and their offspring throughout the centuries are still God's chosen people today, how can a non-Jew ever truly convert and become a Jew when it seems to me that it is based on genetic heritage? Does becoming a Jew make one chosen, or is it based on blood heritage?*

Answer: Converting to Judaism automatically bestows upon a person the distinction of being part of the chosen people. It is not a quality passed on through the blood or inherited through the generations; it is simply a function of one's being Jewish.

But then again, don't forget that pretty much every ethnic group, religion, and nation in the world sees itself as chosen and special for one reason or another. For Jews, being chosen doesn't mean that Jews are better than anyone else; it simply means that Jews believe they were singled out by God to receive the Torah and to observe the myriad commandments in it and their updated rabbinic adaptations throughout the ages. In other words, it is like when your mom singles you out to do more chores in the house because you are considered more responsible than your siblings, or something like that. You simply have more work to do, and it is not because you are better than anyone else in your family.

Therefore, when someone converts to Judaism, they are voluntarily joining the Jewish people who also, at one point in history, voluntarily took on this obligation of observing the commandments in the Torah. Thus, anyone who converts is also chosen just as the Jewish people back at Mt. Sinai exercised their free wills and also decided to be chosen by God and accept the Torah and its obligations. In other words, you can volunteer to be chosen by converting to Judaism! And if you don't believe me about the ability of someone who converts to Judaism to be considered chosen, read the book of Ruth in the Hebrew Bible. She was a Moabite who was considered one of the first converts to Judaism. And she was the great-grandmother of King David!

Question number 3: Dear Rabbi, I'm Catholic and my husband is Jewish. We have a three-year-old daughter whom I insisted that we baptize; however, I also want her to learn about Judaism as well. We sort of celebrate Hanukkah and Passover, but my husband could care less about practicing Judaism. Should I bother trying to teach my daughter about Judaism as well as Catholicism, or should I leave well enough alone and raise my daughter as a Catholic?

Answer: Leave well enough alone. Raise your daughter as a Catholic because that is clearly what you are passionate about. If your husband is interested in passing along his Jewish religious background to his daughter, that should be his decision, not yours. If he feels strongly enough about it, then let him take the initiative. After all, he is the Jew, not you.

Also, traditional Judaism only recognizes children as Jewish if their mother is Jewish. Therefore, raising your daughter to believe that she is Jewish may not only confuse her but also lead her to future frustration and rejection by the rest of the traditional Jewish community later on. Please spare your daughter this heartbreaking misconception.

This might sound funny coming from a rabbi, but stop with the Passover and Hanukkah rituals along with your Christian holiday celebrations. I have met too many adults who were supposedly raised with both religions, and they were almost unanimous in sharing that it was a dismal failure and led them to a very confused and tortured spiritual identity as adults. Your daughter was baptized. She is Catholic, not Jewish. Raise her the way that you clearly intended for her to be raised—as a Catholic. This doesn't mean you have to hide or avoid your husband's Jewish identity, but it is his identity to deal with at this point, not yours. If you wish to talk more about this, I strongly recommend that you contact a local rabbi with whom you can speak directly. Good luck!

Question number 4: *I'm fifteen years old and want to convert to Judaism, but I have heard that no rabbi will teach me unless I'm eighteen. I have many Jewish friends, and I found their Bar/Bat Mitzvahs to be the most spiritual events I have ever seen. I don't feel it is fair to deny me the right to convert to Judaism; doesn't the U.S. Constitution grant everyone the freedom of religion?*

Answer: I am impressed with your zeal, strong commitment, and desire to convert to Judaism. Your arguments are passionate, but unfortunately, they are not necessarily persuasive. You see, even though I would encourage you to continue to learn about Judaism and even begin to take on Jewish practices right now, even at fifteen, I personally would not accept you as a conversion student until you were twenty-one!

Why? Simple—under American law, teenagers become considered adults in a series of stages. At sixteen you can drive, at eighteen you can vote (and be drafted), and at twenty-one you can purchase alcohol. Similarly, there are laws called laws of statutory rape. This is an uncomfortable and graphic subject, but these laws (which vary from state to state) say that even if a young woman is ready to be sexually active and wants to have sex with an older man, simply because she is under a certain age (sometimes seventeen, eighteen, or even twenty-one) the man can be charged with statutory rape even though the young woman was ready and willing to engage in the relationship! This is because that no matter what her age, the law feels that for certain decisions, young people are not mature enough even to decide what to do with their own bodies.

Similarly, although converting to Judaism is nothing like statutory rape, no rabbi (male or female) would ever want to be accused of taking advantage of a teenager and altering their religious identity before they are considered a full adult in our society no matter how willing they were. After all, you didn't say anything about how your family feels about this decision of yours—are they supportive? Perhaps they would be hurt and offended by your decision to change your religion from theirs.

Also, as a Jew, you would be expected to keep Kosher, observe Shabbat, and pray on a regular basis. Would you be able to observe these—and other—Jewish customs and rituals while living in your parents' home? You should know that no rabbi would willingly create a situation where a Jew must—simply because of their age—have no choice but to break Jewish laws and customs because they were not old enough to live by themselves in order to create a Jewish home life experience.

I admire your strong desire to convert, but if you truly want to convert, then start learning about Judaism now. Start taking on as many practices as possible now. Then when you a find a rabbi willing to accept you as a conversion student when you are a little older (either eighteen or twenty-one), you will be that much more ready. You might not like my advice or explanations, but that is the way it is. In fact, waiting till you are older may be harder for you right now, but it is a more mature decision and course of action for you to take.

In fact, anyone who would be willing to accept you as a conversion student now, I believe, would not really be respecting you. Because you could change your mind and make different decisions as you get older. I'm respecting you by allowing you the time to grow and mature in your decision and commitment to convert to Judaism.

You might not have enjoyed what I have said, but I hope you will consider my words. And to be brutally honest, since you probably would not be able to find a rabbi who would work with you as a conversion student, you don't have a choice in the matter. Given this reality, I encourage you to demonstrate your commitment and deepen your understanding and observance of Judaism as much as you can now so that when the time comes, if you are still interested, your conversion process will go that much more smoothly and quickly.

Question number 5: *My fiancé is Jewish and very religious, and even though I am Catholic, I'd still like our future children to be raised as Jews. Is it wrong to convert to Judaism mostly so our children will be*

Jewish when they are born? Is it wrong to do it only for the religion of our children?

Answer: It is not wrong to convert to Judaism only for the sake of your children; however, it is shortsighted, perhaps even hypocritical, and despite what you might think, even insulting to the Jewish religion.

I actively try to dissuade people from converting to Judaism if the only reason they are doing so is to raise their children as Jews. First of all, this is insulting to the Jewish tradition because it implies that Judaism is only important for little kids, not for adults. I would like to believe that the Jewish religion has value and meaning to adults and is not a tradition that is of so little value and interest that it might only be of interest and value to young children. Also, you will communicate a message of hypocrisy to your children that Judaism wasn't good enough for you to take seriously and convert out of your own personal interest and spiritual commitment, but it was acceptable to undergo a superficial conversion for your children. In that sense, you will send the message to your children that Judaism isn't really important if you, their mother, didn't think it was important enough to become Jewish for its own spiritual merits. Also, it is disrespectful to the Jewish tradition because Judaism is a rich and spiritually powerful religion and deserves serious study and commitment in its own right. To enter into the study of Judaism for a trivial goal-oriented reason insults the depth of Judaism's spiritual richness and moral wisdom.

And finally, converting only for your children is also disrespectful to yourself! Why should you have to give up your religious heritage just for the sake of your husband and your future children? Why doesn't he convert to Catholicism? You should take your own spiritual life seriously. If you choose to convert, do so for yourself—not for anyone else or for anything else. Respect yourself!

On the other hand, if you do indeed convert to Judaism only for the sake of your children, I can only hope that the process of studying to become a Jew may, in fact, end up exciting you and lighting a fire of true interest and passion about Judaism. So while you might not be particularly interested in Judaism for its own sake—who knows—maybe you might end up falling in love with Judaism for its own sake. I would like to think so.

I encourage you to talk with your fiancé and discuss this issue of conversion in greater depth and seriousness. You should resolve this issue long before you get married. A superficial conversion for his sake or your future children will not solve any problems, and in fact, this issue may become more intense and difficult the longer you are together.

You should also consider the fact that it is possible to get married and have children and then convert only your children to Judaism. Of course, any rabbi that you choose to convert your children would naturally insist that the children be raised as Jews in a Jewish household with, hopefully, two Jewish parents. In which case, the problems I mentioned above will be even more acute; you will communicate a message of hypocrisy to your children that Judaism wasn't good enough for you, but it is acceptable for them. Your personal example will send the message to your children that Judaism isn't important to you personally for your own life; therefore, your kids may ultimately wonder why should they take it any more seriously.

I don't mean to insult your fiancé in any way, but if this issue of marrying a Jew and raising Jewish children is so important to him, why did he choose to build a relationship with you, a non-Jew? The idea that love conquers all is an unrealistic fantasy; good communication and open, honest dialogue and willingness to compromise are what conquers all. Have some more serious discussions about the role of religion in your lives together. I also encourage you to speak with a rabbi and visit some synagogues before you make any premature decisions. This is a vast and deep subject that clearly is very important to your fiancé—and it should be equally weighty for you. Explore this more and flesh out what your expectations are with each other. Matters of spirit should not be taken lightly. Respect your own spiritual life and the Jewish religion. Make the choices that are right for everyone involved—including you!

Question number 6: Is being Jewish more than a religion? If it is just a religion, why is there Hebrew, Jewish food, and Jewish music? Is Judaism a religion or an ethnic group?

Answer: You asked really good questions! If I understood correctly, you asked if Judaism is only a religion, or is it also an ethnic grouping? The answer is that it is both!

Rabbi Mordecai Kaplan, a famous American rabbi and scholar, once defined Judaism as a religious civilization. The religious part means that Judaism is indeed a religion. There are synagogues, rabbis and cantors, prayers and holidays, Jewish beliefs, and everything else associated with a spiritual way of life. But Judaism is also a civilization. That means that over the past three thousand years, the Jewish people have picked up and added to Jewish civilization all sorts of things from all over the world. For instance, Jews in Eastern Europe ate bagels and smoked salmon like other non-Jewish people living there; but when Jews from Eastern Europe came to America, this food became part of the larger Jewish civilization. Jews who lived in Arab countries for centuries picked up common musical melodies and applied them to Jewish prayers. Even when these Jews left those countries, they brought those melodies with them, and this music then became part of the larger Jewish civilization. Therefore, there are Jewish foods from all over the world, Jewish dances, Jewish clothes, Jewish music, Jewish literature written in special Jewish languages—Hebrew, Yiddish, Ladino, and Judeo-Arabic and others.

Judaism is also an ethnicity, meaning, there is a Jewish peoplehood. Being a Jew doesn't just mean belonging to a synagogue, it means being part of this larger Jewish people scattered all over the world that share these bonds of religion and civilization. So Judaism is both a religion and a civilization. One doesn't have to be religious to be a part of or enjoy the Jewish civilization part.

Question number 7: A long time ago during a difficult period in my life, I converted to Christianity, but I immediately regretted it and even went to a Mikvah [a ritual Jewish bath for spiritual purification]. *But I remember that the church told me that my conversion was irreversible. I want to be Jewish again, and now I feel miserable—is there anything I can do, or is it too late?*

Answer: Thank you for sharing that part of yourself and your past. It must have been a very difficult time for you, and I'm glad that you were able to find solace and relief in an accepting and supportive community even if it was a church. And I want to reassure you that what you experienced and went through is not so unique. I know of many people, even fully practicing Jews today, who converted to Christianity but then returned to Judaism.

The fact that you converted to Christianity and went through baptism is actually a very minor and insignificant matter in terms of the Jewish tradition. In fact, this issue was dealt with by a medieval rabbi named Rashi—short for Shlomo ben Yitzchak—who lived over one thousand years ago. Rashi lived during the Crusades in Europe and ended up making religious decisions as to the status of Jews who had converted to Christianity in order to save their lives. When the crusading knights who had forcibly converted many Jews to Christianity upon pain of death left their towns, many of these Jews wanted to return to being Jews again and didn't know what to do. So Rashi ruled that a Jew, no matter what the circumstances, who decides to convert to another faith is still and always a Jew in the eyes of the Jewish community. The fact that you have even visited a Mikvah in a spiritual and symbolic return to the Jewish tradition is a moving and powerful testament to your desire to return to Jewish life.

The fact that you were told that your conversion to Christianity was irreversible may have upset you, but it means nothing in the Jewish tradition. They can say whatever they want; but if you clearly are not Christian now and do not subscribe to their beliefs, follow their practices, and no longer feel a part of that community, it is irrelevant what any church leaders may tell you.

To address and resolve your concerns, I would urge you to learn more about Judaism and encourage you to take on Jewish ritual practices as a way to continue your return to Jewish life. Observing Shabbat, attending synagogue, keeping Kosher, and giving Tzedakah (charity) are powerful ways to spiritually connect to the Jewish tradition. And I would like you to know that the more you practice Jewish rituals, the less you will feel threatened and uneasy by your past conversion to Christianity. I would also encourage you to seek some professional counseling to address your fears and concerns. While the claims of your former church may have no standing in the Jewish tradition, your fears and concerns are real, and I would urge you to address these feelings. Perhaps even seeking out a local rabbi for further guidance would be helpful. Good luck!

Question number 8: My sister and her husband are both Jewish; however, they have never joined a synagogue, sent their children to religious school, or celebrated their Bar and Bat Mitzvahs. They are completely ignorant of Jewish life and customs. I am Jewish, but my wife is not. Yet we belong to a Reform temple, have sent our children to religious school. They can read and write Hebrew, had Bar and Bat Mitzvahs, and continue to celebrate Jewish holidays. According to Halachah [Jewish law], my niece and nephew are Jewish but utterly ignorant of Judaism. Yet according to Halachah, my children are not Jewish, yet they are knowledgeable and observant of Jewish laws and customs. This situation angers me, and so I ask you, whose children should truly be considered Jews?

Answer: You ask an obvious question and seem intent in trying to provoke some other answer that you can attack. Obviously, your children are more knowledgeable about Judaism than your niece or nephew. However, you are indeed correct that based on a traditional understanding of Jewish law, your children still are technically not considered Jews by the rest of the traditional Jewish community that does not recognize the validity of matrilineal Jewish descent. However, as you know, your sister's children are considered Jewish by the traditional Jewish community despite their complete ignorance of Jewish traditions. It is indeed frustrating, even aggravating and unfair.

However, it may be helpful to think of the Jewish tradition as a kind of game that everyone has the opportunity to play by the rules that they want. Obviously, you are perturbed by the Halachic status of your niece and nephew and your own children. Therefore, I would encourage you to remain active in the Reform, Reconstructionist, or Jewish Renewal community that accepts children such as yours as fully legitimate Jews based on patrilineal descent and a Jewish upbringing. Based on what you indicated in your question, your family does seem to be strongly connected to the Reform Jewish community that accepts the validity of your children's Jewish identity. So what is the problem? It is futile and fruitless to try and seek the acceptance of your children as Jews from the traditional Jewish community, a community that by self-definition does not acknowledge the validity of the form of Judaism you practice. Why beat your head against a wall?

If this situation is unacceptable to you, then go and have your children converted—brought to a Mikvah and symbolically circumcised, all according to traditional Jewish law. Then your children will be considered as equally Halachically Jewish as your niece and nephew. Or if your children are already adults and this situation bothers them, they can go through the traditional rituals of conversion if it makes them feel any better. However, I'm afraid that no rabbi—or anyone—can wave a magic wand and change the traditional understanding of Jewish law in a new way that may make you happier. Is it unfair? Yes, of course, it is; but the traditional Jewish community plays by its own rules of the Jewish tradition. I wish you strength and peace in your spiritual quest for a sense of Jewish legitimacy for your family's Jewish identity.

Question number 9: *My mother is Jewish, and my father was Catholic. And although I wasn't raised in any religion, my mother enjoys and still celebrates Christmas with all of the holiday decorations. My husband, who is Jewish, and I are raising our children as Jews; and my mother has* *agreed to begin celebrating Hanukkah and Passover with us at her home for her grandchildren. But she still insists that we join her for Christmas. I am afraid this is going to confuse my kids. And I have tried to persuade my mother to stop celebrating Christmas, but she won't. What should I do? How am I going to explain this situation to my children?*

Answer: What a complicated situation! If I understand this right, even though your mother is Jewish and has recently agreed to begin celebrating Hanukkah and Passover for your kids, she still celebrates Christmas. I can indeed imagine how difficult it will be for you to explain this to your children!

My advice is don't try to change your mother. You can't and you won't, not after all of this time. But you can change how you and your family celebrate the Jewish holidays. Don't focus and obsess about Christmas at your mother's; instead, make *all* of the Jewish holidays in your home really big deals. Invite your mother to your house for Jewish holidays and then go over the top with Passover and make a big Kasher Seder in your home and have Matzah and no bread. Learn about and celebrate Shavuot, the festival celebrating receiving the Torah at Mt. Sinai. Make sure your family knows about Tisha B'Av and fasts on this date commemorating the destruction of the ancient Temples. And be sure that Rosh HaShanah and Yom Kippur are celebrated in your home as well with big festive meals and attendance at synagogue services. And build a Sukkah this year and eat your meals there. Be sure you attend synagogue for Simchat Torah when we dance with the Torahs and read from the end to the beginning again. And don't forget to dress up for Purim and make a big celebration of it, and of course, there is always Hanukkah!

But most especially, don't forget Shabbat each week—be sure to light candles every Friday night, have a big Shabbat dinner on Friday night with Kiddush and Challot and nice dishes and a fancy white tablecloth and especially your family's favorite food dishes. And go to synagogue on Saturday morning and make Shabbat truly a day of rest, peace, and family activities in your home on Saturday. After all, Shabbat is even more holy than Yom Kippur—and we get to celebrate it every week!

In other words, drown out Christmas at your mother's by ensuring that your children live a life utterly filled to the brim with Jewish celebrations and commemorations and Jewish identity. Make sure they have completely positive, fun-filled experiences with Jewish life. The issue isn't your Jewish mother's celebration of Christmas; it is how much of a Jewish life you can provide in your home throughout the entire year. Marginalize your mom's *celebration* of Christmas—don't marginalize your mother.

Question number 10: *Why are people not considered Jewish if their mother wasn't Jewish but their father was? Where is this law written in the Torah? This law doesn't seem very Jewish to me. It sounds like only a man-made law and not from God.*

Answer: You asked a good question—where is the biblical basis for Jewish matrilineal descent? It is important to understand that the religion described in the Torah is not modern Judaism. The Torah describes an ancient biblical cult based on animal sacrifices at a Temple administered by priests. Modern Judaism is the religion based on the latter rabbinic interpretations and adaptations of the Torah to a post-Temple existence. All of modern Judaism is rabbinic Judaism. The vast majority of what constitutes Judaism today—and for the past two thousand years—does not appear anywhere in the Torah. So therefore, just because something does not appear in the Torah does not mean it isn't Jewish.

As for the issue of matrilineal descent, this tradition is very ancient. For the past two thousand years, Jewish lineage has followed the religion of the mother. Every child of a Jewish mother is 100 percent Jewish, and if the child is a daughter, she is 100 percent Jewish as are all of her subsequent children. This is based on ancient traditions from the Talmud—*not* the Torah. However, this does not mean that there is not material in the Torah to support this position of matrilineal descent.

There has always been a concern in the Hebrew Bible for Israelite men to marry fellow Israelite women. Abraham went to a lot of trouble to have Isaac marry someone from his own people (Genesis 24), and even

Jacob went back to Haran to find someone from his father's clan to marry (Genesis 28). The actual establishment of matrilineal descent in Jewish law probably occurred during the Babylonian exile (beginning 586 BCE) because in the book of Ezra, there was already a concern that the Jewish men have married non-Jewish women (Ezra chapter 10) and their children might not be considered Jewish.

This law of matrilineal descent was finalized during the Talmudic period (approximately 70 to 500 CE) although it reflects earlier traditions that held that Jewish descent was derived solely from the mother's line (perhaps due to the obvious certainty of establishing a child's maternity). The Mishnah, the very first text of rabbinic interpretations written down around 220 CE, provides a Talmudic basis for matrilineal descent when it states, "In the case of any woman whose betrothal with [a man] is not licit [that is, a non-Jew or member of her family] and whose betrothal with others would also not be valid [such as marrying a priest if she were a divorcée, which is not allowed], *the offspring follow her own status (emphasis mine)*; for example, the offspring of . . . a non-Jewish woman" (Mishnah Kiddushin 3:12). This is somewhat difficult to follow, but essentially, it states that the rabbis of the Talmud held that Jewish lineage, and hereditary identity in general, follow after the status of the mother, not the father.

The Gemara, a rabbinic interpretation of the Mishnah (and also part of the Talmud), claims that the law of matrilineal descent actually goes all the way back to the Torah. Deuteronomy 7:3ff says, "You shall not marry with them [referring to Canaanite and non-Israelite women] nor give your daughter to their sons nor take their daughters for your sons—for they will turn your sons away." This refers to the Torah law prohibiting intermarriage for fear that a non-Israelite spouse might lead her Israelite husband away from Jewish religious practice.

The Gemara then states, "How do we know that her children bear her religious identity? Rabbi Yochanon said in the name of Rabbi Shimon bar Yochai: Because the Torah says 'your son.' This means that 'your son' by a Jewish woman is called your son, but your son from a non-Jewish woman is not called your son, but rather *her* son" (Talmud Kiddushin 68b). This is a pretty clear statement of matrilineal descent! Later rabbinic codes written throughout medieval times accepted this interpretation of matrilineal descent. If you should ever want to look them up, two significant rabbis who wrote about this are Rabbi Moses Maimonides (Mishneh Torah, Hilchot Issurei Bi'ah 15:4) and Rabbi Yosef Karo (Shulchan Aruch, Even HaEzer 4), and they both quote these sources above and state pretty clearly that Jewish hereditary identity is based on matrilineal descent.

In modern times, the Orthodox communities and the Conservative movement have continued this tradition. However, according to the liberal denominations of American Judaism—such as Reform, Reconstructionist, and Jewish Renewal—someone is considered Jewish if they had only a Jewish father (and a non-Jewish mother) and provided they were raised as a Jew. Therefore, according to these denominations, someone born to a non-Jewish mother but a Jewish father is Jewish.

As for your feeling that this is only a man-made law and not from God, you are free and entitled to hold any opinions that you wish, and I respect that. However, as you have just read, your views are not consistent with the bulk of the historical Jewish tradition. It doesn't mean that your personal opinions have to be in accord with Judaism, but you should know that your personal opinion is just that—your personal opinion. You may not like this law, but it doesn't mean that this will change the nature of the Jewish tradition. But at least now you know the origins of the law of matrilineal Jewish descent.

Question number 11: What is a secular Jew? How can someone be a Jew without believing in God? I know some Jews who don't believe in God but still celebrate Jewish holidays—but what's to celebrate if you don't believe in God?

Answer: You asked a good question. The term "secular Jew" is indeed bandied about a lot. I suppose a dictionary definition of a "secular Jew" would indeed be someone who is born to a Jewish mother (or both Jewish parents) but who does not practice any aspects of the Jewish religion. There are also secular Catholics and secular Muslims and nonpracticing nonbelievers who are nonetheless affiliated with other religions. These are people born into a particular religious tradition but who do not choose to follow this spiritual path as adults in an active way.

I am also touched by the direct simplicity of your question. For someone who is not religious or spiritually motivated, they could just as easily ask us, "How can any rational person believe in God?" Nowadays, it is easy for people not to believe in God. However, for deeply religious people, it is impossible not to believe in God. If you are indeed of a deeply spiritual nature, then I applaud you and am impressed by your astonishment that anyone, much less a Jew, might not believe in God. Indeed, there is an old Jewish saying that goes, "A Jew can love God or a Jew can hate God, but a Jew cannot ignore God!"

If you are asking a semantic question and are asking how can we apply the label of Jew to someone who does not believe in God, that is easy to answer. As I mentioned above, a Jew is someone, according to a traditional understanding of Judaism, who happens to have been born to a Jewish mother (or both Jewish parents). I am temporarily excluding converts to Judaism in this answer because I presume converts to Judaism do indeed believe in God.

Also, no Jew is *required* to believe in God. That is one of the unique aspects of Judaism; we require no affirmation of personal belief in God. Interestingly enough, the Shema, the central prayer stating the Jewish belief in only one God, only asserts that we believe in the unity of God, not the existence of God as that is already presumed. The Jewish tradition is actually very tolerant and accepting of all Jews no matter their personal theological beliefs.

Of course, while Jewish spiritual practices are predicated on the belief in God, one does not necessarily have to believe in God to practice Judaism. And this leads me to your other question—it is not necessary for a Jew to believe in God if they want to celebrate Jewish holidays. Many Jews are still involved with the Jewish tradition and even ritual celebrations as a way to affirm their Jewish identity, to connect to other Jews, to assert their cultural Jewish identity, or even to identify with the values embedded in the rituals.

For instance, one need not have to believe in God to celebrate a Passover Seder, the ritual meal celebrating the exodus of the Jews from Egypt that, among other things, celebrates the value of freedom and national liberation. There are many different reasons why Jews who are not spiritually inclined might want to still observe some aspects of the Jewish spiritual tradition even if they don't believe in God.

Question number 12: *Our son will be attending a local Catholic high school this year with some of his Jewish friends. Although he is pretty active in our synagogue youth group and has a strong Jewish identity, I'm worried that going to a Catholic high school will somehow undermine his Jewish identity. What are your thoughts?*

Answer: Your feelings of uneasiness may indeed never go away. And after all, how can they? How will you ever know for sure that your son has not strayed from his Jewish identity—until he marries a Jewish girl or until he sends his children to religious school or until your grandchildren celebrate their Bar and Bat Mitzvah? Are you prepared to feel uneasy for that long? You may never resolve these feelings for yourself.

However, you may at least begin to diminish their hold over you by expressing your feelings of concern to your son and not your paranoia. Do not burden your son with your anxiety as he probably has enough of his own about going to high school and being a Jew in a Catholic school. But you should continue to express how much Judaism means to you and live your life in a way that demonstrates your values. You may say that Judaism means a lot to you, but do Jewish values and practices influence your life? How involved with your synagogue are you? How often do you attend services? Do you have regular Shabbat dinners with

Kiddush over the wine and HaMotzi over Challot? Do you observe any aspects of keeping Kosher? Do you continue to improve your own Jewish knowledge by attending adult education classes either at your synagogue or the local Jewish community center? Do you support Jewish causes and give to charitable organizations? If you want your son to value his Jewish identity, you must first value it in yourself.

Since your son's fellow Jewish friends will also be attending this high school with him, you must accept the fact that this is your problem, not your son's. In fact, your continuing anxiety may only have a negative effect on your son—and yourself—if you continue to express it to him and do not work to resolve it in yourself. If you are always worried that he may not be Jewish enough, it may lead your son to develop a poor and even negative self-image of himself as a Jew. He may come to internalize your fears and question his own validity as a Jew, constantly asking himself if he is, in fact, Jewish enough. He may start to wonder whether he will ever be able to do enough for his parents—and in his own eyes—to consider himself a good Jew. Such pressure, external and internal, can alienate people from their positive feelings of identification with the Jewish community. He may even come to reject his Jewish identity if you set such a high standard that he feels that he might never be able to satisfy you.

My advice to you is to focus on the positive aspects of being a Jew and how important they are to you as an adult and how your Jewish identity and personal observances as a Jew affect your life. Your son is at a crucial time in his personal and spiritual development, and your role as a Jewish role model may play a far greater part in his maturation than you can imagine. If you want your son to have a positive and strong identity as a Jew, work and continue to strive to live your own life in the same way. Good luck and I hope that you can rest assured and be confident in your son's spiritual development as a Jew and in your own!

Question number 13: *As I have grown older, I have been more attracted to Jewish life such as attending synagogue services regularly and taking* *adult Jewish education classes. Unfortunately, my husband, who is also Jewish, has no interest in joining me. I love my husband and want to spend time with him, so I feel torn: should I put my husband before my religion? I also want him to join me as a Jewish role model for our college-age children. What should I do?*

Answer: It must indeed be very frustrating for you that your husband is not as spiritually motivated as you are and is not willing to accompany you on your Jewish journey. As sorry as I am to write this, I'm afraid you will also not like reading it—quit trying to influence your husband's religious feelings and work on your own.

You cannot change your husband by directly trying to change him. Instead, I encourage you to continue to develop your own spirituality and knowledge of Judaism as you are already doing. Continue to attend synagogue services as often as you want. Continue to attend adult education classes—learn more about the Torah, Jewish history, prayers, Hebrew, and Kabbalah. Volunteer for your synagogue—join a committee, get involved. Make social connections with other Jews who share your passion and commitment. Invite them over to your home. Create a spiritual community for yourself even if it does not include your husband.

But at the same time, speak with your husband. Tell him how you feel, but do not issue any ultimatums or threats. Simply share with him your frustrations and sadness that he does not share your spirituality, your religious ideals, and your commitments to the Jewish people. Tell him this makes you feel sad, lonely, and bereft of a true spiritual partner but that his noninvolvement will not curtail your activities. You are going to continue to grow as a Jew and spiritual person. Tell him that you still love him and that he is invited to join you whenever he wants. But emphasize that you are continuing to grow as a person and this is what you need to do regardless of how he feels or whether he actually joins you.

And have the same conversation with your children. Talk to them about your feelings about Judaism. Share the fact that you would like them to be more involved Jewishly too. I do not know if they live far from you at college, but invite them home for holidays and Shabbat. Make your home a more Jewish home—not for anyone else but for yourself because only once you have begun to change yourself and made your own life more Jewish do you have any decent chance of influencing your husband and your children. But do not do it for them, do it for you. And only then will you perhaps begin to influence your family.

Question number 14: Although my wife's grandmother was born Jewish, she became a Catholic, and my mother-in-law raised my wife in the Catholic Church as well. However, when we got married, my wife reclaimed her Jewish identity by her own choice. Now we are having some problems with my in-laws because they are not respecting our wishes regarding Jewish holidays. For instance, they still insist on giving us Christmas presents on Christmas Day at their home around the Christmas tree and not Hanukkah presents during Hanukkah. I feel like Christmas is being forced on me, on my wife, and on our children. Do you have any suggestions as to how to handle my in-laws?

Answer: You can't change your in-laws, so don't even try. If they want to give you presents on Christmas in front of the Christmas tree, fine, but that doesn't mean *you* have to give them your gifts at that time. You can honor their customs and wishes without giving up your commitment to a more Jewish celebration of the winter holidays.

Unfortunately, living in America means having Christmas forced on you whether you want it or not. Unless you move to Israel or a non-Christian country, Christmas is a fact of life. However, you and your wife can do a great deal to weaken that influence by emphasizing Jewish holidays and celebrations. Any child who helps to build and decorate a Sukkot will never feel like they are missing something by not trimming a Christmas tree. Any child who asks the Four Questions and participates in the Passover Seder will never feel like they are missing out on a Christmas Eve feast. Any child who celebrates Hanukkah, the Jewish Festival of Lights, will not feel left out by not stringing Christmas lights.

There is a lot you can do to create a Jewish atmosphere in your home. I recommend that you purchase the book *The Art of Jewish Living: Hanukkah* by Dr. Ron Wolfson published by the Federation of Jewish Men's Clubs. Call your local Conservative synagogue for more information about how to order it or visit www.uscj.org. It is filled with wonderful, creative ideas about how to celebrate Hanukkah and not let Christmas dominate December.

Don't try to change your in-laws; it won't work and will only create further resentment. Instead, change your own Jewish practices. Maybe in time your in-laws will get the message. And even if they don't, whatever they do for Christmas—if you can succeed in creating a profoundly fulfilling Jewish environment in your home—won't matter because you will have already succeeded in creating a stronger Jewish identity for your family that their once-a-year Christmas experience cannot challenge.

Question number 15: My four-year-old daughter is starting to ask questions about Christmas and Santa Claus. She is enthralled by our neighbors' Christmas decorations and wants to put up Hanukkah decorations outside our home. We have no problem with such decorations inside our house, but we do not feel it is appropriate to display public Hanukkah decorations outside our home. We want our daughter to see Jewish holidays as fun and positive—are we being too strict here?

Answer: I have a question for you, why is it inappropriate for you and your family to put up Hanukkah decorations outside your house? Is there a neighborhood rule against Jewish holiday displays? Are you afraid of advertising your Jewish identity? Do you live in a Ku Klux Klan neighborhood? Are you afraid of anti-Semitism or of simply sticking out in a Christian neighborhood? Or do you just feel it is tacky and not in good taste? In any case, whether you are explicit or not with your daughter about your discomfort with expressing your Judaism outwardly, she'll figure it out. Whatever you feel about your Jewish identity will be communicated to her whether you intend to or not.

I encourage you to be open with your daughter and with your community. My experience is that most Christians are appreciative of any kind of spiritual religiosity of their neighbors whether they know anything about Jews or Judaism or not. And if you truly do not want to put up any Hanukkah decorations outside of your house, that is okay. You can use this as an opportunity to teach your daughter about not following the crowd, that she can be an individual who does not have to do what everyone else is doing to try and fit in.

But in general, the more you celebrate other Jewish festivals, like Passover and Sukkot and the High Holidays, the less Hanukkah and Christmastime will be a big deal to your daughter. Make Judaism a year-round spiritual experience that you celebrate weekly on Shabbat and on the Jewish holidays, and with regular synagogue attendance if that is possible, or even with observance of the laws of Kashrut—again, if that is possible. Your family's Jewish identity need not be confined to a once-a-year experience at Hanukkah. I wish you luck in coping with the annual December dilemma of Jews living in a Christian country!

Question number 16: My daughter, who is married to a Catholic man, is probably going to convert to Catholicism because she says she wants to be closer to God. I admit that I did not raise her in a very Jewish home; and I tell myself I'm grateful she is happy, healthy, and is a spiritual person. But I still feel heartbroken, and I'm not sure why. Can you help me?

Answer: I'm sorry you feel so brokenhearted about your daughter's imminent conversion to Catholicism. I think you already have a very healthy and appropriate attitude that you stated in your letter—be thankful she is healthy, happy, and still wants to be affiliated with a religious tradition. At least you raised her with awareness of God and to value spirituality, and now she wants to continue to explore that experience even if it isn't on a Jewish path.

You can make yourself feel miserable and guilty if you want to, but I would encourage you not to. There are plenty of young Jews that attend

Jewish schools all their lives and still end up dropping out of Judaism and converting to other religions. Could you have done more while your daughter was growing up? Probably. Would that have been a guarantee that she would have wanted to remain Jewish? Probably not.

My advice to you is to keep the lines of communication open. Be supportive, but don't hide your feelings, and don't let your guilt or upset be a barrier to maintaining a relationship with your daughter and her family. She still is your daughter no matter what her religion is.

Also, explore your own Judaism now. It is never too late. If this event has led you to a religious crisis, then take advantage of it and develop your own Jewish identity, knowledge, and observance. Join a synagogue, get involved with their social group or adult education classes, and make friends in the Jewish community so you can have and be invited to Shabbat and holiday meals. If nothing else, you will simply have a new circle of Jewish friends who may well be able to sympathize with your situation. Will this change your daughter? Probably not, but it might help you feel more comfortable with your own Jewish identity. Let your daughter live out her spiritual destiny—and I would encourage you to do the same for yourself. And who knows, perhaps your renewed interest in Judaism may spark a renewed interest in your daughter.

Question number 17: *Dear Rabbi, my wife and our two-year-old son and I are planning on converting to Judaism together as a family, but not with an Orthodox rabbi. However, I'm concerned that if we ever decide to make Aliyah* [move to Israel to become citizens], *our conversion will not be recognized by the Chief Rabbinate of Israel. I am also troubled that Orthodox Jews will not recognize us as legitimate Jews. What would suggest I do to cope with this problem?*

Answer: Your concerns are, unfortunately, legitimate; but I urge you not to become discouraged or dissuaded from your commitment to a non-Orthodox conversion for the following reasons. First of all, you should not be deterred by a fear of the unknown. We can't base our lives on what may or may not happen in the future or any potential future resistance you and your family may experience someday from the Orthodox Jewish community or the Chief Rabbinate of Israel. I would like to encourage you to continue to live and practice Judaism according to your personal convictions. I think it is just terrific that you feel so closely associated with the Jewish people that both you and your wife want to become Jews as a family. You should always follow your religious and spiritual convictions regardless of what others may or may not feel about your decisions. Your choice of religious affiliation reflects your deepest spiritual values as a human being; therefore, no outside temporal or temporary political concerns should affect your actions. Don't forget that many times throughout Jewish history, Jews have chosen to suffer persecution and even death for the sake of their religious convictions. I urge you and encourage you to hold true to your original, initial religious values.

Secondly, the Chief Rabbinate of Israel has no more and no less religious or moral authority than any other Jewish religious organization in the world. The political and religious turmoil of Israeli life should not affect your religious life here in this country. It is also important to understand that the Chief Rabbinate of Israel maintains its stranglehold over Israeli religious life because of purely political considerations and backroom power deals made by the secular Zionist leaders over sixty years ago in order to gain Orthodox support for the cause of Israeli statehood. Therefore, while the Orthodox Rabbinate of Israel may occasionally try to use their political muscle to force their views on other Jews in Israel and around the world, their pronouncements regarding the acceptance of non-Orthodox conversions should not sway other Jews elsewhere; for to give credence to their views is to yield to their political blackmail.

To give you some more insight into the seamy world of politics and religion in Israel, you should also know that the Orthodox movement in Israel has largely failed to gain more adherents and supporters among the general nonreligious Jewish populace of Israel precisely because they have typically resorted to heavy-handed social and religious actions. It is sad that the very behavior of the religious establishment in Israel that could have made such advances in educating millions of Israeli Jews about Judaism and encouraging their observance of Jewish law and customs has had the opposite effect and become one of the major reasons that there is such a profound and yawning chasm between religious and nonreligious Jews in Israel. The Chief Rabbinate has so perverted the issue of religion in Israel and polarized the two sides that there is no longer any concept of being religiously Jewish in a moderate sense, much as members of the Reform, Reconstructionist, and Conservative movements in the United States understand and practice religion. The delegitimization of these non-Orthodox movements in Israel has nothing to do with religious legitimacy and everything to do with the internal cultural war between the Orthodox establishment and the majority of non-Orthodox Israeli Jews.

It would be a shame for you to base your personal religious actions living here on the politically charged turmoil of Israeli politics. You should also know that as of now, the current language of the Israeli Law of Return that provides that any Jew can move to Israel and naturalize as a citizen indicates that anyone who has converted to Judaism will be accepted as a Jew for civil purposes. It does not specify or require that the conversion be carried out by any particular denomination of Judaism. This means that converts to Judaism under Reform, Reconstructionist, and Conservative auspices can make Aliyah, move to Israel, and become Israeli citizens—and the Chief Rabbinate has no say on this matter at all. While the Orthodox political parties in Israel do periodically try to amend this legal language precisely in order to exclude Jews created from non-Orthodox conversions, their every attempt has been rejected and will probably never be accepted by Israeli lawmakers given the social and political pressure of Jews around the world, the importance of Aliyah to Israel, and the greater unity of the Jewish people. And if, God forbid, this should ever become a problem for your children in the future, there are plenty of sympathetic Orthodox rabbis throughout the world who also recognize the Chief Rabbinate of Israel for what it is and are only too willing to help non-Orthodox Jews gain acceptance in the chaotic structure of the Israeli religious establishment.

I hope that you will continue to live and act according to your own religious convictions and not acquiesce to potential religious blackmail that your children may never experience. Let your own spiritual values serve as your guide. And Mazal Tov on your upcoming conversions to Judaism!

Question number 18: Where in the Torah is the term "chosen people" actually used? Is it true that it makes us different and special, but not better?

Answer: Yes, you are correct. According to Judaism, being chosen simply means that we believe we have a responsibility to observe the commandments of the Torah that other peoples don't have. This means that Jews see themselves as obligated to observe Shabbat and Jewish holidays, keep Kosher, pray daily, give Tzedakah (charity), and study the Torah along with hundreds of other commandments. However, anyone can convert to Judaism and also share this responsibility.

As for the origins of this idea, there are a number of verses in the Hebrew Bible that speak about the choseness of the Jewish people. However, here are some of the clearest examples:

1. Genesis 18:19, "For I have *singled him out* [Abraham] (*emphasis mine*), that he may keep the way of the Lord by doing what is just and right." This verse portrays God wondering whether God should reveal the divine plans to destroy the wicked cities of Sodom and Gomorrah. In doing so, God indicated the choseness of Abraham and his offspring, the Jewish people.
2. Deuteronomy 7:7-8, "It is not because you are the most numerous of peoples that the Lord set His heart on you (the people of Israel) and *chose you* (*emphasis mine*),—indeed, you are the smallest of peoples; but it was because the Lord favored you and kept the promise God made to your ancestors that the Lord freed you with a mighty hand and rescued you from the house of bondage, from the power of Pharaoh king of Egypt." This verse

was actually spoken by Moses who quoted God when he was giving his final speeches to the Israelites at the end of the forty years of wandering in the desert.

3. Joshua 24:22, "Thereupon Joshua said to the people, 'You are witnesses against yourselves that you have by your own act *chosen to serve the Lord (emphasis mine).'*" Joshua, who was Moses's successor, addressed the Israelites telling them that not only did God choose them but that the Israelites also chose God!

4. Nehemiah 9:7, "You are the Lord God, who *chose Abram (emphasis mine)*, who brought him out of the Ur of the Chaldeans and changed his name to Abraham. Finding his heart true, You made a covenant with him to give the land of the Canaanite." This quote is from a prayer that an ancient biblical Jewish leader, Nehemiah, directed to God, also indicating the choseness of the Jewish people via Abraham.

There are many other places in the Hebrew Bible and throughout other classical religious texts that deal with this idea of choseness, but these quotes here make it clear that not only did God choose the Jewish people to observe the commandments of the Torah, but the Jewish people also chose to accept and follow God's commandments!

Question number 19: Although I am Jewish, I was not raised in a religious home. I desperately want to learn more about Judaism, but I am worried that because I am already an adult and so ignorant, I would not be accepted in the Jewish community. Is it too late for me to start? Could you please help me because I don't know where to begin.

Answer: Thank you for writing and seeking some advice. First of all, I want to encourage you in your quest to learn more about your spiritual heritage. I believe that learning about and taking on Jewish spiritual practices can help increase our happiness as human beings, improve the world we live in, and bring holiness into our lives. Secondly, you will definitely be accepted into the Jewish community regardless of your age and background knowledge.

Thirdly, it is definitely not too late for you to learn about Judaism! You should know that I myself, although a rabbi now, did not even know how to read Hebrew or know anything about Judaism until I was twenty! It makes no difference what age you are when you start learning about Judaism. The great Rabbi Akiba, a giant of a Jewish scholar in the Talmud, is fabled to have begun learning how to read and write and studying the Jewish tradition along with his young son; and they even shared the same slate and chalk. And he began when he was forty years old!

Where should you begin? I encourage you seek out a local rabbi for more personal, specific advice, instruction, and to form a relationship with. There is no substitute for direct, personal contact. Then, go Shul shopping. This means check out some of the local neighboring synagogues, or Shuls, in your town and find one that fits you. Find a Jewish community where you feel comfortable, welcome, and accepted. This is very important. Don't stop until you find one that works for you.

Where can you learn more? In addition to learning from a rabbi and being part of a synagogue, go to a Jewish bookstore or check out the Jewish religion bookshelves in a regular bookstore. Browse and find books that appeal to you. For a thorough and exhaustive listing of various Jewish resources available, I encourage you to visit a wonderful Web site: www. convert.org. Although it is aimed at converts to Judaism, it has a fantastic archive of recommended books and information related to Judaism. It would be perfect for you as a beginning. And check out any local Jewish adult education class offered in your area, either at a synagogue, Jewish community center, or local college or university. There is a lot out there, even online courses.

Try observing Jewish rituals and practices. Once you have found a synagogue or Jewish community that you like and feel at home with, start exploring what it means to keep Shabbat, taking off Friday evenings and Saturdays to attend synagogue services. Try to attend a community Shabbat meal or make your own Shabbat meals with all of the various rituals and prayers. Shop around and purchase your own Jewish prayer book and start reading through the prayers in English; see what is there and find some favorites. Read some books about Jewish prayer or ask a rabbi or knowledgeable Jewish friend about prayers and the various services. Start exploring observing Kashrut, the Jewish dietary laws, and avoid mixing milk and meat dishes and stop eating non-Kosher foods like pork or shellfish and learn more about the Jewish Tradition in general. And start volunteering your time at a local charitable agency or donate some money to some worthy causes to fulfill the commandment of Tzedakah, or social and economic justice, to start making this world a better place.

Finally, don't ever let anyone else try to tell you what it means to be a good Jew. There is no such thing as either a good Jew or a bad Jew—be the best person and Jew that you can be in your own eyes. Don't let others persuade you that observing more Jewish rituals makes you a better Jew because, unfortunately, there are plenty of very observant Jews who are unethical people and criminals. Decide for yourself what is valuable, meaningful, and holy to you and practice it. Find a Jewish community where you are welcomed and appreciated, and make it your spiritual and communal home. And above all, keep studying and learning and become the kind of Jew that you ultimately decide that you want to be! Good luck!

Question number 20: I was raised as a Christian, but as an adult, I have grown away from my faith and feel attracted to Judaism. I don't know a lot about Judaism, and unfortunately, I don't live very close to any synagogues or rabbis. I would like to teach my children about religion and God but don't know what to tell them. Thank you for your help.

Answer: It must be very difficult for you and your family given your spiritual soul-searching. Before you decide that you are ready to become a Jew and join a synagogue, I encourage you to raise your concerns and spiritual beliefs with a local pastor or minister. You mentioned that there were no synagogues or rabbis close by where you live, but I assume that you might have connections with a local church. I would encourage you to make another visit back to whatever church you might have previously attended, not for the purpose of trying to dissuade you from your beliefs but so that you will have the opportunity to share your dilemma with your immediate spiritual caregiver.

If, in the course of your discussion, you do not feel that your feelings and beliefs are being respected or addressed, then I encourage you to meet with other local pastors. If necessary, meet with all of them until you can find a spiritual leader that you can trust and feel secure of his or her support.

I believe it is important to belong to a spiritual community wherever you may live and so that your children can grow up not only with a sense of God's presence in their lives, but also with a sense of connection to a caring, supportive spiritual community. It may be different in the various Christian communities than in the Jewish community, but in the Jewish tradition, it is important to belong to a community—any community. The relationships, friendships, and sense of belonging are valuable and necessary to be a healthy, whole person. What you believe is not as important as how you behave, at least that is the Jewish point of view.

In conclusion, don't abandon Christianity just because you have grown away from your previous faith. There is too much to lose by separating yourself from the community. But keep searching for a spiritual leader that you can respect and be respected by. I wish you much luck and strength in your spiritual journey.

Chapter 4

Life Cycle Events and Family Issues
(Sixteen Questions)

No matter who we are or what our circumstances in life are, there seems to be two extremely sensitive areas that manage to push our emotional buttons at some time or other, whether positively or negatively; and they are family relationships and life cycle events. As a former congregational rabbi who provided pastoral counseling for hundreds of congregants and their families, in my experience, no two topics generated more intense feelings than issues surrounding people's family lives and the intense emotional baggage that often accompanied major life cycle events. It is not surprising that these two topics are integrally related.

Issues surrounding our immediate or even extended family are understandable. After all, everyone comes from some kind of family. And in general, whom have we spent more time around and have more shared experiences with—for better or worse—than our parents, siblings, spouse, and children? The people we live with are the source of our greatest joys—and at times the targets and sources of our worst emotional outbursts. We are never more comfortable and display the best of who we are than when we are relaxed and surrounded by our family members. On the other hand, we are also never more aggravated and provoked and reveal the worst side of ourselves than when we are in the company of our family. It is not surprising that many people turn to outside counsel—even rabbis on the Internet—for help and advice regarding family issues.

The same holds true for life cycle events, which is the reason I paired these two related topics. Many Jewish life cycle events are happy, such as celebrations focusing on the birth of children, a Bar or Bat Mitzvah, or a wedding. Yet even these ostensibly celebratory events are not without their underlying tensions and conflicts. Other life cycle events help us deal with sadness and grief, such as divorce, funerals, and mourning, which are fraught with their own emotional challenges.

Historically, fewer people in the United States are formally affiliated with a church or synagogue or any type of organized religion than in the past. It is not surprising that I received many e-mails from people about family problems who could have—and perhaps should have—turned to people they knew directly, such as other family members, coworkers, friends, rabbis, or mental health professionals. As a result of this trend toward alienation from synagogues, churches, and other communal organizations, I found myself performing spiritual and emotional triage via e-mail for hundreds of strangers whom I never met regarding a vast range of family-related emotional issues and life cycle events.

Sadly, what these people probably needed more than anything else was someone to talk to face-to-face and have some personal contact. Family problems can rarely be solved through a dry exchange of communication like e-mail. Rather, what most of these people needed was companionship and someone to be physically present and available to them, to offer them encouragement, empathy, support, and advice. How ironic that the most popular newspaper columns and best-selling books tend to be advice, personal guidance, and self-help related. I suppose this material makes for interesting reading, but rarely does it truly help the people who need such direct assistance and advice the most.

I hope the questions and responses offered below serve to encourage people to create and establish bonds of friendship and trust with their religious clergy or other support networks long before they find themselves desperate enough for their help and are frantic to seek it out anywhere, even from an Internet rabbi. The following questions parallel the life cycle beginning with birth and going through Bar and Bat Mitzvah, marriage, and divorce. Death and mourning are not included here because all of those questions and answers have already been placed in their own separate chapter in this book, chapter 15.

Question number 1: I am pregnant, and a friend of mine wants to throw me a baby shower. However, my mother is adamant that I should not have one because years ago when she was pregnant before me, she had a baby shower; and then she delivered a stillborn. I don't know what to do. Is it okay in Jewish law to have a baby shower and leave all of the presents at my parents' home and not bring them into the house until the baby is born, or is even having a baby shower bad luck to begin with?

Answer: Despite the natural fears and worries of an expectant mother, there is no connection between having a baby shower before the baby is born and any complications during pregnancy. However, there is indeed a Jewish tradition based purely on superstition that having a baby shower before the birth of a child invites the attention of the evil eye. This is indeed nonsense, but there is common sense in this tradition. After all, if there are any complications or worse after birth, the parents won't be traumatized or feel guilt by being in a house filled with baby furniture and gifts that for some tragic reason they are now no longer able to use. And indeed, it sounds like your mother is still coping with the trauma of this experience years ago that may have been reawakened now that you are pregnant and considering a baby shower.

I believe that you have already solved this problem in your question; perhaps you could have a baby shower before the birth of the child and store the gifts elsewhere. That way, you will be able to accommodate your friends and family and have the assurance of having items you may need when the time comes. However, you won't have these items in your home, taking up your physical space and emotional energy. Maybe this is a compromise your mother will accept. I hope that you can offer your mother some comfort at a time that might be triggering a lot of deep feelings inside her that she might have been unprepared to cope with. I'll leave you with the traditional Jewish wish for an expectant mother—B'sha'ah Tovah, which means, "May you deliver at the appropriate time." We don't say Mazal Tov for something that has not happened yet.

Question number 2: What do we need to plan for a home baby-naming ceremony for our daughter who was born last month? Do we need to have a rabbi to perform the blessings, or can we do them ourselves?

Answer: Mazal Tov on the birth of your daughter! There is no official baby-daughter-naming ceremony for the home. There really even isn't one for the synagogue. In a traditional synagogue, all that happens is that the parents receive an Aliyah to the Torah; that is, they are called up to the reading table to recite traditional blessings in Hebrew before and after the chanting of the Torah portion. Then afterward, there is a special prayer that can be chanted by the rabbi or cantor or whoever which is on behalf of the mother and the newborn daughter. This prayer can be found in most traditional prayer books.

In the past several decades, due to a greater sensitivity to the expanding role that women are playing in the communal and professional world of organized Jewish life, people have been creating all kinds of new life cycle opportunities for girls, which did not exist before. The welcoming and naming of a baby girl is one of these gaps in the Jewish tradition that is being filled in with many wonderful, creative ceremonies.

Because there is no single official baby-daughter-naming ceremony, it is up to you as to what you would like to do. These ceremonies—now called Simchat Bat ceremonies or "joy of a daughter" or even Brit Bat or "covenant of a daughter"—usually involve both a naming of the girl and a ceremony by which she is brought into the covenant of our people. I encourage you to explore the myriad versions of such ceremonies available on the Internet or even to work with a local rabbi because as

Jewish professionals, they probably have far more experience, knowledge, and suggestions for you in this matter. Mazal Tov again and good luck!

Question number 3: *In all of the Hebrew Bible, there seems to be only one Moses, one David, one Sarah, one Abraham, etc. Was there a religious reason why parents didn't name their children after famous personalities in ancient times as we do today?*

Answer: The Torah was not a registry at a hospital maternity ward. We don't know what people might have named their children. We only have the stories that are included in the Hebrew Bible. Also, the Torah is not a literal year-by-year description of life in ancient times. In fact, it is not even history; it is the story of the origins of the Jewish people and how they understood God and the covenant between the Jewish people and God. Don't look to get more out of the Torah than what it actually is as that leads to fundamentalism. The Torah is the original source of Judaism. To get the details, it is necessary to study Talmud and Midrash and the last two thousand years' worth of rabbinic literature. For names of children, I recommend getting a good Jewish baby names dictionary. As for popular names in ancient times, who knows? Maybe there were lots of Davids and Sarahs around. But the only ones we know of are the ones in the stories important to us as a Jewish people.

Question number 4: *Can you tell me more about the Jewish practice of circumcision or Brit Milah?*

Answer: The Jewish practice of circumcision is called Brit Milah in Hebrew, and it literally means "covenant of circumcision." It was first commanded by God to Abraham and his male descendants in the book of Genesis 17.

The ceremony itself consists nowadays of the baby being circumcised by a Mohel; this is the title of a man in the Jewish tradition that has been specially trained and certified to perform this ritual. Specifically, the Mohel surgically removes the foreskin of the baby's penis. Since the Torah-derived obligation of performing this act actually devolves upon the father, it is part of the ritual service that the father appoints the Mohel to be his agent in this matter. After the circumcision, the baby is then named, that is, given his Hebrew name. During ceremony, the Sandek, or Kvatter in Yiddish, an honored member of the family, holds the baby on his or her lap. This person is usually considered something akin to the baby's godfather. The word "Kvatter" sort of sounds like the word "father," and the word "Sandek" literally means "companion of the child."

All of the blessings recited by the father and Mohel are done so over a glass of wine; and to help mollify the baby after the circumcision, a drop of wine, or a napkin dipped in the wine, is usually placed in the baby's mouth to suck on. It is also considered a Mitzvah, or commandment, to provide a nice meal immediately afterward to celebrate the bringing of a baby boy into the Jewish people's covenant with God. This is called a Seudat Mitzvah, or a "commanded banquet."

The circumcision usually takes place on the eighth day after birth as commanded in the Torah. However, if there are health considerations, for example, if the baby is not healthy enough to withstand the circumcision on that day, it may be postponed. If the baby is healthy enough, the Brit Milah is performed exactly and always on the eighth day—never earlier—even if that day happens to be Shabbat, a holiday, or even Yom Kippur.

Question number 5: Why does it say in the Torah that boys should be circumcised on the eighth day? I have read that the blood-clotting factor is actually above normal eight days after a child has been born. Is this the reason Brit Milah is on the eighth day?

Answer: That is indeed fascinating about the blood-clotting factor being higher on the eighth day! While I doubt the ancient Israelites knew of this factor, it probably would have been irrelevant to them because Brit

Milah, or circumcision, is considered a divine commandment issued by God. However, the number 8 is the sum of 7 plus 1. Why is this important? Because the numbers have significant meaning unrelated to any medical or scientific reasons that the ancient Israelites were probably unaware of. The number 7 is symbolic of completeness and holiness as symbolized in the seven days of creation, or seven days of the week, seven wedding blessings, seven circles the bride makes around the groom, and so on. Seven added to one, which is symbolic of the One God, makes for wholeness and completeness! It might sound simple, but there is tremendous significance to numbers in the Hebrew Bible.

Regardless of the reasons, the Torah makes it quite clear that circumcision is to be performed on all Jewish baby boys on the eighth day when God said, "And he that is eight days old shall be circumcised among you, every male throughout your generation" (Genesis 17:12). Later on, the rabbis in the Talmud declared that if a child is unhealthy or sick or for some reason a circumcision might prove life threatening, circumcision can be delayed as long as necessary until the child is healthy enough to withstand this simple medical procedure.

Question number 6: My sister and her husband don't have children, and I recently learned that they named their new puppy after our grandfather. And this has upset me terribly. I believe only human beings should be named in the honor of a departed loved one. Am I overreacting?

Answer: Wow, what an interesting question. Whatever happened to just naming a dog Rover? This is a question for a family psychotherapist more than a rabbi. Honestly, I can see both sides of the issue. For some people, pets can indeed be like members of one's family. Therefore, from this perspective, it does seem to make sense that naming one's dog after deceased family members is, in a way, like continuing their names and memories. And people should be able to name their pets whatever they want to. They are just pets after all.

On the other hand, I can also understand your point of view. Naming an animal, a dog, after someone that you knew and loved might indeed seem insulting and disrespectful to the memory of your grandfather. Dealing with death and memories can touch us in very deep places. Also, you are indeed correct that the Jewish traditional custom is to name children—human beings—after deceased family members as a way to carry on their name. So I can definitely understand your feelings. And I do not think you are overreacting; you are merely expressing your legitimate natural feelings on this issue.

But please keep in mind that there is no correct answer to this question. Rather, I hope that you and your sister can work out your feelings so that this won't cause a rupture in your relationship. It would be sad to cause a breach in your family over this issue, yet your sister should at least appreciate and be sensitive to your feelings. Yet you should also recognize that, well, a name is still just a name no matter who had it before and your sister has the right to name her animals anything she wants. I hope that you can work it out together amicably.

Question number 7: When was the Bar Mitzvah invented? Did it come from the Talmud?

Answer: The term "Bar Mitzvah" literally means "son of a commandment" in Hebrew. It refers to a young man who has reached the age of thirteen whereby, according to Jewish law, he is now obligated to observe all of the statutes and rules of Jewish law.

In ancient times, this was probably not celebrated to any great extent just as we don't have special parties for teenagers when they turn eighteen signifying their new status as eligible to vote in this country or be drafted. In ancient times, the simplest and most public way that any young man could demonstrate to the community that he was now subject to all of the obligations of Jewish law was to be called up to recite the blessings over the chanting of a Torah portion since only adult Jews can receive this honor.

This concept of Bar Mitzvah is not mentioned anywhere in the Hebrew Bible. It is a concept that the rabbis of the Talmud created perhaps over two thousand years ago. Over time, a Bar Mitzvah developed into an occasion to celebrate. Some people in the United States now feel that the Bar or Bat Mitzvah party has overshadowed the ritual significance of the Bar Mitzvah celebration in a synagogue or temple and that the spiritual aspect of this event has been lost. While this may be true, the Bar Mitzvah ceremony originated as simply a public way to demonstrate to the larger Jewish community that a young boy—and in modern times, a young girl—is able to fully participate in Jewish ritual life, enjoying all of the responsibilities and privileges of a Jewish adult.

Question number 8: *Can I have my Bar Mitzvah at home? I read it can be done without a special ceremony.*

Answer: The Hebrew words "Bar" or "Bat Mitzvah" literally mean "son or daughter of the commandments," and it refers to the age when a Jewish boy and girl are supposed to begin observing the Jewish commandments that adults do. At the age of thirteen, a Jewish boy and girl becomes obligated to observe Jewish laws, customs, and rituals whether there is a public or private celebration or not. This traditional Jewish obligation to observe Jewish commandments just happens by itself, like being able to vote when you turn eighteen—you don't have to do anything special except register to vote. By the way, in some traditional Jewish communities, a girl is considered an adult and can celebrate her Bat Mitzvah when she turns twelve because the rabbis in earlier times recognized that girls generally mature faster than boys, both physically and emotionally. However, some synagogues don't want to differentiate between boys and girls and holding their Bar and Bat Mitzvah celebrations when they are different ages, and so they have policies in place to ensure that boys and girls are completely equal in this matter. And everyone waits till they are thirteen years old before celebrating their Bat or Bat Mitzvah.

In the Jewish tradition, this is considered an opportunity to celebrate when a young man and woman becomes an adult in the Jewish community. The basic Jewish ritual is to be called up to chant blessings before and after the reading of a Torah portion on Shabbat in a synagogue. This is called receiving an Aliyah, literally, to go up to the table or stand where the Torah is read. It is simply a public way of demonstrating that a thirteen-year-old boy (or twelve-year-old girl) is now old enough to participate in this religious ritual. This is the traditional way of celebrating a Bar Mitzvah. Of course, Bar and Bat Mitzvah boys and girls can participate in far more of the Shabbat service than just receiving an Aliyah, such as leading substantial parts of the worship service and writing and delivering an original interpretation of the weekly Torah portion. And it does not even need to take place on Shabbat; it can take place at any worship service when the Torah is read in public such as a Monday or Thursday in traditional synagogues.

And yes, you can also celebrate this life cycle event privately in your home. In which case, you and your family can create any kind of creative ritual experience or celebration you would like. However, I have to be honest—as a rabbi, it doesn't make much sense for me to celebrate a Bar Mitzvah in the privacy of one's own home without many family or guests from the larger Jewish community present. After all, the point of being a Bar Mitzvah, an adult in the Jewish community, is the ability to participate in *communal* religious events. And the celebration of a Bar Mitzvah doesn't make much sense if it is not in the context of a Jewish community. I would encourage you to speak to a local rabbi for their opinion and advice. Whatever your choice, good luck and Mazal Tov!

Question number 9: Can you explain to me about the concept of the B'sheret or "soul mate"? I've looked everywhere and can't find anything.

Answer: The word "B'sheret" is actually Yiddish, and it loosely translates as "fate" or "destiny." B'sheret can refer to any kind of seeming coincidence or fate. Meeting someone who ends up helping you get a job is also considered B'sheret. It is most often used in connection with someone meeting his or her future spouse, so it is understandable why you assumed that the word "B'sheret" actually means "soul mate."

There is actually quite a bit of rabbinic literature about people searching for and finding their appropriate spouse. I would recommend that you expand your search of relevant concepts to include Jewish matchmaking, making couples, and marriages.

However, here are a few popular stories sprinkled throughout rabbinic literature that deal with the idea of someone finding their destined marriage partner. One rabbi in the Talmud claimed that forty days before an embryo is formed, a divine voice calls out announcing that the daughter of so-and-so is to be the future wife of such-and-such that this embryo will turn out to be. Another rabbi claimed that a wife is selected in heaven for each man according to his deeds in life (Babylonian Talmud, Tractate Sotah 2a). The Talmudic rabbi named Raba once heard a certain man praying, "May that young woman join me in wedlock." Raba said to him, "You need not pray that—if she is your proper match, she will not escape you" (Talmud, Moed Katan 18b). A Roman woman once asked Rabbi Yosi bar Halfta, "I understand that God made the world in six days. But what has God been doing since then?" The rabbi replied, "God has been joining couples, determining who should be married to whom" (Talmud, Moed Katan 18b). There are many more examples of such rabbinic statements and stories about people finding the right spouse for them available on the Internet and books dealing with Jewish weddings (see "Suggested Readings" at the end of this book).

Question number 10: Should nonpracticing Jews be allowed to have a religious wedding?

Answer: Absolutely! Nonpracticing Jews should not only be allowed but also encouraged to have a religious wedding! Even if they are nonpracticing now does not mean that this important and significant life cycle event will not touch their hearts and souls and possibly lead them to becoming more open to Jewish ritual life in the future. After all, if Jewish rituals were reserved for only the so-called religious practicing Jews, then Judaism would truly be out of reach for millions of Jews and soon die out.

Also, to prevent Jews, even nonpracticing Jews, from experiencing the depth and spiritual power of their own religious rituals would deny them the opportunity to ever taste the sweetness of their own tradition—and then how would they ever possibly be enticed to learn more? I have personally met and worked with literally hundreds of Jews who became far more religious after attending or experiencing an unfamiliar Jewish ritual event. That was the spark that led them to catch the fire of Torah.

And the fact that you used the word "allowed," I interpret to mean that you personally do not believe nonpracticing Jews should be allowed access to their own spiritual heritage. However, I must respectfully disagree with your attitude. If Jewish rituals are reserved for only the religious, this would create Jewish ritual apartheid and create two separate classes of Jews: the so-called religious and the so-called nonreligious. It would also create tremendous resentment and practically guarantee that no nonpracticing Jew would ever want to breach the barriers and experience Judaism for him or herself. I would encourage you to soften your heart and recognize that the greatest possible Mitzvah is to allow and *encourage* nonpracticing Jews to celebrate major life cycle events enhanced by the spiritual depth of their underutilized religious tradition.

Question number 11: What is the meaning of the word "Aufruf"?

Answer: "Aufruf" is a Yiddish word which means "stand up," "get up." It is traditional that on the Shabbat before a wedding, the groom receives an Aliyah to the Torah. That is, he is called up out of his seat to chant the blessings before and after the Torah reading. This is an opportunity for a special blessing to be made on his and his fiancée's behalf. In some traditions, the groom also recites the Haftarah, a selection from the prophetic section of the Hebrew Bible. An Aufruf is simply a public way to announce and celebrate a wedding in advance in a communal setting.

Question number 12*: Can you explain the custom of why the bride circles the groom three or seven times at a Jewish wedding? I understand that it is taken from the book of Jeremiah or Hosea, but how did this tradition start? Thanks for your help!*

Answer: There are some numbers in the Jewish tradition that simply have a holy or lucky association. While you may have indeed found texts in the Hebrew Bible that support the three or seven circles of the bride around the groom in a Jewish wedding, the actual anthropological explanation of such customs is that the circling of the bride around the groom is just that—a custom. Seven is a holy number because of its association with the seven days of the week, Shabbat being the seventh day, and the seven days of creation. Therefore, a nice reason for number 7 is that a bride and groom are creating a new married world for themselves and a new family. And finally, there are exactly seven wedding blessings that are recited to consecrate a Jewish marriage.

Why three circles in some traditions? Because it is less onerous for the bride to schlep around her groom that many times and number 3 is also a holy number because there were three patriarchs: Abraham, Isaac, and Jacob. Also, Abraham traveled three days with Isaac before almost sacrificing him to God. There are three Matzot on the Seder plate at Passover, and the people of Israel prepared themselves three days before getting the Torah at Sinai. And there are three identifiable classes or tribes of Jews today used for ritual purposes—Kohen, Levi, and Yisrael—and the list goes on and on.

The whole point of circling in general is to show that a bride is now creating a new life and a new sacred circle centered around her new husband-to-be. Any biblical verses that you may have found that purport to explain the origins of the number of circles a bride makes around the groom were found after the fact and highlighted in order to justify a long-standing tradition. For some more explanations about these numbers and why the bride circles the groom, I urge you to consult the book *The Jewish Way in Love and Marriage* by Rabbi Hayim Donin.

Question number 13: My daughter is getting married next week, and my future in-laws are planning to throw candy at the bride and groom at the end of the ceremony. Can they do this? I thought that this tradition was only for Bar Mitzvahs!

Answer: Believe it or not, your daughter's future in-laws are reviving an ancient tradition! It was also traditional to throw candy and, yes, even rice or corn at a newly married couple for the same reasons we do it for B'nai Mitzvah celebrations—so that their new life together should be sweet and fertile! After all, rice, corn, and wheat kernels were originally thrown as a symbol of fertility. Enjoy the wedding and Mazal Tov!

Question number 14: What is the significance of the groom breaking the glass at the end of the wedding ceremony?

Answer: There are many explanations for this tradition. Rabbis pick and choose among the ones they want to share at weddings. Here are a few reasons I have heard and used myself:

1. It is a fulfillment of Psalm 137:5, which states, "If I forget you, O Jerusalem . . . and do not raise you above my highest joy." This refers to the desire to always remember the past destruction of Jerusalem even in moments of celebration such as a wedding. The broken glass is therefore a symbol of the destroyed Temple in the past.
2. It is also based on a story in the Talmud where a rabbi married off his daughter, but the wedding guests got so drunk and lighthearted that they were in danger of losing sight of the holiness of the event. So this rabbi took an expensive vase and

shattered it, and that got everyone's attention real quick! So the breaking of the glass is a reminder of the holiness and seriousness of the enterprise of marriage.

3. It is symbolic of the fragility of life and relationships and the need to respect a spouse and constantly work to strengthen a marital relationship.

4. It is symbolic of the hard, painful times of life and marriage that cannot be avoided. However, by living together as a married couple, it is possible to overcome these difficult times through mutual love and support.

5. It is an ancient superstition to break the glass and appease the evil spirits that might want to harm the couple, so instead, we break a glass to divert their attention from the bride and groom.

6. Anthropologically speaking, breaking the glass is symbolic of the sexual consummation of the marriage that is about to take place. Of course, this is one explanation I do *not* share at a wedding or with the guests in a public setting!

There are many Jewish wedding books out that may give you additional explanations. And if you are attending a Jewish wedding anytime soon, be sure to shout out Mazal Tov as the glass shatters!

Question number 15: A judge married my husband and me, but now we would like to have a Jewish religious wedding. The only problem is that his ex-wife refuses to grant my husband a Get [Jewish divorce document]. What should we do?

Answer: I'm glad to hear that you and your husband are interested in sanctifying your marriage with a religious wedding, and I am equally saddened to hear that your plans seem to be frustrated by the bitter attitude of your husband's ex-wife. The first thing that you should do is to find a local rabbi who may be able to provide you with immediate and personal advice, support, and counsel. I can give you a few hints, but I strongly urge you to find someone that you know and trust to help you through this. One thing a local rabbi may be able to do for you is to help you negotiate with your husband's ex-wife or with someone else that she chooses to arrange this. Perhaps the less personally involved you all are in this process, the easier it may be. Nearly all rabbis will insist that all parties involved in a marriage should be religiously divorced before performing a new religious wedding.

However, even if your husband's ex-wife absolutely refuses to have anything to do with a Get, technically speaking, this is not an obstacle to your getting married under a Chuppah, that is, the traditional wedding canopy. This is because traditionally a husband does not need to give a Get before he can get remarried. Rather, it is the ex-wife who needs to *receive* a Get from her ex-husband should she ever decide she wants to have a Jewish religious marriage in the future. So from a very traditional point of view, your husband's ex-wife's refusal to be involved in receiving a Get is irrelevant to your plans! This is based on the very ancient biblical precedent that a man could have more than one wife (consider Jacob and two wives, Rachel and Leah, in the Torah). However, even in the Hebrew Bible, a woman can only have one husband.

However, you all probably should try to resolve this issue with your husband's ex-wife in order to begin your religious marriage on a note of peaceful relations. As a last resort, there is such a thing in Jewish law as a Get Zikui, which literally means the "vacating of a Get." Essentially, a Get Zikui is used in exactly the situation you described. It is when a husband wants to give his a wife a Get, but she refuses. Therefore, it is possible to arrange that a Beit Din, a rabbinic tribunal, receives the Get in place of your husband's ex-wife, thus fulfilling his obligation to give a Get even if his ex-wife won't accept it. As to how and why a Beit Din can do this in the ex-wife's place even if she herself refused to accept it is kind of complicated, but any traditional rabbi should be able to explain it to you. So to be perfectly frank, this is your husband's ex-wife's problem—not yours or your husband's! She may regret her attitude later if she should want to get remarried, in which case I urge your husband to be lenient and forgiving. I hope this helps you, and I strongly urge you again to find a local rabbi who may be able to help you.

Question number 16*: My ex-husband will not give me a Get. What options do I have if I ever plan to remarry in the Jewish community?*

Answer: Depending upon which branch of American Judaism you are affiliated with, different rabbis of different denominations will give you different advice. From a purely traditional point of view, you cannot get remarried in a religious ceremony without a Get from your ex-husband. No traditional rabbi will perform the ceremony.

However, even in traditional Jewish communities, Orthodox rabbis have often acted in concert to place social or even financial pressure on a recalcitrant husband in an effort to forcibly persuade him to grant a Get to his ex-wife. And in Israel, rabbis and rabbinic courts have the civil authority to actually jail a man who refuses to give his ex-wife a religious divorce. However, that has only happened in extreme cases.

However, if your husband proves to be recalcitrant, at least within the more liberal branches of American Judaism such as the Conservative, Reconstructionist, and Reform movements, it is possible, although rare, to Jewishly nullify your original marriage even if your ex-husband refuses to give you a Get. If your marriage is nullified in this fashion, then there is no need for a Get, and you can get married without one. Rest assured that if you had children with your ex-husband, they will not be considered illegitimate! So go to the rabbi of your choice for more direct, personal advice and guidance in this manner, and rest assured, it can be resolved.

Chapter 5

Ethical Issues (Thirteen Questions)

Religion is all about correct behavior—or at least it should be. However, despite the prevalence of many traditional Jewish laws intended to provide guidance and direction in our lives, human life is infinitely more complex and varied than can be encompassed in any body of law no matter how old or comprehensive. And the definitions of what constitutes appropriate, ethical, or moral behavior vary depending upon culture, country, religion, and region. How does one ever know what is the right thing to do? Perhaps no religious tradition, no matter how old or vast, can encompass or anticipate the entirety of socially vexing, challenging situations that may arise regarding appropriate, acceptable conduct between fellow human beings. I would like to believe that most people want to do the right thing in social situations, but it is not always clear exactly what that conduct should be.

The Jewish tradition defines ethical, appropriate behavior as Derech Eretz, which literally means "the way of the land." In other words, the way one behaves has an organic connection to our lives and the places we live. The ancient rabbis literally wrote dozens of volumes filled with laws and advice as to how Jews—or anyone for that matter—should go about living an ethical life. In the past several centuries, an entire social and scholarly movement devoted to ethical, pious behavior arose in the Talmudic academies of Eastern Europe called the Musar or ethical movement whose adherents committed themselves fully to a conscientious life of strict piety and principled conduct.

But what does ethical behavior entail nowadays? Modern life has only grown more complex, and the web of social relationships that bind us to one another only more complex and heterogeneous. The following questions are a potpourri of various moral and ethical dilemmas from various people of all walks of life. My answers reflect my personal and professional attempt to interpret and apply the established laws and precedents of the Jewish tradition to these situations. Other rabbis may well have responded entirely differently to these questions based on their personal experience and understanding of the Jewish tradition. I can only hope that we may all learn and grow from studying and considering all of these unique situations and range of solutions. The questions in this chapter begin with basic, general questions about ethical choices and then progress into questions about the details and finer points of specific situations.

Question number 1: What is the basis for determining whether a choice is right or wrong?

Answer: Excellent question! First of all, it depends on the situation. If it is a personal matter, one in which there is no Jewish or civil or even criminal law regarding it, then first you might consider what your conscience tells you. In other words, will your choice hurt someone? Will it make them feel bad? Will it make you feel bad? Is it a choice that might feel bad now but is actually the best, healthy, and appropriate decision to make for your long-term health and happiness? You might think about all of these when you try to figure out what your inner sense of right and wrong are telling you.

Also, you might want to read the Torah. Is this a matter that is dealt with in the Hebrew Bible? For instance, the Torah tells us not to hate people in our hearts (Leviticus 19:17) and that we should love people as we love ourselves (Leviticus 19:18). It also says that we should not go about as gossipmongers (Leviticus 19:16) and respect our elders (Leviticus 19:15). So perhaps the situation is described in the Torah.

And finally, is what you plan to do illegal in some way? Does it violate American criminal or civil law? After all, the Jewish tradition tells us we must follow civil law. The phrase Dina D'Malchuta Dina is Aramaic for "The law of the land we live in is the law we must also follow" (Talmud, Baba Kamma 113a). Therefore, as Jews we must always abide by the legitimate laws of the country we live in.

If you are still having trouble, I would encourage you to share your dilemma with friends and family or a trusted member of the clergy or a rabbi if you are Jewish to get some more insight, or even a mental health professional. Help and advice are available if we are willing to ask for it.

Question number 2: I read somewhere that making someone blush is like killing them because the blood rushes to their face for everyone to see, so in a way, you have publicly killed them. Do you know where this passage is from?

Answer: You have a good memory for the sources you read! The rabbinic source that you are referring to is from the Talmud Tractate Baba Metzia 58b as well as a slightly different formulation in Sanhedrin 99a. In Baba Metzia, it states, "The one who causes someone's face to go white in public (that is, embarrass them and make the blood run from their face)—it is as if they shed blood." In other words, the blood that you caused to leave their face through socially embarrassing them has been symbolically shed by you as if you had physically injured them. In the Sanhedrin source, it says, "The one who causes someone's face to go white in public has no share in the world to come." When people die, the pallor of their skin becomes white. Therefore, these sources imply that causing someone to feel such shame is tantamount to murder! The point of both of these passages is that we should avoid humiliating or embarrassing anyone because we want to spare people feelings of shame and disgrace that may be so great they may feel as if they could die on the spot out of social discomfort.

Question number 3: *What should I do about Jews disrespecting other Jews and disregarding commandments that are written in the Talmud? I just celebrated my Bar Mitzvah, and I take Judaism and the commandments seriously.*

Answer: There is a lot that you can do, but it takes a lot of courage and self-confidence. The first thing you can do is to ignore it. After all, it makes no difference what other people do or say regarding traditional Jewish holy texts. Their words or actions do not diminish the holiness of the contents of these traditional religious works. But I agree, it can be very frustrating and upsetting when you see other people, whether they be your friends or other Jews, disrespecting the words of traditional Jewish texts that are clearly far more important to you than it seems they are to them.

Another thing you can do is to speak out about your frustrations and talk to these people who are acting in a way that is bothering you. According to the Torah (Leviticus 19:17-19), we must not be angry with people in our hearts but rebuke them and share our feelings of frustration with them. Maybe we can influence their behavior or maybe not, but we have to try. In fact, the following verses from the book of Leviticus (19:17-19) contain a lot of wisdom about how to act in the very situation you describe. Here is how I would explain these verses, line by line, phrase by phrase:

1. "You shall not hate your fellow person in your heart"—If you become angry with your friend for some reason, you are not permitted to simply remain passive and hate this person quietly, privately, in the deepest recesses of your heart.
2. "Rebuke your fellow person"—For if you should then try to rebuke your friend, maybe you'll discover that what they said or did was a mistake, or perhaps they didn't even intend it. The best possible result from this action is that your fellow person will recognize the hurt they caused you, and they will apologize.

3. "But incur no guilt because of him"—This is a difficult clause to understand and bears more study. However, it probably means that you shouldn't embarrass the person you are trying to rebuke, or else you risk committing a sin yourself in going overboard in telling them what you think they did wrong.

4. "You shall not take vengeance or bear a grudge against your countrymen"—If you do in fact avoid rebuking your friend, your anger and hatred may build up inside you, and you may end up seeking revenge or bearing a grudge against him or her that may lead to further anger or violence. This is why the Torah places these verses in this order. Seeking vengeance or bearing a grudge is a logical potential consequence of not rebuking your fellow person or expressing your wounded feelings directly to him or her.

5. "Love your fellow as yourself: I am the Lord."—The ultimate goal is not to hate your friend but to love him or her and, therefore, imitate God. This is the ideal outcome of this biblical flowchart of actions and consequences. If we can successfully deal with our anger, we will avoid hatred by seeking a healthy confrontation with our fellow person. This in turn will enable us to restore harmony to our societal relationships that is what the Torah seeks to create.

In conclusion, you may wish to ignore the behavior that you find so challenging in other people, or you may even choose to talk to them and share your feelings of frustration that they are not observing Jewish traditions in the way that you feel they should. But please recognize that the only person you can ever truly influence and change for the better is yourself. Only you can do the right thing; we can't always demand or expect others to behave in a way that we think they should!

Question number 4: How does Judaism treat the issue of the humane treatment of animals? Does Judaism take into account the unique character of a family's relationship with a pet such as a dog or cat? What about our relationship with working animals, such as Seeing Eye or bomb-sniffing dogs?

Answer: There is a whole category of laws relating to the humane treatment of animals in Jewish law called Tzar Ba'alei Hayyim, that is, avoiding causing pain to a living creature. Basically, it is forbidden to treat animals cruelly or to cause them any pain. Consider the following Torah sources below that I have paraphrased regarding the injunction to avoid hurting animals:

1. Exodus 23:5—You should help your enemy's donkey that falls or stumbles under its load even though you may hate the animal's owner because you both must work to ensure the animal is not suffering.
2. Deuteronomy 5:14—On the Shabbat, not only should the Jewish people rest, but also even work animals get to rest one day a week.
3. Deuteronomy 22:6-7—When gathering wild bird's eggs to eat, one needs to send the mother bird away while stealing her eggs, for the ancient rabbis interpreted this to mean that we should be merciful toward the feelings of even a bird for her eggs.
4. Deuteronomy 22:10—When farming, one should not yoke a donkey together with an ox as that is cruel to the donkey who would be unable to pull the same burden as the much larger and stronger ox.
5. Deuteronomy 25:4—When plowing your fields, you should not muzzle an ox to prevent it from eating as it is working.

The traditional sources don't differentiate between pets and working animals because in earlier times, all domesticated animals were working animals to a certain extent. The point of these sources is that even animals that we use either for their labor or the hide or food they provide us must be treated in a humane and ethical manner.

Question number 5: *What is the Jewish view of teen pregnancy and abortion? Also, what current trends in modern society do you find troubling or disturbing from a Jewish perspective?*

Answer: You ask excellent and difficult questions! First of all, please recognize that I am paraphrasing and summarizing a great deal of the Jewish tradition in my answer below. Also, as one lone rabbi, I am not necessarily the sole voice of Judaism that is recognized by millions of Jews around the world. But I can give you an idea of the direction of Jewish thinking in general about the issues of teen pregnancy and abortion.

In short, as surprising as this might sound, the Jewish tradition actually does not explicitly prohibit premarital or teen sex because the ancient Jewish tradition advocated early marriage and sexual relations as a valid form of creating a marital bond between a man and woman. In other words, if you had sex with someone, you were automatically married to him or her as a result. There was no such thing as fooling around in ancient times without accidently marrying your partner. However, it is fair to say that the general weight of traditional Jewish texts abhor immature unmarried teenagers engaging in sexual relationships that they are not mature enough to deal with emotionally—not to speak of the potentially weighty consequences that can result if they have a child. It is sad that teenagers who are barely able to care for themselves may be suddenly faced with the prospect of having to care for a baby or make a decision as to whether to have an abortion.

As far as abortion in concerned, while modern traditional Jewish leaders may have social and political reasons for opposing it, the traditional Jewish sources actually support the legality of a woman's right to have an abortion. While there are many traditional Jewish sources that elucidate this issue, the best example is from the Torah (Exodus 21:22-27) that states that if a man accidently injures a pregnant woman and causes her to miscarry, then that man is only fined and not executed. The death penalty was always the punishment meted out for murder in the Torah. The fact that the man only has to pay a fine demonstrates that even as far back as the Torah, a fetus was not considered an equivalent life of an already-born human being. Of course, there are many conditions and other considerations that apply to the modern debate about abortion, but this is the essential traditional Jewish approach to abortion.

Finally, as to what is troubling or disturbing in modern society from a Jewish perspective, there are about a million current trends and issues that are challenging to traditional Jewish ethical and moral values in Western culture today. How about the prevalence of so much poverty, homelessness, and hunger in the United States alone? How about the level of violence caused by guns or otherwise in our schools? How about current polls that suggest that a majority of American students think it is okay to cheat on tests in school? How about the fact that in such a wealthy society filled with opportunities for spiritual growth and development, so many people still feel so alienated from God and a spiritual life? These are things that upset me as a rabbi and a Jew and, I hope, my fellow Jews.

Question number 6: *Are there any references in the Jewish tradition to self-defense, and when is it appropriate to resort to it?*

Answer: There are many Jewish sources dealing with self-defense. As Jews living in a Christian society, we are all familiar with the statement of Jesus when he says, "If someone slaps you on the right cheek, turn and offer him your left" (Matthew 5:39). However, as Jews, our tradition enjoins us to defend ourselves. This principle is based on a situation described in the Torah relating to the case of a thief who sneaks into a house at night. Exodus 22:1 states, "If a thief is seized while tunneling (that is, sneaking into a house), and he is beaten to death (by the homeowner) where he is found, there is no bloodguilt in his case." This means that there is no bloodguilt upon the homeowner because it was not clear whether the intruder had come to steal property or to commit murder. In other words, the homeowner was entitled to the right of self-defense. The Talmud in Sanhedrin 72b discusses this situation in greater detail:

> Our rabbis have taught: If a thief is found breaking in."
> (Exodus 22:1) From this verse I know that the law (about killing in self-defense) applies only to a case of breaking into a person's home. How do I know that it might apply to (the case

where the thief was found someplace else, like) on the roof, in a courtyard, or an attached enclosure? Because the verse continues, "where the thief is found . . ." implying wherever he is found as a thief. If so, then why does the verse state "breaking in (to someone's house)"? Because his breaking in constitutes a formal warning.

In other words, this passage from the Talmud states that if an intruder enters your home and you have no idea whether all he wants to do is take some of your property or hurt or even kill you or any of your family members, then you as the homeowner, according to Talmudic law, do not need to call out, "Hey! Stop, get out of here!" or warn the person that you have a gun or something because the very fact that they broke into your home at night relieves you of your obligation to warn them that you might have no choice but to resort to deadly force in the interests of self-defense.

An even clearer example that demonstrates that deadly force is permitted in the interests of self-defense actually comes from a Midrash, or rabbinic folktale. The Midrash states, "If someone comes to kill you, then rise early and kill him for behold, he is a murderous pursuer" (Bamidbar Rabbah 16:17). You should know that this is not always the case in American law and that the laws of self-defense vary from state to state, so don't confuse ancient Jewish laws of self-defense with modern American criminal law. But this is the essence of the traditional Jewish sources indicating that at times and in certain situations, it is appropriate to resort to violence in self-defense.

Question number 7: The other day, a friend and I beat up some skinheads at our school that had attacked one of my friends who is also Jewish. Afterward, I felt awful that I had sunk to their level. I was trying to stand up for my friend and fight against racism, but now I am confused. Is what I did wrong?

Answer: It sounds awful the problems that you are having in your school with skinheads and racist attacks. And that is terrible that they

114 Rabbi Daniel Kohn

attacked your friend just because he or she was a Jew. But I have to ask, where were the teachers and administrators of your school? Does the principal know about what is going on? If nothing else, you should try to get some adults in authority involved in this situation as it sounds like this situation could escalate and become far more dangerous as time goes on.

Was it wrong for you and your friend to beat up some of the skinheads? Maybe. That is a complicated question—if you were defending yourself, then it is always okay to defend yourself as long as it is reasonable and proportional to the threat. However, if you were attacking out of revenge and seeking to get some kind of emotional satisfaction, then it was not okay. If you are able to avoid violence by simply walking away, then you should always seek to steer clear of confrontations that may lead to fighting.

Again, get the school authorities involved even if it happened off campus or not during school hours. Even if the skinheads are not students, your safety and that of your friend's is the responsibility of the school. By going to the authorities, you are not tattling on anyone or being a coward—you are doing what is right. Let the school administration do its job and maybe even get these racist bullies in serious trouble. Let the school administration and adult community work with you and for you. Don't become violent bullies yourself in the process.

When you take this situation into your own hands and beat up some skinheads on your own, I would agree with you—you are sinking to their level. If you are being confronted and are defending yourself and have no other option but to resort to violence, then by all means, do what you need to do. But don't go overboard and recognize that even simple schoolyard fights can end in serious injury, escalation of the violence, and even lawsuits and jail time. Would a policeman or a lawyer or even your principal agree with what I have told you here? Probably not but I don't know, so I'll end with emphasizing what you yourself felt in your own guts—don't sink to their level.

Question number 8: *Where do you draw the line for compassion regarding an abuser and their victim? Must we always forgive a criminal? I have been a victim of domestic violence for many years and have only recently gained the courage to get on with my life. Should I still try to find compassion toward my abuser?*

Answer: I am so sorry to hear that you were a victim of abuse. I wish you the strength and courage to continue with your efforts to get on with your life in a different, hopefully more healthy and supportive environment. It makes my blood boil to learn of situations of domestic abuse, of how a family relationship—which is supposed to be a model of the loving and intimate relationship between God and human beings—has been perverted and debased through abuse.

Should you forgive your abuser? No one can answer that but you. I have neither the right nor the arrogance to assume that I can—or should—tell you how to feel inside toward someone who has caused you such pain and anguish over such a long period of time.

As Jews, we are not real big on the Christian concept of turning the other cheek. On the other hand, the Torah does say, "Do not hate your fellow in your heart—you shall rebuke him" (Leviticus 19:17). The point of this verse is not to keep hatred and anger inside where it causes internal emotional harm to us. Rather, we must express it in healthy, appropriate ways. It seems to me that you are already expressing your anger in healthy ways—you seem to be getting along in your life—and I can only encourage you to seek serious professional counseling and support to help you deal with the residual anger and pain you may feel for years to come.

But should you forgive your abuser? I would say if, and only when, you feel ready to—if that time ever comes. When the anger and hatred becomes too much of an emotional burden for you to continue carrying around and becomes emotionally unhealthy and corrosive, then you'll know it, and it will be time to put it aside. But in the meantime, anger toward your abuser can be a healthy expression of your soul's endeavor to heal itself. Just don't feel *guilty* about your anger during this time. It is like the scar tissue over a wound. It will go away in time, but you need it temporarily to help protect the vulnerable insides underneath the scab. But it may always leave a scar.

Question number 9: As a police officer, I sometimes participate in elaborate sting operations intended to fool people and lure them into committing a crime that they might or might not have committed if we were not arranging this sting operation. My problem is that I feel guilty about being part of the entrapment because I am not God to judge these people. Is it wrong for me to be part of this? Should I help catch these potential criminals? Am I part of God's plan for making the world more just?

Answer: While I can understand your feelings of conscience in this matter, I want you to know that according to the Jewish tradition, you are doing absolutely the right thing. Just consider what the Torah says in Deuteronomy 16:18-20, "You shall appoint magistrates and officials for your tribes, in all the settlements that the Lord your God is giving you, and they shall govern the people with due justice . . . Justice, Justice shall you pursue!"

In other words, while God may set the absolute standards for justice, there is no justice here in our world unless we take action to ensure that this is so. We need to establish courts, judges, and even police to ensure that justice prevails in our society. The concept of "Judge not so that ye be not judged" is a quote from Jesus (Matthew 7:1) and is a uniquely Christian value. If we as human beings and as Jews do not become partners with God in ensuring the establishment and maintenance of justice in this world, then who will? While the standards of absolute and divine justice has been established by God, the establishment and pursuit of that justice is in our hands! Thank you for the work you are doing to keep our society safer.

Question number 10: Why doesn't the United States just assassinate evil leaders of other countries, like the president of Iran or North Korea, to alleviate the suffering of the people in those countries? What is the Jewish perspective on this issue?

Answer: There are many traditional sources that actually deal with this challenging question of competing values, but perhaps one of the easiest to find is in the Torah that states:

> (Moses) saw an Egyptian beating a Hebrew, one of his kinsmen. He turned this way and that and seeing no one about, he struck down the Egyptian and him in the sand. When he went out the next day, he found two Hebrews fighting; so he said to the offender, "Why do you strike your fellow?" He retorted, "Who made you chief and ruler over us? Do you mean to kill me as you killed the Egyptian?" (Exodus 2:11-14)

Moses might have thought he was doing the right thing when he killed the Egyptian hurting the Israelites, but it was still murder. And the Torah is filled with examples and quotes about not murdering. This is because murder is tantamount to the destruction of the divine image. Even someone evil deserves to be judged in a court of law and not assassinated outright. Regarding murder, the Torah states in a number of places that the murderer shall suffer capital punishment. Here are only a couple of examples of this biblical perspective:

1. Genesis 9:5-6, (God tells Noah after the flood) "For your own life-blood I will require a reckoning: I will require it of every . . . man, too, will I require a reckoning for human life, of every man for that of his fellow man! Whoever sheds the blood of man, by man shall his blood be shed; for in His image did God make man."
2. Exodus 21:12, (God commands the Israelites) "He who fatally strikes a man shall be put to death."

Despite the fact that there are innocent people suffering in other countries due to the misrule of their leaders, from a purely Jewish religious perspective, they should not simply be assassinated. They should face justice and a court of law. I hope this helps answer your question.

Question number 11: Does Israel have the right to destroy the home of a Palestinian who is involved in an act of terror? This only deepens hatred of Israel among the surviving family members. Amnesty International has charged Israel with illegally detaining Palestinians in their prisons and using torture. How can I maintain the feeling that Israel is a wonderful place and central to my religion and still acknowledge the horrible nature of the acts I have mentioned? Of course, I grieve and feel anger when Jews are attacked just because they are Jews. But Palestinians are people too. What does the Jewish tradition have to say about my emotional conflict?

Answer: It is important to make a distinction between Israel as a Jewish state that was founded to be a haven for all Jews seeking persecution from anti-Semitism and the governmental policies of Israel that you find offensive. It is possible to be a Zionist and have very strong feelings of attachment and connection to the State of Israel, a country that is the homeland of the Jewish people, and at the same time be outraged by the behavior of the government of Israel that formulates and carries out the political and military policies that you find hateful.

It is also completely natural and legitimate to agree with Amnesty International's condemnation of the Israeli government's unethical treatment of Palestinians and still support the right of the State of Israel to exist. Similarly, back in the 1960s and 1970s, it was possible to oppose the Vietnam War and the U.S. government while still being a patriotic American who supported the continued existence of the United States. It is also not a contradiction to support the United State and still oppose the current war in Iraq.

In fact, the Haftarah (selection from the prophets of the Hebrew Bible chanted in synagogue) of Yom Kippur is a section from the prophet Isaiah's condemnation of the ancient priests, Jews, and governments of the Jewish kings who did not act morally or ethically. Your question and cry of outrage is an ancient one. You can read it yourself in Isaiah chapters 57 and 58.

There should be no conflict in your mind regarding wh
opposing emotional and intellectual viewpoints; in fac
Jewish to demand and expect ethical behavior from other ﺟﻮ
from the Israeli government. And you are right to demand nothing ﻟﻮ
than completely ethical and moral behavior from the Jewish state. Some
people would claim that the very essence of patriotism, either toward
this country or Zionist or religious feelings of connection to Israel, is to
actually criticize the immoral and illegal behavior of governments out
of our very love and loyalty to them! To expect or settle for anything less
is to pervert Jewish values of morality and universal justice. No one is
above moral behavior—even the Israeli government and the Jewish state.
And I agree with you, of course. Palestinians are people too. And it is a
cornerstone of our religious tradition that all human beings are created
in the image of God (see Genesis 1:27) and deserve all of the rights and
privileges that we would demand and expect for ourselves.

*Question number 12: What is the general Jewish view on war and
peace?*

Answer: Peace is preferable to war. However, sometimes war is
unavoidable in the interests of trying to maintain peace. In the Hebrew
Bible, God commanded war against a people called the Amalekites,
who were to be considered the eternal enemy of the Jewish people (see
Deuteronomy 25:17-19) for their inhumane and cruel attacks upon the
Israelites when they were at their weakest, just having left Egypt in the
great exodus and flight from slavery. The rabbis of the Talmud, in fact,
differentiated between three types of war:

1. Obligatory war: These were the wars that God commanded the
    Israelites to wage to drive out the Canaanites from the land of
    Israel over three thousand years ago. This ancient law, to drive
    out the Canaanites, however, was understood to be a one-time
    command for that generation alone. Also, the war against the
    Amalekites was also included in this variety.

2. Defensive war: When people attack Jews, since it is a commandment to protect one's life, it is not only permitted but also obligatory to fight a war of self-defense. Even a bride and groom are obligated to cut short their honeymoon to engage in a war of self-defense of the Jewish people. Israel's War of Independence in 1948-49 was just such a war, for the very day after Israel declared independence, it was invaded by five neighboring Arab countries and had to fight for its very survival.

3. Optional war: The rabbis in the Talmud applied this category of war to the wars of King David in the Hebrew Bible and the Maccabees in Greek and Roman times who fought to enlarge the borders of their kingdoms.

Even in these kinds of wars, however, the rabbis emphasized that peace is always superior to war because the Talmud states that peace is the greatest of all blessings because every other kind of blessing in the entire world can be summed up and included in the divine gift of peace.

Question number 13: What are some important biblical passages dealing with Shalom (peace)? What is the significance of peace in the Jewish tradition?

Answer: Peace is one of the most important values in the Jewish tradition going all the way back to the Hebrew Bible. For instance, in Psalm 34:13, it states, "Depart from evil and do good, seek out *peace* and pursue it!" In Zechariah 8:10-16, the prophet wrote, "These are the things that you should do: Speak the truth to every man and his fellow; execute the judgment of truth and *peace* in your gates." And the prophet Isaiah also stated (Isaiah 52:7), "How beautiful upon the mountains are the feet of the messenger that brings good tidings, that announces *peace*, the harbinger of good tidings, that announces salvation; that says to the people of Zion: 'Your God reigns!'"

The rabbis of the Talmud further emphasized the primary importance of peace in the Jewish tradition in the following passages:

1. Avot 1:18—"Rabban Shimon ben Gamliel said, On three things does the world stand: on justice, on truth, and on *peace.*" In this passage, peace makes it as one of the top three values in the Jewish tradition.

2. Tractate Shabbat 6:4—"A person shall not go out of his house (on Shabbat) carrying a sword, a bow, a spear, or a shield. And if he goes out, he is guilty of sin. Rabbi Eliezer said: But these are mere ornaments for a person (and not intended to be used)! The sages replied: They are nothing but a disgrace, as it says, 'You shall beat your swords into plowshares and your spears into pruning hooks; one nation shall not lift up a sword against another nation: They shall never again know war' (Isaiah 2:4)". The rabbis here quote another famous passage from the prophet Isaiah to show that even ornamental weapons contradict the Jewish value of emphasizing peace in our lives.

3. Tractate Berachot 64a—"Rabbi Elazar said in the name of Rabbi Hanina: Scholars increase *peace (emphasis mine)* in the world, as it says, 'And all of your children will be learned in (the ways of) God, and great will be the *peace* of your children' (Isaiah 54:13). Don't read "your children" (Banayikh in Hebrew); rather, read it as if it said, "your builders" (Bonayikh)". This is a difficult passage to understand since it is based on a Hebrew play on words, but the essence of it claims that anyone who studies the Jewish tradition cannot help but create more peace as they learn more about the commitment of the Jewish tradition to peace in this world.

4. Midrash Vayikra Rabbah 9:9—"Rabbi Shimon bar Yohai said: Great is *peace* because all of the other blessings are included in it, as it says, 'God will grant strength to His people: God will bless his people with *peace*' (Psalm 29:11)." In other words, while God might give qualities of strength to people, the ultimate quality and blessing is that of peace.

Chapter 6

Questions from Kids and Teens
(Sixteen Questions)

Young people often embrace technology more quickly and easily than do adults, and when AOL launched the "Ask a Rabbi" service, it was not surprising to me that nearly half of all the questions I received came from young people, specifically children and teenagers. And it was not surprising to me that many of the questions that they posed often did not fit into any of the nice and neat categories that comprise most of the other chapters in this book, although I'm sure it has been fairly easy to identify questions in other chapters that were sent in by young people based on the simple questions and sometimes adorably naive language of their questions.

Kids, teens, and children have lots of questions about Judaism and religion because they are still trying to figure it all out. They are working on establishing a sense of their own identity as individuals as Jews and want guidance and direction as they grow increasingly aware of the world they live in, the community that they are part of, and grow more sophisticated about the ways of other people and religions around them. It is for this reason that I felt it appropriate to devote an entire section to the unique, unclassifiable questions, issues, and challenges posed by kids and sometimes even the adults who raise and work with kids and wanted some more advice and insight. Even if you are not a kid, I hope that these questions and answers may still address subjects that are of value and interest to everyone.

In terms of editing the questions—I haven't, at least, not very much. I have corrected spelling, grammar, and capitalization mistakes—like any good English teacher—but I left the essence of the questions as I received them. And of course, I changed or omitted all identifying features so as to preserve their anonymity. Oftentimes, the spelling and syntactical mistakes were the only clues I had about the identity of the person writing me the e-mail question. Sometimes, the mistakes themselves were instructive and helped me understand how to couch a particular answer. So I hope the highly creative writing does not dissuade you from reading their questions—or my answers!

Question number 1: Hi, I am nine years old, and I have a question for you. Why did God talk to Adam and Eve, Moses, and lots of other people but not to us?

Answer: Thank you for asking such a good question! I don't know, but maybe I can suggest some ideas for you to think about which might help you answer the question for yourself. Although we usually think that Adam and Eve and Abraham, Moses, and others in the Hebrew Bible were closer to God than we are today since they seemed to talk to God all the time, maybe these famous, important people were actually not as religiously mature as we are today! What I mean is that maybe they were like little kids, and God was like their mother or father who gave them lots of religious advice because they weren't very knowledgeable about Judaism and needed more help.

But nowadays, we have had over three thousands years of Jewish history and generations of rabbis who wrote all kinds of religious books to help us in our religious life. We are like adults now in terms of Jewish history, and maybe God feels like parents sometimes do after their children grow up, that their kids don't need their help all the time. God is still there, but God simply chooses not to get as involved as God used to so as to allow us to be more independent.

Or for a different answer, perhaps God does continue to speak to us all the time—but maybe we are the ones who aren't always listening. For instance, sometimes when we do something wrong, we might feel bad about it afterward. Maybe this ability to feel bad about things we have done wrong this comes from God. God might not literally say, "Hey, that is wrong! Don't do that!" But maybe our ability to know the difference between right and wrong somehow still comes from God, and so whenever we have the feeling that we are doing the right thing, maybe that feeling comes from God!

And finally, maybe God does not literally speak to us; rather, God helps us in the difficult times in our lives, and that is how God shows that God is still around and present in our lives. In other words, when we feel really bad about something or are very depressed but somehow we get through it okay, maybe God helped us through it. God can give us strength to carry on when we seem to lose all hope. And maybe God is somehow pleased when, in a moment of our great joy, we thank God for all of the good things in our life. God might not always speak to us—but we can always speak to God. This is one of the reasons why we pray to God in Judaism.

I don't know if I answered your question, but I hope I gave you some interesting things to think about. Please tell your parents that a wonderful book that you all could read together is called *Teaching Your Children about God* by Rabbi David Wolpe. It is a wonderful book and may help answer many other questions you have about God.

Question number 2: Where does God live?

Answer: Where does God live? I could answer your question with another question—where does God *not* live? According to the Jewish tradition, God is everywhere. As it says in Isaiah 6:3, "The whole earth is filled with God's glory." Even King Solomon who built the Temple in Jerusalem asked, "Can God possibly live in a building?" Obviously, the answer is no. God is everywhere in the universe—especially in the shape of human beings. We all have been created in the image of God. Whenever we interact with other people, we must learn to see that they were also created in the image of God. God is also inside of us. We may not always be aware of God's presence, so the challenge is for us to try and listen very carefully. And maybe we can understand what God is saying to us deep inside ourselves. And God does not live in the sense that human beings live because God does not die. One famous rabbi wrote over a thousand years ago that "God was is, is and will always be" because God was never born and will not die. God is eternal and therefore does not live anywhere. God is always everywhere! Perhaps most importantly of all, God lives inside of us. Our lives are a gift from God, and so there is always a little spark of God inside of us and all living creatures.

Question number 3: Hello, Rabbi. I am twelve years old and Jewish, but I'm not sure that God exists. I really want to believe in God, but I find it difficult sometimes. I still say the prayers, attend synagogue on the holidays, and celebrate the various holidays. My question is can you prove that God exists for me? And does my questioning the existence of God make me a bad Jew, or not even Jewish?

Answer: Questioning the existence of God does not make you a bad Jew—quite the opposite! Judaism encourages people to question their faith and ask lots of difficult questions. In fact, the name of the Jewish people, "Israel," literally means "to wrestle with God" (see the Torah story about this in Genesis 32:29)—so you are just fulfilling the destiny of the Jewish people! But if you are expecting me or anyone else to be able to prove the existence of God with rational arguments, I'm afraid that you are going to be disappointed. There are no absolute proofs to demonstrate the existence of God. Unfortunately, it just doesn't work that way.

You should also know that belief in God is not necessarily the most important part of Judaism or living a spiritual life. Our tradition emphasizes appropriate moral, holy behavior in our lives, not necessarily believing in God. How you behave is more important than what you believe. So it is great that you are still able to practice Judaism even with your doubts about God's existence.

There is an amazing story that the ancient rabbis of the Talmud made up a long time ago that says that God would rather us (the Jewish people) keep the Mitzvot (the commandments) and *not* believe in God because the observance of the commandments will ultimately lead us to believe in God. Maybe that is true, I don't know; and while I don't believe there is such a thing as a good or bad Jew, you should know that you are a very honest Jew for asking these questions!

Question number 4: What should I say to my teenage son who, after years of sending him to Hebrew school, says there is no God?

Answer: You should tell your son how much you love, support, and understand that life can be challenging and that you want him to know that you will always be there for him. But I do have to ask you—with great respect and kindness—what exactly did you expect Hebrew school to do for your teenager? Brainwash him into believing in God? Produce a teenager who mouths theological platitudes that he does not believe? Would you prefer that he lie to you about his spiritual beliefs? Synagogue-based religious education can teach children to read Hebrew, to pray, to observe Jewish holidays and other religious rituals and observances. And the students might even have fun in the process. But to expect that a part-time, after-school, couple-of-days-a-week supplementary school can instill theological beliefs about the nature of the universe in the students is perhaps asking for too much. Synagogue-based religious schools have a hard enough time as it is teaching children about Judaism, helping them develop a positive sense of Jewish identity, and perhaps preparing them for their Bar and Bat Mitzvah celebrations; but please don't foist the job of ensuring doctrinal conformity on Hebrew schools. As a rabbi,

I am happy if the kids in my religious school can even remember the Hebrew Aleph-Bet a few weeks after their Bar or Bat Mitzvah!

Personally, I think your teen's Hebrew school education was a success—he is unafraid to share with you, his parent, what he truly believes. Your son feels comfortable enough in your relationship to express his confusion and doubts about life and reality. Congratulations on maintaining a positive and healthy relationship with your teenager! I'm serious! And just because your son said he doesn't believe in God is not a failure either of the religious school or of your religious home life. This is an opportunity! Now is when you have the greatest chance to affect the religious and spiritual development of your teenager as a parent and an adult who has a lifetime of experience to draw on. Cultivating a belief in God is *your* job! Have you ever initiated a conversation about your personal spiritual beliefs with your son about God? Have you shared your feelings, thoughts, doubts, and insights and experiences about God with him? Don't wait—now your teen has the religious background necessary to understand and truly explore and consider sophisticated theological premises. If you want to affect the spiritual life and future of your teenager, you will never have a better opportunity.

Finally, it is completely natural, appropriate, and healthy for your teenager to express a doubt in the belief in God. This is age-appropriate behavior—to rebel against what he has learned in religious school and also to express his doubts in the ideal of divine personification in universal cosmic justice. Maybe he is even rebelling against you and your religious beliefs, which is still a normal and healthy stage of growth for a teenager. Besides, how many people in this world are absolutely convinced as to the belief in God? You may indeed be among those few with clear and unwavering faiths. But that kind of faith takes years of life experience to develop, or naïveté. Maybe your teen will develop such faith in time. But it is only natural and appropriate that at this early stage in his life that he does not yet have it. You can help them see the world through your eyes. Your child's doubts about God are a God-given opportunity. I encourage you to take advantage of your teenager's openness and honesty—you may not get another chance.

Question number 5: Dear Rabbi, I am nineteen years old, and although I celebrated my Bat Mitzvah and continue to observe Jewish holidays, lately I have been questioning the existence of God. I don't understand how God can exist when there are innocent people dying every day and wicked people prospering. Also, everyone claims his or her religion is the only true one; how can we be sure Judaism is the only true religion?

Answer: Regarding your first question, no one knows why bad things happen to good people. An awful lot of books have been written about this! In fact, a popular book published a number of years ago with this very title dealt with this issue, *When Bad Things Happen to Good People* by Rabbi Harold Kushner. I encourage you to read it.

Regarding this issue of the existence of evil and God's existence, perhaps I can suggest a way of looking at the world that might offer a little bit of perspective for you. You don't have to accept what I'm sharing with you, but I just want to offer an alternative point of view. There are basically two kinds of bad things that happen to good people. The first is bad things that other humans cause and can prevent or stop. I call this human evil because humans create this kind of evil and humans can stop it. The other kind of bad things that happen to people are those caused by nature or accidents, like terminal diseases, hurricanes, or earthquakes that couldn't have been prevented. I call this natural evil because this is the way nature works.

As for human evil, since humans caused these bad things to happen, humans can stop it. Many people try to blame God for not stopping the Holocaust, but God didn't cause the Holocaust—people did! The Nazis made the Holocaust happen, along with willing German citizens and the collaborators of many other countries that the Nazis occupied. And people were responsible for putting an end to it—the Allied armies of the United States, Britain, France, Russia, and other countries. And in fact, the Holocaust only ended because Germany lost World War II. So people did, in fact, stop that evil.

As for natural evil, there is no answer. Bad things can happen to good people with no reason and no way to stop it. This can be tragic and heartbreaking, but this is also the nature of reality in our world. We might not be able to prevent accidents, cure all of the world's diseases, or stop tsunamis and earthquakes, but we can try to help people in their suffering when bad things do happen to them. We can work to alleviate their pain and ensure that they do not suffer needlessly and try to prevent such natural causes of suffering from affecting people in the future.

Regarding your second question, no one ever claimed that Judaism was the one true religion for everyone. Judaism is a religion that is right for Jews and anyone else who feels moved to convert and join the Jewish people. Every religion espouses a unique way in which to understand and approach God. Our religion is also a very special, unique way of understanding and appreciating God in this world. We also understand—or at least believe—that God wants us to do everything in our power to alleviate the pain and suffering of other people and creatures in this world and to try and perfect it. This is our understanding of God and what we believe God wants of us. We cannot nor should we force other people to accept our religion as the one and only true religion in the world. As Jews, it is also part of our religious tradition to respect the beliefs of other religious communities in the world—even if they don't respect ours.

Question number 6: Although I am fifteen years old and Christian, I have spent the last two years of my life trying to find answers about God because I feel I need some help. I have read the holy books of other religions. And recently, I have begun to study about Judaism, and I really enjoy what I am learning. Christianity no longer satisfies the thirst I have for God. So I am turning to you, Rabbi, to counsel me in this matter. How do I properly ask God to help me? I am crying out to God, and I have no strength left. Please help me in any way that you can.

Answer: Thank you for your e-mail. Your letter clearly reveals the depth of your soul and the seriousness of your spiritual longing. But I have to be honest with you—just because you want something so terribly does not always mean that you may be able to find it. Who wouldn't want to have a sense of the Divine in their lives and in their hearts? Many people seek God's presence in their lives, all their lives, and there is no guarantee that they will find it. That is a tough message to hear, but it is a realistic one. And Judaism is a religion based on a realistic assessment of this world and the lives we lead.

You mentioned that you have been searching for the answers to your questions. You should know that Judaism is a tradition that values the questions more than the answers. This is because answers tend to actually stifle further inquiry and questioning. So from a traditional Jewish standpoint, formulating good questions is half of the journey to finding God. I would caution you against finding satisfaction with any answers that you might find because continuing to question means that you are still growing and developing spiritually.

The language of your e-mail is so beautiful, poetic, and heartfelt that it reminded me of reading the Psalms from the Hebrew Bible. The book of Psalms is a collection of ancient biblical poems written by people who also desperately longed for God's presence and help. Perhaps reading the book of Psalms might bring you some solace and comfort in your spiritual quest. And perhaps God is a lot closer than you might imagine. As it says in the Hebrew Bible, 1 Kings 19:11-12, "And behold, the Lord passed by. There was a great and mighty wind, splitting mountains and shattering rocks by the power of the Lord; but the Lord was not in the wind. After the wind, an earthquake—but the Lord was not in the earthquake. After the earthquake, a fire—but the Lord was not in the fire. After the fire—a still, small voice." You may be looking for the wind, earthquake, and fire but missing the "still, small voice" of God inside you. As Jacob in the Torah said when he awoke from his dream (Genesis 28:16), "Surely, God is in the place—but I, I did not know!" God is all around us already; the challenge is to wake up spiritually and open our eyes and see God everywhere! I wish you lots of luck and strength in your spiritual journey through life.

Question number 7: *My brother has believed in God all of his life. But recently, he has been asking a lot of questions, and I don't think he* *believes in God anymore. He says that since there is no proof that God exists, the Torah may all be just myths. How can I help him? I still want him to believe in God because if he doesn't, I am scared that God will punish him. Please help!*

Answer: It is perfectly normal for your brother to question whether God exists. As hard as it may be for you to understand right now, it is a natural part of growing up for young boys and girls to question all kinds of things that they used to believe in. Many children question the answers their teachers give them in school or the things that their parents tell them to do. And it is perfectly normal for people to question whether God exists.

It must be very scary for you to see your brother asking these questions, but I want to assure you that God will not punish your brother for doubting God's existence. That is not the way God works in the Jewish tradition. God gives us the freedom to ask any question we want and accept any answer we want even if we end up not believing in God! Just because people might not believe in God doesn't mean that God doesn't care for them.

I would like to recommend that you continue to tell your brother how much you love and care for him no matter what he believes. Also, don't be afraid to share your fears and concerns with him. I'm sure that he will appreciate your love and support. And don't be afraid to share these fears with your parents too. But don't be afraid if he doesn't believe in God just because you want him to. You must give him the freedom to believe in what he wants—just as you have the freedom to express your concerns about him as well.

Question number 8: Hi, Rabbi! I am fourteen years old, and I don't know a lot about Judaism. I never had my Bat Mitzvah because I can't read Hebrew because I quit my temple's Hebrew school, and I still feel bad about that. But I would like to become more involved in my religion now, but I am the only Jewish kid in my high school. So I would appreciate some advice. Thanks for your answer!

Answer: Thanks for having the courage to write and share a little about yourself. It takes a lot of guts—and insight—to figure out what it is that you might be missing in your life and trying to figure out a way to include it. Please don't feel ashamed because you never celebrated your Bat Mitzvah or that you don't know Hebrew. First of all, you should know it is never too late to celebrate your Bat Mitzvah and you are never too old to get more involved in Jewish life. When I was a rabbi of a synagogue, one elderly woman in the congregation celebrated her Bat Mitzvah when she was eighty-three years old! I'm going to suggest a bunch of different ideas regarding how to get more involved in Judaism, so please feel free to pick and choose among the various options I suggest, or I hope I spark your imagination to come up with some new ones!

1. Get involved in your synagogue's youth group. Just because you didn't continue with your Hebrew studies at your temple doesn't mean you cannot or should not get involved in your local teen social group. There are a lot of Jewish teen organizations out there either connected to your synagogue or connected with a regional Jewish youth organization, and you should join one.
2. Talk to your rabbi. Believe it or not, rabbis can be great resources to help you get connected to other kids in your community. Maybe your rabbi doesn't relate well to teens, and that could be, but at least give it a shot. Maybe she or he can help. At least your rabbi is a good place to start.
3. Do some Jewish homework. Start to add a Jewish book or two into your reading this year or over the summer. Not a heavy, intense history book or anything too boring. There are lots of novels about Judaism that are accessible to teens, like Chaim Potok's *The Chosen*. Check your temple's library or even the public library for some ideas.
4. Hit the Web. There is *so* much Jewish stuff on the Web. A great place to start is www.MyJewishLearning.com or www.Jewish.com.

Just because you are not involved in your synagogue's Hebrew school doesn't mean you cannot connect to other Jewish teens and begin developing a better sense of your Jewish identity. But it means you are going to have to get off your duff and make an effort yourself. It won't come to you on a silver platter; you're going to have to push yourself a little. But you know what? It is definitely worth the effort! Good luck!

Question number 9: There is a kid in my class who's Jewish, and everyone hates him, what should I do?

Answer: It is unfortunate that the other children in your class hate one of your fellow classmates. I have no idea how old you are or what grade you are in, but I do know that sometimes groups of kids gang up on other kids sometimes for no reason at all. Do these kids just passively hate this other classmate, or are they actually doing mean things to him and making his life miserable? Perhaps it doesn't really make a difference, but if these other kids are actually harassing your Jewish classmate, then maybe you really do need to do something for your Jewish classmate.

It is also unclear to me if the other members of your class hate this child just because he is Jewish. If this is the case, then that is indeed very upsetting and sad. I also have no idea if *you* are Jewish or not and maybe no one else in your class knows about it. Whether you are Jewish or not, it doesn't really make a difference; the fact that you are upset that other kids are acting unjustly toward another classmate already tells me that you have a strong sense of justice and want to do the right thing. There are a couple of things you can do if you want to get the rest of your class to stop hating this kid. However, I must warn you that my suggestions might not work, but if you feel very strongly about this, I would urge you to act and do what you know is right.

First, you might simply try talking to a few of the kids in your class and let them know that you are unhappy with how they have been treating this child and that you won't go along with them. It can be very scary and takes a lot of guts to stand up to other kids, but if you feel that is the right thing to do, you should do it. Maybe by taking such a courageous stand, you might get some of the other kids to feel badly and ashamed about how they have been treating this kid. Maybe some of these other kids don't even really hate this Jewish child either and are just going along with one or two other bullies in their social group, but they don't have the courage to speak up about how they feel. Sometimes, all it takes is for one courageous person—like you—to tell them that they are wrong, and maybe that will be enough to convince these other kids to reconsider their actions. You could be the one to stop all of this.

If you are uncomfortable with that, you might talk to the teacher or your principal and tell them what you see is happening. You know, when people hate someone just because of their religion or their skin color, that is called bigotry and racism. It might seem pretty harmless now, but if no one ever challenges your classmates who hate this child, their feelings of hate will only grow as they get older and may lead them to say and do terrible things toward Jews in the future. Your teacher and principal ought to know about this, and maybe they can deal with the situation and help deal with this problem in an appropriate way.

And the least that you can do is to talk to this Jewish kid and let him know he is not alone. Maybe he feels horrible that he is being singled out. He might feel terribly alone with no friends in his class. Maybe you could make him feel better by letting him know he isn't alone and that he does have a friend—you—and that you are willing to take his side and that you disagree with the rest of your classmates and that at least you do not hate him.

And of course, talk to your parents and ask them for advice. They might have some other suggestions about how to help this other child in your class. But ultimately, I am sure you will do the right thing. I hope and pray that you have the courage to stand up to hatred, wherever you may find it.

Question number 10: As a religious schoolteacher in a temple, what should I teach my nine-year-old students about Tisha B'Av [Jewish fast day commemorating the destruction of the Temple in Jerusalem]?

Answer: The historical truth. I recommend that you teach them any of the following ideas about Tisha B'Av, the day the two ancient Temples in Jerusalem were destroyed and which remains a fast day in the Jewish calendar.

First of all, teach them that the Temple in Jerusalem was the center of Jewish life in ancient times. It was where the Kohanim (priests) and Levites (Temple workers) helped ordinary Jews offer animal sacrifices to God. However, twice in Jewish history, the Jews became involved in wars and that this Temple was destroyed. The first time, the Jews fought the Babylonians, and the First Temple was destroyed in 586 BCE. But later on, the Jews were able to rebuild it and worship there again. Hundreds of years later, the Jews fought a war against the Romans, and the Second Temple was destroyed in 70 CE. What is even more amazing is that both of these Temples were destroyed on exactly the same day but in different years.

Because these two Temples were destroyed, the Jews were very sad and fasted because no one feels like eating or drinking when they are really sad. Even to this day, some Jews continue to refrain from eating or drinking on Tisha B'Av, the ninth day of the Hebrew month of Av, to commemorate the destruction of both of these ancient Temples in Jerusalem. In addition, we read the book of Lamentations from the Hebrew Bible to remind us of how sad we were and still are on the anniversary of when the Temple was destroyed. The book of Lamentations was written a long ago possibly by the prophet Jeremiah who was alive when the First Temple was destroyed and felt so awful he wrote this book to help express his sadness.

Sometimes, it is okay and healthy to feel sad. It helps us feel better in the long run when we acknowledge our sad feelings. But in general, we have plenty of happy holidays in the Jewish calendar, but this is why we continue to commemorate this sad day when both of the Temples were destroyed long ago. Judaism recognizes that there are times we are happy and times we are sad, and both of them can be part of our spiritual practices.

Question number 11: *Help me, Rabbi! My teacher gave us a question to answer that I don't understand. I am only twelve years old, and I can't figure this out. Here is the question: "All things are mortal but the Jews; all other forces pass, but he remains. What is the secret of his immortality?" Thank you for your help.*

Answer: Thank you for your question, but I want you to know that it is my policy not to help school-aged children with their homework through this "Ask a Rabbi" service. I'm sure your teacher would not give you an assignment without providing you with some clues or resources as to how to answer this question. However, I will give you some ideas that I hope will kick-start your imagination and give you some suggestions about where to continue your research.

First of all, no one is immortal. However, the Jewish people can be thought of as immortal, which means "living forever" in the sense that the Jewish people has existed as a unified, recognizable people for over three thousand years. That is longer than any other people on this planet. As for the secret of the Jewish people's immortality—no one knows. But the sentence that you quoted is very similar to a line written by Mark Twain in an article he wrote for *Harper's Magazine* around one hundred years ago. Mark Twain was writing about his amazement at how long the Jewish faith and tradition and people have survived for so many thousands of years. So my advice to you is to answer the question in this way—why do you think that the Jewish people are still around after so many thousands of years? Are the ancient Egyptians who built the pyramids still around? Or the Greeks who carved all of those wonderful statues so long ago, or the Roman Empire that conquered most of Europe, the Middle East, and North Africa? Why did all of those cultures disappear, but the Jewish people are still around? That is the real question that I think your teacher wants you to answer. Now go track down Mark Twain's article and read it for yourself for more insight into how to answer your teacher's question.

Question number 12: *I heard a story that one time at a Jewish day school, a thirteen-year-old boy was fooling around and gave his girlfriend* *a ring and recited the traditional wedding formula as he did it. When the families found out, they had to get a Get* [Jewish divorce document] *since the two kids were considered officially married. Could this story be true? And if so, shouldn't it be a little more difficult to get married than that?*

Answer: I have also heard this story. And who knows, maybe it could be true. But if it is, it seems to be that the families and rabbis who dealt with this situation were being a little too uptight and narrow-minded about how to deal with kids, Jewish education, and Jewish traditions. My guess is that this is the equivalent of a Jewish urban myth, that is, a story that seems plausible and that gets passed along and reappears from time to time but is really just a fairy tale. Because I heard this story years ago, my guess is that it is a hoax.

So why does it keep reappearing? Because this story illustrates the seriousness of treating Jewish laws and religious rituals lightly or joking about with them. Unintentionally, I think it pokes fun at an overly serious interpretation and application of Jewish law by taking a silly situation and turning it into a serious matter. So don't worry—I don't think you are going to run into too many thirteen-year-old divorcées out there on the school yard!

Question number 13: Dear Rabbi, I am trying to eat only Kosher food, but it is difficult since I am living with Christian parents. I try to pick out Kosher foods when I go shopping with my mom, but sometimes I have no idea if the ingredients are Kosher. My parents won't let me get two sets of dishes, and although my parents are trying to help me, I'm not sure what to do. Do you have any suggestions on how I can maintain a Kosher lifestyle until I finish high school?

Answer: What a challenging home life you must have! Forgive me for asking, but it is quite intriguing to me that you are keeping Kosher yet you state that your parents are Christian. How did you come to be Jewish? Did you formally convert as a teenager with a rabbi with or without your parents' consent? Or are you interested in converting to Judaism when you are old enough and are trying to prepare for that eventuality? Or are you simply interested in observing the Jewish dietary laws out of your own personal spiritual beliefs having nothing to do with a desire to become a Jew later in life?

It is not my place to judge your motivations, so the least that I can do is try to help you. And I do have a suggestion for you since you do want to try and keep Kosher while living as a teenager in your parents' un-Kosher home. You might not like my suggestion, but I recommend that you become a vegetarian until the time that you can establish and maintain your own private Kosher kitchen. When you eat vegetarian, you are already ensuring that none of the food you eat will be non-Kosher. If you and your parents take care to purchase vegetarian food products, then that will guarantee that you won't eat any non-Kosher foods.

In fact, some Jewish scholars and rabbis claim that being a vegetarian is the Jewish ideal. Adam and Eve were vegetarians in the Garden of Eden. It was not until the time of Noah in the Torah after the flood that God allowed humans to start eating meat since God realized that violence and killing was part of the human character. It might not be the advice you were looking for, but I encourage you to go vegetarian; it is easier and one step closer to being fully Kosher until the time you can fully keep Kosher on your own.

Question number 14: *I am thirteen years old, and I have experienced many difficulties in my life. And I was wondering, what should I do when people tease me about being Jewish?*

Answer: It must be very hard for you to deal with the hurtful comments people may make to you because you are Jewish. I also grew up with lots of hateful, negative comments about being Jewish that were also very painful for me. Unfortunately, there is no magic formula that I can share with you that will make these people stop teasing you or will make it any easier for you. But I do have two suggestions.

The first suggestion may be hard, but it also may be the most effective: whenever anyone says anything to you about you being Jewish that makes you feel bad or uncomfortable, tell them how much it hurts you. Tell them that it makes you feel bad and that you don't understand why they would want to say such cruel and unfriendly things to you. Maybe if you can find the courage to tell them how you feel and expose your feelings, it may make them think twice before they say something again. I am assuming these are people you know and may be positively affected by your words.

If they are not people you know or your words don't have any effect on them, then the second suggestion I have for you is to ignore them. Instead of focusing on the negative part of being Jewish, focus on how fun and exciting being Jewish can be. For instance, get more involved in your synagogue, learn more about your Jewish identity, and join a Jewish youth group. In other words, do something to make yourself feel proud of your Jewish identity. Don't let these other insensitive, cruel people make you feel bad about being Jewish; it is a great honor and distinction to be a Jew! So enjoy it, do things that are Jewish that will help you feel proud and excited to be Jewish. Maybe it won't stop people from saying nasty things or teasing you, but you will feel a lot better about who you are!

Question number 15: Although I feel grown-up, why should it matter so much to my parents that I only date Jewish guys? After all, I'm only fifteen years old! There are so few Jews in my school that there is practically no one to date. Thanks for your help.

Answer: It must seem very unfair to you that your parents only want you to date other Jews especially when there are so few of them at your school. I'm not saying whether your parents are right or wrong, but maybe your parents want you to marry someone who is Jewish someday. Maybe they want you to get into the habit of only dating Jewish boys so that as you grow up, you'll still continue to date only Jewish men and, one day, eventually fall in love with someone who is Jewish and want to marry him.

I don't want to seem like I'm trying to control your social life too, but interfaith dating is a serious issue for young Jews because although you might not ever intend to fall in love and marry a non-Jew, it can happen easily enough. It is indeed quite a big commitment to date only Jews, but it is not all that difficult if you feel strongly about living an observant, committed Jewish life. The dating habits you develop now are likely to affect your dating habits in the future as an adult. And the more often you date non-Jews, the higher the probability that you will end up falling in love with and marrying a non-Jew. No one can predict when he or she will eventually fall in love and want to get married. But if you feel strongly about your Jewish identity, maybe your parents are right—it is logical that you should want your future husband to share that same commitment to being Jewish as well. Good luck!

Question number 16*: I am in the ninth grade, and it has gotten progressively more difficult for me to accept Judaism. Why should I believe the Torah, a three-thousand-year-old book, instead of scientific facts today? I don't like putting my faith into something unless I'm sure that it is valid. How can I blindly put my faith in something without any verification? Doesn't this kind of faith lead to extremism and terrorism?*

Answer: You ask some very good questions—and make a very common mistake. Most people think that the Hebrew Bible is a historically accurate book of history, and many assume that the story of the creation of the universe is a statement of fact. The Torah, however, is not science; nor was it ever intended to be seen as a book of science—even in ancient times. Instead, the Torah and the whole Hebrew Bible is a book of theology, morals, and the story of the origins of the Jewish people. If you want to know how the world was created and origins of the universe, then by all means read a book of modern science, astrophysics, and evolution. Torah and science do not contradict each other: science explains *how* the world and universe came into being, but the Torah deals with *why* it is here and what we, as human beings and Jews, are supposed to do with our lives.

It is simplistic and too easy to equate Judaism with the nonsense ideas called creationism, which is the literal belief that God created the world in exactly six days with all of the details as outlined in the first chapter of Genesis. There have been generations of religious, knowledgeable Jews who have never made the mistake of reading the Torah as a book that demands that we disregard the fruits of science and rational thought in place of some blind allegiance to the pseudoscientific fundamentalist fantasy of what is now called creationism.

I actually agree with you that blind, uncritical faith can lead to extremism and terrorism. We are living in times that make this connection all too obvious and deadly, which is why I urge young Jews to study Judaism from a critical, intellectual perspective and to accept nothing on faith alone. Use your brain—that is why God gave us one: to think with! If you study the Torah and Judaism from this perspective, then I don't think you will be in such a hurry to dismiss it. Enjoy your study of both science and the Torah!

Chapter 7

Sex (Eleven Questions)

You must have suspected that we were bound to get to this topic at some point! During my tenure as an Internet rabbi, people young and old, teenagers and adults frequently sent in questions about sex in the Jewish tradition. Who would not want to know more about this juicy topic? I was surprised by the questions that I received on this topic, especially by the candor and even innocence of some of the questions and also by how much personal information people were willing to share. Sex in the Jewish tradition is not an easy or simple topic, and the issues these questions raised were often complex and challenging.

In order to demonstrate the existence of sometimes shockingly explicit traditional sources regarding sexuality in the Jewish tradition, I often supported my answers with numerous quotations and citations from the Torah, Talmud, and other classical Jewish texts. I wanted to demonstrate that my responses were not simply answers that I invented or that I was foisting off my personal opinions as traditional Jewish positions.

And despite the heartfelt and touchingly frantic requests for simple, quick answers, I resisted the urge to tell anyone what they should do or which choices they should make in their personal or romantic lives. I believed then—and still do—that it was not my job as a rabbi to tell anyone how he or she was supposed to behave or how to live their lives.

Just because I was sharing a particular answer or range of options with them did not mean that they were obligated to believe what I told them, accept my advice or that they should feel compelled to behave in any particular way. Rather, I believed that my legitimate role was to share with them the wisdom and insights of the Jewish tradition so that they could make up their own minds and provide them with some knowledge and guidance from Jewish sources to consider as they weighed their options. I may have provided them with some conventional sources, but the responsibility for choosing a course of action was theirs alone.

There was a certain irony in the fact that people were seeking advice about the most intimate of all human affairs through e-mail, the single most isolating and distancing of all forms of communication and interaction. The questions in this chapter start with questions about foreplay and premarital sex and progress into the topic of marriage and marital sexuality. I hope that the answers I provided for these questioners helped to provide them with a little direction in what was clearly a turbulent and emotionally intense time in their lives, one which even prompted them to seek advice from an anonymous Internet rabbi. Similarly, I hope that these answers provide you with ideas and traditional Jewish sources to consider and weigh in your own lives regarding this most intimate and powerful topics.

Question number 1: Please help me, Rabbi. I'm a young Jewish man who is having trouble finding Jewish girls to date because I live in an area with few other Jewish families. I desperately want to masturbate, but I don't want to have sex until I'm married. How can I fulfill my sexual urges without having premarital sex?

Answer: I can sympathize with your challenges. Many Jews living in small isolated communities also confront this same issue—where to find other Jewish singles to date and hopefully marry? I have no idea how old you are, if you are in high school or college, or whether you currently attend any kind of college or university; but you might consider locating the closest institution of higher learning in your area and see if they have a Jewish student organization on campus or possibly think about moving to an area with a larger Jewish community. If there are few Jews where you live, you ought to consider moving to another place where there are more potential Jewish dating partners. You might also want to explore some of the online Internet Jewish dating services. Nowadays, distance does not need to be a limiting factor in your romantic life.

Regarding the issue of masturbation, I hope you are not overly strict or angry with yourself because of your sexual needs. The only traditional Jewish issue involved in masturbation is the concept called wasting a man's seed. From a rabbinic point of view, semen should not be wasted; that is, a man should not have an orgasm unless he is having sex with his wife where it might lead to conception of a child. However, according to modern liberal rabbinic authorities, when the issue of having children is not part of your consideration, for instance, if you have no sexual partner or in a nonmarital relationship, since the man's seed would not go toward procreation in the first place, then the issue of wasting one's seed is irrelevant.

Please note, however, that not everyone would agree with you that masturbation should be considered premarital sex. Some people consider masturbation and sex with another person to be entirely separate categories of sexual activities; therefore, engaging in masturbation would not violate your desire to avoid premarital sex. Although masturbation is indeed frowned upon (based on the story of Onan in the Torah who "spilled his seed" and was punished by God, see Genesis 38), it is not absolutely forbidden in rabbinic literature. There are actually a number of colorful and explicit stories of men and women masturbating in rabbinic literature. You should also know that nearly all modern physicians and psychologists today agree that there is absolutely nothing wrong with masturbation and that it should even be considered a healthy, safe sexual outlet. In fact, there has been much discussion among the rabbinic leadership in the liberal Jewish movements in recent times about officially adopting a new rabbinic view about masturbation, officially permitting it in situations like yours where legitimate sexual needs cannot be met according to traditional Jewish standards. In either case, I wish you luck in the future and hope that you will indeed make the necessary life changes in the future that will ensure that you are able to establish a healthy and active social life with other young Jews.

Question number 2: I am in a very serious relationship with my girlfriend, and she wants to have sex and do other things like oral sex. Is this something we are allowed to do in Judaism? We are not married, and I'm not sure what to do.

Answer: I certainly cannot tell you what to do, but I would like to share a few thoughts and perspectives from the Jewish tradition that may help you and your girlfriend decide on your own what you feel comfortable doing together. In earlier times in traditional Jewish communities, it was normal for young men and women to get married much younger than is somewhat more common today, even when they were teenagers, so that the natural teenage sexual drives would be channeled toward marriage. Nowadays, when it is normal for most young men and women to wait until they are older to marry, the issue of finding an appropriate outlet for the natural and healthy sexual desires of young men and women is very complex. On one hand, according to a strict and conservative interpretation, the Jewish tradition does not permit premarital sex. On the other hand, the Jewish tradition recognizes the needs of young men and women to explore and channel their sexual energies.

I cannot tell you or your girlfriend whether you should or should not have premarital sex as that should be your decision as a couple. However, I will share with you some of my thoughts about sex that have been influenced by the values expressed in our religious tradition. Whether during or outside of marriage, sex should be between two loving, consenting partners and entered into as an expression of love—not so that one person can prove something as in "do it to prove you love me" or wanting to have sex to prove to yourself that you are macho.

Also, sex should not be engaged in for any other type of exploitative reasons. In other words, both people should feel ready and not pressured into it whether the pressure comes from one's partner or from friends, movies, TV, the Internet, or elsewhere. It is a really good thing that you are thinking about all of these issues beforehand. It is my own fervent belief that sexual intimacy is a very special thing that should not be wasted or underestimated. Good sex is more than just mere physical pleasure—it creates a unique bond of intimacy and vulnerability between two people. This value is part of what drives the strong prohibitions against premarital sex in our tradition.

There are also some other issues to consider these days in regard to premarital sex that you should keep in mind. In an age of AIDS and other sexually transmitted diseases, you should keep in mind the very real and very dangerous aspects of sexual contact and take appropriate precautions. These are things that you and your partner need to be able to talk about, and if you don't feel comfortable discussing these issues, then it may be some indication that neither of you are ready to approach sex seriously enough. A very good book to read about sex and the Jewish tradition is a book by Rabbi Michael Gold called *Does God Belong in the Bedroom?* I hope this has helped you and your girlfriend think about the issues involved when considering the future of your romantic relationship.

Question number 3: *I am a female college student, and next semester I'm planning on renting an apartment with my best friend who is a man. We would be living together as roommates and not as a boy and girlfriend. In fact, we are not even interested in each other sexually. The problem is my dad; he is dead set against my plans and says it is against Jewish law for a man and woman to live together unless they're married. Since my dad is helping me with my college expenses, I need his consent. That's why I'm writing to you. Is my dad right? Would I really be breaking Jewish law?*

Answer: Jewish law is irrelevant in this situation. Rather, this is about your father's feelings about what is right and appropriate for you and the fact that he is supporting you financially right now. This is actually about the commandment to "honor your father and mother" (Exodus 20:11). Right now, your father is asking you to live your life in a way that will respect his feelings of what he considers to be appropriate behavior.

On the other hand, you are an adult now. You are—and should be—free to make your own decisions as to your living arrangements. But then again, if your father is supporting you, it only seems fair and right that you should listen to what he has to say. And remember, he is your father and probably does not want you to live with a man out of love and concern for your modesty as a young woman. Don't forget that he does have the power to stop supporting you financially and thereby perhaps forcibly prevent you from sharing your apartment with a male roommate. However, it would be very sad if your relationship and ability to communicate with your father degenerated to that point.

From the point of view of Jewish law, your father is correct. It is considered inappropriate for a man and woman to be secluded together, alone, if they are not married even if they have no sexual feelings toward one another. There is a lot of material in ancient rabbinic sources about the inappropriateness of a man and woman spending time in private together if they are not married. But your father is using this information selectively—what this means is that from a very traditional point of view regarding Jewish law, no Jewish woman of marriageable age should ever be left alone with any single, available man in any social situation. These kinds of laws regarding a young woman's modesty were enacted to protect young women's modesty and chastity in earlier times where appearance and social propriety were more highly valued. Nowadays, many young Jews in this country are more liberal in their personal lives or not very familiar with traditional Jewish lifestyles or perhaps not committed to living their lives based on what are perceived to be old-fashioned values of modesty between the sexes. While I have no idea whether you or your family are traditional Jews, the few personal comments you made in your question lead me to believe that neither you nor your father are particularly observant traditional Jews. Therefore, it appears somewhat selective and arbitrary for your father to apply this Jewish legal concept regarding your modesty only to the situation of your living with a male roommate. But he is right about traditional Jewish law being against unmarried men and women sharing living quarters. But then again, are you a traditional Jew, and is this a value you want to live your life by? I can't answer that—only you can.

My advice to you is work out your living situation arrangement with your father and your potential male roommate without dragging Jewish law into it. While it is appropriate to consider the issues of modesty and privacy, this has more to do with respecting your father's wishes and the fact that you still want and might need his financial support during your college years. I wish you strength, patience, and wisdom to work out an acceptable and appropriate arrangement that works for you and your father.

Question number 4: Dear Rabbi, I am in love with two young men, and while I have not had sex with either of them yet, one of them is starting to become upset that we have not being seeing each other as often as he would like. I know I have to choose between them eventually, but how do I know whom to choose?

Answer: Boy, that is a tough question. I'm not sure why you are asking a rabbi for advice and not your mother or father, but I'm happy to put in my two cents' worth! Go with your gut feelings about the guys. Who do you feel truly cares about you as a person and not simply about eventually sleeping with you? Which one do you feel that you can truly open up your heart and soul to and share your vulnerabilities with? Which one do you enjoy spending more time with and feel more like your true self with? And which one do you feel that you could imagine a life together with forever? I'm not saying you have to marry the guy, but it is never too early to begin searching your own heart for what you want in a life partner. Know yourself, and then you will know who is right for you.

Question number 5: Is it okay to have sex with more than one girl at a time as long as you like them both?

Answer: Do you mean at the same time on the same bed? Or do you mean dating two women during the same period of time and having a sexual relationship with each of them but at different times? In either case, the answer is no. This is because the Jewish ideal of love and romantic relationships is based on fidelity. The more committed one is to a partner and the more exclusive the relationship, the more holy it is. Having a sexual relationship with two different women at the same time is therefore a less holy relationship.

My advice to you would be to pick one girl. Demonstrate some maturity and responsibility in your romantic life. It is not fair to either of these women to double-time them, and it is ultimately not good for you in the long run. It may only lead to you growing less satisfied with any one woman and lead to your being unfaithful to future partners, even your future wife, as a response to any dissatisfactions you may experience in your sexual life in a relationship with any one particular woman. Look, you asked for my opinion, and I gave it to you based on the Jewish tradition. But you have to make your own decisions about your life. But you might ask yourself, what advice would you give to your future wife if she were to ask you the same question about two guys that you asked me?

Question number 6: Does the Torah prohibit fornication between two consenting adult lovers?

Answer: "Fornication" is not a word you hear or read every day! Therefore, to put it into simpler language, the Torah does not recognize nonmarital sexuality between two people who are not married to each other. Quite apart from the crimes of rape, incest, or adultery, according to the Torah, sex between two consenting adults is by itself the act of consummating a marital relationship! This is what is called today common law marriage and is recognized as such by many states in the United States. In other words, according to the Torah, at that time in ancient Israelite society over three thousand years ago, having sex with another unmarried consenting adult automatically made one husband and wife. That is why there is no such thing as premarital sex in the

Torah. The moment you have sex with a legitimate potential marriage partner, you become married in that very instant.

The rabbis of the Talmud, however, who came nearly a millennium after the time of the Torah, did acknowledge and recognize the ability of two consenting adults to engage in a sexual relationship and not automatically consummate a marital relationship. And they strongly condemned such nonmarital consensual sexuality because it precluded the holiness that the rabbis insisted could only be created through a sacred marital relationship.

Is nonmartial sex prohibited in the Jewish tradition? Despite what you may have heard or read, the Torah itself did not prohibit nonmarital sex primarily because it didn't recognize such a category of sexual relationships. However, the rabbis of the Talmud *did* recognize such a nonmarital sexual relationship and generally discouraged them. Nowadays, the answer to your question depends upon the individual modern rabbi you ask because we can all find different parts of the Jewish tradition to support whatever we want to say. Just like a good lawyer can support any side of an argument and find some legal precedence or principle to justify their position, the same is true of rabbis and perhaps even more so.

My personal answer to your question is that the sexual relationship you ask about is not prohibited in the Jewish tradition, but it is awfully sad and lonely since it is not practiced in a sanctified, long-term, loving relationship in the framework of marriage. The Jewish tradition insists that holiness in sexuality can only be achieved through marriage, through a relationship in which the partners have committed themselves to an exclusive emotional and sexual relationship. You may indeed be able to achieve this kind of relationship now without marriage. If so, then why not get married? Because there is a bond of intimacy and vulnerability that can only exist when partners make a serious lifelong commitment to each other to sanctify their relationship through marriage. Is a consenting sexual relationship forbidden? No, but it is far less holy than it could be and leaves both partners emotionally vulnerable.

Question number 7: Dear Rabbi, I am upset because recently a Christian friend told me that I am sinning because I am in a relationship with a woman and we are not married. I have heard that sex outside of marriage is not forbidden in Judaism. Do you know more about this? Can you give me some quotes from the Hebrew Bible or elsewhere about this? Thank you.

Answer: In general, I believe that a person's sex life is no one else's business—except your partner. Obviously, your friend has no business commenting on your personal romantic life whatsoever. In fact, I would encourage you to be as blunt or as diplomatic as you like in expressing to them the message that they should mind their own business.

However, for your own information, nonmarital relationships are treated somewhat matter-of-factly in the Hebrew Bible. For example, Judah, the son of Jacob, has sex with his daughter-in-law, Tamar, because he thinks she is a harlot (see Genesis 38:15ff). Later on, King David shares his bed in his old age with the young Abishag the Shunamite in order to stay warm (see 1 Kings 1:1-4). In each case, the sexual liaison is treated lightly, even casually. The Torah's main concern regarding nonmarital sexuality was that a young woman would lose her virginity that in biblical times constituted the essence of her value as a candidate for marriage. A woman's virginity was even taken into account in the Ketubah, the wedding contract. According to the Mishnah, the first ancient rabbinic text of Jewish law, a virgin was to receive two hundred silver coins from her husband if divorced or widowed to be paid by the surviving family while a nonvirgin or divorcée received only one hundred silver coins (Mishnah Ketubot 1:2). Thus, nonmarital sex was significant in a financial and social context. In fact, it is possible to claim that the Torah never explicitly forbids premarital sex, for every such instance was viewed as an act of establishing a marital bond. The Torah states,

> If a man comes upon a virgin who is not engaged and he seized her and lies with her, and they are discovered, the man who lay with her shall pay the girl's father 50 shekels of silver, and she shall be his wife. Because he has violated her, he can never have the right to divorce her. (Deuteronomy 22:28-29)

Although this is presented in the context of rape, whose criminal and moral repugnance is dealt with elsewhere in the Jewish tradition, here the Torah is focusing on the fact that the very act of having sex establishes a marital bond. The Talmud states that among the various legitimate ways that a man may establish a marital relationship with a woman is to have sex with her. The Mishnah states, "A woman is acquired (that is, married by a man) in three ways: by a document (a wedding contract), silver or money (a gift to the woman by the man of some value, such as a ring) or sexual relations" (Mishnah Kiddushin 1:1).

Because women were not recognized as legally or financially independent in ancient times, marriage was viewed as a form of acquisition for the man whereby legal responsibility for a young woman shifted from the father or other older male relative to the husband. As this passage from the Mishnah makes clear, having sex with a woman was another legitimate legal means by which a man could marry a woman. Even to this day, cohabitation without the benefit of sanctioned nuptials is still recognized in many states as common law marriage if a couple has been living together for a significant amount of time. Therefore, in biblical times, there was no such thing as premarital sex for the very act of having sex transformed it into a marital bond. I hope that this answers your question and gives you some background and understanding about the role of nonmarital sexuality in traditional Jewish sources.

Question number 8: I am going to be married soon, and while I'm not the most traditional young Jewish woman, I'm interested in learning more about the custom of going to a Mikvah [Jewish ritual bath] before my wedding. Can you tell me more about this specifically why I should go and what to do there? Thank you.

Answer: Mazal Tov on your upcoming wedding! I think it is great that you are interested in learning more about the Mikvah. Visiting a Mikvah before a wedding is a way that Jewish women spiritually prepare themselves for their wedding and married life and is a symbolic way to mark a formal entrance into a marital sexual life. There is an enormous amount of information available to you about the laws and customs associated with this practice of visiting the Mikvah that is called in Hebrew Taharat HaMishpachah, which literally means "purity of the family." Visiting the Mikvah before your wedding is just one aspect of this body of laws and practices. By the way, I have read that traditional Jewish women who are still single but sexually active have also begun to visit the Mikvah as a way to laying claim to a formerly traditional marriage custom and adapting it to a new modern Jewish traditional lifestyle. Some excellent books that you might want to read that can give you an insight into this practice include the following:

1. *The New Jewish Wedding* by Rabbi Anita Diamont. This is an excellent book for all Jewish couples getting married, and I highly recommend it for planning all aspects of your wedding. There is also a wonderful chapter in it on going to the Mikvah. If you only consult one book, this should be it.

2. "Waters of Life," an article by Rachel Adler printed in the *First Jewish Catalogue* by Michael Strassfeld and Richard Siegel. It is a very philosophical approach to the Mikvah experience that presents this ancient practice in modern feminist symbolism.

3. The *Encyclopedia Judaica* entry on Mikvah. The *Encyclopedia Judaica* is a seventeen-volume reference set first published in the early 1970s but is still the most authoritative reference collection about all aspects of Jewish life and history available. You can probably find a set of these volumes in a local synagogue library. The article on the Mikvah will give you lots of traditional sources and a scholarly overview on the concept.

These sources above make good reading, but here is my own brief overview of the laws of Taharat HaMishpachah. The Torah mandates that women should not have sex with their husbands during the time that they are menstruating just as men are prohibited from having sex with their wives if they have a nocturnal emission. To ensure that a woman's period was completed, the rabbis in the Talmud standardized the whole process and added on additional days prohibiting sex after a woman's period was done just to be on the safe side. Currently, traditional Jewish law states that as soon as a woman has her period, she should abstain from having sex with her husband for five days during which she is presumed to be having her period and then continue abstaining for another seven days to be sure that the flow of blood has ceased. Thus, a woman who is fairly regular in her period would end up not having sex with her husband for twelve days of each menstrual cycle.

In either case, on the evening of the twelfth day, a woman then goes to the Mikvah, a ritual bath whose waters come from a natural source, such as rainwater, spring water, or melted ice. Rivers, lakes, and oceans are also natural Mikvahs but are awfully cold! The woman then removes anything from her body that might interfere with the water coming into contact with all parts of her body. This includes not just removing her clothes but jewelry and makeup and even combing out any braids or knots in her hair. A blessing is said, and she immerses herself. The tradition is that she should then return and resume her sexual life with her husband that very night.

Although this should be obvious, the practice of going to the Mikvah was intended only for married women. And you may have noticed that the period of abstaining from sex ends just when a woman is most fertile, approximately twelve to fourteen days after her period. However, many traditional but not necessarily Orthodox Jews who observe going to the Mikvah feel that the seven additional days after the first five days of a woman's period is a little excessive; and therefore, they only wait an additional one day to visit the Mikvah upon the conclusion of their menstrual cycle, thus abstaining from sex with their husbands for only a total of six days out of each month.

The Mikvah is not just for women. Some men also visit the Mikvah on a regular basis, either before marriage or Jewish holidays, as a way to enhance their own spiritual awareness and appreciation of these holy days. Also, immersion in a Mikvah for both men and women—and children—is the final step that candidates for conversion take when they complete the process of converting to Judaism.

Some scholars believe that the laws regarding Mikvah and women derive from ancient blood taboos and biblical ideas of ritual purity and impurity. However, what is important for you to know is that none of this matters today. Blood taboos and concepts of ritual purity and impurity no longer have any relevance to the practice of going to the Mikvah today. The only reason you should practice this is for your own personal spiritual enhancement of your sexual life or for a sense of spiritual awareness. While my answer to your question was probably far more than you wanted to know, I wanted you to understand that the practice of visiting the Mikvah before one's wedding is just a small part of a much larger set of marital customs and laws practiced by traditional Jewish women for centuries. Good luck on your upcoming wedding, and I hope that you will indeed look into visiting a Mikvah before your wedding day! It is a wonderful and powerful ritual to prepare for and celebrate your wedding and marriage.

Question number 9: Since the Sabbath is a day of rest, doesn't that mean sex should be forbidden since it is technically "work" for procreation? Wouldn't it be considered a violation of the Sabbath to have sex on such a holy time?

Answer: I can't help but start with a joke—if having sex is "work" for you, then you are not doing it right! But seriously, I am sorry to inform you that you are wrong. Having sex is definitely *not* work on Shabbat. And besides, there are other pleasures derived from sexual intercourse other than procreation. The Jewish tradition is far more progressive and honest about sexuality than you might imagine.

The Talmud encourages husbands and wives to *have* sex on Shabbat! The ancient rabbis saw the relationship between God and the Jewish people in explicitly sexual terms—God is the husband, and the people of Israel are God's wife. The Shabbat is a day for mystical union between God and Israel; therefore, it is considered an especially propitious time for married couples to have sex. It says in the Talmud that "a husband should fulfill his marital obligation (meaning, having sex) *every* Friday night" (Talmud, Ketubot 62b). Far from being a burden, sex on Shabbat was considered a double Mitzvah—observing Shabbat as God's day of rest from creation is the first, and having sex fulfills the commandment to "be fruitful and multiply" (Genesis 1:28).

Question number 10: What is the historical Jewish position on the issue of sexual harassment?

Answer: Sexual harassment was never dealt with specifically in Jewish law. The closest the Torah comes to prohibiting anything that we might recognize as sexual harassment can be read between the lines of Leviticus 18 that includes a long list of forbidden incestuous sexual relations. In Hebrew, these laws are called Gilui Arayot, or literally, "revealing nakedness." The presumption is that if these incestuous unions are forbidden, how much the more so any kind of behavior that might even lead to such a relationship in the first place, including threatening language and behavior.

An example of what sexual harassment can be seen in Genesis 39 where the wife of Potiphar was attracted to Joseph and continually said to him, "Lie with me!" (Genesis 39:7) When Joseph kept refusing, she eventually accused him of rape and had him imprisoned. And another example later on in the Hebrew Bible was when Amnon, one of King David's sons, constantly pleaded and begged his half sister, Tamar, to lie with him; and because she refused, he eventually raped her (see 2 Samuel 13). Each of these incidents was seen as examples of wicked, immoral behavior.

In addition, the laws of Lashon HaRah, or "evil tongue" prohibit people from saying hurtful, insulting things or engaging in social violent, hostile speech. Also, the laws of Tzniut, or laws relating to personal modesty, prevent one from dealing directly with sexual, immodest matters; and the laws of Kedushah, or "holiness" forbid inappropriate and hurtful sexual relations between people. Therefore, while one cannot point to a specific law in the Jewish tradition that deals directly with sexual harassment, it is clear from these other areas of Jewish law that it is absolutely forbidden.

Question number 11: *I am doing research in ancient religious texts and was wondering if you can tell me if there were any ancient customs or laws against women cutting their hair in the Hebrew Bible. For example, was there any particular Jewish rule that required women to have either short or long hair? And did the custom of women covering or veiling their heads or faces have anything to do with hair?*

Answer: There are no laws prohibiting a Jewish woman from cutting her hair in the Hebrew Bible. However, there is an assumption that women should keep their hair covered, whether long or short, as a sign of sexual modesty. Cutting one's hair was considered a dramatic act of grief; and the only instance of this related to a woman is in the Torah where a non-Jewish woman who has been seized as a captive in war by an Israelite man is required to shave her head, cut her fingernails, and wear special clothes signifying mourning for her parents for a month before the Israelite man who captured her is allowed to marry her (see Deuteronomy 21:12). Some medieval Jewish commentators claim that the rule about shaving her head is precisely to make her less attractive so that the Israelite man might have the opportunity to reconsider whether he truly wants to marry this woman he captured in the heat of battle and pillaging. In general, having exposed, uncovered hair was considered lascivious and dangerously provocative for a woman both in biblical and Talmudic times.

In the Middle Ages in Europe, some traditional Jewish communities felt that a woman's hair was the essence of her beauty and attractiveness. Therefore, as a sign of modesty, women in these communities completely covered their hair after marriage either with a wig or a kerchief. Some women in these communities even shaved their heads after marriage and wore a wig in order never to attract undue attention from men who were not their husbands. In fact, many women in ultra-Orthodox traditional Jewish communities both in the United States and Israel still follow these customs about hiding their natural hair from the gaze of other men.

Chapter 8

The Hebrew Bible and Torah Study
(Twenty-five Questions)

While everyone talks about "the Bible," Jews and Christians are often actually referring to two different books. To Jews, *the* Bible is the Hebrew Bible or as it is called in Hebrew, the Tanach. It is composed of three major sections—the Torah, or Five Books of Moses; the writings of the prophets; and the section simply called the Writings, including such diverse works as Psalms, Proverbs, Job, the book of Ruth, Esther, Chronicles, and more.

Christians who refer to "*the* Bible" may indeed be referring to the Hebrew Bible, but it is more likely they are talking about the Christian Bible that consists of the four Gospels, Acts of the Apostles, and the numerous Epistles of Paul. Christians call their Bible the New Testament in contrast to the Hebrew Bible, which they call the Old Testament. However, the stories and theology of the Christian Bible are nearly incomprehensible without a familiarity with the Hebrew Bible. Therefore, the study of the Hebrew Bible is of keen interest to both Christians and Jews. And even the Koran includes a significant number of references to the Hebrew Bible as well as variations of a number of stories from the Torah.

For Jews, the study of the Hebrew Bible is considered a commandment (called a Mitzvah in Hebrew) written in the Torah itself. Deuteronomy

6:7 states that every Israelite should "teach these words to your children," which was understood to refer to the Torah itself. The later rabbis who formulated the basis of modern Judaism emphasized the study of the Hebrew Bible as a fundamental principle of Jewish life and equated its study with all of the religious customs of the Jewish religion. Without a familiarity of the Hebrew Bible, modern Judaism is nearly incomprehensible. However, modern Judaism is very different from the religious practices described in the Torah.

Modern Judaism is the product of generations of ancient rabbis who lived in the Middle East nearly two thousand years ago who devoted their lives to studying and interpreting the Hebrew Bible and adapting the ancient practices of the Torah to evolving historical circumstances and sensibilities. For instance, over time, animal sacrifices were replaced with heartfelt prayer and devotion. Also, Jewish religious leadership once provided by the priests and Levites was replaced over time by the rabbis who wrote the Talmud and other works of classical rabbinic literature. However, you would never know this from just reading the Torah by itself. Therefore, while the Torah is the foundation of modern Jewish practice, it is not the only religious document sufficient for practicing modern Judaism.

Therefore, the study of Torah—and the entire Hebrew Bible—is of particular interest to Christians and Jews, and the number of questions that I received on the topic was sufficient to warrant an entire chapter devoted to just questions about "*the* Bible." The questions in this chapter have been arranged to correspond to the order of the stories and books in the Hebrew Bible itself.

Question number 1: Was the Torah written by God or by several people?

Answer: The answer to this very question is the reason that there are so many different denominations of Judaism today. Now I tend to try and avoid characterizing the theological positions of other people, not to mention other movements in Judaism, but I'll try to give you a brief synopsis of what I understand to be each of the main American Jewish movements' approach to the authorship and source of the Torah because there is no one answer to your question.

According to Orthodox Jews, God wrote the Torah. The word "Orthodox" literally means "correct doctrine," and the basic Orthodox understanding is that the Torah was communicated orally, word for word to Moses on Mt. Sinai thousands of years ago. This scroll was written down in its entirety, without error, by Moses and passed along by the Jewish people from generation to generation; and our Torah is the exact record of this divine message.

According to most Reform Jews, human beings wrote the Torah. The classical Reform approach to the Torah is that it is a completely human-authored document by probably a number of different people over a long period of time, however written with divine inspiration. Therefore, while many of the rituals and laws described are not necessarily obligatory upon each and every Jew, unless they themselves choose to observe them, the ethics and morals contained in the Torah are the most important divine aspects of the Torah that are still applicable even in modern times and forever.

According to Conservative Jews, the Torah is a product of both human and divine activity. The briefest, most concise summary of the Conservative approach to the authorship of the Torah is that the deeper meaning of the Torah is divine and that its ultimate source is God, but the physical, written literary work that we call the Torah is the product of human beings who tried to communicate their experience of what happened to the Israelites at Mt. Sinai to future generations. Therefore, the Torah is how the Jewish people experienced revelation and contact with God and how they tried to express their experiences.

Other denominations such as Reconstructionism and Jewish Renewal are similar to various elements of the latter two approaches. In conclusion, the answer to your question as to whether God or several people wrote the Torah, the answer is yes to both of them—it just depends on which Jewish denominational point of view you prefer.

Question number 2: I have only just learned about the documentary hypothesis regarding the authorship of the Torah that claims that there were a number of different ancient versions of the Torah that were written by different people and all combined together. What is the value of this hypothesis, and is it accepted in the academic world?

Answer: The documentary hypothesis is indeed nearly universally accepted in the world of modern biblical academic studies nowadays. The documentary hypothesis holds that the Torah is actually a literally work that was created in ancient times by priests and Levites who combined together at least four major separate historical and religious documents telling the stories and laws of the ancient Israelites. These four documents were then edited together in a process called redacting in ancient times to form the Torah as we have it now. There are probably more than just four documents that comprise the Torah, but the main ones are called the J, E, P, and D documents. This is what they stand for and why they have these single letters as names:

1. The J document is called this because the name of God used throughout the stories in it is called, in English, Jehovah, which happens to be a modern mispronunciation of the holy four-Hebrew-letter name of God.
2. The E document is called this because the name of God used throughout the stories in it is Elohim, another name for God used in other stories in the Torah.
3. The P document is called this as it stands for the priestly document because it contains the sections of the Torah that focus primarily on animal sacrifices and matters relating to ritual purity and impurity.
4. The D document is called this because it consists primarily of the book of Deuteronomy, which is written in a unique style all its own.

Biblical scholars continue to argue that shorter, less easily defined but nonetheless discrete documents were also woven into the Torah in addition to the J, E, P, and D documents. These basic core documents of the Torah were probably collective efforts written over long periods of time by lots of different people in various literary circles in ancient Israelite society, like different families of priests, prophets, or groups of royal advisors to the Israelite or Judean kings. During the Babylonian exile, these groups joined together and redacted their various holy documents together to produce the Torah. According to most modern biblical scholars, this is how the Torah that we have nowadays came into being. For more information, visit any major library or search online for more details.

Question number 3: *Archeologists studying prehistoric man seem to suggest that human beings lived on the earth before Adam and Eve. How can we counter their arguments?*

Answer: I don't want to counter their arguments at all! It is obvious that the archeologists, anthropologists, and paleontologists are right because the Hebrew Bible is *not* a book of history. It describes how the Israelites understood the role of God in the construction of the universe. The creation story in the Torah is based on ancient traditional spiritual beliefs of how the world was organized and arranged by God. The Torah was never intended to be read as a book of science, nor should it be viewed as having anything to do with modern science today. The Hebrew Bible is a book about God, morals, and ethics; therefore, it is not surprising it says nothing about dinosaurs or prehistoric man or any other branch of science for that matter.

To put it in other words, the story of Adam and Eve is a myth that is true but not factual. What does this mean? It means that the story of Adam and Eve is not a historical descriptive story of what actually happened. Therefore, it is not factual. However, the story of Adam and Eve is true in the sense that it is a story that explains how human beings learned to exercise their free will and learned about the consequences of their actions in this life. It also explains why humanity doesn't live in a state of divine bliss and ease in the Garden of Eden and why people die. These truths about human life are the truth in the story of Adam and Eve and the Garden of Eden. In fact, the whole Torah itself is a kind of myth that explains humanity's relationship with God. It is definitely *not* history—at least in the very early parts.

Even Rashi, the classic medieval Jewish commentator on the Torah (whose real name was Rabbi Shlomo ben Yitzchak who died in 1105) states explicitly in his very first comment on the first verse of the Torah that the Torah is *not* a record of the chronological creative acts of God. In other words, nearly one thousand years ago, even Rashi knew the Torah wasn't meant to be science! Therefore, the so-called theory of creationism—that is, the idea that the events described in Genesis should be accepted as literal, descriptive, scientific truth—is a complete misreading and misunderstanding of the purpose of the Torah.

And even Rambam (whose real name was Rabbi Moses Maimonides who died in 1204), the classic medieval codifier of Jewish law and theologian, understood that science and Torah don't conflict with each other in any way. Science tells us *how* the world came into existence whereas the Torah teaches us *why* it came into being. Therefore, I have no problem with scientists and the study of early human ancestors because science and Judaism are not in conflict.

Question number 4: When God said, "Let Us create man in Our image," who was God talking to?

Answer: It is indeed very puzzling that God speaks in the plural when God says, "Let Us make man in Our image" in Genesis 1:27. There are two possible explanations for this unusual expression.

1. Maybe God was using the royal "we" just as a king or queen of a country would use. In other words, it is the appropriate form of speech for a ruler that suggests the power and authority of the

speaker and does not really mean "we" in sense of God speaking to other people or angels.

2. According to a Midrash, or the ancient imaginative rabbinic explanations of the Torah, God was actually speaking to the angels and consulting with them about how to create human beings. According to these Midrashim, this shows God's humility because God wanted to confer with angelic creatures of lesser stature before engaging in certain acts of creation. The rabbis taught that if God was so humble in this majestic act of creation, how much the more so should we human beings practice humility and emulate God's example!

Indeed, it is quite a puzzling expression the use of "we" when God speaks in this story. I don't know if anyone really knows why this is the case. But it sure makes for a great discussion, doesn't it?

Question number 5: A friend recently asked me about the significance of the snake in Judaism. He claimed that the snake represents evil in Christianity. Does the snake have any significance in the Jewish religion? Also, what is the Jewish view of Eve's sin of eating the forbidden fruit?

Answer: The Jewish tradition doesn't attach any particularly negative symbolic significance to the snake. In fact, the coiled serpent is the symbol for the Israelite tribe of Dan; and in one story in the Torah, the image of a snake has life-healing powers when Israelites who had been bitten by poisonous snakes merely had to gaze upon a bronze image of a serpent to be healed (see the book of Numbers 24)! In Judaism, there is no evil other than the evil actions of human beings.

In regard to the Jewish view of the Garden of Eden and Adam and Eve's transgression, it is quite different than the classic Christian understanding. While I am no expert on Christianity, it is clear that Christianity views Eve's actions as a sin—the sin of disobeying God as the original sin for which all human beings must now suffer and are still tainted.

In the Jewish tradition, Eve's only transgression was that she did indeed disobey God's order not to eat from the Tree of Knowledge of Good and Evil. By the way, it is also clear from the Hebrew in the Torah that Adam was with her the entire time and at no time tried to stop her! Therefore, it is incorrect to blame Eve alone for this transgression. And even the transgression and punishment weren't so bad, really. All that happened to Adam and Eve is that they were expelled from the Garden and had to live ordinary human lives. In other words, they had to leave home and grow up and live as responsible human beings just as little children eventually grow up, become teenagers, leave their parents' home, and make their own way in life.

Also, if they had never eaten from the forbidden tree, they would have never discovered their capacity to act with free will in the world. And according to the Jewish tradition, God doesn't want human beings who have no choice but to act in such a way that they will always do what is good and right. God wants us to *choose* to do good and actively shun evil. When Adam and Eve lived in the Garden, they were like robots without the experience of ever having acted on their own free will. Therefore, it was actually a blessing to have been expelled from the Garden of Eden! Adam and Eve were the first humans to act on their free will—and this is ultimately what God wanted. Eve wasn't bad, nor was the serpent evil although everyone in the story ended up being punished by God for disobedience. In fact, it is possible to claim that Eve was the liberator of all humanity! In fact, a Midrash, or rabbinic interpretation of the Torah, states, "Come, let us celebrate our ancestors (i.e., Adam and Eve) for if they had not sinned, we should not have come into the world!" (Talmud, Avodah Zarah 5a). In other words, perhaps one of the benefits of their sin was learning to procreate and have children! Quite a different reading than the classic Christian understanding, isn't it?

Question number 6*: I'm not clear on the Cain and Abel story in chapter 4 of Genesis. What exactly did Cain do to anger God? As I understand it, both Cain and Abel gave what they could from what they produced or herded as a gift to God. In addition to this, why, after Cain slew Abel, did the Lord* *protect him from the wrath of others—especially if the Lord was already upset with him? The entire Genesis story makes sense up until this point to me. Any assistance you could offer would greatly be appreciated.*

Answer: Before I answer, I just have to say that I'm really impressed if you find that the initial chapters of the book of Genesis make sense! They are deceptively complicated, even contradictory, and have been the focus of a tremendous amount of scholarly inquiry for many centuries. However, I'll do the best I can to answer your questions. It is actually possible to figure out Cain's sin by reading the story closely. The Torah states that Abel offered the best or choicest of his flock as an offering to God whereas Cain only offered ordinary, regular ol' produce of his field as a gift to God. Perhaps it is because Abel thought to offer the best he had that God decided to snub Cain's ordinary offering. Who knows, ultimately? This is one possible answer.

Why did God protect Cain? Because it is not at all clear from the context of the story that Cain's killing of Abel was premeditated murder, for which the punishment described later on in the Torah is indeed death. However, manslaughter was not a crime that necessarily mandated the death penalty. In fact, later on in the Torah, cities of refuge were established just for the purpose of protecting inadvertent manslaughterers from the revenge of their victim's family. In our story, perhaps God's placing a special mark on Cain was a form of protection from this kind of family revenge, although since they were from the same family, it is unclear who would have sought to kill him in revenge. And don't forget that Cain did not escape punishment completely—he was forced into exile from both human society and God's presence.

Question number 7: How old was Isaac when Abraham almost sacrificed him?

Answer: When we read the story of the near sacrifice of Isaac by his father, Abraham, in the Torah in the book of Genesis 22, it seems like Isaac is a young boy. However, a rabbinic Midrash, or folktale, claims that he was actually 37 years old! The Talmudic rabbis determined this age from some of the verses that indicate that Sarah was 90 years old when she gave birth to Isaac. Also, since her death is reported immediately after the story of the binding of Isaac in chapter 23, the rabbis surmise that she must have died immediately after she found out what had almost happened to Isaac. The Hebrew Bible then says that she was 127 years old when she died. Therefore, the rabbis simply subtracted 90 from 127 to get 37! Is this true? Who knows! Did this story really happen? Again, who knows, but at least we can get an age for Isaac at the time of his near sacrifice no matter how counterintuitive it might seem.

Question number 8: When did the exodus of the Israelites from Egypt take place? And who was the Egyptian Pharaoh who was in power at the time of the exodus?

Answer: No one really knows the historical dates of these events mostly because there is nearly no external or nonbiblical evidence of the events described in the Torah. All we have is the Torah; and the Torah is not a work of history but rather a book of *historiosophy*, that is, a theological representation of the history of the ancient origins of the Israelites. Its purpose is to not preserve history but to show how the Israelites understood God's actions in history.

However, many ancient historians agree that *if* the events in the story of Exodus were even remotely historically accurate, then the Israelites left Egypt approximately 1250 BCE. And *if* there was any involvement with the ancient Egyptians, then the Pharaoh who *might* have been in power at that time based on Egyptian history was Ramses II. However, all of this is very sketchy and based on scant archeological evidence based on Egyptian writings.

Question number 9: Why does the number 40 keep coming up in Jewish history, such as forty days of rain in the story of Noah and the flood or forty years of wandering in the desert?

Answer: Don't forget the forty days that Moses was up on Mt. Sinai talking to God or the forty days that the Israelite spies were snooping around the land of Canaan! Certain numbers seemed to have had magical or supernatural fascination to ancient Jews and the Israelites. For example, we drink four cups of wine, ask four questions, and tell the short story of the four sons who ask about the Passover story at the Pesach Seder. Then there are seven days of creation as well as seven days of the week plus ten plagues, ten commandments, ten spies who spread slander about the land of Israel, and so on. And if you do the math, 40 is the sum of 10 x 4! Forty is one of these interesting recurring significant numbers in the Jewish tradition.

The frequent appearance of the number 40 and other significant numbers in the Torah is a literary device that is not intended to convey exact measurements but rather to denote that all of history is unfolding according to God's plan. According to the Hebrew Bible, history is not haphazard and fate is not blind. Rather, God is directing history and human affairs. This is what the repetition of various numbers in biblical events is trying to tell us. The Hebrew Bible is not trying to detail an exact chronology of what happened; rather, it is trying to convey spiritual truths through these narratives. They are not history but rather *historiosophy*—the philosophy and theology of God's involvement in human history. The recurrence of special numbers in so many different Torah stories is a subtle clue that things just don't happen for any reason, but rather God is the architect of all human history and events.

Question number 10: I am troubled by the law in the Torah that commands "an eye for an eye" (Exodus 21:24). Where is this law discussed in the Talmud?

Answer: The original material where the rabbis dealt with this law of "an eye for an eye" is the beginning of the eighth chapter of the Talmud Tractate Baba Kamma. And you should know that the Talmudic rabbis were also troubled by this rather harsh, punitive law!

To provide you with a very brief Jewish understanding of this concept, it is important to remember that in ancient biblical times, this law of "an eye for an eye" was actually profoundly humane and a great innovation in ancient Middle Eastern law. This is because other Ancient Near Eastern societies legislated social class differences in their legal systems. For instance, if a low-class person accidentally put out the eye of a high-class person, the low-class person could be executed! But if a high-class person injured a low-class person, he might get off with merely paying a small fine. The Torah was the first ancient law code that established that all such crimes must be dealt with on a level of complete equality between people with no regard to their social status.

Also, the law of "eye for an eye" determines that no one can be punished or injured worse than the original injury they caused, so it actually sets a limit to retaliatory punishment. In other words, if someone injured someone else's eye, then the retaliatory punishment could not mandate cutting off someone's hand or foot, for example. It had to be equivalent punishment.

And finally, the rabbis of the Talmud chose to read this law not literally but instead as referring to equivalent *monetary* compensation. Therefore, they understood it to mean that if someone put out another person's eye, the offender had to pay for the damage to that person's eye and that alone. That is, they were required to pay a fine or monetary compensation that was equivalent to the loss of sight in that person's eye. It is a lot more humane to think of it this way, isn't it?

Question number 11: Could you please explain the origin of the Kohanim, or ancient Jewish priests, and their duties? Also, why are they not allowed to enter cemeteries, and why do they get special honors bestowed upon them in synagogue services?

Answer: The Hebrew word "Kohen" actually means "priest." There are various scattered references to the elevation of the Kohanim to be the priests of the Jewish people throughout the Torah. Basically, the Kohanim were a subclan of the tribe of the Levites, one of the twelve tribes of the ancient Israelites. Descended from Aaron, the brother of Moses, and his family, the Kohanim were responsible in ancient times for officiating at the animal sacrifices in the Tabernacle and the Temple in Jerusalem when it was eventually built. Priests also were entitled to eat specific portions of each sacrifice since these were holy offerings, and they were required to remain in a state of ritual purity at all times. This necessitated avoiding contact with dead un-Kosher animals as well as human corpses. This is why Kohanim traditionally did not enter cemeteries in ancient times except for the funerals of their own family members.

After the destruction of the Second Temple in 70 CE by the Romans, the Kohanim essentially lost their jobs since there was no longer a temple to officiate in. However, to lessen the severity of the blow, many social honors were accorded to the descendants of Kohanim, such as the privilege of receiving the first Aliyah in the Torah reading service in synagogues. An Aliyah is the honor of reciting blessings over the public reading of the Torah and the privilege of Duchaning, that is, a tradition in some traditional synagogues where the Kohanim of the congregation bless the congregation in synagogues on festivals. Even though the ritual laws of purity no longer apply, the custom—and only a custom—of refraining from entering cemeteries except for the funerals of their own family were maintained and still observed by some people who claim descent from these priestly families even to this day as a reminder of this ancient status.

Question number 12: *How does Leviticus 7:8-9 apply to modern life today?*

Answer: These verses and this chapter of Leviticus have *nothing* to do with modern Jewish life or practice. This may be surprising to you, but not everything in the Torah is relevant to modern Jewish life. These particular verses refers to a priest keeping the skin of an animal sacrifice that he might offer to God on behalf of someone else for his own personal use. The Kohanim, the ancient Israelite priests who officiated at animal sacrifices, actually slaughtered the animal brought for sacrifice and cut it into designated portions to be burned on the altar or returned parts of the animal to the Israelite who brought the sacrifice to be roasted and eaten. The Kohanim made their livelihood through these activities. Therefore, the Kohanim were given certain portions of the animal sacrifices as their own food and the skins for their own use or to sell. These verses actually do not apply in any way to today's life or even Jewish religious practice in modern times.

In the Hebrew Bible, the standard, accepted way to express praise or thanks to God was to slaughter an animal and burn part of it on an altar and eat the remaining elements. Animal sacrifice was understood as the primary mode of communication with the divine. But even this ancient custom evolved during biblical times. In the book of Genesis, people sacrificed to God wherever they happened to be. They would build an altar from stones they found and then make their sacrifice. In the books of Exodus, Leviticus, and Numbers, after the Israelites left Egypt and were wandering in the desert, the Torah states that the Israelites could only make sacrifices in the Tabernacle, the portable altar and sanctuary; and only the Levites and the priests could officiate at such sacrifices. Depending on the sacrifice, the priests and Levites would also get to eat a portion of the sacrificed animal. Also, oil, meal, and water offerings were also acceptable forms of sacrifices. In the book of Deuteronomy, it says that after the Israelites enter into the land of Israel, they would be permitted to sacrifice in only the one place that God would eventually choose. Although it took many centuries before a place was finally chosen, that place ended up being Jerusalem. The story of how King David came to determine the exact spot where the Temple was to be built is described in 2 Samuel 24.

After King Solomon ended up building the Temple on Mt. Zion in Jerusalem, this became the only place where Israelites could sacrifice. Although the Israelites continued to sacrifice in other places outside of the Temple, this was considered sinful and a violation of the Torah's laws. The Babylonians ultimately conquered and destroyed Jerusalem and the Temple in 586 BCE. With the destruction of the Temple, all animal sacrifices came to a complete halt. Only years later when the Jews were allowed to rebuild this Temple, called the Second Temple, did animal sacrifices resume around the year 517 BCE. It was this Second Temple that the Maccabees fought to purify after the Greeks had performed pagan rituals there and which King Herod rebuilt and expanded in his reign. However, in the year 70 CE, the Romans destroyed Jerusalem and this Second Temple in a great war against the Jews. Since the year 70 CE when the Second Temple was destroyed, there have never been any more animal sacrifices in Judaism.

However, just because animal sacrifices came to a halt does not mean that Judaism did not progress and develop further. In fact, the birth of modern Judaism came about directly as a result of this destruction of the Second Temple and the end of animal sacrifices. The rabbis who lived at this time developed and adapted Judaism to the new post-animal sacrifice age. Rabbinic Judaism replaced animal sacrifices with prayer. The rabbis replaced the Temple in Jerusalem with local synagogues, and instead of a single priestly caste, all Jews became fit and worthy of communicating with God directly through prayer.

A typical story that illustrates this new rabbinic Judaism goes like this (from a rabbinic text called Avot DeRabbi Natan 11a):

> Rabban Yochanon ben Zakkai was once walking with his student, Rabbi Joshua near Jerusalem after the destruction of the Temple. Rabbi Joshua looked at the Temple ruins and said, "Woe to us! The place which atoned for the sins of the people Israel through animal sacrifice lies in ruins!" Then Rabban Yochanon ben Zakkai comforted him and said, "Don't be sad, my son. There is another way of gaining atonement even though the Temple is destroyed. We must now gain atonement through deeds of loving-kindness." For it is written, "Loving-kindness I desire, not sacrifice." (Hosea 6:6)

While Jews have historically hoped and prayed for a return to this sacrificial system, Judaism has long since evolved into a nonsacrificial religion based on prayer and acts of kindness and charity. I know this is a long answer to a short question, but I wanted to provide you with a complete picture! Not everything you read in the Torah is relevant to modern Jewish life.

Question number 13: When does the Jubilee year spoken of in the Torah begin and end, and is there anything special we are supposed to do during this year? What is the year of Jubilee all about, and when was the last one?

Answer: According to the Torah, specifically in the book of Leviticus 25, the Jubilee is a special year that falls every forty-nine years and is celebrated on the fiftieth year (that is 7 x 7 of years). On the Jubilee year, it is to be a Sabbath of Sabbath years. Not only were all agricultural activities to cease and all monetary loans cancelled, but also slaves were to be set free; and legally purchased plots of land in Israel were to revert automatically back to their first owners going all the way back to the original tribes to whom they were given, as described in the book of Joshua in the Hebrew Bible, so that the land would remain in the same Israelite tribe in perpetuity.

Modern biblical scholars doubt whether the events stated in Leviticus 25 that were supposed to take place on the Jubilee year ever actually happened historically at any point in biblical or Jewish history. After all, it is never mentioned in any Jewish literary or historical sources that any of these things ever happened. As I'm sure you can imagine, freeing all of the slaves and rearranging the ownership of all previously sold property over the past fifty years would have had quite a major impact on the economy at any time! But since no ancient legal or historical sources ever mention this as happening, many scholars think that these laws were ideals and were never acted on. Therefore, there is no date of the last Jubilee ever having taken place because there is no source ever anywhere indicating any Jubilee year may have been celebrated.

Question number 14: *What are the symbols for each of the tribes of Israel? Can you describe them to me?*

Answer: The source of the symbols of each of the twelve Israelite tribes is actually not mentioned anywhere explicitly in the Hebrew Bible. Rather, the symbols or their flags were derived from a rabbinic Midrash, or folktale, from a book called Bamidbar Rabbah 2:7. This fanciful interpretation quotes many different verses from the Torah in an effort to link each of the twelve tribes with some kind of relevant visual symbol. The symbols of each of the tribes are—in their original birth order—as follows:

1. Reuven's symbol was a mandrake, a kind of plant reputed to have magical or medicinal properties.
2. Shimon's symbol was an outline of the town of Shechem, or modern-day Nablus.
3. Levi's symbol was a priestly breastplate with twelve gemstones on it representing each of the tribes.
4. Judah's symbol was a lion.
5. Dan's symbol was a coiled serpent.
6. Naftali's symbol was a deer.
7. Gad's symbol was an image of tents in a camp.
8. Asher's symbol was an olive tree.
9. Issachar's symbol was the sun and moon.
10. Zevulun's symbol was a sailing ship.
11. Joseph's tribe was split into two tribes for his two sons: the tribe of Ephraim was a bull, and the tribe of Manasseh was an ox.
12. Benjamin's symbol was a wolf.

These symbols often adorn synagogue stained glass windows or as themes in the artwork and tapestries on the walls. A famous example of these symbols is the stained glass windows in the chapel of Hadassah Hospital in Jerusalem designed by the famous Jewish artist Marc Chagall. I hope that you will now be able to identify the tribes by their symbols!

Question number 15: What happened to the Ark of the Covenant? I've read that the Ethiopians took the Ark to their own country during the reign of King Manasseh. Does the Hebrew Bible offer any information about this?

Answer: The ancient Ark of the Covenant was a holy container that was described in the Torah (Exodus 25) and created during the era when the Israelites wandered for forty years in the desert. It is described as being covered in beaten gold inside and out and contained the original Ten Commandments and other items from the years of wandering in the desert. It was ultimately placed in the Holy of Holies, the central and holiest inner repository of the ancient Temple in Jerusalem built by King Solomon. However, as the historical narratives of the Hebrew Bible make clear, the city of Jerusalem and the Temple was captured, looted, and destroyed by the Babylonians in 586 BCE. From there, the Ark was lost forever to the Jewish people and to history. No one knows what happened to it. It was probably melted down for its gold and destroyed at some point, so the film *Raiders of the Lost Ark* is a cute fantasy about the continued existence of this Ark but utterly incorrect. I've never heard this theory that the Ethiopians took the Ark during the reign of the Judean king Manasseh, who incidentally lived, ruled, and died long before the Babylonians destroyed the Temple and stole the Ark.

Question number 16: What is the verse from Isaiah 53:5 referring to? It states, "But he was wounded because of our transgressions, he was crushed because of our iniquities: the chastisement of our welfare was upon him, and with his stripes we were healed." Is this referring to Jesus Christ? If not, who else?

Answer: The prophet Isaiah in Isaiah 53:5 in no way refers to Jesus. I don't mean to be rude or insulting, but the idea that Isaiah was referring to Jesus contradicts the entire institution and nature of ancient biblical prophecy and shows a complete ignorance and understanding about the role and function of biblical prophets in general.

The biblical prophet Isaiah in chapters 52 and 53 was referring symbolically to the entire people of Israel—not an individual person. Written during the period of the Babylonian exile in the sixth century BCE, the Jews were living in Babylonia and felt isolated from God and unsure as to why they were suffering through this exile and the loss of the Temple in Jerusalem. But Isaiah gave them hope, justifying their suffering in order to let them know that God planned all of this but would eventually restore them to their former land and way of life in Israel and Jerusalem. The "he" being referred to in Isaiah is actually "they"—the entire Jewish people personified as a single person. This was a common biblical literary convention employed by many other biblical prophets. According to Isaiah, God would soon forgive the Jewish people and allow them to return to Israel and Jerusalem at the end of this period of exile as a result of their suffering in exile, that is, their "stripes" or pain of exile that was expunging their sin of idolatry.

It is crucial to understand that biblical prophets were not fortune-tellers or prognosticators of the future. They were not making predictions about what would happen in time to come. The idea that a biblical prophet was trying to anticipate the coming of Jesus is utterly contradictory and foreign to the institution of Israelite prophecy. Rather, biblical prophets spoke what they believed to be the word of God relating only to events in their own contemporary times. All prophecies were completely contextual, relating exclusively to the historical time period in which the prophet lived. Isaiah's prophecies are eternal only in the sense that they give meaning to anyone who is suffering and needs hope, and Isaiah articulates an aspect of biblical theology that holds that God judges nations for their moral sins but is ultimately forgiving. Although this verse from Isaiah is often used as a crucial proof of Jesus Christ embedded in the Hebrew Bible, the reality is that it has nothing to do with Christianity whatsoever.

Question number 17: *Who is the author of Kohelet, that is, the book of Ecclesiastes? Why do they think it is King Solomon? If it wasn't him, then who was it?*

Answer: Kohelet is indeed the Hebrew name for the book of Ecclesiastes. Although the biblical author of this book calls himself Kohelet, this is not really a name. It is actually a title and means "the gatherer" or someone who assembles people in order to make a speech to them. However, the word "Kohelet" has been picked up by the Jewish tradition to refer to an actual person with this name. Some people think Kohelet was King Solomon because Kohelet calls himself a king in Jerusalem and also because Kohelet speaks of his search and pursuit of wisdom, which was equated with Solomon's reputation as a wise king.

However, it probably was not King Solomon because it was common for ancient writers to ascribe their literary works to other more famous people so that their book would be accepted and more widely read and circulated. There are also linguistic inconsistencies that would make it unlikely that King Solomon actually wrote Kohelet. The specific words and phrases in the Hebrew of Kohelet only came to be used hundreds of years after King Solomon actually lived. It would as if George Washington and Thomas Jefferson used the slang words "cool" or "far out" in their time, which they obviously didn't!

Then who wrote Kohelet? I don't know—and no one else does either. From a traditional point of view, God wrote it and all the rest of the Hebrew Bible. However, from an academic, intellectually critical point of view, Kohelet was probably written by an erudite Jew, perhaps even a member of the Davidic royal family in the ninth or tenth century BCE. It shares many characteristics of what biblical scholars call wisdom literature, a genre of writing popular among Egyptians and Mesopotamians at this same time. It makes sense that the cosmopolitan Israelite culture at that time would be strongly influenced by the high culture of these larger empires surrounding the tiny kingdoms of Israel and Judah. But as to who specifically wrote it? I don't think we'll ever know.

Question number 18: In Proverbs 1:8, it differentiates between the "instruction of the father" and the "law of the mother." Are there different traditions unique to each of the parents in Judaism?

Answer: No. There is no separate tradition in Judaism for anything called the instruction of the father or law of the mother. What you are referring to in the book of Proverbs is simply a form of biblical poetry called parallelism. In other words, in the Hebrew Bible, they would say the same thing twice using different terms as a form of poetic emphasis and conceptual alliteration.

For example, look at the last poem of Moses in the Torah in Deuteronomy 32:1. Moses begins by saying, "Give ear, O heavens, let me speak"; then the verse continues and says the exact same thing again with slightly different words, "Let the earth hear the words I utter." There is no difference between these two phrases. It is just a fancy way for Moses to say that he wants the entire world to hear what he is about to say from heaven to earth. Therefore, the instruction of the father is parallel to and means the same thing as the law of the mother. The basic idea is that a child should listen to the instruction of both of his or her parents.

Question number 19: What is the Jewish understanding of reward and punishment as described in Daniel chapter 12?

Answer: Although the book of Daniel is part of the Hebrew Bible, it is unique because it is part of a special kind of biblical literature called apocalyptic, meaning, that it purports to contain hidden, secret information. Therefore, much of this ancient apocalyptic literature is written in symbolic code, that is, using phrases and ideas that were meant to be obscure and difficult to understand to the uninitiated outside of the group for whom it was intended. That is why all of us modern Jews have a hard time figuring out exactly what Daniel was trying to say because Daniel was trying to be vague and mysterious on purpose!

Scholars believe that the particular section of the book of Daniel you are asking about, chapter 12, was written during the persecution of the Jews in Israel by the leader of the Seleucid Greeks from Syria, Antiochus IV Epiphanes. This was the persecution that led to the Maccabee revolt around 167 BCE. Apparently, the prophet Daniel was horrified and upset by the death of so many innocent Jews at the hands of the Seleucid Greeks for simply trying to live religiously observant lives as Jews. Therefore, he articulated a theological vision in which those who had died as Jewish martyrs would be resurrected to life again as a kind of reward for their suffering (see Daniel 12:2).

However, there were also Jews who were called Hellenizers back then; that is, they were Jews who actively embraced Hellenistic or Greek culture and maybe even Greek religion. These Hellenistic Jews were considered traitors by their more traditional coreligionists, and Daniel claimed that these traitors would suffer for their disloyal actions in life. This reckoning would happen one day in the future at the time of some great divine reckoning or apocalypse, a cataclysmic meting out of justice for the entire world when all injustices in this world would be settled by God. This is the subject of chapter 12 in the book of Daniel—all described in a very confusing code of obscure literary or political allusions and hidden references. After all, if the Seleucid Greeks realized that Daniel was essentially fomenting rebellion and resistance, he might have suffered the same fate as his countrymen whose fate he was bemoaning!

Question number 20: Were the books of Tobit, Judith, and Maccabees and Wisdom of Solomon ever part of the Hebrew Bible?

Answer: No. The books of Tobit, Judith, Maccabees, and others were never part of the Hebrew Bible because at the time that they were written, perhaps around the first century BCE, there was no recognized or universally accepted canon, or official list of books, for the Hebrew Bible. When the books of the Hebrew Bible were finally chosen by the Talmudic rabbis years later, these books just didn't make the cut.

The process of canonization, or the choosing of the holy biblical books for the Hebrew scriptures, was a long process about which we as moderns do not know all that much about. However, most scholars guess that there were probably many holy books that were popular around two thousand years ago or so. Slowly, the rabbis at the time began to discuss which books were holier than others. So slowly, a canon or list of holy books seemed to develop over the centuries until at some point, around two thousand years ago, the process apparently concluded. The results were the Hebrew scriptures as we have them today.

However, many books were left out. Why? We don't know. Maybe they were considered too modern to the rabbis back then, or maybe they contained political or religious messages that the rabbis did not feel were appropriate. In any case, those books that were left over still continued to exist and were read, studied, and copied throughout the ages. In fact, early on in the development of the Catholic Church, the Early Church Fathers decided that a number of these leftover books should be included in the Christian Bible. These leftover books were called the Apocrypha, which is a Greek word that implies that these books dealt with hidden or secret messages. The word "Apocrypha" is derived from a Greek word that means "secret." So don't worry—there was no secret conspiracy to deprive the world of any biblical books!

Question number 21: *When were the Books of the Maccabees translated from Greek back into Hebrew?*

Answer: There are actually several books called the Books of the Maccabees, possibly as many as eight different books! However, the first two are the most important in the Jewish tradition. The first book of Maccabees was originally written in Hebrew, and the second book of Maccabees was originally written in Greek.

The Hasmonaean family commissioned the writing of the first book of Maccabees shortly after their military success commemorated by the celebration of Hanukkah approximately 163 BCE. They wanted to glorify their military victory over the Hellenistic Seleucids who had been religiously persecuting the Jews, and so the Hasmonaean family probably paid someone to write up their exploits much in the way that ancient kings would preserve their acts in a book of royal annals. This book was the book of 1 Maccabees, that is, the first one. It was probably written in Hebrew. But over time, the original Hebrew was lost, and only the Greek translations remain. It is possible that the Greek version was translated from the original Hebrew at the very time the original Hebrew was composed.

The second book of Maccabees was an independent but parallel work written originally and only in Greek by a Jewish historian named Jason of Cyrene perhaps a few decades after the time of the Maccabean rebellion. It focuses on just the Hanukkah story and is filled with Hellenistic literary conventions, perhaps made-up material and exaggerations. Its purpose was to address the Jewish population of Israel and who lived scattered throughout the kingdoms of the Mediterranean world called the Diaspora who were already Hellenized, that is, living Jewish lives but strongly influenced by Greek or Hellenistic culture, to make them feel proud of their loyalty to the Jewish tradition despite their acceptance of the Hellenistic way of life. This book, 2 Maccabees, was never translated from Greek into Hebrew except in modern times for the Hebrew-speaking academic community of modern Israel. The other various versions of the Books of the Maccabees were also written in Greek as well as Aramaic and Syriac, but they are far less important in the Jewish tradition than the first two versions.

Question number 22: How important is the Book of Enoch, and how accurate or true do you think it is?

Answer: To be honest, not that important or accurate. Although I must admit that I have not spent a lot of time studying this book because it is not part of the Hebrew Bible, nor is it a particularly important part of the Jewish tradition. The Book of Enoch is one of many books that were composed long after the Five Books of Moses and the rest of the entire Hebrew Bible had come to be considered holy and canonical. These later books were called the Pseudepigrapha because their authors pretended that their books had been written by much earlier biblical figures. That is, they wrote their books using pseudonyms or false names. However, the rabbis at this time, around two thousand years ago, never considered these works holy; and thus they were never included in the Hebrew Bible and certainly not the Torah! Therefore, the Book of Enoch is not one in which I, or probably many other rabbis or fellow Jews, place much importance on or even have any ideas as to its accuracy—much less its content! It is briefly quoted in the Christian Bible. So it may be important to Christianity but not to Judaism.

Question number 23: I am trying to find information on the Dead Sea Scrolls. What is the Jewish view of the doctrines described in the Dead Sea Scrolls? Are they accepted?

Answer: Current scholarship holds that the Dead Sea Scrolls were from the library of the Essenes, a monastic sect of Jews that separated itself from the larger society and lived in isolation in the Judean desert from around 100 BCE till they were wiped out by the Roman army in 68 CE during the Great Revolt of the Jews against the Romans.

This Jewish sect basically believed that they were the only true followers of God's will. They wrote several commentaries on various books of the Hebrew Bible and some of their own manuals about how to behave in their community and books of their unique philosophy and theology. They believed that a great cataclysmic war between the divine forces of good and the forces of evil was coming. They described themselves as the Sons of Light and their enemies, such as the Romans and perhaps other non-Essene Jews, as the Sons of Darkness. They adhered to a strict code of asceticism and ritual purity.

Because the Essenes withdrew from the larger Jewish society, their ideas were limited to their immediate population, perhaps never larger than several hundred or thousand. Therefore, it is unclear how much they may have influenced rabbinic or modern Judaism or even early Christianity. Because these scrolls were discovered only in the 1940s, their doctrines are of academic interest mostly. They have had no religious impact upon modern Jewish theology today in modern life. Rather, they are instructive in revealing how varied were the numerous theologies of the many splintered Jewish sects in existence at that time. So to answer your question, are their ideas accepted in modern Jewish life? No. They are of historical and academic interest only.

Question number 24: *What is the Septuagint?*

Answer: The Septuagint is the Greek translation of the Torah written around the first century BCE. As the legend has it, seventy-two Jewish scholars, or six from each of the twelve Israelite tribes, were commissioned to translate the Hebrew Bible into Greek; and according to the legend, a miracle occurred in that each Jewish scholar produced the same exact, word-for-word Greek translation. Therefore, this translation is called the Septuagint, Greek for "seventy" (and interestingly enough, not seventy-two) because seventy just happens to be the closest round number!

Question number 25: *I know the Temple in Jerusalem was destroyed a long time ago, but will there ever be another Jewish temple built there? And if so, who will serve as the priests and Levites there? How will they know if they are descended from the tribe of Levi?*

Answer: The possibility of the ancient Temple ever being rebuilt and animal sacrifices resuming is slight, if not nonexistent. For the past two thousand years, although the Jewish people have kept alive the memory of the hope of rebuilding the Temple in Jerusalem on its ancient site, it has always remained just that—a memory of a hope and not an active desire.

The Temple will never be rebuilt for two reasons—one is religious, and the other is political. The religious reason is that Judaism has developed and changed over the past two thousand years in such a way that animal sacrifice is not even a realistic possibility anymore in the Jewish religion. All of modern Judaism is predicated on prayer, spiritual practices, and

Rabbi Daniel Kohn

acts of loving kindness—not animal sacrifice. Animal sacrifice is simply not a relevant expression of Jewish spirituality anymore. We may still kill animals for food, but for many people, the idea of slaughtering an animal for a purely spiritual purpose is cruel and inhumane.

The political reason the Temple will never be rebuilt is that over one thousand years ago, Muslims built religious shrines and a mosque on the ancient site of the Temple; and short of a world war, they cannot nor will they ever be removed or demolished to rebuild an ancient Jewish Temple that no one even wants anymore. While many radical Palestinians still continually claim that the Jews are out to destroy their holy Islamic shrines, nothing could be further from the truth. The Israeli authorities take great pains to ensure the safety and stability of these Muslim holy sites out of a very realistic fear that should anything ever happen to endanger them, the collective wrath of millions of Muslims could lead to a catastrophic war in the Middle East.

Having said this, it is important to admit that there are small groups of lunatic fundamentalist, perhaps even messianic Jews, who actively hope for the rebuilding of a Third Temple in Jerusalem on that very same spot. To that end, they have been studying all of the ancient details of animal sacrifice so that should the time ever arrive, they will be ready! However, they are just a small fringe group in Judaism. Few Jews in the world even know of their existence because their numbers are so few and their ideas so preposterous. But sadly, some of these nutcases did actually try and blow up the Dome of the Rock and the Al-Aqsa Mosque in 1984. But the Israeli police foiled this plot, and the would-be Jewish terrorists are still languishing in Israeli jails.

As for the problem of who will serve as the Levites, or Temple workers, and Kohanim, or officiating priests, in such a hypothetical future Third Temple—that is indeed a challenging, although moot, question because in ancient times, these tribal and clan identities were maintained through heredity, family traditions, and genealogical records. Because the religious importance of maintaining such records disappeared two thousand years ago due to the destruction of the Second Temple by the

Romans, very few people truly know their tribal identity. However, many families that have the last names of Levi or Kohen or other variations of these names may indeed be descendants of the tribe of Levi and the families of Kohanim. It is good to know that they'll be ready should the time ever come when they will be needed!

Chapter 9

Jewish History and Denominations of Judaism (Twenty-five Questions)

Jews have been around for a long time; subsequently, there is a lot of Jewish history! Beginning with Abraham nearly four thousand years ago, the story of the Jewish people covers a lot of territory, both in material and geographical information. After nearly two thousand years of history in the land of Israel, the Jewish people—through exile and dispersion—migrated to virtually all parts of the globe. Jews have lived not just in the Middle East but also in Europe, Africa, India—even China and the Far East as well as South and North America. And each community has its own unique, rich, and complicated tale to tell.

Although there has been much suffering in Jewish history due to the ongoing presence of anti-Semitism, Jewish history is by no means one of only woe and melancholy. Jewish history is filled with great intellectual flowerings, literary and legal output, even wars and conquests and great contributions to societies all over the world. There are probably as many books about different eras and climes of Jewish history as there have been years of Jewish history!

And just as the story of the Jewish people has been varied and mixed over the centuries, the shape and nature of the Jewish religion that the Jewish people have practiced over the centuries has also evolved and changed a great deal. This is the reason that I have combined two closely related topics in one chapter, that of Jewish history with that of the major American Jewish denominations. In fact, one Jewish joke goes that if you put two Jews in one room, you'll end up getting at least three different opinions about any topic! Similarly, another joke tells of a single Jew stranded on a desert island. When eventually rescued, his rescuers discover that he had built not one, but two different synagogues in which to worship. When asked about it, he responded, "That synagogue I worship in. The other one—I wouldn't step foot in!"

For almost as long as there has been an organized central form of Jewish spiritual life, there has been fractures, divergences, divisions, and denominational splinter movements. Judaism has not remained monolithic throughout the ages. Internal Jewish religious movements have come and gone. The major denominations of American Judaism today are but the latest forms of an ongoing undulation of movements and countermovements that have swirled throughout Jewish history. If this is confusing, the questions and answers below indicate the general state of this bewilderment shared by many Jews and non-Jews alike. In terms of the organization of this chapter, questions and answers dealing with the different denominations of Judaism are toward the end preceded by questions about Jewish history.

Question number 1: Any idea why we read Hebrew from right to left?

Answer: Yeah, I have one or two ideas on the topic. In the early days of writing, many thousands of years ago, writing was first inscribed on stones or tablets for public display. The writing used to start on the right side, go across to the left, then continue on from left back to the right side again, and so on without a break! In other words, it zigzagged across a tablet. This was called in Greek boustrophedon that means "as the ox plows," that is, as an ox would plow a field going one direction, turn around, and then go down the next row. Early writing emulated this pattern.

188 Rabbi Daniel Kohn

Later on, the lines of written texts began to be cut off at the ends. In the ancient Middle East, all of the languages there used to be written from right to left. If you think about the fact that most humans are right-handed, then it makes sense that writing should begin on the right side of a page or a clay tablet because that is where your right hand naturally rests. However, in the Western world, the convention ended up being that one should begin on the left side of a tablet, not the right. However, it remained on the right side for Middle Eastern languages such as Hebrew, Aramaic, Arabic, and Farsi (the language of Iran) and Pashto (the main language of Afghanistan) and others.

Question number 2: I have always believed that Judaism was the oldest religion in the world, but someone recently told me it is Hinduism. Is that right?

Answer: Judaism could not possibly be the oldest religion in the world. After all, there were polytheistic religions long before Judaism existed. There was also the Egyptian religion, the religion of Mesopotamia, the religions of South and Central America, and other ancient animistic religions. Scholars speculate that even the Neanderthals had some kind of religion! And Hinduism also probably existed long before Judaism.

From your question, it sounds like you are somehow disappointed to learn that Judaism is not the oldest religious in the world and that this somehow detracts from its power and importance. But so what? Judaism is a profoundly unique and special religion even if it isn't the oldest religion in the world. It doesn't have to win any antiquity contest to be spiritually significant. The Jewish people, however, are probably among the oldest continuous ethnic-religious groups in the world, along with the Indians, Chinese, and others! So don't worry, we "win" in other "oldest" contest categories!

Question number 3: When was the first Talit made and worn, and who made it? I know the Torah describes the fringes, or Tzitzit, but when did the Talit itself begin to be used and by whom?

Answer: Good question! The answer is no one knows when the first ever Talit, or prayer shawl, was made or worn. I would assume it was made by the Israelites in the desert when they received the Mitzvah to make the Talit in the prescribed manner as described in Numbers 15:37-41.

But from an anthropological and critical historical perspective, the Talit and its fringes were probably already in existence and in use long before the Israelites began using them as religious garments. Biblical scholars believe that this kind of cloak and fringes were a part of the local Canaanite culture and that the Israelites adopted this practice when they moved into the area and gave it a uniquely Jewish spiritual interpretation.

The oldest Talitot that had ever survived are remnants that were discovered along with the Dead Sea Scrolls caves in the Judean desert in Israel dating back to perhaps around 100 BCE, but that is fairly modern when it comes to biblical history that stretches back another thousand or even two thousand years before that! Sorry but I don't think that anyone can really answer your questions!

Question number 4: How was the synagogue first started?

Answer: Good question! I don't know. In fact, there are not many people who do know because the first synagogues are very old. In ancient times back in the days of the Hebrew Bible, the Israelites didn't have synagogues; they sacrificed animals to God in one central Temple located in Jerusalem. In 586 BCE, the Babylonians destroyed the Temple and exiled the Israelites far away to Babylonia. Maybe back then, almost 2,500 years ago is when the first synagogue began by the exiled Israelites in Babylonia who prayed for a return to Israel. This is a topic of ongoing study and scholarship.

When the Jews were allowed to return to Israel, they rebuilt the Temple and began animal sacrifices again around 500 BCE. But it seems that Jews also began to build synagogues around the land of Israel around two thousand years ago even when this Second Temple was still up and running. In fact, archeologists have found stone remains of synagogues from this time period when people still sacrificed animals. However, when the Romans in 70 CE destroyed the Second Temple, all Jews began to build and assemble in synagogues all over the world. But they all probably got a head start in the centuries or decades before this time.

Question number 5: The word "Jew," as I understand it, literally means "someone from the tribe of Judah." Are all Jews today descended from the tribe of Judah? Or do we even remember what tribes we're from?

Answer: To properly answer your question, I have to provide a brief historical explanation so you will understand. Around 1000 BCE, King David established a kingdom of the united twelve tribes of Israel. However, there was a civil war, and ten tribes split to make their own kingdom. Later on, this split-off kingdom was conquered, and the ten tribes were scattered and assimilated into other peoples. They forgot their language, nationality, and history and thus were lost to history. These are the ten so-called lost tribes of Israel.

The only two tribes left at this time were the tribe of Judah and the priestly tribe of Levi. Therefore, the survivors throughout Jewish history have been called Jews, meaning, as you correctly note, "from the tribe of Judah" (the etymology is clearer in the Hebrew) and Levites "from the tribe of Levi." A subclan of the tribe of Levi is the priestly clan called the Kohanim, literally, "priests." The job of the Kohanim in ancient times was, among other things, to bless the people using the special hand symbol that you may already be familiar with from watching Mr. Spock the Vulcan on the original series of *Star Trek*. The Kohanim were from the tribe of Levi but had no special priestly status. The Levites, while not priests, were Temple workers and helped the Kohanim do their jobs.

So today, it is generally accepted that if people have a family tradition of being a Kohen or Levi or have a last name that is some derivation of that name, they may well be descended from the tribe of Levi.

Everyone else is probably from the tribe of Judah, which is the vast majority of Jews today. Kohanim and Levites are a fraction of the Jewish population. The only reason some people care about this today is that in some traditional Jewish communities, members of a synagogue who claim ancestry from either the Kohanim or Levites receive some traditional ritual honors. But other than this, there is no practical difference nowadays between the original ancestries of any two Jews. After all, according to the Torah, all Jews are descended from Abraham and Sarah!

Question 6: I saw a show on TV about the ten lost tribes of Israel. Some people think that some of the tribes went to South America because Spanish conquerors that first met with the native tribes claimed that they had greeted them with Hebrew prayers. Also, some of the Aztec or Mayan temples are apparently similar to ancient Israelite architecture. Is it probable or even possible that some of the lost tribes could have found their way across the Atlantic to settle there?

Answer: No. It is not possible or even remotely probable that the ten lost tribes of Israel made their way over to the Americas from the Middle East three thousand years ago. I'm sure that the TV producers were able to cash in on such nonsense, but quite frankly, such shows greatly distort historical reality.

The truth of the matter is that in biblical times from 922 to 722 BCE, there were two Israelite kingdoms in the land of Israel. In the south, the Kingdom of Judah consisted largely of the tribes of Judah and Benjamin and a sprinkling of the tribe of Levi, or the priests and Temple workers. In the north, the Kingdom of Israel consisted of the other ten tribes. In 722 BCE, the Assyrian Empire (based in modern-day Syria and northern Iraq) conquered the Kingdom of Israel but not the southern Kingdom of Judah. At that time, it was common practice to deport and exile the captive native population to other lands in order to destroy their sense of national identity and prevent rebellions. These ten tribes of Israel were exiled back to Assyria and lands throughout the Middle East to areas that are now Lebanon, Syria, Turkey, and Iraq. Many of these people fled south to the Kingdom of Judah where they were absorbed into the tribes of Judah and Benjamin. However, this Assyrian policy or deliberate assimilation of conquered peoples worked quite well. These tribes were lost in that they did not remain a united population. They forgot their culture, language, and religion, scattered as they were throughout the region.

However, some tribes in Eastern India and Burma (as well as other peoples in Africa) claim descent from one or more of these lost tribes, such as the tribe of Ephraim; and some of these people have even begun to officially convert to Judaism and move to Israel. The Israeli government and other organizations have even welcomed these long-lost brethren back to the Holy Land. However, I believe that the attitude of the Israeli government has more to do with Israeli politics than with a sincere belief in the ancient biblical heritage of these people, and many of the members of these so-called lost tribes may also be motivated to immigrate to a more Western, developed country for financial reasons.

Be this as it may, my description above is generally how most biblical scholars understand how and why these tribes were lost. There are no conspiracies, nor was there a mass exodus of ancient Israelites to foreign lands. These tribes died with a whimper over two thousand years ago. TV programs notwithstanding, the ten lost tribes are indeed still lost to the Jewish people and Jewish history forever.

Question number 7: What is Hellenism, and how did it influence Jewish thought?

Answer: Hellenism is the combination of classical Greek thought, philosophy, art, religion, architecture, and culture as it was combined with local, indigenous Middle Eastern culture and religion in ancient times. It was a major cultural phenomenon over 2,300 years ago and originated in the aftermath of Alexander the Great's conquest of Egypt and the Middle East when he forcibly introduced Greek culture in the region. For example, in addition to the many classical Greek gods and goddesses, Hellenism embraced the Egyptian and Mesopotamian pantheon of gods as well. It was so important and had such a major impact on Jewish thought that many, many books have been devoted to the subject of the question that you ask!

I will share only one major contribution of Hellenism to Judaism among many. Greek culture and scholarship was the first sophisticated literary culture in ancient times to subject their literature to close, intensive scrutiny and study. The ancient Greek scholars even developed principles of literary analysis of the classical Greek texts such as the Homeric epics of the *Iliad* and the *Odyssey*. Greek scholars would devote their lives to the study of the Homeric epics, applying principles of deduction and analysis in order to divine the hidden meanings inherent in the poems. These same principles and devotion to the close study of sacred texts influenced Talmudic, rabbinic culture, and so the ancient rabbis adopted many of these same principles and ideas and applied them to the study of the Torah. In a way, you could say that the Talmud is an indirect result of the influence of Hellenism on Jewish culture! It was also during this period that the Torah was translated into Greek known as the Septuagint. Of course, not everyone embraced Hellenism; just ask the Maccabees who started a war in order to prevent and reduce Hellenistic influence in Israel in ancient times, but that is another story!

Question number 8: What was King Herod really like? I have read that the Jews he ruled hated him since he was a puppet of Rome and killed many of his own family members as well as rabbis. Was he truly evil or just an opportunist?

Answer: You ask a very sophisticated question; and the answer is that King Herod, who was installed as king of the Roman province of Judea in ancient times, was probably a murderous, paranoid, frustrated, dangerous despot as well as an opportunistic tyrant who grabbed power when he was offered it and ruled with an iron hand in Judea. Nearly every Roman-era artifact and architectural ruin you might come across in Israel today is due to Herod's fanatical obsession with building public works.

Depending upon which historian you read and which point of view you care to view him from, Herod was all of these things. For a direct experience of trying to decide about Herod on your own, I urge you to read some of the excellent English translations of Josephus, a Jewish historian who, although he was not a contemporary of Herod's, lived in the period immediately following his reign. If you can't sit through Josephus's *Antiquities of the Jews*, I recommend reading at least the very first section of Josephus's *The Jewish War* where he talks at length about Herod and describes his reign.

As in all things in history, we'll just never know. Think about how President Bill Clinton will be judged—as someone who helped the economy of the United States, or as simply a lecherous president who was impeached? Or President George W. Bush for that matter—will he be remembered as someone who championed freedom and democracy around the world or as a president who led America into an unpopular war in Iraq? The truth is in the eye of the beholder, and only time will tell. As for King Herod, we may never know.

Question number 9: Who really killed Jesus Christ? Was it the Jews or the Romans? Why don't Jews believe Jesus is the son of God?

Answer: To answer your first question in a nutshell before a longer explanation, no, the Jews did not kill Jesus. The Roman authorities in the province of Judea executed Jesus probably sometime in the first century of the Common Era.

However, before I explain in more detail, I want to impress upon you how loath I am to answer this question. Because the Christian church has blamed Jews for the death of Jesus up until modern times and hundreds of thousands of Jews have been murdered by Christians throughout history because of this very question, no Jew should ever have to be asked this question. It is a question that engenders subconscious yet visceral negative feelings in most Jews. Every Gentile who asks a Jew this question must understand that this is a very hostile and loaded question.

I should also point out that precisely because of this long-held prejudice that the Jews were responsible for the death of Jesus, the Catholic Vatican Council II in 1965 officially exonerated the Jewish people from any guilt involved in his crucifixion. Also, you should know that other than the Christian Bible, no other external or contemporary historical evidence exists—save for one ambiguous paragraph in Josephus's history (an ancient Jewish historian in Roman times)—about Jesus. In addition, many enlightened academic Christian scholars even question the actual historical existence of Jesus.

Keeping these things in mind, if Jesus's life is as it was described in the Christian Bible, then it is plausible that while Jews may not have executed Jesus, they were certainly involved in events leading up to his death. This is because the time described in the Gospels was during the Roman occupation of Judea. Many Jews at this time wanted to avoid provoking Roman hostilities at all costs to prevent revolts, reprisals, and bloodshed by the Roman army. Because Jesus was popularly acclaimed to be the king of the Jews (at a time when Jews were not allowed any form of self-government), this would have been perceived by Romans and Jews alike as a call for popular rebellion against the Romans. Many Jews cannot have looked upon such a call to arms against Rome with favor as they would have been fearful of their lives and worried about the stability of the already precarious relationship between Jews and the Roman Empire.

The situation described in the Gospels seems to indicate that part of the Jewish community at that time actively sought to hand Jesus over to the Romans as a potential rebel against Roman rule for execution. Also, at this time, Jews were not allowed by the occupying Roman authorities to carry out capital punishment. Rome kept the right to exact this ultimate act of punishment for itself. And it appears that the Romans were only too willing to help out and execute Jesus. The Jewish authorities of the Roman province of Judea were only involved in having Jesus arrested by the Romans to try and prevent clashes and violence between the Jews and the much stronger Roman army. The Romans executed Jesus as a so-called king of the Jews because they considered him a political threat to Roman rule in Judea. Please keep in mind that if the situation as described in the Gospels is historically accurate, then this is probably why these things happened, but it is not at all clear whether these events as described in the Gospels have any historical validity or accuracy.

To answer your second question as to why Jews do not believe Jesus is the son of God is because Jesus, his life and message, is not part of Judaism. Asking why Jews don't accept Jesus is tantamount to asking why don't Buddhists or Hindus or Shintos accept Jesus as the son of God. Jesus and his message are part of the Christian religion—not Judaism. The idea that God could or would in any way want to become incarnate in a human being is simply unfathomable in the Jewish tradition. It makes absolutely no sense from a Jewish perspective.

This is the short answer. The longer answer is that the message and role of Jesus conflict with basic Jewish religious concepts. Here is a brief synopsis of why Jews do not accept Jesus as the son of God:

1. According to Christian teachings, Jesus, who was the son of God, was also the Messiah. According to Judaism, the Mashiach, which literally means "the anointed one," is a semimythical figure that will one day come to bring about the complete and absolute end of all war, violence, and hatred in the world. However, the state of the world today contradicts this, and nowhere in the Jewish tradition does it state that this Mashiach will be anyone other than a completely ordinary human being.
2. According to Christian teachings, man is evil and born into sin as a result of the original sin of Adam and Eve eating from the forbidden tree in the Garden of Eden. However, according to Judaism, human beings were not expected by God to be perfect. And if people do sin, then they can do Teshuvah, or repentance,

and thus be forgiven by God. This happens once a year on Yom Kippur, the Day of Atonement, in the Jewish calendar. There is no need for Jesus to remove sin in the Jewish tradition.

3. According to Christian teachings, God rejected the Jewish people as God's chosen people when they refused to accept Jesus. However, according to the Torah and biblical prophets, God's covenant with the Jewish people is eternal and can and will never be abrogated.

So in conclusion, no, the Jews did not kill Jesus, the Romans did. And the Jewish people never accepted Jesus as the son of God and probably never will because it is a complete contradiction of the most basic foundations of Judaism.

Question number 10: I have read that ancient historians such as Josephus, Tacitus, and Pliny have all affirmed the historical existence of Jesus; yet you have claimed in previous answers that there are no sources outside of the Christian Bible referring to Jesus, which do not seem to be correct. Would you care to comment?

Answer: Why, yes, I would care to comment and thank you for your question! I am impressed with your familiarity with ancient historians and previous answers that I have written. Unfortunately, none of these great ancient writers actually lived during the time of Jesus's life. In addition, their references are rarely taken seriously by modern academic historians for two reasons: they often repeat information that they had received from other sources (kind of like literary hearsay), and the accepted style of historical writing in ancient times was based on fanciful embellishment, not dispassionate scholarship. Hellenistic histories make great reading and are indeed important sources of historical information, but they are far from what we would call dispassionate eyewitnesses or even reliable sources of history.

Please understand that I am not impugning your beliefs or the validity of Christianity in any way. I am merely restating what Paul Tillich, one of the most respected Christian theologians of the last century, said in his book *Systematic Theology*. He concludes that it is impossible to historically substantiate the existence of Jesus. However, that is utterly irrelevant to Tillich. Instead, what are important are the ideas that Jesus is claimed to have asserted and the lesson of the story of his life. The historical veracity of his life is irrelevant in comparison to the spiritual significance of the story of Jesus. After all, it is called the greatest story ever told! Christianity is valid and relevant whether Jesus ever lived or not. A great Christian theologian said this, not me! Please feel free to believe whatever you may choose to believe and base it on whatever you may choose to base it on. Whatever I may choose to claim about the historicity of Jesus should be completely irrelevant to you. I wish you peace and tranquility in your spiritual life undisturbed by my heretical assertions.

Question number 11: *What is Kiddush HaShem?*

Answer: "Kiddush HaShem" is Hebrew for "sanctifying the name (of God)." It is a euphemism to describe religious martyrdom that means dying or giving your life for a religious cause. There is a well-known Midrash about Kiddush HaShem based on a passage in the Torah from Leviticus 18:5. The verse reads, "And you shall observe My statutes and commandments, which if a man shall do he will *live* through them." The Midrash of Tanchuma in Parasha Mas'ai chapter 1 quotes this verse from the Torah and then adds in a few words at the end, "'He will live through them'—*and not die by them.*" In other words, our tradition informs us that the laws of the Torah are intended to bring us life, not death. However, the Jewish people have endured profoundly tragic times and experiences that have tested the truth of this Midrashic interpretation. There have been times when Jews have not only been willing, but have also been commanded to give their lives for a cause.

In medieval times, Rabbi Moses Maimonides wrote a great deal about Kiddush HaShem in his book the Mishneh Torah, Yesodei HaTorah 5:1-3. Basing himself on older Talmudic laws, he wrote that if a non-Jew were to force a Jew to violate any of the commandments in the Torah or suffer death—the Jew should violate these laws of the Torah and not be killed! However, there are three exceptions to this general principle to save your own life: if a Jew was to be forced to commit an act of idolatry, incest or rape, and murder.

In other words, one can transgress any commandment in order to survive except these three above. However, this changes depending upon different circumstances. First of all, it depends upon whether the transgression of the Torah law is to be committed in public or private. If it is in private and no one else would know that you broke one of these laws to save your own life, then do it. But if it is in public and other people may see you setting a bad example, even in times of war and persecution against Jews, then a Jew is supposed to allow themselves be killed rather than be forced to engage in an act of public idolatry, incest or rape, or murder. The overarching factor in all of these cases seems to be the biblical injunction not to profane God's name—especially in public. Sadly, the Jewish people have had a lot of experience with martyrdom, or dying for their faith. This was true in Roman times, during the Crusades in Europe, and even during the Holocaust. I hope this answers your question.

Question number 12: *Why were the Jews pestered so badly by the crusaders if they were innocent?*

Answer: Not only were the Jews "pestered" by the crusaders, but they were also persecuted, massacred, forced to convert to Christianity upon pain of death and their children were kidnapped, forcibly baptized and raised as Christians. The age of the Crusades is one of the most tragic times in Jewish history prior to the Holocaust. The word "pestered" is hardly the word to use to describe the thousands of Jews who were murdered in the name of Jesus at that time.

Why did this happen? Because for the most part, other than the few armies of true knights and fighting nobility, most of the so-called armies of the crusaders were a vast spectrum of thugs, thieves, naive true believers, camp followers, and peasants. Since the Muslims who lived in the Holy Land were at some distance from Europe, many of these self-styled Christian soldiers found it far easier and more convenient to slaughter the infidels who were closer at hand—the Jews. For the most part, the Jews had lived in peace with their Christian neighbors throughout Europe for literally centuries. The Crusades ended this period of peace and quiet. It was the first time in Jewish history that Jews were persecuted and attacked just because they were Jews.

Some of the most horrific tales of torture, murder, and slaughter came out of the Jewish communities during the Crusades. Many fast days were established in the Jewish calendar at that time to remember those who had been killed. Unfortunately, as so often seems to happen in Jewish history, the horror of the Crusades was ultimately eclipsed by far worse and horrific persecutions and massacres. However, from the early medieval times until the Holocaust, the era of the Crusades was considered the most tragic and terrible periods of all Jewish history.

Question number 13: *Who are the Marranos, and are they Sephardic Jews?*

Answer: The word "Marrano" in Ladino (a mixture of Hebrew and Spanish) means "swine," and it was used by Catholics to describe those Jews who converted to Christianity to avoid being expelled from Spain in the great Edict of Expulsion of 1492. Although many people still use this word "Marrano," it is a derogatory term. Instead, most Jews in academia prefer to call these Jews Conversos, literally, "those who converted to Christianity" or even Crypto-Jews, meaning, Jews who secretly observed their Jewish rituals in secret, sometimes even in their basements or crypts to hide them from their suspicious Catholic neighbors and the Spanish Inquisition.

The Catholics called these Jews swine because they believed that their conversions were insincere and that they were still practicing Judaism in secret as many of them did. As a result, the Spanish Inquisition, the Catholic Church's religious secret police, set out to prove that these Conversos were violating church law and their oaths of conversion to Christianity by still practicing Judaism. Many Jews suffered horribly through torture, and thousands died as the Inquisition extracted forced, oftentimes false, confessions from these Conversos. If found guilty, many of these Conversos were burned at the stake in an execution called an auto-de-fé, or an act of faith, in which their dying proved their faithfulness to Catholicism.

By the way, the term "Sephardic" refers to all Jews descended from those original Jews who lived in medieval Spain. It has sometimes been used to refer to Jews that also came from North Africa and Arab countries in the Middle East, but these Jews prefer the term "Edot HaMizrah," or "tribes of the East." In fact, the word "Sephardic" comes from the Hebrew word for Spain that is "Sepharad." Jews who came from Western and Eastern Europe are called Ashkenazic Jews. There are numerous but ultimately minor differences of ritual custom and versions of prayers that differentiate between Sephardic, Edot HaMizrah, and Ashkenazic Jews. Therefore, any Jew who is descended from Conversos is by definition a Sephardic Jew since the only Jews to have become Conversos were Sephardim living in Spain.

Question number 14: I heard that there was once a Jewish pope, is that really true?

Answer: Yes, sort of. A long time ago, there was a man named Peter Pierleone (1090-1138) who lived in Italy and was the great-grandson of a Jew who had converted to Christianity. He came from a powerful and rich family in Rome at this time and eventually became a priest and then a cardinal in 1120. In 1130, as a result of complicated internal political struggles within the Vatican and Italian politics, Pierleone was actually elected to be the pope and took the name of Anacletus II. He was criticized by his enemies because they claimed that he was still a Jew and that he was out to destroy the Catholic Church, but he remained the pope until his death in 1138. In the Jewish tradition, he gave rise to a number of legends about a Jewish pope; however, according to Jewish tradition, he was not Jewish.

Question number 15: *What is a Golem? Is this a fictional character that has been handed down and is specific to Jewish culture in Europe?*

Answer: The word "Golem" is Hebrew for "raw material" and refers to medieval Jewish legends about a human being that was made in an artificial way and brought to life through mystical means, usually through the creative power of speech and the letters that spell God's name. There are many legends about Golems in rabbinic and mystical literature. However, the most famous legend concerns Rabbi Judah Loew of Prague who lived in the sixteenth century. He is supposed to have created a Golem to protect the Jewish people from anti-Semites. There is also a very famous silent black-and-white film from the early part of this century made in Germany entitled *The Golem*, which by the way is filled with negative European stereotypes about Jews.

Some scholars claim that the legend of the Golem is actually a fantasy invented by the Jewish people during the medieval period to compensate for the lack of political power that the Jews suffered from in Christian Europe. The Golem is an all-powerful creature able to destroy the enemies of the Jewish people easily. However, as the legend developed, it also began to include a cautionary note about the use of power: that once you have it and start to use it, it cannot be controlled. Thus, the ending of the story of the Golem is that even the rabbi who brought this creature to life—like God—could not control the forces that he unleashed on the world, and the Golem ended up destroying the Jewish ghetto in Prague. In the end, the message seems to be that one should leave such yearnings—for power and the ability to create life—in the hands of God. While the Golem legend is unique to Jewish literature, the fantasy of bringing a lifeless lump of material to life is not confined to the Jewish tradition. Just look at Mary Shelly who wrote *Frankenstein* in 1818, and there may well be lots of other non-Jewish precedents for such a creature.

Question number 16: What can you tell me about the life and mind of Shabbatai Tzvi?

Answer: There is an excellent book all about the life and mental maladies that afflicted Shabbatai Tzvi written by Gershom Scholem called simply *Shabbatai Tzvi*. For a shorter version, I also recommend that you read the article about him in the *Encyclopedia Judaica*, a seventeen-volume reference set available in most synagogue libraries—or check out his entry on wikipedia.org.

However, to briefly answer your question, Shabbatai Tzvi was a very charismatic Jewish leader who lived in the mid-1600s in Greece and Israel. Most modern scholars believe that he suffered from manic depression or what is now called bipolar disorder. During his manic moods, he must have been very inspiring and charismatic as he attracted thousands of followers who acknowledged his spiritual leadership.

In the beginning part of his life, his mental disorder caused him to exhibit strange behavior such as violating traditional Jewish laws of Kashrut that caused him to be expelled by a number of Jewish communities. Only when a man named Nathan of Gaza became his chief propagandist did people begin to proclaim him the Messiah. His charisma was such that hundreds of thousands of Jews believed that he was the Messiah. Even Christian sources in Europe prophesied that the year 1666 was to be a year of the second coming of Jesus and they based much of their proofs on the phenomenon of Shabbatai Tzvi and the excitement he was raising among Jews all over the world.

Despite his periods of mania and charismatic leadership, he also endured months or even years in a depressive state. However, his short-lived messianic career ended abruptly when the Sultan of the Ottoman Empire offered him the choice of converting to Islam or being executed. Even after he ultimately converted to Islam, many Jews secretly continued to believe he was the Messiah. His life makes fascinating reading and influenced some of the trends of modern Judaism today.

Question number 17: Was there ever a Jewish mob?

Answer: Indeed there was. Bugsy Siegel and Meyer Lansky were two famous Jewish figures from the world of organized crime in this country in the early 1930s and '40s. There have been many books written about the presence of Jews in the mafia and several movies as well, such as *Bugsy* and *Once Upon a Time in America*. Some people claim that without the Jewish mafia, there would be no Las Vegas today since Jewish gangsters essentially created it.

Question number 18: What is the Jewish position in regard to brotherhood and our growing multicultural society?

Answer: The Hebrew Bible contains numerous expressions regarding the brotherhood of all people. The most famous passage is Leviticus 19:18, "Love your fellow as yourself." And in Exodus 22:20 and 23:9, it emphasizes how Jews must not oppress the strangers in our midst because Jews know what it was like to be strangers in Egypt. In addition, there are many passages in rabbinic literature in which the Talmudic rabbis expressed their lofty ideals of human brotherhood. Hillel in Pirkei Avot 1:12 declared that we must all "love our fellow creatures" (meaning all humans, not just Jews). It also says in Pirkei Avot 2:15, "Let your fellow man's honor be as dear to you as your own." The best expression of the rabbinic concept of brotherly love is in a minor volume of the Talmud called Avot DeRebbi Natan chapter 23, "Who is mighty? Whoever turns an enemy into a friend."

Question number 19: What does Judaism teach about African-Americans and interracial marriages?

Answer: Judaism makes absolutely no distinction between people based on skin color or ethnic origins. In fact, Jews come in a great variety of ethnic and racial types. There are Jews from Cochin, India, who are indistinguishable from their Hindu Indian neighbors; Ethiopian Jews are as equally dark skinned as their fellow Ethiopian Christian neighbors. Jews from Arab countries look very similar to other Arab peoples, and there are plenty of Jews who have blond hair and blue eyes. A few hundred years ago, there was even a thriving Jewish community in China, and those Jews were also indistinguishable from their fellow non-Jewish Chinese neighbors. How could Judaism possibly differentiate among different peoples and groups of Jews when we all appear so dissimilar?

The Jewish tradition has absolutely no opinion whatsoever on interracial marriages. The closest that you can possibly come to any kind of mention of what we would call an interracial marriage is a rabbinic tradition regarding Moses's second wife in the Torah. In Numbers 12:1, it says that after Moses's first wife died, he married a Cushite woman; and his brother and sister, Aaron and Miriam, grumbled about it but were then punished. According to an ancient understanding of biblical geography, the land of Cush supposedly refers to the southern Arabian Peninsula, and some rabbis claim that the reason Aaron and Miriam spoke negatively about their brother Moses was because his second wife was darker skinned than Moses. However, they were severely punished and rebuked for their actions; so if anything, we can read into this story that God, God's Self, condoned interracial marriage!

The bottom line is that the skin color or ethnic origins of Jews are irrelevant. Of course, the Jewish tradition does not accept interfaith marriages, but that is based on religious differences, not skin color or ethnicity. However, when a non-Jew converts and becomes a Jew by choice, then no matter what their racial or ethnic background, they are a complete and fully legitimate Jew. Therefore, an interracial Jewish marriage between two Jews is simply that—a Jewish marriage!

Question number 20: Where did Jewish law come from, and what are the main denominations of American Judaism?

Answer: I tend to try and avoid characterizing the theological positions of other people, not to mention other movements in Judaism. But I'll try to give you a brief synopsis of what I understand to be each of the main American Jewish movements' approach to the Torah and the origin of Halachah or Jewish law.

The word "Orthodox" literally means "correct doctrine," and the basic Orthodox understanding is that the Torah was communicated orally, word for word, to Moses on Mt. Sinai and that this message was written down in its entirety without error by Moses and passed along by the Jewish people from generation to generation and that our Torah today is the exact record of this divine message. The Orthodox movement began nearly two hundred years ago in Europe precisely to discourage as many Jews as possible from abandoning or changing traditional laws and practices in response to modernity. Orthodox Jews, therefore, have a strong aversion to changing or deviating from ancient, traditional practices as they believe they may end up violating the literal will of God. It is actually one of the smaller organized denominations in terms of numbers of adherents in the United States today.

The classical Reform approach to the Torah is that it is a completely human-authored document written with divine inspiration. Therefore, while many of the rituals and laws described are not necessarily obligatory upon each and every Jew, unless they themselves choose to observe them, the ethics and morals contained in the Torah are the most important divine aspects of the Torah. The Reform movement emphasizes the ethical and moral teachings of the classical biblical prophets such as Isaiah and Amos more than the ritual laws of the Torah. The Reform movement began over two hundred years ago in Europe with the aim of trying to reform and change ancient rituals to be less conspicuous and more in line with modern sensibilities. It is currently the largest denomination in the United States today with possibly over a million members.

The briefest, most concise summary of the Conservative approach to the authorship of the Torah is that the Torah is divine and that its ultimate source is God, but the Torah is the work of human beings who tried to communicate their experience of what happened at Mt. Sinai to future generations. Therefore, the Torah is how the Jewish people experienced revelation and how they tried to express their experiences. In other words, the Torah is how the collective Jewish people remembered what happened at Mt. Sinai even if it is not exactly what might have happened there, but since no one really knows what happened at Mt. Sinai, we shouldn't try to read the Torah as if it were a book of literal history. The Conservative movement began in the 1880s in the United States in response to the Reform movement as an effort to conserve or preserve as many of the traditional practices as possible but allowing for gradual change and adaptation to modern circumstances. Fifty years ago, it was the largest denomination in the United States, but over the past few decades, it has shrunk to around half a million or more.

The Reconstructionist movement was founded in 1968. And its approach to the origins of the Torah are similar to the Conservative movement, but they emphasize a greater role of human beings and the role of history in shaping how we understand and act on the laws of the Torah today. The founder of this movement, Rabbi Mordecai Kaplan, expressed the basis of this new movement when he declared that Judaism is an "evolving religious civilization." That is, it continues to change over time. It is based on a spiritual approach to life; and more than being simply a religion, it is also a civilization with literature, art, music, and dance. Another one of the mottos of this movement is that the "past has a vote, not a veto" in determining how Jewish law should be practiced in contemporary times. The Reconstructionist movement is the second smallest of the organized denominations, and every one of its congregations chooses how they, as a community, will interpret and express their Jewish identity—with guidance from their rabbis.

The Jewish Renewal movement is probably the smallest of all of the denominations and far less organized and cohesive than the other movements, but it also traces its roots to the 1960s in the United States. It was established by a number of wayward ultra-Orthodox rabbis who drew inspiration from Far Eastern religions and Jewish mysticism (Kabbalah). Their approach to the origins of the Torah is similar to the Reform movement; and their communities and practices tend to be more focused on an ecstatic experience of worship, focusing on singing, dancing, and meditation. In other words, the quality of one's spiritual experience is more important than the form that they take.

Question number 21: How is the Conservative movement different from the Orthodox movement in terms of observance of Shabbat?

Answer: Not that different, believe it or not. After all, Halachah (Jewish law) is still Halachah no matter who is observing it. The Conservative movement was established in the late 1880s in the United States precisely to conserve as many traditional Jewish religious practices as possible in modern times. However, in the past half century or so, the Conservative movement has generated a number of original Halachic opinions that Conservative Jews may choose to follow if they wish. For example, one of them is a very controversial decision in 1950 to allow Conservative Jews to drive to synagogue on Shabbat if they live too far to walk. Another decision in 1955 was to allow the use of electricity on Shabbat but only for activities that do not violate the true essence of Shabbat, like turning on and off lights or calling close friends and family on the phone to foster a sense of community. These are just a few, but in general, the Conservative and Orthodox movements are very similar in their stance on Shabbat observance. Whether the adherents of each movement actually pay attention to what their religious leaders teach, however, is a different story for both movements!

Question number 22: Why do some Orthodox rabbis think that Conservative Jews are not Jews? I am a Conservative Jew, and I am very concerned.

Answer: I believe you may be referring to a recent news story about an Orthodox group of rabbis called the Union of Orthodox Rabbis who declared that Reform and Conservative Judaism are illegitimate forms of Judaism. I hope you are not too upset about it because the statements of such people and groups are utterly irrelevant and should have no meaning for you and anyone else who does not recognize the role of these people and authority over you. I would like to explain why you shouldn't worry about this recent statement and why it is irrelevant.

The Union of Orthodox Rabbis is a small fringe group of right-wing reactionary rabbis in New York who represent no one but themselves. Their name sounds like they represent all Orthodox Jews, but they most certainly do not. In fact, many mainstream Orthodox rabbis and organizations have gone out of their way to disassociate themselves with this group precisely because of their hyperbolic, bombastic statements of hate and exclusion directed toward fellow Jews.

This particular group has a long history of trying to delegitimize non-Orthodox Jewish movements. When they were first established over a century years ago in 1903, their first official pronouncement was to declare Solomon Schechter, the greatest and most visionary leader of the Jewish Theological Seminary and the Conservative movement, a heretic; and they excommunicated him! Such ridiculous stances obviously did not in any way affect the dynamic growth of the Conservative movement or diminish Solomon Schechter's enormous contribution to the development of American Judaism. This group admits that they made these current bombastic statements at the request of some unnamed ultra-Orthodox rabbis in Israel in an effort to delegitimize non-Orthodox Jews in Israel so that they could achieve their own internal political goals in Israel.

In addition, this group is saying nothing new. Such fringe groups as well as other Orthodox groups have claimed over the past one hundred years that Conservative and Reform Judaism were not legitimate forms of Judaism. And finally to clarify some of the confusion, this group did not say Reform or Conservative Jews were not Jews; they were misquoted. Rather, they declared that Reform and Conservative Judaism—the organizational, institutional movements—were not legitimate and that everyone should quit these synagogues and become Orthodox. Very convincing, wouldn't you say?

Ultimately, who cares what they say about Reform and Conservative Jews? Jews who are not Orthodox should derive their sense of personal Jewish legitimacy from their own actions in life—no one else has the right or is able to suddenly declare that they are somehow no longer legitimate Jews! After all, who made this group the sole arbiter of who can be considered legitimate or not? Our sense of self-worth and value should come from inside ourselves. I wouldn't worry too much about what anyone says about Reform or Conservative Jews. It is irrelevant and ridiculous. I feel no less legitimate now than I did a week ago! And I hope you can feel the same way too.

Question number 23: Where do Orthodox laws and customs come from? Are they in the Hebrew Bible?

Answer: You ask an excellent question! Modern Judaism is not at all synonymous with the religion depicted in the Hebrew Bible. Modern Judaism is the result of nearly three thousand years of growth, development, and interpretation. Our current forms of Jewish practice developed over a long period of time. So no, Orthodox laws and customs are not found in the Hebrew Bible—at least, not exactly.

In order to understand this, we first have to recognize that the religion practiced by the Israelites until the destruction of the Second Temple in 70 CE by the Romans as described in the Torah was a cult replete with priests and animal sacrifices. When this cult and the Temple came to a traumatic and abrupt end in 70 CE, the first rabbis—the teachers and interpreters of the Torah—became the new spiritual leaders of the Jewish people. These rabbis wrote the Talmud that is basically an interpretation and update of the biblical laws. Subsequent generations of rabbis and scholars have continued this process of interpretation and adapted Jewish law to suit modern times. In fact, if you exclude all of the laws of the Torah that deal with animal sacrifices or laws related specifically to agricultural products grown in the land of Israel that are not relevant to Jews living in the Diaspora (outside of Israel), then that leaves less than half of the original 613 commandments in the Torah that can still be followed!

Orthodoxy, as a movement, is actually a relatively modern phenomenon starting barely two centuries ago. The Orthodox movement developed as a reaction to the Reform movement that began in Germany in the mid-1800s. As the Reform movement changed certain traditional Jewish laws, the Orthodox movement developed as a counter-Reform movement to preserve the strict, traditional interpretation of Jewish law. While Orthodox rabbis also actually engage in the process of updating Jewish law, the process is much slower and far more minimal and conservative.

Since the beginning, the Orthodox movement in general has tended toward stricter interpretations of traditional Jewish practices over time in reaction to what Orthodox leaders perceive as a threat to traditional Jewish values, namely, the growing liberal nature of Western culture—specifically the greater role of women; the increased role of sexual suggestiveness in clothing, entertainment, and marketing; and an emphasis on material culture. However, even the Orthodox world has split into various groupings, such as modern Orthodoxy and traditional Orthodoxy. As confusing as this might all be, the final answer is that Orthodox laws and customs are those commandments from the Torah that can still be observed in a modern context as they have been interpreted throughout the Talmudic and medieval periods and continuing into modern times.

Question number 24: Why does the Reform movement not celebrate the second day of Rosh HaShanah? I also heard that a Kipah [head covering] is not always worn in a Reform temple. If so, why?

Answer: Two very good questions! In ancient times, all of the Jewish holidays in the Torah were actually celebrated for only one day. However, when uncertainties developed in late antiquity and the early medieval period regarding the establishment of the Jewish calendar, the rabbis decided that all Jewish holidays should be observed for two days in the Diaspora, that is, Jewish communities outside the land of Israel.

However, over one hundred years ago as the Jewish population of Palestine, the land that would eventually become the State of Israel, increased and grew, the early pre-Israeli Orthodox Jewish leaders decided that with so many Jews returning to live in Israel due to Zionism, they should also return to the ancient practice of observing only one day of each Jewish holiday. Interestingly enough, even in Israel, Orthodox Jews continue to observe two days of Rosh HaShanah because this practice was also considered to be very ancient.

In modern times, the Reform movement, citing the burden of keeping two days of every Jewish holiday as well as harkening back to those earlier times, issued a decision allowing Reform congregations to reduce all traditional two-day holidays back to one-day celebrations. Not all Reform temples or rabbis have chosen to reduce such two-day holidays as the two nights of the Passover Seder or two days of Shavuot back to one day, so there is no unanimity even in the Reform movement about this topic.

As to your second question, you are also correct that in general, Reform Judaism doesn't require the wearing of a Kipah (Yarmulke, or head covering) because it is not actually a Mitzvah, or commandment, to have one's head covered in Judaism. While the custom is very ancient and has assumed the status of law today, Reform Judaism has determined that a Kipah need not be required for male or female worshippers unless they choose to do so. This decision was made partly to reflect the fact that wearing a Kipah is not actually a commandment and also to help Reform Jews who might feel uncomfortable wearing such an obvious garment and identification as a Jew feel less conspicuous. The wearing of a Kipah originated in ancient times as a way to indicate awareness of God's presence presumably as a simplistic reminder of God who dwells above us in the heaven and as a way of showing humility because apparently, Roman slaves were required to wear a head covering to indicate their subservient status. Ancient Jews adopted this custom to indicate a subservient status to God. Although anyone is free to wear a Kipah in a Reform temple if they want to, it is not required.

Question number 25: What can you tell me about Messianic Judaism? I don't know much about it, but I am very confused; how can they even call it Judaism?

Answer: Messianic Judaism is Christianity; it is not Judaism. The only reason Messianic Jews (really Christians) call it Messianic Judaism is to fool Jews into thinking that it is just like Judaism so they will join them. Messianic Judaism may have some Jews involved in it, but it is mostly Christians and is funded entirely by conversion-focused evangelical Christian churches. Most Jews perceive Messianic Judaism as an evangelical Christian church that attempts to subtly and deceitfully encourage Jews to convert to Christianity.

Messianic Jews are very insightful and effective in their marketing strategies. They have adopted all of the language and symbols of Judaism to try and make Jews feel like they are in a synagogue. Messianic Jews even call their houses of worship synagogues, not churches, and even have some Hebrew prayers and spiritual leaders that they call rabbis. But is it Judaism? Absolutely not—don't be fooled. Messianic Judaism is also called Jews for Jesus, and although they might call themselves Jews, it is important to know that these movements are not accepted as legitimate forms of Judaism by the majority of Jews in the world.

The Jews and Christians who are involved in Messianic Judaism may be very sincere in their belief that people can be Jews and believe in Jesus as the Messiah at the same time. However, according to the Jewish tradition, it is not possible. People who believe in Jesus as the Messiah are not Jews; they are called Christians. Judaism doesn't require us to believe in many things, but belief in Jesus as the Messiah is definitely one of those beliefs that separates Jews and Christians.

So why are some Jews possibly attracted to Messianic Judaism? Because the churches of Messianic Judaism are friendly, warm, and very spiritually oriented houses of worship. There is a tremendous sense of community, and they are very effective at making people feel welcome and at home. Who wouldn't feel good in such a place that is so appreciative and friendly? In other words, they have many features that sadly most American synagogues do not possess. And Jews who feel alienated from Judaism may desperately desire to feel a close spiritual connection to God and feel part of a spiritual community. Unfortunately, many American synagogues are perceived as cold, unfriendly, and not very spiritually oriented. They can also be very cliqueish and unwelcoming to visitors and prospective members. The fact that some Jews are attracted to Messianic Judaism should serve as a warning flag to the American Jewish community that we must make our synagogues more user-friendly for Jews by making them more accessible, friendly, and more spiritually focused institutions where Jews can feel truly at home.

I hope this helps answer your question. There are many books and articles written about Messianic Judaism such as *The Real Messiah? A Jewish Response to Missionaries* by Rabbi Aryeh Kaplan. There is also an organization called JewsforJudaism.org that was created to help the Jewish community counter the tactics of Messianic Jews. I hope this answers your question.

Chapter 10

Jewish Law and Mysticism
(Twelve Questions)

One of the unique aspects of Judaism is that the Jewish tradition is filled with hundreds, if not literally thousands, of Mitzvot, or commandments, telling the Jewish people exactly how to behave all times of the day every day throughout each year. In fact, the five books of the Torah contain the very first commandments—all 613 of them. However, over time this number grew substantially. After the era of the Hebrew Bible, the early rabbis began interpreting and explaining these commandments and in the process generated even more. And once this era of the Talmud was completed around the fifth century CE, the early and later medieval rabbis continued this process, and it continues on even into the present day. This entire corpus of Jewish law is called Halachah in Hebrew, derived from a word meaning "to walk" or "to go." Hence, Halachah is the path, or way, that a Jew goes through life.

While there may be no system of courts or even police to ensure compliance with these Jewish laws (hence, they are all voluntary nowadays), the language of a legal system remains from those early days of the Hebrew Bible and the Talmud. The vast compendium of Jewish traditional texts are written in the language of legal codes and interpretations, and the many rabbis who have written commentaries on them made their own judgments as to how the Jews in their local Jewish communities should observe these religious legal traditions throughout Jewish history.

One of the many challenges to practicing the Jewish religion is that there is no pope that is a universally recognized religious authority that determines how the Jewish people should interpret the millennia of Jewish law and how to observe it. As a result, every rabbi and every Jewish community has always been free to determine just exactly how they want to construe and live out the laws governing Jewish life. Therefore, the Jewish community throughout the world has been constantly riven by cultural, theological, and denominational conflicts over the centuries.

For example, Jews who trace their ancestry to Western and Eastern Europe are called Ashkenazic Jews, and their practices differ somewhat from Jews who trace their ancestry to North Africa and the Middle East called Edot HaMizrach that are the tribes of the East. In addition, the practices, customs, and even the clothes of ultra-Orthodox Hasidic Jews from Eastern Europe are very different from the practices of the Jews of India, called B'nai Yisrael—yet they are all still Jews. And in America, the various denominations of Reform, Conservative, Orthodox, Jewish Renewal, and Reconstructionist are all very different from one another due precisely to the fact that there is no one central, worldwide Jewish authority who determines exactly how all Jews should behave or even what they should believe. Halachah today is quite vast and varied; as a result, the questions that I received that directly relate to issues of Halachah were equally diverse and sundry, covering a wide range of topics.

It was interesting to note how many people's questions about Jewish law also related to a very different topic and some would even claim the opposite of Jewish law—that of Jewish mysticism. Jewish mysticism is usually called Kabbalah in Hebrew, which literally means "that which is received," for the Jewish mystical tradition is said to have originated with the earliest biblical and Talmudic figures and was passed on and handed down through the ages from master to disciple until the present day.

But mysticism in general is not unique to Judaism. Religious mystical traditions usually begin in historical eras characterized by political persecutions or great national tragedies and disasters. As a result, religious mystical traditions attempt to answer a basic underlying theological question that is on the minds of all the members of that community at that time, namely, why does the world suck? Or to be more poetic, why does God no longer seem to care about our suffering in the world? Due to the long and pervasive nature of anti-Semitism and Jewish national tragedies throughout history, Kabbalah has never been far from many rabbis' and scholars' minds and imaginations.

There have been discrete and distinct eras in Jewish mystical literature addressing the specific needs and questions of a particular generation and locale. In modern times, meaning the last sixty years of so many Jews of the baby boomer generation and especially Generation X and Y (sometimes called Generation "Why?") have begun to develop an interest in Kabbalah as a result of spiritual yearnings unlocked during the progressive and radical years of the 1960s. Many Jewish spiritual seekers who became enamored of Far Eastern religions and their theological traditions began to seek out the same riches in their own religion—and Jewish spiritual leaders, rabbis, and scholars were only too happy to oblige them. Today, there is a renewed interest in all things relating to Kabbalah, and many people are eager to learn more about it, even popular non-Jewish Hollywood celebrities!

In my experience as a rabbi, many Jews seem to get turned on to Judaism as a result of their interest in Kabbalah, which then leads them to developing a greater interest in observing Jewish rituals, customs, holidays, and practices—in other words, Halachah! Thus, in arranging these questions and answers, it seemed natural to combine these seemingly different topics of Halachah and Kabbalah. In terms of the organization of this particular chapter, all of the questions of Halachah precede those dealing with Kabbalah.

218 | Rabbi Daniel Kohn

Question number 1: *What is the origin of the Hebrew phrase, "Kol Yisrael Arevim Zeh B'zeh," and what does it mean? Who said it, and under what circumstances?*

Answer: The phrase you referred to is found in a number of places throughout the Babylonian Talmud, specifically in the tractates or volumes of Shevu'ot 39a, Sotah 37a, Rosh HaShanah 29a in the Rashi commentary there and in Sanhedrin 27b and other places in rabbinic Midrashic literature. So it is an often-quoted phrase in rabbinic literature.

Basically, it means "All of Israel is responsible for one another" or that all Jews are interconnected in some way. It is used to denote the spiritual, political, and social unity of the Jewish people. What one Jew does affects every other Jew, and that each of us is responsible for the actions of one another. Essentially, it is the answer to the rhetorical question that the biblical figure Cain asked God. When God asked him where was his brother, Abel, whom he had just killed, Cain responded to God, "Am I my brother's keeper?" To which the Jewish tradition ultimately answers, yes! Kol Yisrael Arevim Zeh B'zeh—All of Israel is responsible for one another! You are indeed your brother's keeper! Each of us is!

Question number 2: *Can you tell me the location of the passage, "If you save a life, you save the world"?*

Answer: The actual quote is, "All who destroy a single life—it is as if they had destroyed a whole world. But all who preserve (or it could be translated as save or rescue) a single life—it is as if they had preserved the whole world." This quote comes from the Mishnah, a part of the Talmud. It is located in Tractate Sanhedrin 4:5. It is from a larger passage that was used to exhort witnesses in a court of law to tell the truth and nothing but the truth in capital cases because literally, matters of life and death rested on the veracity of their testimony.

Question number 3: *I was taught that you were not supposed to shoot someone even if it would save your life. If someone said, "Shoot this one person, or I will shoot these ten people," what are you supposed to do?*

Answer: You are correct, and that is exactly what the Jewish tradition says to do. According to the Talmud, Jews can break any Jewish law to save their own life except for three! These are committing a sexual crime, worshipping idols, and committing murder (Babylonian Talmud Sanhedrin 74a). In other words, the Talmud tells us that we should be prepared to die rather than commit these three heinous crimes. Even if someone were to hold a gun to our heads and tell us to do this, we should allow ourselves to be killed—provided self-defense is not a feasible option—rather than violate these three basic crimes. Specifically in the case you mentioned, Jewish law seems to indicate that we should permit ourselves to be killed rather than be forced into becoming a murderer. After all, as the Talmud says in Tractate Sanhedrin 73a, is the blood of the would-be victim of your forced shooting any less red than yours? In other words, you both have an equal right to life. The value of life is extremely important in the Jewish tradition, and sometimes the lives of other people are more important than ours depending upon the circumstances.

Question number 4: *I have read that if a Jewish court kills one man in seventy years it is a bloodthirsty court. Can you explain what this means?*

Answer: The quote you are looking for is from the Mishnah that is the core of the Talmud. Tractate Makkot 1:10 states, "A Sanhedrin (ancient rabbinic court) which executed a person once in seven years was called destructive. Rabbi Eleazar ben Azariah said, 'Once in seventy years!' Rabbi Tarfon and Rabbi Akiba said, 'If we were members of a Sanhedrin, we would never put a person to death.'"

It is clear that despite the fact the Torah often prescribed death to people for various crimes and religious violations, the Talmudic rabbis felt very uncomfortable with actually carrying out such death penalties. Therefore, any court that actually sentenced a person to death—even once in seventy years—was considered to be a bloody court. Meaning, that even once in seventy years was too much and too frequent for anyone to ever be put to death. And as you saw above, Rabbi Tarfon and Rabbi Akiba would never have sentenced anyone to death because they were opposed to the death penalty on principle. So if you are looking for traditional sources to oppose the modern practice of capital punishment, you found one!

Question number 5: What does the Jewish religion think of abortion?

Answer: The Jewish tradition permits abortion in certain circumstances. The basis for this is actually found in the Torah. In Exodus 21:22-23, the Torah describes a case where a man accidentally injured a pregnant woman and caused her to miscarry. However, the only punishment for the man was that he had to pay a fine to the husband whose wife miscarried. But in all other cases in the Torah where someone kills another human being, the punishment is death. This example was understood by the Jewish tradition to demonstrate that a fetus is not yet considered a full or complete human life.

In fact, the Talmud speaks in a number of places about abortion. Even during childbirth, if the labor is actually dangerous to the life of the mother, the Jewish tradition permits what we would call late-term abortion in order to save the life of the mother. The principle in the Jewish tradition is that the fetus about to be born is unintentionally pursing the mother with murderous intent. In other words, if delivering the baby would mean the certain death of the mother, then abortion is permissible. Therefore, believe it or not, for purposes of self-defense, a pregnant/delivering mother and her caregivers can perform an abortion to save the life of the mother.

However, as soon as the baby's head emerges or the majority of the body, it is no longer permitted to abort the life of the newly emerging baby. This is based on the Jewish principle that one life does not take precedence over another. This means that as soon as the baby is born, it is considered a viable full human being with all of the rights that any other human being has. But the baby has to be born first or least its head or most of its body if it is born feet first.

Subsequent generations of rabbis have interpreted Jewish law to be less tolerant of abortion even to the point of only permitting it in the most extreme cases of danger to the mother. This is because the permissibility of abortion conflicts with the Jewish emphasis and value of life. However, the classical Jewish sources do indeed recognize the validity of abortion in certain cases. For more information, I urge you to read the classic book on this topic *Birth Control in Jewish Law: Marital Relations, Contraception, and Abortion as Set Forth in the Classic Texts of Jewish Law* by David Michael Feldman.

Question number 6: Why is fishing permitted while other types of hunting are banned?

Answer: According to the Torah, it is prohibited to eat any Kosher land animal or bird that has not been butchered in the prescribed way called Shechitah, or "slaughter." Hunting of these animals and birds is prohibited because depending on the method of capture, it might wound or kill the animal, and if it dies, it will not have been slaughtered by this method of Shechitah and not be Kosher. In addition, for an animal to be Kosher, it must be unblemished and uninjured before slaughter. This is why hunting is prohibited; the animal that is wounded or killed can't be eaten according to the laws of Kashrut. However, trapping an animal in such a way that it wouldn't be injured or killed is permitted. In general, nearly all Kosher land animals and birds were and still are raised as domesticated creatures bound for slaughter and not hunted in the wild. Fishing as a sport and industry of food collection is permitted because there are no prescribed ways to slaughter a fish other than to simply have it die as a result of it being removed from the water. Fishing, therefore, doesn't injure or kill the fish in such a way that would render it unfit to be eaten afterward.

Question number 7: *I recently learned that baptism is not a Christian invention. John the Baptist, as a Jew, was acting in the long tradition of Jewish practice. It seems that ritual cleansing, as well as baptism for converts to Judaism, was part of Jewish practice for centuries. Is there some equivalent rite today within Judaism?*

Answer: Baptism does indeed derive from a Jewish practice. From biblical times onward, Jews were commanded to visit a ritual bath called a Mikvah, which literally means "a pool of gathered waters," in order to spiritually purify themselves. In ancient times, anyone could visit a Mikvah in order to spiritually purify him or herself before making animal sacrifices in the ancient Temple in Jerusalem.

What made and continues to ensure that a Mikvah is Kosher or fit according to Jewish law is the source of the water—it must to come from a pure, natural source such as rain, spring water, or snowmelt. These waters are called living waters or natural waters in Jewish sources. And this water cannot be pumped or drawn; they could only be used for a Mikvah if they are collected in a reservoir or run downhill naturally to a pool for collection.

Despite the cessation of animal sacrifices, Jews have continued to practice going to the Mikvah for spiritual purification even to this day. Nowadays, mostly traditional Jewish women visit the Mikvah upon the conclusion of their menses and traditional Jewish men before Jewish holidays. Also, converts to Judaism immerse themselves in a Mikvah as the final act of becoming a Jew. Early Christian leaders adopted this practice, but you are indeed right—it originated as a thoroughly Jewish custom that is still practiced today. And there is no equivalent rite in Judaism in place of this practice; it continues to remain a part of Jewish ritual life!

Question number 8: In the Torah Numbers 15:37-41, it says to use a blue or purple thread on each corner of the Tzitzit, or the fringes on a Jewish prayer shawl. However, nowhere does it state what shade of blue or where or what animal to get this dye from. In my research on the Internet, it says that the formula for the blue dye has been lost and that white is okay. How can it be okay when God said to use blue?

Answer: Modern, contemporary Judaism is not identical to whatever it says to do in the Torah. The Torah describes biblical Judaism, a religion based on priests, animal sacrifices, and agricultural life in the land of Israel in ancient times. That society came to a traumatic end nearly two thousand years ago when the Roman Empire destroyed the ancient Temple in Jerusalem and dispersed a sizeable portion of the Jewish people throughout the rest of the world, forever putting an end to animal sacrifices and any semblance that Judaism could ever again follow the biblical dictates of animal sacrifices.

At that time, the rabbis or the teachers emerged as the new spiritual leaders of the Jewish people. The rabbis spent generations interpreting the Torah, updating and adapting its laws to contemporary reality. Among the various laws that they covered was the law dealing with the blue thread, called in Hebrew Techelet, in the Tzitzit or fringes of the Talit, the traditional prayer shawl. Since the Torah does not specify which shade of blue to use, the rabbis relied upon the oral tradition, verbal details not included in the Torah but passed down through the generations of religious leaders. But as you correctly note, over time, the recipe for creating that dye was lost. Therefore, rather than possibly violate the color chart or particular hue that God might have had in mind, the Talmudic rabbis—as they did with all other things in the Torah—accepted the responsibility of continuing to provide guidance to the Jewish people in matters that were unclear. Therefore, they decided to abandon the idea of using any kind of blue dye and instead use all-white Tzitzit in order to be safe and conservative.

Interestingly enough, there are a number of contemporary Jewish groups who claim to have rediscovered this ancient recipe for the blue dye, and it is now possible to purchase a Talit with a thread of blue just like it is described in the Torah. Therefore, Jews today have the choice as to whether they want to buy a Talit that adheres to the letter of the rabbinic interpretation of the Torah, meaning all-white Tzitzit, or one that adheres to the general spirit of the Torah that include Tzitzit with a thread of blue.

Question number 9: *What is the role of women in the Jewish faith?*

Answer: That is a very complicated question. In fact, there are many excellent books on this topic. The best that I have found so far is called *Women in the Talmud* by Judith Abrams and another one is *Daughters of the King* edited by Susan Grossman. You should also read *A Jewish Feminist Reader* edited by Susanna Heschel as well as another book about this by Blu Greenberg called *On Women and Judaism*.

Now, to answer your question very briefly, in the ancient traditional Jewish sources, women were not seen as legally or intellectually competent or independent. Therefore, their rights and responsibilities were limited—as were, by the way, all women in ancient traditional societies and religions including Christianity and Islam. However, even despite this handicap and in comparison to other contemporary religions and societies, women were treated very well in the Jewish world throughout Jewish history.

In the Torah, although women were subservient to men—particularly to their fathers, brothers, or husbands—they still played major roles in the stories of the Hebrew Bible. For example, in the Torah, although Rebecca was subservient to her husband, Isaac, she played a key role in convincing her son Jacob to wrest his older brother Esau's birthright from Isaac in his old age. Miriam, the sister of Moses, led the Israelite women in song and dance in triumph after the Egyptian army was drowned in the Sea of Reeds. And one of the most famous ancient judges and military leaders of the Israelites was a woman named Deborah. And if it had not been for the determination of Ruth, a Moabite who converted to Judaism, she would never have ended up founding the line that ultimately led to the birth of King David.

Despite the legal status of women as semi-second-class citizens in Jewish life, the Talmud is filled with stories of strong, intelligent, and resourceful women, such as Beruriah, the wife of Rabbi Meir, and Yalta, the wife of Rav Nachman. Texts from medieval times reveal Jewish women to be active members of society such as the diary of Glückel of Hameln, who lived in the late 1600s, and Donna Gracia Nasi, a noble Portuguese Jewish woman in the 1500s who used her wealth to help free Jews wherever they experienced oppression.

In the realm of Jewish ritual, women's responsibilities were traditionally confined to the home and family life. In Halachah, women were exempt from fulfilling commandments that had to be performed at a certain time due to the concern that their home and family responsibilities would interfere with their religious obligations. Traditionally, women were excluded from counting in a Minyon, which is a quorum of ten adult Jews required to recite certain prayers, and could not receive an Aliyah to the Torah or lead parts of the worship service or even sit with men in the synagogue. However, as the role of women in contemporary modern life has evolved and changed to become more egalitarian, this has begun to affect Jewish ritual life as well.

In modern times, because the role of women has changed so dramatically in contemporary Western society over the last several decades, these changes have begun to affect women in Judaism, particularly their role in the synagogue and ritual events. The Reform, Reconstructionist, and Conservative movements in the United States have taken great strides forward in equalizing the role of women in every aspect of Jewish rituals and laws. The first girl ever to celebrate a Bat Mitzvah took place in the United States over a century ago. Women have achieved larger and more powerful roles in public and synagogue life too. The Reform and Reconstructionist movements in the United States were the first denominations to permit women to study for and become ordained as rabbis in the Jewish community in the 1970s. The Conservative movement followed suit in the 1980s, and this process of growing egalitarianism continues where even in the Orthodox world where there is growing internal pressure to change the role of women in more traditional, conservative communities and enable them to serve in greater religious leadership capacities. In conclusion, despite the initial legal hurdles that women faced in fully participating in Jewish life, the role of women in Jewish life has continued to evolve and expand over time.

Question number 10: *I once heard a rabbi tell a story about the seven righteous men who held up the world. Could you tell me where to find it? Thank you very much.*

Answer: You are referring to someone who is known as a Lamed-vavnik, meaning "one of thirty-six," in the Jewish mystical tradition. According to Kabbalah, there are thirty-six Tzadikim, or righteous people, in every generation upon whom the survival of the world depends.

This is an ancient tradition originally derived from the Babylonian Talmud (Sanhedrin 97b) that states, "Abbaye said, there are not less than thirty-six righteous men in the world who receive the Divine Presence." The number 36 was not arbitrarily chosen. It is obviously 2 x 18 that equals 18 that in Hebrew letters is the word "Chai" or "life" in Hebrew. Therefore, double Chai or double life in the symbolism of Hebrew letters and numbers is 36.

Interestingly, the number 36 doesn't seem to be the essential part of this tradition because Rabbi Shimon bar Yochai, another rabbi from the time of the Talmud, said, "The world never lacks thirty righteous men" (Genesis Rabba 35:2); and Rabbi Yehotzadak claimed, "The world exists by the merit of forty-five righteous" (Babylonian Talmud, Hullin 92a). The Kabbalists and Hasidim adopted this tradition of righteous people spiritually supporting the existence of the world in later medieval times. I do not know any specific Hasidic sources for the Lamed Vav'nickim or these thirty-six righteous men, but if you want to know more about them, I would encourage you to do your research in Hasidic and Kabbalistic sources.

Question number 11: What is Kabbalah?

Answer: "Kabbalah" is a Hebrew word that literally means "that which is received." It refers to a body of traditional Jewish literature that is supposed to have been passed down through the ages from one generation of scholars to another through a special chain of individual transmission from master to disciple. "Kabbalah" is another word for Jewish mysticism.

Mysticism exists in many religions and is not unique to Judaism. Religious mysticism in the Jewish tradition arose in various times of Jewish history when the Jewish people felt cut off from God, like during times of wars and persecutions. Mystical texts and wisdom are filled with explanations for why there is—or was perceived to be—such a gap between human beings and God. Oftentimes, mystical texts in Kabbalah offer prescriptions for how to close this gap and achieve a spiritual or vision-induced closeness to God through special religious practices or the recitation of special prayers and formulas and even descriptions of ascetic practices and instructions on how to enter into trances via meditation.

There have been several distinct periods of Jewish mysticism beginning with the generations of rabbis who wrote the Talmud two thousand years ago who tried to induce mystical visions of God's mysterious chariot as described in the first chapter of the prophet Ezekiel in the Hebrew Bible. Later on, in thirteenth-century Spain, a mystical community produced the Zohar, the classical work of Jewish mysticism that consists of lots of different books but primarily mystical interpretations of the books of the Torah. Another important era of Jewish mysticism was the sixteenth century in a small town called Tzefat in northern Israel where Rabbi Isaac Luria created a sensation with his radically new and attractive vision of Kabbalah. It was Lurianic Kabbalah that inspired the Hasidic movement in the eighteenth and nineteenth centuries in Eastern Europe and is currently the formulation of Kabbalah that most Jews and scholars teach and practice today.

There are lots of various rules and restrictions associated with the study of Kabbalah, such as you could only be thoroughly learned in the Hebrew Bible and Talmud, married and over forty to be eligible to study Kabbalah. Many of these restrictive traditions arose after a particularly famous false Messiah roiled the Jewish community of Europe and the Middle East in the 1660s named Shabbatai Tzvi. This man's charismatic leadership and popularity was predicated on familiarity with Lurianic Kabbalah, and after he was obviously revealed as a false Messiah and thousands of Jews were left in despair, Jewish communal leaders blamed Kabbalistic teachings for this catastrophe in the Jewish community and sought to limit its dissemination.

However, since the 1960s and new generations of Jews hungry for authentic Jewish mystical wisdom and spiritual teachings, the study of Kabbalah has become popular and easily accessible again. New, brilliant academic scholars of Kabbalah have been translating and publishing quite a bit about Jewish mysticism, and there has been a kind of renaissance of Kabbalistic studies both in universities and in synagogues around the world. But it is not magic. And it will not enable anyone to cheat death and live forever, nor will it confer instantaneous spiritual enlightenment. However, Kabbalah is a fascinating legitimate branch of traditional Jewish literature and is filled with spiritual insights. So if you want to learn more about it, unlike times in the past, you don't have to look too far or hard to find books and classes on Jewish mysticism! Enjoy your studies!

Question number 12: Why is Kabbalah so popular now? Is it considered a cult? Are there any cults in Judaism?

Answer: I think that Kabbalah has become popular in recent years for a number of reasons. First, many Jews are unsatisfied with the traditional denominations of American Judaism that they feel are lacking in spirituality. Kabbalah is completely devoted to spiritual matters, and this attracts people. Many leaders from the ultra-Orthodox community are also realizing this and are trying to teach more about Kabbalah as a way to gain new followers.

Secondly, for many centuries the Kabbalistic texts were written only in Aramaic and Hebrew that most common Jews could not read. In recent decades, many of these ancient texts have been translated into English, so now they are accessible to the majority of Jews in the world who are curious about these texts. In addition, lots of rabbis, scholars, and Jewish teachers are writing books of Judaica about Kabbalistic topics with enticing titles to attract these readers.

Thirdly, the study of Kabbalah has been sometimes falsely portrayed as a secret shortcut to achieve spiritual insights into life. Nothing could be further from the truth; the Jewish mystical tradition is predicated on expertise and great familiarity with a vast number of traditional Jewish texts and makes extreme demands regarding personal religious practice on its adherents. Still, many people don't know this and are interested in finding an accelerated path to enlightenment and spiritual equanimity.

And finally, there are some Jewish Kabbalistic organizations that do seem like cults such as the Kabbalah Centre in Los Angeles that has attracted celebrities like the rock singer Madonna among others. Cults are characterized as internally focused communities led by strong, charismatic leaders who claim that their way is the only path to truth or salvation. While the Kabbalah Centre in LA and its many branches may not be as extreme as this, it certainly uses Kabbalah to attract people, but hopefully not for evil or malicious purposes.

And finally, yes, there have been cults in Judaism in the past; and some would argue that certain Jewish institutions and organizations today have many cultlike characteristics. Some critics of the ultra-Orthodox Hasidic communities also claim that they were once and may still be indeed cults. However, unless they are actively advocating violence or mass suicide or other self-destructive acts, for the most part, the wider Jewish community and outside authorities have not taken steps to intervene in the internal affairs of these communities. And let's face it, last year's cult may be next year's mainstream religious movement!

Chapter 11

Shabbat, Jewish Festivals, and the Hebrew Calendar (Twenty-four Questions)

Jewish life revolves around the annually recurring cycles of the Hebrew calendar. As Rabbi Abraham Joshua Heschel, a major Jewish theologian of the twentieth century, wrote in his book *The Sabbath*, the Shabbat is a "cathedral in time" for the Jewish people. The same is true of all Jewish holidays. Rather than sanctifying holy places or locations, ever since the destruction of the Second Temple by the Romans in Jerusalem in the year 70 CE, the Jewish people have established holy times in the week and calendar so that certain times are sacred, not actual physical locations or buildings.

While most Jews do not ordinarily think of the Sabbath day, which begins sundown Friday night and concludes at dark on Saturday night, as a holiday, Shabbat is actually the holiest day of the week and year in the Jewish hierarchy of holy days. Based on many biblical sources and additional Talmudic additions, the Shabbat was legislated by the ancient rabbis to be as complete a day of rest and cessation from normal, regular, productive, everyday activities as humanly possible. As a result, confusion abounds as to what religious Jews can and cannot do on Shabbat.

In addition, similar rules regarding abstaining from standard weekday activities also apply to the major Jewish holidays although somewhat less restrictive. Part of the problem is that the Torah speaks about ceasing from "work" on Shabbat and the festivals. Unfortunately, this has led to more confusion as what may constitute one person's definition of work is another person's personal form of rest and recreational activity. Therefore, some of the questions in this chapter deal with trying to establish just exactly what one can or should not do on these holy days in order to honor the spirit and letter of Jewish law.

Another ongoing source of confusion is related to the fact that the dates of Jewish holidays seem to wander through the commonly used Gregorian calendar, which was formally the Julian calendar but finally more accurately fixed by Pope Gregory in the sixteenth century. There does not seem to be any fixed or established dates for the Jewish holidays; sometimes the Jewish High Holidays come earlier in the fall and sometimes later. This is a result of the fact that our standard calendar is purely a solar calendar that no longer follows the phases of the moon whereas the Hebrew calendar is based on the cycles of the moon and is routinely adjusted to correspond and stay in sync with the solar seasons. For more information about this fascinating but confusing state of affairs, read the questions and answers below.

Furthermore, despite the fact that there are two major Jewish High Holy Days (Rosh HaShanah and Yom Kippur) and three Pilgrimage Festivals (Pesach, Shavuot, and Sukkot) and several smaller, minor holidays (Purim and Hanukkah), the majority of questions that I received focused on the Jewish holiday of Pesach. This is because it is perhaps one of the most historically popular of all Jewish festivals, and unlike all of the other Jewish holidays, Passover is the only one that is accompanied by its own unique set of dietary restrictions over and above the ordinary rules of Kashrut (see chapter 13 for more information about Kashrut or "Appendix A: Kashrut Explained"). Because of this, all questions related to Pesach do not appear in this chapter but instead have been grouped together in chapter 12.

The order of the questions in this chapter is as follows: First, there are general questions about the Hebrew calendar followed by questions about Shabbat. After this, I placed questions about the holidays in the order they come according their sequence and progression in the Jewish calendar beginning in the fall with the High Holidays—Sukkot, Hanukkah, Purim (Passover is in chapter 12)—continuing with Shavuot in the early summer and back to the fall again.

As I have written in other places, even though many people wrote to me asking for specific advice and guidance, I did not believe that it was my job to tell them what to do. I believed that it was my role as a rabbi to share the wisdom and insights of the Jewish tradition so that they could make up their own minds as to how to live their own Jewish lives and best express their Jewish identity. I offer these questions and answers regarding the Jewish holy days in that same spirit.

Question number 1: Why is the lunar calendar used for festivals and the High Holidays whereas it is the solar calendar that we use for weekly Sabbaths? Was the choice of Saturday for Shabbat made by the rabbis, or did it come from the Torah?

Answer: Actually, the Hebrew calendar is a lunar calendar adjusted to the solar calendar. The original biblical calendar is based on the cycles of the moon. For example, Exodus 12:1 indicates that the Hebrew calendar was initially based on solely the lunar cycle. However, the Jewish calendar is not a pure lunar calendar because the festival of Pesach must fall in the spring (see Deuteronomy 16:1), but the seasons are determined by the solar calendar. If the Jewish calendar were purely a lunar calendar, then because the lunar calendar is approximately 11 days shorter than the solar calendar, each year, the festival of Pesach would fall 11 days earlier than the previous year. That is because a lunar year is 354 and 1/3 days long whereas a solar year 365 and 1/4 days long. The difference between them is approximately 11 days. If the Jewish calendar were purely a lunar calendar, after three years, Pesach would fall one month earlier; and after nine years, Pesach would fall in the winter! Because the seasons are based on the solar calendar—but the original biblical calendar is based primarily on the lunar calendar—the Jewish calendar is actually a lunar calendar that is *adjusted* to the solar calendar to make sure all of the Jewish holidays fall in the right season.

As for the choice of Saturday being Shabbat, the occurrence of Shabbat is based neither on the lunar or solar schedule; it is a seven-day cycle that recurs that is unrelated to the cycle of the moon or the sun. However, the concept of a seven-day cycle is very ancient and is also found in early Babylonian calendars. It is based on the five main visible bodies in the nighttime sky: the sun, the moon, and the five planets visible to naked eye—Mercury, Venus, Mars, Jupiter, and Saturn. In fact, our current English names for each of the days of the week still resembles the ancient practice of dedicating each day of the week to that planet or god in either Norse or Roman mythology associated with it, for example, Sun-day, Moon-day, Tui's-day, Woden's-day, Thor's-day, Fria's-day, and Saturn's day. The choice of Saturday for Shabbat predates the rabbis and quite possibly even the Torah. Apparently, the selection of Saturday as the Shabbat is a very ancient tradition, and our cycle of weekdays originated possibly long before recorded calendars and records.

Question number 2: What year is it in the Jewish calendar? My understanding is that the Jewish calendar began in 3761 BCE. How was that date determined, and what does that make the current year of 2007? I would appreciate your help.

Answer: The current year of 2007 according to the Jewish calendar is 5768, and this represents the number of years according to the Jewish tradition from the creation of the world until the present time. This calendar system was first mentioned in Jewish texts by Hai Gaon, a leader of the Babylonian Jewish community in the eleventh century. However, he claimed that this Hebrew calendar was actually first introduced long before him by Hillel II, a leader of the Jews in the land of Israel who lived around the fourth century CE. However, Hai Gaon is probably referring to the complicated calculations required to establish the Hebrew calendar and keep it on track, not the actual count of the years.

A more credible explanation of how the current Hebrew calendar year was established from the years of creation is probably due, ironically enough, to Christian influence. The Protestant Archbishop of Armagh, a man named James Ussher, the Anglican Primate of All Ireland who lived around the seventeenth century, produced a careful chronology of all human history in his work *Annals of the World* (1650). He is credited with having counted all of the generations of humans mentioned in the Hebrew Bible, counting up all the life spans listed and determining an exact year, date, day of the week, and time for the creation of the world, which he determined to be the evening of Sunday, October 23, 4004 BCE! This preoccupation with determining an absolute calendar—as opposed to simply counting the years of the reigns of kings—probably influenced the Jewish community to determine a similar calendar, thus yielding the current Hebrew calendar date of 5768 years from the creation of the world.

Please note, however, that only a minority of the Jewish community accepts this year as an actual date marking the creation of the world. However, the Jewish community has continued to use this calendar—despite the fact that scientists are pretty sure the world is actually 4.56 billion years old—because it is an ancient and traditional calendar that the entire Jewish community accepts and continues to use. And quite honestly, if the entire Jewish community around the world can agree to even this one thing, then it is worth keeping and using!

Question number 3*: Could you tell me the importance of Shabbat for a Jew?*

Answer: Shabbat is one of the most important of all of the Jewish laws and customs for the reasons explained in the Torah. According to Genesis 2:1-4, God ceased from creation and rested on the seventh day. Therefore, observing the Shabbat is a way to imitate God. In other words, we are more godlike when we too rest on Shabbat. Observing Shabbat is also a way to remember the exodus from Egypt. According to Deuteronomy 5:12-15, the Shabbat reminds us that we were slaves in Egypt and that

God redeemed us. That is, as slaves in Egypt, the Israelites could not stop and rest on any day of the week. Only as free people could the Israelites rest from their daily work on the Shabbat. Therefore, observing Shabbat serves to deepen our historical appreciation of the history of the Israelites as well as sensitize us to the needs of other people who also need rest and rejuvenation. Finally, it is a day for us to take a break from our busy weekday lives and seek restoration in restful, spiritually focused activities, whether that includes communal worship services, reading, studying Jewish texts, walking, or even sleeping and taking naps! For more information, I encourage you to browse the shelves of your local synagogue or the religion section of any bookstore as there are literally entire shelves filled with books about Shabbat!

Question number 4: What does Exodus 31:13 mean when it says that the Shabbat is a sign between God and the Jewish people? Can you explain this?

Answer: When Jews observe the Sabbath, it is a visible sign that they believe in and are keeping faith with their unique relationship to God as described in the Torah. In other words, it is a symbol that the covenant between God and the people of Israel is still intact—at least from the Jewish perspective. Whether God needs this sign as a reminder of this special relationship is not clear; however, it is certainly a reinforcing ritual within the Jewish religion. That is, when Jews continue to observe the Sabbath throughout the generations, this helps reinforce the sense of God's presence in our midst and reminds us of our covenantal relationship we share with God.

For example, wearing a wedding ring is a visible, outward sign that a person is married. Maybe people wear it to show other people that they are married and not single and unavailable to date. Maybe they wear it for themselves because it is a piece of beautiful jewelry and it reminds them constantly of their marriage and their partner. Even if someone takes off their wedding ring, they are still married, but it is a token of their involvement in this relationship that reminds them every time they see it that they are married and have a special relationship with their spouse and no one else. The Shabbat is similar to a wedding ring, for it shows that the Jewish people are still committed to this ongoing relationship with God. It is a sign both to remind us, the Jewish people, of this relationship as well as other people of our spiritual values. Perhaps God doesn't need this sign; but it certainly helps us, the Jewish people, remember that we are in a committed relationship with God!

Question number 5: *Why are the Jewish people commanded to sacrifice more animals as offerings to God on Rosh Hodesh than on Shabbat? I thought Shabbat was considered to be the most important day in the Jewish calendar of holidays.*

Answer: Although Shabbat is considered the holiest of all days, just because a holiday has more sacrifices does not mean it is more holy. After all, Shabbat is even more holy than Yom Kippur, but there were many more sacrifices on Yom Kippur and even Sukkot than there were on Shabbat.

Rosh Hodesh, the holiday celebrating the beginning of a new moon and thus a new Jewish month, is important and special in general because the Jewish calendar is primarily a lunar calendar that is then adjusted to the solar calendar. All of the Jewish holidays are determined by what day of the particular Hebrew month they fall on. Passover falls on the fifteenth day of Nisan, which is determined by when the new moon or new month begins. Therefore, the determination and celebration of each month in Judaism is a very big deal. And we still commemorate it to this day with special prayers and a special Torah reading in the synagogue. Anyway, Rosh Hodesh actually has exactly the same number of sacrifices as Shabbat—three: one in the morning of the day, an additional or Musaf sacrifice, and then one in the afternoon.

The way you can tell when animal sacrifices used to be offered in the Temple in Jerusalem in ancient times is based on the number of Amidah prayers, or the special section of standing prayers at the core of every major Jewish worship service we say on any given day. Ignoring the evening, or Ma'ariv or evening service, because that is a complicated side issue, on Shabbat we say an Amidah prayer in the morning for Shacharit (or dawn), for Musaf (the additional prayer service), and Mincha (the afternoon service). Therefore, there were three sacrifices on both Shabbat and Rosh Hodesh because each day today has three daytime Amidah prayers that we say.

A much better way to determine the holiness or importance of each day in Judaism is to count the number of Aliyot or divisions of readings to the Torah there are on any given Jewish holiday. The more Aliyot there are for each day, the more holy it is. Weekday Torah readings have three Aliyot; Rosh Hodesh has four Aliyot; Passover, Shavuot, Sukkot, Rosh HaShanah have five Aliyot; Yom Kippur when it falls on a weekday has six Aliyot; and Shabbat is the only day with seven Aliyot! Therefore, you are indeed correct—Shabbat is the holiest day of the Jewish calendar, and it comes every week.

Question number 6*: Why are we not supposed to touch or handle money on Shabbat? Who made this a rule?*

Answer: The prohibition of handling money actually does not come from the Torah but rather stems from the biblical prohibition against doing business on Shabbat (see Nehemiah 13:15-22). Therefore, the handling of money is prohibited as an additional restriction to prevent the accidental conduct of business on Shabbat.

Now the reason that business is prohibited is that on Shabbat, Jews are commanded to emulate God's activities as described in the Torah (see Genesis 2:1-4). Because God ceased from all creative, productive activity on Shabbat, so too are we, the Jewish people, supposed to cease from all creative, productive weekday activities on Shabbat. The clearest definition of what defines our regular workweek is whatever we do for our regular business that we do during the week. Therefore, Shabbat should be a different special day of rest and holiness. And what better way to emphasize and observe this distinction than by refraining from the single most characteristic weekday activity there is—shopping! Although many people find shopping recreational and relaxing, it is predicated on doing business; therefore, the rabbis of the Talmud added the use of money to the list of prohibited activities on Shabbat. This prohibition against the use of money and shopping is also related to the restriction against writing on Shabbat because in ancient times—and even today—nearly all purchases involved the writing or printing of some sort of receipt. Therefore, using money was an additional stricture to prevent people from writing as well! These rabbinic rulings were established over two thousand years ago in order to help Jews enjoy Shabbat free from the distractions of weekday activities.

Question number 7: *I am moving into my first apartment and living on my own for the first time ever. This might sound funny, but growing up, it was always my mother who lit the Shabbat candles on Friday nights. One time I tried to light the candles, but my grandmother told me that lighting the Shabbat candles is a "woman's job." My father then told me that if no women are present to light the candles, I am exempt from having to light Shabbat candles. My question is should I light candles myself in my apartment on Friday nights because no women will be present, or am I really exempt from having to light Shabbat candles as a single man living on my own?*

Answer: Far be it from me to disagree with your grandmother or your father! But in this case, they are both wrong. Rather, this is a clear difference between folk Judaism—the customs and rituals assumed to be ancient, authentic unchangeable laws—and actual Halachah, Jewish law as created and passed down through the centuries by the rabbis and scholars the way they intended it to actually be practiced.

In this case, everyone—male and female alike—has the exact same obligation to light Shabbat candles. This Mitzvah, or commandment, is incumbent upon all Jews regardless of their gender. Therefore, you should light your own Shabbat candles every Shabbat. That is the Mitzvah; it is irrelevant who actually lights them. And when your mom, sisters, or grandmother or other women friends or family visit, let them light the candles.

The reason that this myth began about only women being able to light the Shabbat candles is that for so many centuries, women have been excluded from many Jewish rituals and customs so that the few things they were permitted to do in traditional Jewish law became sacrosanct. Also, because it was assumed in ancient times that men would be praying in the synagogue on Friday night around candle-lighting time, the women were the only ones at home to actually light the Shabbat candles at the right time. That is the history behind the myth that only women could light Shabbat candles. Now you know better. Enjoy your Shabbat candle lighting in your new apartment!

Question number 8: *Why is the Challah bread loaves that we eat on Friday nights braided?*

Answer: One symbolic reason is that braided Challah represents the intertwining of God, the Torah, and the people of Israel together in a single unified whole. Or like a Havdalah candle, the braided wick candle used to mark the conclusion of Shabbat on Saturday night, it represents the intertwining of Shabbat and the weekdays and how the holiness of Jewish time weaves in and out of the regular workweek pattern of our lives.

For a more academic answer, in the book *Jewish Magic and Superstition*, Joshua Trachtenberg writes very convincingly that braided bread loaves in the Jewish tradition came from premedieval Germany. Their origin is actually in Germanic pagan cultic practices. When ancient German tribes developed and eventually moved away from actual child sacrifices to their pagan gods, they burned the braided hair of young virgins that they cut off when they reached the age of menstruation as a substitute for the young girls themselves. Eventually over time, instead of actually burning the hair of these girls, they instead offered bread that had been baked in the shape of braided hair. After they eventually stopped even offering these braided loaves of bread as sacrifices to their gods or perhaps with the advent of Christianity, the German people kept baking braided bread this way because these ancient traditions can take on a life of their own. Even later, when Jews moved into the Rhineland and other areas of modern Germany well over a thousand years ago, they adopted this local custom of baking braided loaves of bread and kept it alive in Jewish rituals. While the rest of the German people eventually gave up this medieval practice, the Jews adopted it as their own, and it became associated with Friday night Challah loaves. Fascinating if true! But who really knows?

Question number 9: *What's the best way to blow a Shofar?*

Answer: In the immortal words of Lauren Bacall in the film *To Have and Have Not*, "Just put your lips together and blow." But seriously, learning to blow a Shofar is not that difficult. But it takes some experimentation and practice, like learning any musical instrument. However, it cannot easily be described by e-mail. I recommend that you find someone who can instruct you in person such as a cantor or rabbi of a local synagogue. Good luck!

Question number 10: *Can you please give me a brief history on the Shofar and why, when, and how it is used? I'm especially interested in the different calls and patterns of the sounds. Thank you.*

Answer: The Shofar is a hornlike musical instrument similar to a trumpet that is fashioned literally from the horn of either a ram or gazelle. The Shofar is mentioned nearly seventy times in the Hebrew Bible. Some of the places it is mentioned are in connection with the proclamation of the Jubilee year: "Sound the Shofar . . . and proclaim liberty throughout the land unto all the inhabitants thereof" (Leviticus 25:9-10). This verse is also inscribed on the Liberty Bell in Philadelphia. The Shofar was used to announce the new Jewish year of Rosh HaShanah (Numbers 29:1) as a musical instrument in the ancient Temple in Jerusalem (Psalm 98:6) and as a call to war (Judges 3:12ff). It is currently used in Jewish practice during the Hebrew month of Elul, the month before Rosh HaShanah. The Shofar is blown every morning during regular weekday services each day of the Hebrew month of Elul as spiritual preparation for the Jewish New Year to usher in the season of repentance. It is also blown on Rosh HaShanah itself in celebration of the new year and to inspire awe and reverence.

The Shofar is used to make four distinct calls in modern Jewish liturgy. Two of these sounds were mentioned in the Hebrew Bible, and the last two were derived through interpretation by the Talmudic rabbis over two thousand years ago. The call known as Tekiah is a long blast (Numbers 10:5-8), and the Teruah is a set of three short wavering blasts. The third call of Shevarim is a blast of at least nine staccato notes. The final note, "Tekiah Gedolah," literally means "a big or long Tekiah call," one long blast held as long as the Shofar blower can sustain. The ancient rabbis debated the meaning of these names and exactly how they should be sounded in detail, but ultimately, the calls that we now use and hear were a result of these discussions and debates long ago. All of these calls are sounded throughout Rosh HaShanah in specific series so as to add up to one hundred Shofar calls each day of the holiday. And at the end of Yom Kippur, one long note is sounded to signal the end of the holiday and the fast.

Question number 11: What are the prohibitions and restrictions for Yom Kippur?

Answer: They are exactly the same as the traditional thirty-nine major categories of forbidden activities on Shabbat that were established by the rabbis in the Talmud over two thousand years ago. Since Yom Kippur is called the Sabbath of Sabbaths, it is observed just like Shabbat, however, with just a few more thrown in that focus on the unique themes and observances of the Day of Atonement. First of all, here are the Talmudic forbidden categories of activities on Shabbat that includes other actions that may be similar to them as well:

1. Plowing—leveling or preparing ground for planting, including digging for any reason
2. Sowing—promoting the growth of plants, including watering them
3. Reaping—detaching fruit or vegetables from their roots, stalks, or branches
4. Sheaf-making—gathering produce together in piles
5. Threshing—removing a husk or shell from nuts, fruits, or vegetables unless for immediate consumption
6. Winnowing—removing less desirable parts from a fruit, nut, or vegetable unless for immediate consumption
7. Selecting—picking out better, more appetizing fruits or vegetables from a pile
8. Sifting—systematically removing bad or inedible parts from food
9. Grinding—crushing fresh pepper, grinding coffee, grating cheese, and other such activities
10. Kneading—mixing a liquid with a dry powder to form a dough mixture
11. Baking—cooking anything as well as boiling or roasting
12. Sheep-shearing—cutting your own hair or fingernails
13. Bleaching—soaking clothes, rubbing, and wringing to remove stains
14. Combing raw materials—preparing raw wool to make yarn and thread
15. Dyeing—adding food coloring or painting a picture or even applying makeup
16. Spinning—making thread, string, or rope
17. Weaving—knitting, crocheting, embroidering, and even braiding hair
18. Making two loops (part of sewing or weaving, any sewing activity)
19. Weaving two threads together (any sewing activity)
20. Separating into threads (any preparation for sewing)
21. Tying a knot (refers only to permanent knots, so you can tie your shoelaces)

22. Untying a knot (and yes, you can take off your shoes as well by undoing the laces because this only refers to permanent knots)
23. Sewing—either making something new or repairing a garment
24. Tearing (includes cloth, any kind of garment, or even paper)
25. Trapping or hunting of any kind of animal, fish, or insect
26. Slaughtering—killing of any kind of animal, fish, or insect
27. Skinning—separating the skin of a dead animal from the carcass
28. Tanning—making raw materials more durable, including pickling food or even oiling boots
29. Scraping pelts—removing any roughness from a material, including scrubbing pots and pans
30. Marking out—marking any surface for either writing or cutting
31. Cutting to shape—cutting or tearing a material into a pattern
32. Writing—making any signs on any material, including writing, drawing, painting, typing, and printing
33. Erasing—removing any signs on any material including wiping a chalk or dry erase board
34. Building—making any kind of structure, including hammering a nail or putting up a tent
35. Demolishing—knocking down a structure or clearing space to prepare for future building
36. Kindling a fire—lighting a flame, poking a fire, regulating a flame or stove top burner, putting wood on a fire, smoking a cigarette
37. Extinguishing—putting out any kind of already burning material unless there is a potential loss of life
38. Striking the final hammer blow—putting the finishing touch to a newly manufactured article and can include any activity that makes something that was previously useable ready to be used on Shabbat
39. Carrying from the private to the public domain and vice versa—carrying objects in one's pocket, over the arm, by hand, in a bag or case for instance from your home to the synagogue

Of course, none of these restrictions apply if there is any danger to someone's life, for saving and preserving a life takes precedence over any and all Jewish ritual concerns. If you can believe it, there are even more restrictions and special cases in addition to these thirty-nine categories listed above, and there are literally hundreds if not thousands of books about the Shabbat in Jewish law. However, this is the basic outline of prohibited activities on Shabbat as defined by the rabbis in the Talmud nearly two thousand years ago.

As for Yom Kippur, all of these restrictions above apply no matter when Yom Kippur happens to fall during the week either on Saturday, that is Shabbat, or a regular weekday. And it also includes five additional prohibitions that are unique to Yom Kippur and they are the following:

1. It is forbidden to eat or drink for the entire twenty-four hours of the day (actually, it is twenty-five hours because it begins at sunset of Yom Kippur and then concludes when you can see three stars in the sky the next night, which is about an hour after sundown).
2. It is forbidden to wear leather shoes.
3. It is forbidden to anoint oneself, that is, using cosmetics, perfume, or cologne.
4. It is forbidden to wash or bathe for pleasure except for hygiene.
5. It is forbidden to have sex with one's spouse.

There are many reasons offered by rabbis as to why we observe these particular abstentions on Yom Kippur, but one explanation of all of them is that we refrain from the regular activities of our lives that enable us to sustain our lives and live in comfort. By observing these five specific abstentions, we confront the fragility of our own mortal existence. In addition, refraining from these activities temporarily free us from our connections to the physical world and provide us an opportunity to raise ourselves to a higher spiritual level if only for one day. All year long, we rarely go for more than a few hours at a time without eating or drinking or longer than a day without bathing, wearing shoes, and applying perfumes and colognes. But Yom Kippur is the one single day out of the year when we purposely strive to acknowledge that we are more than our mere physical bodies. In addition to having a physical body that needs constant care and attention, we also possess a nonphysical, spiritual side that also needs nourishment and attention.

There are many more reasons that have been suggested for these five prohibitions that give Yom Kippur its unique character; however, the basic, underlying purpose is that these practices aid people in achieving a sense of spirituality and lending a feeling of otherness to the day even if it means feeling somewhat faint or light-headed from lack of food! But I should also conclude by pointing out that none of these five Yom Kippur restrictions apply if there is any danger or even suspicion that someone's health may be threatened. I hope this helps answer your question.

Question number 12: *What is the practice of fasting, and why is it practiced?*

Answer: Fasting is a sign of mourning and spiritual purification. The Hebrew Bible speaks of people who fasted in order to spiritually prepare themselves for difficult encounters in life, such as Queen Esther before she went to see the King of Persia without an invitation (Esther chapter 4) or King David when he was worried about the failing health of his sick infant son (2 Samuel chapter 12). In antiquity during times of drought, people fasted as a sign of communal penance and atonement in the hopes that God would send rain.

In modern religious practice, there are two main full-day, twenty-five-hour fasts in the Jewish calendar. One takes place during the summer in July or August depending upon the Hebrew calendar and commemorates the destruction of both of the ancient Temples in Jerusalem. This fast is called after the date it falls on in the Hebrew calendar—Tisha B'Av, or the ninth day of the Hebrew month of Av. This is the date that the First Temple was destroyed by the Babylonians in 586 BCE, and amazingly enough, it is also the same date that the Second Temple was destroyed by the Romans in 70 CE coincidentally! In this case, fasting is a sign of mourning and grief. The other full fast day takes place on the Jewish

High Holy Day of Yom Kippur, the Day of Atonement where it is clearly a practice of spiritual purification. Yom Kippur usually falls in the early fall of each year. These full-day fasts are actually twenty-five-hour fasts, slightly longer than a full day because they begin just before sundown of the day and then conclude with the appearance of stars in the sky on the evening of the next night.

There are also four other half-day fasts, that is, from-sunrise-to-sunset fasts in the Jewish calendar. Each of these half-day fasts commemorates historical events in Jewish history. The Fast of Gedalyah, which takes place in the fall the day after the festival of Rosh HaShanah, memorializes the assassination of Gedalyah, the last Jewish ruler of the just-conquered Kingdom of Judah. Jewish loyalists murdered Gedalyah after the Babylonians installed him as a puppet ruler after deposing and exiling the last Davidic king of Israel, Zedekiah. This happened in the middle of the sixth century BCE.

The fast of the tenth of Tevet marks the day that the Babylonians broke through the outer walls of Jerusalem in their siege of the Holy City in 586 BCE that ultimately led to the destruction of the First Temple and the exile of the Jewish king, nobility, and upper classes of the population of Judah. The fast of the seventeenth of Tammuz marks the day that the Romans broke through the outer walls of Jerusalem in their siege of the city in 70 CE that ultimately led to the destruction of the Second Temple and the end of biblical Judaism as it was practiced for over a thousand years. The final half-day fast is actually a custom instituted by the Talmudic rabbis to commemorate the fast of Queen Esther as described in the book of Esther. Before seeking an uninvited audience with the King of Persia, for which she could have lost her life, Esther fasted as a symbol of trying to curry divine favor (Esther 4:16). She ultimately succeeded and saved the Jews of Persia from a massacre.

These are the six public fasts in the Jewish tradition, meaning they are incumbent upon all Jews who choose to observe them. However, the Talmud lists a whole series of personal, private fasts for individual events in a person's life such as fasting the day of one's wedding up until the celebration or after the night of a bad dream. I hope this answers your questions about fasting in the Jewish tradition.

Question number 13: This is a question about Yom Kippur. I am currently breast-feeding my son and would like to know what are the rules about fasting for a nursing mother. On the one hand, it's only one day; but on the other hand, my son will not get proper nutrition for that day. I can give him a bottle, but it is rather inconvenient to prepare that much breast milk in advance. What is your opinion?

Answer: According to some ancient rabbinic authorities, a woman who had recently given birth was considered as if she was recovering from an illness and should be fed on Yom Kippur. And according to the Mishnah, one of the earliest compilations of rabbinic legal traditions, a sick person should be provided with food and water even if they claim they are feeling well enough to fast! This is because any matters of health and even doubtful concerns about health immediately override all ritual restrictions. However, some rabbis extended this definition to a woman who had recently given birth as being similar to someone recovering from an illness to only the first week or so after the birth of a child. After that, she is like everyone else as regards to fasting. Since you don't mention how old your breast-feeding son is, I don't know whether you fall into this category or not.

However, bear this in mind regarding your situation: all Jewish rituals are voluntary nowadays. If you want to fast or observe other traditional Jewish customs for Yom Kippur, then that is great, and I hope you derive much spiritual satisfaction from your commitment and practices. If you don't fast for whatever reason you find compelling, I'm not about to tell you that what you are practicing is right or wrong. If you want to find someone who will tell you exactly how you should live your Jewish life, there is no dearth of spiritual leaders who will be more than happy to dictate to you every single detail down to the smallest jot and tittle of how you should behave as a Jew in private and public. But I'm not one of them. I want to give you the resources to make up your own mind and decide for yourself. Therefore, this decision is ultimately yours to make.

My personal opinion is that any woman following childbirth who is still breast-feeding her child should obviously take the health of the child into account when making decisions about fasting. However, you yourself noted that it is only for one day, and there are other ways to continue to nourish your child with your breast milk without causing him to suffer as a result of your fasting. It may be inconvenient and annoying for you, but there are ways for you to fast and to still preserve the health of your child during this one day. On the other hand, if you feel that fasting would either be too burdensome for yourself or be detrimental to the health of your infant son, rest assured that there are plenty of Jewish legal sources that can be interpreted to apply to your situation, enabling you to continue to eat and drink on Yom Kippur. The bottom line is, according to a strict interpretation of traditional Jewish legal sources, you probably ought to fast. However, if you choose not to, there are plenty of sources to support that decision as well. Whatever you choose, I hope that you have a meaningful and spiritually fulfilling Yom Kippur!

Question number 14: *What does Kol Nidrei mean? And why is it chanted three times?*

Answer: The Kol Nidrei prayer that is recited on the eve of the Jewish High Holy Day of Yom Kippur isn't really a prayer; it is a legal formula. It is very ancient, going back possibly to medieval Spain or before. Around the year 1492, many Jews felt coerced to convert to Christianity upon pain of death or to avoid expulsion. Therefore, many Jews converted simply to save their lives or possibly to continue their comfortable lives in Spain. Afterward, after the danger had passed or they had moved to other countries where they could openly practice Judaism again, many Jews wanted to return to and join the Jewish community. However, by converting to Christianity—even though it had been under pain of death or expulsion—they had violated the Jewish tradition by renouncing their faith. Therefore, this legal formula of Kol Nidrei was created and chanted before the evening services of Yom Kippur in order to allow these errant Jews to rejoin the Jewish community and pray with their fellow Jews on Yom Kippur.

"Kol Nidrei" literally means "all vows," and the text of the formula essentially states that any oaths that we have taken in the past year that are between us and God should be annulled and forgiven by God. However, I want to emphasize that this formula applies only to vows that affect no other human beings, only those vows between God and human beings. Kol Nidrei is used to exempt us from the personal, private promises and vows we made to ourselves or to God, perhaps such as breaking a diet or violating some Jewish religious ritual or not living up to a personal goal.

This legal formula of Kol Nidrei was considered necessary in earlier times because the Jewish tradition takes language and words very seriously. When we make a vow, not only do we back it up with our word of honor; but in the eyes of the tradition, if we violate that vow, we have also violated Jewish law! Therefore, vows and promises are taken very seriously, and we can only dissolve these commitments by being forgiven by God. This is the purpose of Kol Nidrei. It is chanted three times because this is the normal procedure with Jewish legal rites to ensure that they take effect and that no mistake was made in any of the recitations.

The language of Kol Nidrei is Aramaic that was once long ago the common tongue of Jews in ancient times. Because it is a legal formula, it must be recited before Yom Kippur actually begins as it is forbidden to conduct legal matters on a Jewish holiday. Hence, Kol Nidrei services always begin just before sundown on the evening of Yom Kippur. The Talit is also worn to heighten the dramatic effect of the recitation of Kol Nidrei. Although the Talit is never worn at nighttime Jewish prayer services, because Kol Nidrei is recited before sundown, it is still the daytime; and thus, it is still permitted to wear the Talit. However, we continue to wear it for the rest of the evening so as not to appear anxious to take off such a holy garment. It is the only night of the year when we wear a Talit in the evening.

Question number 15: *What does Hoshanah Rabbah mean, and what is it about?*

Answer: "Hoshanah Rabbah" is Aramaic for the great Hoshanah, and the Hebrew word "Hoshanah" means "Please save us"! Hoshanot is the name for special religious poems we recite on each day of the festival of Sukkot, when worshippers take up their Lulav, which is the palm branch with willow and myrtle branches, and Etrog, which is a citron fruit, and make a circular procession around the sanctuary singing a different Hoshanah poem for each day of the Sukkot holiday. Hoshanah Rabbah is the last day of the Sukkot festival and is a special minor holiday by itself.

On Hoshanah Rabbah, worshippers circle the sanctuary seven times singing all seven Hoshanot poems from the previous seven days of the holiday. At the end, the three willow branches of the Lulav or a new bunch of five willow branches are taken and thrashed on the floor five times. The practical and symbolic effect is that just as the branches lose their leaves during the thrashing, so too do we strive to rid ourselves of our sins. Hoshanah Rabbah is considered a mini-Yom Kippur, and some parts of the Jewish tradition claim that our spiritual judgment is ultimately concluded on Hoshanah Rabbah even though it falls nearly two weeks after Yom Kippur.

Because the practices of Hoshanah Rabbah are so detailed and complicated, I urge you to contact a local rabbi who may be able to explain these customs in greater detail. An excellent book that will give you a very sophisticated and detailed explanation of what to do for Hoshanah Rabbah is *A Guide to Jewish Religious Practice* by Rabbi Isaac Klein or *The Jewish Holidays* by Michael Strassfeld.

Question number 16: *Are you only allowed to get only one present on Hanukkah every night, or is it as many presents as your parents give you each night?*

Answer: Since giving presents on Hanukkah is not even a Jewish custom, your family can follow whatever custom you want. Jews only give gifts on Hanukkah in America because the Jewish community has been influenced by the Christian custom of giving gifts on Christmas. Since Christmas often falls close to Hanukkah, this custom rubbed off on the Jewish community. Some families give one a night, other families give only one gift on the first night, and some do not give any gifts at all! I also know some families who don't give each other gifts but instead make it a practice to give Tzedakah, or charity or money or practical items to charitable organizations to the needy. So consider yourself lucky that your family practices gift giving on Hanukkah at all!

Question number 17: During this Christmas season, I have several Jewish friends, and I'd like to give them a holiday gift. I am not Jewish, so I would appreciate any advice about what would be appropriate and tasteful to let them know that they are special to me.

Answer: Because the practice of giving gifts on Christmas or Hanukkah—or any other Jewish holiday—is an alien custom in the Jewish tradition, there are no traditional or even thematically appropriate gifts to give to Jews on any particular holiday except the holiday of Purim, which falls in the early spring; but that is a different story altogether.

Rather, the traditional way that Jews pay homage to one another is to make charitable donations to causes that the person being honored finds important. So my advice to you is to try to determine what charitable organizations your friends support and make a donation in their name or figure out what causes they are passionate about and donate some money to an organization that supports that cause. Most charitable organizations usually send a card to the person informing them that a monetary gift has been made in their name. Rather than give someone a gift they may or may not need or even want, use your money to bring some real good into this world—help fight homelessness, poverty, and hunger or a terminal or debilitating disease or support a worthy political cause. That is an appropriate holiday gift for anyone!

Question number 18: *I recently read an interesting story about the legend of Hanukkah. It had something to do with Judah Maccabee fighting the Greeks and capturing the sacred Temple in Jerusalem and finding only a single flagon of holy olive oil used to light the Menorah. When did this happen? Did the Menorah have seven branches or nine like modern Hanukkah Menorahs? And did the light in the Menorah last for eight days straight? I am confused by this story and would appreciate an accurate version. Thank you.*

Answer: The story that you are referring to is found in the Babylonian Talmud Tractate Shabbat 21b and reads as follows:

> What is Hanukkah? Our rabbis taught on the twenty-fifth of Kislev, these eight days of Hanukkah (we) are not (to give) eulogies on them and not to fast on them; for when the Greeks entered the sanctuary, they defiled all of the oil that was in the sanctuary. But when the kingdom of the house of the Hasmoneans was victorious, they checked and did not find except one jug of oil that had on it the seal of the High Priest (to attest to its purity) and there was not in it enough except for one day. A miracle was performed and they kindled from it for eight days. The next (year), they established them (these days) and made them holidays with Psalms of Praise.

This is the entire story of the Hanukkah miracle of oil. Everything else is later embellishments, explanations, and interpretations by other people. This is the only source for this story of the jug of oil. For more details about the military victories of the Maccabees, whose real family name was the Hasmoneans, you can read extensive details in the books of the Maccabees that unfortunately are not part of the Hebrew Bible. Rather, they are found in a volume of ancient postbiblical works called the Apocrypha. However, these books, while they detail the military story of the Maccabees, make no mention of the story of the jug of oil. The tale of Hanukkah as you describe in your question is actually an amalgam of these two different literary sources—one is the story of the military victory of the Maccabees, and the other is the Talmudic story of the miracle of the oil.

As for your other questions, there do indeed seem to be some details that are missing in the Talmudic story. For example, the story indicates that the oil that the Maccabees burned in the Menorah only lasted one night. Back then, the Menorah that the Maccabees was lighting had seven branches as that was the official lampstand of the ancient Temple to enable the priests to attend to their duties at night. The story omits some details that in ancient times everyone simply already knew, namely, that the little jug of oil was poured into all seven braches of the Menorah; all of the seven lights burned for that one evening and then went out in all seven branches toward the morning as happened every night. The next night, the Maccabees then refilled the Menorah oil cups with oil from the same little jug that they thought was empty, but it turned out there was just enough to light all seven of the Menorah branches for another night. And the same thing happened for eight nights in a row. The miracle was that the little jug of oil had enough in it to fill and keep the Menorah light eight nights in a row—not burning continuously as you and probably others have assumed due to the lack of details in this Talmudic story. And the Menorah in the story only had seven branches, one for each day of the week as described in the Torah. Our modern-day Hanukkiyah candle stands have nine branches as they were created specifically to celebrate this story of the Maccabees—one branch to commemorate each night of the miracle of the oil and a special ninth candle stand called a Shamash, or servant or helper candle, that is used to light the other eight candles. I hope I cleared up some of your misunderstandings about the Hanukkah story!

Question number 19: I recently learned that the miracle of the oil in the Hanukkah story was made up a long time ago. If this is so, why do we even bother to light the candles and say a blessing that implies that God had something to do with this made-up event? Also, the blessing over the candle lighting implies that God gave us the commandment to kindle the lights of Hanukkah. I can appreciate the miracle of the spiritual and

military victory of the holiday without the farce of lighting the candles. I
have been disturbed about this for some time. Please help me understand.
I want to believe again in the miracle of the Hanukkah story!

Answer: The lighting of the Hanukkah Menorah, which is more
accurately called a Hanukkiyah, is not a farce; it has profound spiritual
and religious significance. While I can appreciate your sense of letdown
at learning of the more likely historical events underlying this story, I
urge you to reconsider the historical elements that led to the Talmudic
rabbis shifting the focus of the Hanukkah story from that of a military
victory to that of a divine miracle of a cruse of oil. Here are the main
points of the historical reality behind the popular Hanukkah story:

1. The Maccabees did indeed fight a war against the Syrian
    Greeks called the Seleucids from 167 to 163 BCE, and Judah
    Maccabee did indeed cleanse the holy Temple in Jerusalem of
    pagan, non-Jewish idols and forms of worship. The Maccabees
    did indeed hold an eight-day celebration of their military victory
    that was also a rededication of the Temple to Jewish worship.
    This is the basic story of Hanukkah as is popularly known.
2. However, what Jewish children in Sunday school are often
    not taught is that after peace had been reestablished with the
    Seleucid Greeks after the Maccabean rebellion, the Maccabees
    refused to retire their arms. They kept the elements of their
    guerilla army intact and continued the war as a civil war against
    the Seleucid Greeks and Hellenized, or Greek-influenced, Jews
    in Jerusalem. This civil war lasted eight more years; and only the
    last Maccabee son, Shimon, was left alive of the original family
    that initiated the rebellion. But he eventually seized control of
    Jerusalem, declared himself Ethnarch (which means political
    leader of the Jewish community) as well as the Greek title of
    Strategos (head of the Jewish army) and finally Kohen Gadol
    (Jewish high priest). Shimon Hasmon, the last of the Maccabees,
    then commissioned an official history of their victory called the
    Book of Maccabees or, as it is now referred to, 1 Maccabees. It
    was unabashedly pro-Maccabean because they paid for it, and

therefore, it is pure propaganda. But as the closest literary source to the actual events, it is probably very accurate in its depiction of events.

3. The Jewish loyalists who had fought with the Maccabees against the Seleucid Greeks who called themselves Hasidim—the original Jews to use this term—were scandalized by Shimon Maccabee and his descendants for seizing for themselves both spiritual and temporal powers, that is, claiming the title of both king and high priest. They essentially believed in a kind of separation of church and state or perhaps Temple and kingdom! These Hasidim formed a new political party in opposition to the Maccabees called the Pharisees that literally means, "the Separatists." These Pharisees over time eventually evolved into the rabbis who wrote the Mishnah and Talmud—and they kept their hatred for the Maccabees alive. After all, the Maccabees in their eyes had committed blasphemy by combining the powers of the kingship with that of the priesthood.

4. Over the next one hundred years that this independent Maccabean kingdom existed, the Maccabees—that is, Shimon and his sons and grandsons—used their military might to expand the Jewish kingdom, forcibly converting conquered peoples, such as the neighboring Idumeans, to Judaism and waging unremitting war against their other neighbors. They epitomized the worst in military dictatorship and religious authoritarianism. The more successful the Maccabees became, the wealthier and more Hellenistic, or Greek influenced, they became. Although they had begun by opposing Hellenism, they ended up becoming the single most powerful Hellenizing force in Jewish society. They ended up being just as Hellenistic and Greek as the Seleucids that they had once fought against.

5. Eventually, due to internal political intrigues, the Maccabean Kingdom became weakened and was eventually conquered by the Romans; and by the time the rabbis wrote the Talmud, the land of Israel had known tremendous loss of life and destruction due to several vainglorious military rebellions against the much more powerful Roman Empire. The martial memories of the

Maccabees were no longer seen as reminders of a glorious past but dangerous, seditious influences that must be suppressed at all costs to ensure the tenuous peace between the Jews and Rome. The rabbis were afraid to glorify a martial past while still occupied and oppressed by a militarily dominant Rome.

6. The rabbis probably invented the myth of the cruse of oil, and it served to obscure the truth about Hanukkah for centuries. The Talmudic rabbis may have deliberately concealed the military narrative and Hellenistic causes of Hanukkah in order to maintain the holiday but shifted its focus away from the Maccabees and on God and more religious themes out of a greater need to ensure the survival of the Jewish people in the land of Israel. They co-opted the holiday of Hanukkah by eviscerating its true military origins and replacing them with more acceptable passive religious themes. This was the only way that they could ensure Jewish survival. And indeed, if that meant obscuring the bellicose origins of the holiday, they felt that Jewish survival was worth it.

Perhaps this is what you might keep in mind this next Hanukkah when you are tempted to think of Hanukkah as a farce. The story of the miracle of oil might be imaginative history, but it has true spiritual significance and importance. I hope my answer at least provided a context for appreciating the story of Hanukkah and our celebration of it over the centuries.

Question number 20: *Is it okay to use a Hanukkiyah on a night other than Hanukkah?*

Answer: I can't tell you what to do or not to do with your Hanukkiyah. However, if you were willing to take direction from me, my answer would be no. The Hanukkiyah should be reserved for use only on Hanukkah. To use it on another occasion is to diminish the special nature of the Hanukkiyah, just like we do not blow the Shofar on other days apart from Rosh HaShanah just for fun, build a Sukkah in the spring because it is more pleasant to be outside then. Or in nonreligious terms, we don't often bake and serve a wedding cake at an ordinary party just for fun. Certain objects and acts are special and sacred because they are reserved only for their special days. That way they retain their unique symbolic meanings and emotional significance in our lives.

Question number 21: I have often wondered why, if the Jewish people received the Torah on Mt. Sinai on the holiday of Shavuot, we complete the reading of the Torah and begin reading it again on the holiday of Simchat Torah, which comes after the holiday of Sukkot four months later.

Answer: You ask an excellent question! Why don't we finish the Torah reading and begin again on Shavuot? To answer your question with another similar logical question, why don't we end and begin the Torah reading on Rosh HaShanah, the new Jewish year, which would make even better sense?

The answer? It is possible that perhaps once in early Jewish history that is exactly what happened. Perhaps some Jewish communities did indeed begin and end the yearly Torah reading cycle on Shavuot, the anniversary of the giving of the Torah on Mt. Sinai. But the early, possibly medieval, rabbis wanted to make the beginning and ending of the Torah reading a special and unique day unto itself. By finishing and beginning the reading of the Torah on Shavuot, this joyous act of completion and renewal would overshadow the unique historical and agricultural themes of the holiday of Shavuot. Doing the same thing on Rosh HaShanah would also take away from the themes of repentance and self-examination during the High Holy Days. Simchat Torah, a holiday that falls at the end of the seven days of Sukkot, which is the fall harvest festival, provides an opportunity and a holiday to celebrate this event without detracting from Sukkot or any other holiday.

In fact, Simchat Torah only became its own semiholiday about a thousand years ago. It used to be just the second day of the festival of Shemini Atzeret, a holiday that falls at the end of Sukkot. However, during the

Middle Ages in Europe, ancient Jewish sources started referring to this day as Simchat Torah and described all kinds of new special rituals to mark the conclusion and beginning of the reading of the Torah. So Simchat Torah kind of had a spontaneous origin among the Jewish people in early medieval times and not as a planned-out or divinely commanded celebration from the Torah or even the Talmud.

Question number 22: What is the Halachah regarding working on the holiday of Shavuot? Are there Shabbat-like restrictions?

Answer: According to the Mishnah (Megillah 1:5), the only difference between Shabbat and a Yom Tov or a Jewish holiday is the preparation of food. The holidays that the Mishnah is referring to are Pesach, Shavuot, Sukkot, and Rosh HaShanah. As you are probably aware, there are thirty-nine major categories of activities that are prohibited on Shabbat that cover a full range of human productive activities. The purpose for restricting all of these activities was to emulate God—just as God rested from creation of the world on the seventh day, so too are the Jewish people supposed to rest and cease from all productive activities on Shabbat. Jewish holidays are very similar to Shabbat but somewhat different.

According to the rabbis of the Talmud, on Jewish holidays that do not fall on Shabbat, we are permitted to bake and engage in all kinds of food preparation as well as carry objects from public to private domains and vice versa. This is because the rabbis felt that it was part of the delight and joy of the holidays to be able to cook and eat freshly prepared food on the holidays, especially since nearly all of these Jewish festivals are two-day holidays. While it is relatively easy to cook all of your meals for Shabbat in advance, it is somewhat more challenging to cook all of your meals for a two-day Jewish holiday in advance. Therefore, cooking was permitted so that the Jewish holidays would truly be joyful and pleasant with hot, freshly cooked meals.

However, even though it is permitted to bake and cook food on Jewish holidays, the rabbis still did not allow the indiscriminate lighting and extinguishing of fires. Therefore, when cooking on a holiday, the stove top burners are traditionally left on; and although they can be adjusted in their heat, they should not be turned off and on. The same is true for ovens as well. Also, fire can be transferred from flame to flame but not ignited anew or extinguished. Therefore, on two-day holidays, we light the second-day set of evening holiday candles from the already burning flame of a twenty-four-hour Yahrzeit or memorial candle that was lit just before the holiday candles on the first night.

And to facilitate socializing and to encourage people to organize communal holiday meals, the rabbis also permitted the carrying of objects during the holiday such as dishes of food and so on. And since we can carry food on the holidays, the rabbis also permitted other items to be carried, like the Lulav and Etrog for Sukkot and the Shofar on Rosh HaShanah. That is why these objects can be brought to the synagogue and used on the holidays, but not on Shabbat when we are not permitted to carry. I know what I am describing may seem like a collection of lots of complicated little details, but it is helpful to have a full picture of what and why the rabbis in the Talmud permitted what they did for holidays.

Question number 23: My daughter is planning a wedding next year sometime in the spring. I recall learning once that there is a period of time in the spring in which Jewish weddings should not be scheduled. When is this period of time, and what is it all about?

Answer: The period of time you are referring to is called Sefirat HaOmer, or in English, "the counting of the Omer." This is a period of seven weeks immediately following the first day of Pesach until the festival of Shavuot. For historical reasons, this was considered a period of national mourning for the Jewish people during which time it was considered inappropriate to celebrate weddings or schedule festive private celebrations. In fact, many traditional Jewish men grow beards during this time, which is a sign of mourning.

The reason this is considered a sad time in the Jewish calendar is that in ancient times, the Romans, upon defeating a Jewish rebellion led by the Jewish general Bar Kochba in 135 CE, instituted a series of persecutions aimed at the Jewish people; and they came into force during this period of time. One of the persecutory proclamations forbid the teaching of Torah upon pain of death; however, a number of prominent rabbis were publicly tortured and executed for violating this decree. Later on in medieval times, many of the Crusades launched by Christian knights to liberate the Holy Land from Muslims ended up leading to the slaughter and destruction of numerous Jewish communities throughout Europe. All of these tragic events occurred precisely at this season of the counting of the Omer in between Pesach and Shavuot.

However, there is a tradition that the Jewish rebel leader Bar Kochba and his forces achieved a minor military victory against the Romans at this same time, and another tradition claims that a plague that was ravaging the Jewish people at this same time during the Roman persecutions finally ended on the thirty-third day of this period of the Omer. Therefore, for this one single day during the counting of the Omer, the mourning practices are temporarily suspended. This day is called Lag B'Omer because the word "Lag" is a word made up of Hebrew letters that stand for the number 33. It is just a coincidence that it is the word "lag" in English, like to lag behind or tarry. According to some Jewish traditions, on the thirty-third day of the Omer and following all the way up to the festival of Shavuot, it is permitted to celebrate weddings and other happy occasions. Therefore, I encourage you to consult with the officiating rabbi at your daughter's wedding and inquire about these dates. In either case, Mazal Tov in advance!

Question number 24*: I recently read in a guide to synagogue customs that the fifteenth day of Av is listed as a partial Jewish holiday. I can find no reference to that date. What is this holiday?*

Answer: The fifteenth of the Hebrew month of Av, along with Yom Kippur, was actually considered a happy Jewish holiday! It says in the Mishnah the following:

Rabban Gamliel said: There were no greater days than the fifteenth of Av and Yom Kippur. For on them, the daughters of Israel would wear white clothes, or lend them to those who didn't have any . . . and go out into the vineyards and say, "Young man, raise your eyes and look! Whom do you choose? Look not upon beauty, but rather, cast your eyes upon family (background) . . . beauty is vain, and prettiness is empty." (Mishnah Ta'anit 4:8)

In other words, this was a Talmudic Jewish version of Sadie Hawkins Day where young Jewish men and women would meet outside in the fields to socialize and to hopefully find a bride or a groom! This is why it is considered a semiholiday even though this practice probably ceased centuries ago.

Chapter 12

Pesach (Fourteen Questions)

The Jewish holiday of Passover, or Pesach in Hebrew, merits its own separate chapter due to the complexity involved in two major areas related to its observance. The first area of complexity relates to the myriad rituals, details, customs, and specific laws that pertain to the celebration of the Seder meals. Pesach celebrates the exodus of the Israelites from slavery in Egypt over three thousand years ago, and the first two evenings of the holiday (or only the first evening if you live in Israel) is devoted to the retelling of this event complete with its own script called a Haggadah, derived from the word "to tell," and the eating of symbolic ritual foods related to the story of the exodus. These scripted holiday meals are so complex and richly detailed that the very name Seder is Hebrew for order to ensure all of the rites and traditions are followed in their proper order. I received so many questions about the Pesach Seder meals that I wrote and posted a special guide about the Pesach Seder online in an effort to proactively anticipate future questions. It is no longer available on the Internet; however, I have included it as "Appendix B: A Guide to the Pesach Seder" at the end of this book. In fact, I would encourage anyone who is not familiar with Pesach and the Seder rituals to read it first so as to better understand the questions and answers in this chapter.

The second area of complexity related to Pesach deals with an additional set of dietary laws of Kashrut that are unique to this holiday.

For the eight days of Passover (or seven if you live in Israel or adhere to the Reform movement's calendar of holidays), Jews are prohibited from eating any food that contains the five grains of wheat, barley, rye, oats, and spelt (grains considered native to the land of Israel) that have been leavened with yeast. These foods are collectively called Hametz, or just leavened foods. According to the Torah, during this one-week holiday that usually falls in the early spring, observant Jews are prohibited from eating food that contains Hametz. In simple terms, it means no bread, crackers, or pastries for a week—only Matzah, or unleavened bread that is ironically enough made from wheat, but it is not leavened with yeast. Therefore, for one long week out of the year, many religiously observant Jews turn their homes inside and out in order to adhere to these strict and complicated dietary laws. For Jews who take the laws of Kashrut seriously and for those who also observe the additional dietary laws of Pesach, it can be quite a challenge to shop for and then cook an entire week's worth of Pesach festival meals, avoiding any foods with Hametz in it. This has given rise to an entire industry of Kosher-for-Pesach foods and special Kosher certifications for these kinds of foods as well.

For these two reasons, all questions about Pesach are grouped together here in this chapter rather than being scattered throughout the chapter dealing with Kashrut or other Jewish holidays. I hope that this organization makes it easer to locate and understand the unique facets of the Jewish holiday of Pesach. The questions and answers in this chapter begin with general questions about Pesach and then focus on more detail-oriented questions about the Seder meal and the laws of Kosher-for-Pesach food.

Question number 1: What criterion determines when Pesach occurs from year to year?

Answer: Pesach always falls on the fifteenth day of the Hebrew month of Nisan. Because the Jewish calendar is based on the moon and lunar cycles, it is fairly consistent. It is actually only our secular Gregorian calendar that is based only on the sun that messes up the keeping track of the lunar year.

However, Pesach must always fall during the spring as it says in the Torah, "Observe the month of Aviv (spring) and keep the Pesach to the Lord your God" (Deuteronomy 16:1). However, because the Jewish calendar is a lunar calendar, the Jewish holidays fall behind the solar calendar by eleven days because the lunar year is eleven days shorter than a solar year. However, the Jewish calendar is adjusted to the solar seasons; therefore, every three to four years there is a Jewish leap year in which we add in one extra month. At that time, the Jewish holidays are then suddenly thrust forward and observed a full month later than they were the previous year. Therefore, the Jewish holidays basically slowly fall back or begin earlier for a few years and are then thrown forward and begin later by one month every three to four years.

In terms of Pesach, it always falls around the springtime; but as mentioned above, every year it begins to fall eleven days earlier each year for a few years until an extra Jewish leap month is added into the calendar. And it is then celebrated a full month later the next year and begins this slow and subtle shifting through the Gregorian calendar in an endless cycle. So whenever you want to know when Pesach starts, don't try to figure this out at home—check a Jewish calendar!

Question number 2: *I am confused—do we celebrate Pesach for seven or eight days?*

Answer: It says in the Torah to celebrate Pesach seven days, "Seven days you shall eat Matzah" (Exodus 12:15). However, in ancient times, the dates of Jewish holidays were established by direct observation of the phases of the moon. When Jews in the Diaspora lived too far away from the land of Israel to receive word as to when exactly to observe the Jewish festivals based on direct observations of the cycles of the moon, the rabbis of the Talmud decided to add an additional day of celebration to all Jewish holidays to be on the safe side. That is, if the Jews who lived far away from Israel observed two days of every Jewish holiday, then at least one of the days was bound to fall on the actual date of the holiday as determined by the cycle of the moon. So all over the world—except in Israel—Pesach is observed for eight days.

In the modern State of Israel, for nearly one hundred years, Jews have returned to observing only one day of each Jewish holiday as a powerful symbolic statement that the Jewish people have returned to their ancestral homeland and no longer live in the Diaspora, far away from the original homeland of the Israelites. Therefore, in Israel, Pesach is observed for only seven days. However, to further complicate the picture, the Reform movement in the United States and other countries around the world where there are Reform temples decided that since the Jews of Israel have returned to this ancient custom, there is no reason for other Jews living in the Diaspora to continue observing two days of every Jewish holiday either. Besides, it is a burden to keep all of the holidays for twice as long. So therefore, most Jews affiliated with the Reform movement observe only seven days of Pesach, like the Jews of Israel. However, most traditional Jews outside of Israel—Conservative, Reconstructionist, and Orthodox Jews—continue to observe the ancient Diaspora custom of keeping eight days of Pesach. I hope that my answer did not confuse you more!

Question number 3: *Why do we burn Hametz before Pesach begins, and what is its purpose?*

Answer: Before Pesach begins, it is a commandment to get rid of all of our Hametz, or leavened food products, as it says in the Torah, "You shall put away leavened food from out of your houses" (Exodus 12:15). There are lots of ways to do this. First, we eat up as much of the leavened food products as we can that we happen to have in our kitchen in advance of the holiday. We can give it away to neighbors or to charitable food pantries, and we can even sell the remaining Hametz in our house to non-Jews. Then as a figurative completion of this removal, the night before Pesach, we do a symbolic search for the remaining crumbs of any leftover Hametz throughout our homes and find prepositioned pieces of bread that we then gather up. The next day, the morning of the eve of Pesach, we say a special formula and blessing that is found inside the Haggadah; and then we burn the little pieces of Hametz to symbolically demonstrate that we are getting rid of it entirely. This is why we burn the Hametz.

A more spiritual or sermonic explanation of this ritual is that the Hametz is symbolic of our puffed-up egos. After all, Hametz foods are derived from yeast-risen dough. While our egos can play healthy roles in our emotional and psychological lives, sometimes we all overindulge and get a little too full of ourselves, and our egos can get too puffed up than what is healthy. Therefore, every now and then, it is good and appropriate to practice some humility and acknowledge our modest individual roles in the grand scheme of human history. Getting rid of and burning the Hametz is a symbolic way to deflate our egos for a little while, and eating the flat bread of Matzah helps us acquire a more humble perspective of our lives. However, Hametz-based foods can be delicious, and there is no reason to deny ourselves these foods forever. Therefore, Pesach is a temporary abstention of these foods in service of a higher goal—not just serving God but reducing the size of our egos temporarily in the service of God in which we acknowledge our subservient position to the Divine. And this is also why we burn the Hametz before Pesach.

Question number 4: *Why do we have two Seders during Pesach? Is one more important than the other?*

Answer: No. We have two Seders because there are two festival days of Pesach at the beginning of this eight-day holiday. In other words, the first two days of Pesach are considered holy days or festivals followed by four semiholy intermediate days during which we still cannot eat bread, only Matzah. The last two days of Pesach are again festival days. Religious Jews do not work on these holy festival days on either the first two and last two days of the week of Pesach. They attend synagogue services and recite special prayers and read special selections about the holiday from the Torah. During the four intermediate days of Pesach, called Hol HaMoed in Hebrew that literally means the "regular days of the holiday," there are no boundaries on work and we resume our normal lives—except that the dietary restrictions of Pesach still apply.

In ancient times, there used to be only seven days of Pesach. Back then there was only one day of the Pesach festival at the beginning and one day of festival at the end, with five intermediate days of Hol HaMoed in between. Since there was only this one day of festival at the beginning of Pesach in ancient times, they used to only have only one Seder meal the evening of the first night of the holiday. But when Jews began to live far away from the land of Israel, scattered throughout the world, the rabbis were worried that the Jewish calendar wouldn't get communicated to all of the Jews at the right times. They wanted to make sure that all Jews would always be celebrating the holidays on the right days, so they expanded all major Jewish festivals (like Rosh HaShanah, Pesach, Shavuot, and Sukkot) from one day to two days just to be on the safe side. When they did that, the one Seder night of Pesach expanded to become two nights; therefore, the rabbis simply established two Seders. They are both completely equal with no difference between them. Since the creation of the State of Israel, Jews who live in Israel have gone back to the ancient custom of having only one Seder. Some Reform temples have done the same here in the United States. So some Jews today only celebrate one Seder like they used to in ancient times.

Question number 5: The Pesach Haggadah says that when Pesach falls on a Saturday night, the final blessing of Havdalah [the ceremony on Saturday night marking the end of the Sabbath] *should be recited at the beginning of a Seder on Saturday evening. Yet there is no mention of the other Havdalah blessings and customs. My family loves celebrating the Havdalah ritual using the special braided candle on Saturday nights! Even though the Haggadah instructions don't mention this candle, may we still light a Havdalah candle before lighting candles for the Saturday night Seder and conduct the entire Havdalah ritual?*

Answer: Wow! What a detailed question about a complicated topic! I'll do my best to answer all of your questions, but I want to warn you that my answer may be kind of long in order to do it justice. There is a good reason that the instructions in your Haggadah do not mention a Havdalah candle on Saturday night before one begins the Pesach Seder—that is because you are not supposed to use one! The Havdalah ceremony or the separation ritual that is performed on a Saturday night that also happens to fall on the festival of Pesach is a very special and unique situation, and we do not observe all of the regular rituals we are used to doing at the conclusion of ordinary Shabbats on Saturday night throughout the rest of the year.

On an ordinary end of Shabbat on Saturday night, we celebrate Havdalah with four blessings:

1. The blessing over the wine—because all rituals of holiness connected to Shabbat and holidays are sanctified with the blessing over wine
2. The blessing over spices—because there is a tradition that our ability to enjoy the extra-special quality of Shabbat departs from us on Saturday night at the conclusion of Shabbat; therefore, the sweet smelling spices help ease the loss of this ability
3. The blessing over light using a special multiwick candle to symbolize the intertwining of holiness and the mundane and Shabbat and regular weekdays in our lives
4. The blessing thanking God for creating the major separations in Jewish life—between holiness and the mundane, between light and darkness, between the people of Israel and other nations, and between Shabbat and the other days of the week

On the Pesach Seder that every few years or so falls on Saturday night, depending upon the version of the Haggadah your family uses, it should clearly explain the order of the unique Havdalah ceremony for Saturday nights whenever this fairly rare occasion occurs. The Havdalah service is actually merged into the Kiddush for the Pesach Seder. The order of the various intertwined rituals is as follows:

1. First, you recite the blessing over wine that praises God and concludes, "Who creates the fruit of the vine."
2. Next, you say the official paragraph of Kiddush for Pesach found in the Haggadah.
3. Before drinking the wine, we insert the blessing over light here that praises God and concludes, "Who creates the light of the fire." However, instead of using the special multiwick candle for this blessing, we simply look at an ambient light from whatever light source you are using that evening—perhaps your dining room chandelier or other light source. Why? Hang on—I'll explain that just below.
4. After this, we then recite the special concluding paragraph of Havdalah, thanking God for the major separations in Jewish life. However, it is a little bit different than the ordinary end-of-Shabbat paragraph because we are not celebrating the passing of Shabbat into a weekday but rather the transition from a Shabbat to another holiday. Therefore, this blessing praises God and includes a phrase thanking God "who separates between the holiness of Shabbat and the holiness of a holiday."
5. Finally, at the end of this merged Kiddush and Havdalah ritual, we say the blessing of Shehecheyanu, thanking God for keeping us in life to celebrate this moment. Only then do we finally get to drink the wine of Kiddush and Havdalah.

Now, back to your original question—why no special Havdalah candle with the braided wicks on the Saturday night that falls during the Pesach Seder? This is because on the festival of Pesach, as with other Jewish holidays, there is an ancient prohibition against lighting new lights such as other candles and extinguishing flames as well (except in the case of danger). Therefore, we do not use or light the special braided wick Havdalah candle at the beginning of the Pesach Seder that falls on a Saturday night. Instead, we use the ambient light from other sources as I mentioned above.

You should know that this situation of combining Pesach Kiddush with Havdalah on a Saturday night was so complicated that the ancient rabbis also worried about keeping this all straight and came up with a Hebrew mnemonic device to help them remember the arrangement of all of these blessings for Kiddish and Havdalah that are interspersed when Pesach begins on Saturday night. In Hebrew, the nonsense mnemonic word they came up with is "Yaknehaz." This stands for the official order of these blessings that is *Ya*yin, *K*iddush, *N*er, *H*avdalah, and *Z*'man. Or in English, wine (for Kiddush), Kiddush (the actual blessing of the Pesach holiday), candle (for Havdalah on Saturday night to conclude the Shabbat), Havdalah (the special prayer blessing the transition from Shabbat to a holiday), and the blessing of time called Shehecheyanu.

This word "Yaknehaz" does not have any meaning in Hebrew; but apparently, it is similar to a Yiddish phrase that was familiar to Ashkenazic Jews in the Middle Ages who spoke this language, a combination of Hebrew and German. To them, it sounded like the Yiddish words "Yag und Haz," which means, "hound and hare," or a dog and a rabbit. This explains why many medieval manuscripts of Pesach Haggadot are sometimes illustrated on some pages with pictures of a dog chasing a rabbit. Although each of these creatures is un-Kosher and in general Jews did not own dogs as pets or use them in their professions, the illustrations of these animals helped Jews remember the complicated order of blessings when the Pesach Seder would fall on a Saturday night. I know this was a long and complicated answer, but I hope this helps explain the differences between a regular Havdalah on an ordinary Saturday night and the special merged Havdalah and Kiddush ceremony we make on the Saturday night that falls on the eve of a Pesach Seder.

Question number 6: What is the significance of lettuce on the Seder plate? Why is it that all Seder plates do not have lettuce?

Answer: That is a good question. The lettuce in question is called in Hebrew Chazeret; and in some of the ancient Jewish sources on Pesach, sometimes the ancient rabbis wrote about Maror, the bitter herbs, and Chazeret as if they were the same thing. Since there was some confusion as to what "Chazeret" actually was—whether it was simply Maror or something else entirely—the rabbis decided that it must be another kind of bitter herb. So they compromised. On some Seder plates, there is a spot for both Maror and Chazeret in which case, chopped horseradish goes in the Maror spot and romaine lettuce goes in the Chazeret spot. Romaine lettuce is considered a bitter herb because although it tastes sweet initially, it leaves a bitter aftertaste. This is similar to the experience of the Israelites when they first went down into Egypt during the time of Joseph; it was a pleasant experience at first because they were connected to Joseph, the second-in-command to the Pharaoh because of the whole famine story described at the end of the book of Genesis. But after many years, they became slaves, thus, the bitter aftertaste. In Seder plates with only a spot for Maror then the horseradish is placed there.

Question number 7: Since Matzah is made of wheat flour and water, why is wheat among the non-Kosher foods for Pesach? Also, if the Matzah is Kosher for Pesach, why couldn't I bake more Matzah during Pesach with wheat flour? Why is the wheat flour forbidden during Pesach?

Question: You raise an excellent question! This is one of the most complex and perplexing aspects of Pesach—the very grain that is the most forbidden is the *only* grain that can be used to make Matzah to celebrate Pesach! Of course, the difference is that the flour used to make Matzah has absolutely no yeast in it whatsoever and is not allowed to rise. Actually, the five grains that are prohibited on Pesach as Hametz, or leavened foods, are the only five grains that can be used to make Kosher-for-Pesach Matzah; and they are wheat, rye, barley, oats, and spelt. The reason we eat Matzah is to fulfill the commandment in the Torah because it is both a symbol of our slavery and freedom.

From the perspective of Jewish law on Pesach, you cannot bake more Matzah during the eight-day holiday of Pesach because once the holiday begins, all flour from the five forbidden grains are indeed forbidden! Therefore, in ancient times, if you ran of out Matzah during Pesach, you couldn't make any more because the wheat and other kinds of flour were forbidden to own, cook with, or eat. Nowadays, you can just go to a store and buy more Matzah. This is because all Matzah that we eat during Pesach, even nowadays, has to have been made before Pesach began.

Spiritually speaking, the difference between Hametz—this forbidden leavened food made from the five grains of wheat, rye, barley, oats, and spelt with yeast—and Matzah in Hebrew is very minor: just rearrange the Hebrew letters and add a little dash in the Hebrew letter Hey to make it the letter Chet. The two Hebrew words of "Matzah" and "Hametz" are very similar in spelling and appearance. The rabbis in the Talmud pointed out that Hametz is the symbol of the Yetzer HaRah, the selfish inclination to indulge one's appetites. Sometimes this selfish inclination can actually be a positive force in the world, leading us to strive and achieve great accomplishments in our lives. But by overindulging, a good thing becomes bad and takes over our lives. Therefore, every year, we must separate ourselves from the Hametz in our lives to remind ourselves of its proper place. This is why wheat and the other grains are forbidden during Pesach.

Question number 8: Why do we use only wine or grape juice for the Kiddush and the Four Cups on Pesach? Why not another kind of alcohol?

Answer: Here are four reasons why we use only wine or grape juice to say the blessings that sanctify the Shabbat and Jewish holidays called Kiddush:

1. We use wine because it is an ancient tradition. Jews have used wine for Kiddush for over two thousand years! When traditions are this long and this ancient, many people—Jews included—don't feel that we should change it. We preserve this ancient tradition therefore because it makes us feel connected to our ancestors two thousand years ago and helps us to feel a part of the unbroken Jewish tradition. And we hope that Jews will continue to be drinking wine for Kiddush and Pesach for the next two thousand years.

2. We always use wine for Kiddush and the Four Cups on Pesach because one of the effects of drinking wine in small amounts, at least for many people, is that it helps us relax and feel good and even happy. And since the Torah commands us to rejoice on Shabbat and the holidays, what better way to fulfill this commandment than through wine and some alcohol? When we drink too much, however, we don't feel so good. Therefore, we should only drink as much as will help us to feel a little happier and relaxed. Some people however don't like the taste of wine. Therefore, it is okay to drink grape juice instead even though it doesn't have the same effect as wine, but it is still a grape product. Interestingly enough, the decision allowing the use of grape juice for Kiddush instead of wine is of rather modern origin. It came about as a result of the law of Prohibition against alcohol in the United States in the 1930s; and the leading rabbis at that time therefore ruled that grape juice, because it came from grapes and had a similar makeup as wine (minus the alcohol), was still acceptable for Jewish ritual purposes.

3. Wine is made from grapes, and the Torah (in Deuteronomy 8:8) says that grapes are one of the seven native fruits of the land of Israel. Therefore, we drink wine for Kiddush and the Four Cups at the Pesach Seder to remind us of our ancestral homeland, the land of Israel, and to help us continue to feel connected to our homeland. Although grapes grow in many places throughout the United States and all over the world, for Jews, grapes remind us of our Holy Land.

4. Wine is an alcoholic beverage that was highly prized and valued in the ancient world even before the time of the Hebrew Bible. It was considered one of the most important, valuable, and crucial drink in the ancient world, not only because of its alcoholic content but also because it took so much time, energy, and effort to create it. It wasn't a naturally occurring drink, like water or an easy-to-produce drink like a fruit juice that you simply had to squeeze to make. It required the grapes from the earth and the winemaking skills of human beings. To the ancient Jews, it was the perfect model of a divine partnership between God and human

beings. Therefore, it was considered an especially appropriate drink to celebrate Shabbat and holidays with, for these are days that are bestowed by God upon the Jewish people to enjoy and praise God's gifts of creation. This is why we make Kiddush over wine!

Question number 9: *My adult children have become vegetarians and do not even eat eggs. Cooking for Pesach is difficult enough, but having to avoid eggs makes it nearly impossible. It seems that all Pesach foods and recipes include eggs! Are there Pesach noodles that don't have eggs? Where could I find them?*

Answer: From what you described, it sounds as if your children may be lacto-vegetarians that means they don't drink milk or eat eggs or possibly even vegans, which means that they will not eat or even use any products derived from animals.

In either case, it is still possible to enjoy a healthy and satisfying Seder and Pesach without having to use eggs. As a vegetarian myself who must watch my cholesterol, all of my Pesach holidays have been meat and largely egg free, so I know it is possible to do so and not suffer in the least. It is simply a matter of educating yourself about the different kinds of cookbooks and recipes available—and there are many—that can guide you on how to prepare vegetarian, egg-free meals for Pesach. The only reason eggs are used so often in Pesach recipes is that they serve as a binder of other materials often in place of flour and other Hametz-derived foods. However, it is possible to use other foods and products as binders in recipes. Many of these vegetarian Kosher-for-Pesach cookbooks have helpful substitution hints.

It is interesting that you specifically mention Kosher-for-Pesach noodles because pasta—even special Pesach pasta—is not necessarily a traditional Pesach food! However, if you are absolutely set on having Kosher-for-Pesach noodles for your Pesach meals, there is not much I can do to help you. There are no Kosher-for-Pesach food companies that produce egg-free noodles for Pesach that I am aware of. They may be out there, but you will have to do your homework and probably spend some time on the Internet doing research. I have never had Kosher-for-Pesach noodles for Pesach, so it is not necessarily a must to eat noodles on Pesach. My Pesach meals are made nearly exclusively from fresh vegetables and fruits. The food is healthier, less heavy, tastier, and far more nutritious. I urge you to expand your culinary horizons and explore some more creative ways to enjoy a vegetarian, egg-free Pesach holiday. It will help your children feel at home, and it is also much healthier to cook with more fruits and vegetables. Good luck and have a happy, healthy, and Kosher Pesach!

Question number 10: *Why don't we eat lamb at the Pesach Seder if it is a Torah commandment and not a rabbinic interpretation?*

Answer: Today, we are all rabbinic Jews, not biblical Jews. Despite what the Torah might say, Judaism is the religion of the rabbis who interpreted the Torah. Even though the Torah says we are to eat lamb on Pesach (see Exodus 12:3-4) in ancient times, the only place that the Pesach sacrifice of this lamb could take place was in the ancient Temple in Jerusalem where it would be both slaughtered and eaten. Because the Romans in 70 CE destroyed the Temple, it is no longer possible to make this sacrifice.

Even in the absence of the Temple, the Talmudic rabbis determined that Jews should not eat lamb for any meal on Pesach because it is too similar to the actual Pesach sacrifice, and it might appear that the person was trying to perform a commandment that could no longer be fulfilled according to Jewish law. In addition, in the Middle Ages, a group of Jews broke away from traditional rabbinic Judaism and claimed that they would only follow the commandments explicitly commanded in the Torah. These Jews called Karaites did not follow the rabbis or the Talmud and created a bitter schism among Jews that lasted for nearly two centuries. Therefore, the later rabbis further enforced this ban on eating lamb on Pesach in order to underscore the difference between

276 Rabbi Daniel Kohn

rabbinic and Karaite Jews. Therefore, the *only* Kosher meat that is actually prohibited to eat at the Seders is lamb.

Question number 11: *Why is it that we can use peanut oil on Pesach but not peanut butter? And why are legumes prohibited on Pesach?*

Answer: You asked a great question! First of all, the custom of not eating legumes such as rice, peanuts, corn, peas, and beans on Pesach is purely a custom for Ashkenazic or European Jews that developed in the thirteenth century in France. It is also only a custom—not Jewish law. No one really knows the reason, but many rabbis have invented reasons over the centuries to try and explain the origin of this custom. At least a dozen completely different reasons have been suggested for this custom; therefore, it is highly probable that there is no one original, real reason. In fact, over fifty medieval rabbis disagreed with this custom and called it a stupid custom! But somehow or other, it caught on and is still practiced today.

The original custom is for Ashkenazic Jews to refrain from eating the legumes themselves—not their by-products. This means that the custom is not to eat peanuts, but the use of peanut oil is perfectly acceptable. Peanut butter is a direct use of the peanuts and not a secondary food product, which is why it is included in the original prohibition. Rabbi David Golinkin, a Conservative rabbi in Israel, wrote a legal opinion in 1988 dealing in great depth with this question of legumes for Ashkenazic Jews on Pesach and determined that there is no compelling Halachic or legal Jewish basis for this custom and ought to be discarded! Other Orthodox rabbis in Israel have also come around on this topic and issued rulings permitting Ashkenazic Jews to eat legumes on Pesach. Rabbi Golinkin's reasoning (which I find fascinating and convincing) is that observing this custom of refraining from eating legumes:

1. focuses on a mere custom of secondary importance and takes away from the actual Mitzvah, or commandment, of avoiding actual Hametz during Pesach;

2. further reduces the kinds of foods that Jews can eat on Pesach and therefore reduces the joy of the holiday;
3. encourages price gouging by Kosher food manufacturers who take advantage of this custom by raising the prices on foods with Kosher-for-Pesach certifications certifying that they do not contain any legumes;
4. further divides Jews from different ethnic origins in a world already split among many groups and factions;
5. and finally, has no Halachic or Jewish legal basis whatsoever!

The only reason to continue to observe this custom is to observe an ancient traditional custom. That is all. Also, please be aware that legumes, called in Hebrew Kitniyot, are Kosher for Sephardim and Edot HaMizrah, that is, Jews who come from North Africa and the Middle East. Therefore, serving and eating Kitniyot on Pesach will not make someone's dishes un-Kosher for Pesach.

Question number 12: I have heard that it is permitted in Jewish law to eat non-Kosher-for-Pesach food, that is, food with Hametz at the very end of Pesach and then put them away for the next Pesach. Is that right? If so, does that mean that I can use any of my dishes and utensils that I have used throughout the year on Pesach as long as I haven't used them for a full year? And what about using dairy dishes and utensils for meat food and vice versa if I haven't used them for a year? Does not using a set of dishes for a whole year make them Kosher for other kinds of food?

Answer: The simple answer to your many questions is no. To put it another way, you cannot eat meat food on dairy dishes and then simply wait a year and use those dairy dishes for regular dairy food again or the other way around. Therefore, you cannot eat non-Kosher-for-Pesach food on your Pesach plates after Pesach is over and then simply wait a year and use them again for Pesach. Kosher dishes that come into contact with food that they are supposed to be separate from renders those dishes Treyfe or not Kosher anymore. Sometimes they can be cleaned and made Kosher again but sometimes not.

In terms of Pesach, dishes that have been used throughout the year to eat Hametz food have to undergo a stringent cleansing process to be made Kosher for Pesach. First, they have to be scrubbed clean of any Hametz food remnants. Second, they have to be taken out of active use for twenty-four hours to let whatever remaining microscopic amounts of the Hametz food particles go stale. Third, the dish then has to go through a Koshering or cleaning process based on the principle of "As it absorbs, in that way will it be extruded." This means that metal pots that cook wet, hot food have to be immersed in boiling water for at least twenty minutes. Glasses that only contained cold liquids have to be immersed in cold water for seventy-two hours straight. An oven, which is used in extremely hot, dry temperatures, must be cleaned with a blowtorch or put on a self-cleaning cycle or set to high or five hundred degrees or the maximum setting for that oven for a half hour. If a dish or utensil—such as a ceramic bowl or wooden spoon—cannot undergo this process without cracking, breaking, or being destroyed, then this item cannot be made Kosher for Pesach, and a replacement item must be purchased and used only for Pesach.

Now, after having said all of this—what you have heard is somewhat true about Pesach dishes but not the way you heard it. The one exception to all of these rules regarding preparing dishes to be Kosher for Pesach has to do with very fine, expensive china dishes. Based on the principle that the Jewish tradition does not want the Jewish people to be financially overwhelmed by observing the rituals of Pesach, the ancient rabbis determined that for especially fine china, which would be destroyed in the Kashering process, it would be too great a loss of money to have to replace it with all Kosher-for-Pesach china. Therefore, the rabbis said if there are no other alternatives, it is possible to make fine, expensive china Kosher for Pesach even if they were not Kosher for Pesach before this.

First, one has to follow the first two steps above of thoroughly cleaning and letting these fine china dishes sit unused for twenty-four hours. Then put the china dishes away for one full year to let any possible microscopic Hametz food remnants that these dishes absorbed go completely bad and stale. This way, the remaining Hametz food substances that have been absorbed into the china are no longer even considered food. One year later, you can bring out this china and use it for Pesach and only for Pesach throughout the rest of their lifetime of use. If you put Hametz food back on it, you must follow the same process of putting aside the dishes again for another year. The cycle of purposely eating Hametz food on Pesach dishes that you described is unfathomable to me, but even based on what I just wrote, it still would not be acceptable because Pesach is an eight-day holiday. Even if you followed these steps above for fine china, these dishes would still be eight days shy of sitting unused for a full year. You still would not be able to use them for the next successive Pesach holiday. They would have to wait nearly two years before you could use them again. And if you did this as a regular practice, it defeats the original purpose of the rabbinic leniency regarding fine china dishes on Pesach that can be made into Kosher-for-Pesach dishes just once. If someone does this every year, it is clear that they are using this leniency to disregard the Pesach Kashrut laws. Therefore, to answer your first question again—no, you should not make a regular habit of switching your china back and forth from Hametz to Pesach even if it is every two years.

Question number 13: Could you please explain the background of Elijah the prophet? Why is Elijah not in the Hebrew Bible in the section with other prophets? He certainly is of significance to the Jewish people! And regarding those other prophets in the Hebrew Bible, could you please provide me with time frames for them? What I don't understand is if Elijah was part of the Pesach story, why isn't he mentioned anywhere in the Torah?

Answer: Elijah was a Hebrew prophet who lived during the seventh century BCE in the northern Kingdom of Israel. He persistently criticized King Ahab and his foreign wife Jezebel for their worship of pagan gods and performed many miracles on behalf of God and ordinary people. What is unusual about his story is that the Hebrew Bible implies that he never died. Instead, he was taken directly up to heaven in a flaming chariot of God (see 2 Kings 2). Because of this, he is considered a figure of some mystery in the Jewish tradition.

His story is told in the Hebrew Bible in the book of 1 Kings and a little bit in 2 Kings. By the way, not all of the prophets who figure prominently in the history of the people of Israel have their own books. There is a distinction between preliterary and literary prophets. Literary prophets simply refer to the prophets who wrote down their own words or had them recorded. Other prophets such as Elijah, Elisha, and Nathan are considered preliterary simply because they didn't write down their words, nor were they preserved in a separate book.

Elijah is not mentioned once in the Five Books of Moses. In terms of history, he lived six hundred years after the time of Moses. Elijah actually had nothing whatsoever to do with the story of the exodus of Israelites from Egypt. So what does Elijah have to do with Pesach? It is all because of a very strange detail about the Pesach Seder. Almost two thousand years ago, the rabbis of the Talmud argued over whether Jews should drink four or five cups of wine at the Pesach Seder based on some complex arguments over the interpretation of certain verses in the Torah. Since they couldn't decide, these rabbis compromised and decided to pour a fifth cup but not drink it. The rabbis believed that someday in the future, before the Messiah comes, the prophet Elijah will return to earth from heaven in advance to prepare the way. According to the Talmud, one of the ways that Elijah will prepare the way of the Messiah is to settle all of the rabbinic legal disputes of the rabbis. In other words, whatever they couldn't decide, Elijah will settle once and for all. Therefore, this cup of Elijah is actually the fifth cup about which Elijah will decide whether it should be drunk or not. The cup of Elijah at the Pesach Seder is actually not intended for Elijah to drink but rather the cup that Elijah will ultimately make a decision about whether we should drink it or not as part of our Pesach Seder.

However, over the years, Elijah morphed into the Jewish version of Santa Claus in popular Jewish imagination, visiting all of the homes of Jews all over the world on the eve of Pesach and drinking this fifth cup of wine poured for him at the Seder. This is a gross distortion of the role of Elijah and this fifth cup, but at least now you know its real origins and the role Elijah plays or rather does *not* play in the story of the exodus of the Jews from Egypt.

Question number 14*: Why do we read Shir HaShirim on Shabbat Pesach?*

Answer: Shir HaShirim, or the Song of Songs from the Hebrew Bible, is a collection of poems about love and springtime; and since Pesach is a springtime holiday, it is appropriate to read a book all about that season. The rabbis also interpreted the Song of Songs metaphorically as a love song between God and the people of Israel. Therefore, we read it on Pesach for that is the anniversary of when the people of Israel and God first entered into a relationship during the exodus of Egypt. The rabbis understand this relationship as similar to that of marriage. Therefore, Song of Songs symbolically refers to this love relationship between the Jewish people and God that began at Pesach over three thousand years ago.

Chapter 13

Kashrut: Jewish Dietary Laws
(Twenty-one Questions)

The Hebrew word "Kosher" means "fit" or "acceptable." Therefore, Kashrut refers to food that is considered fit or acceptable to be eaten by Jews. Although Islam has a similar practice of regulating the diet of its followers as well as other Asian religions that insist on vegetarianism, the idea that the consumption of food can or even should be connected to one's spiritual faith—as opposed to health—is foreign to the vast majority of people in this country. And to tell you the truth, it is also confusing for many Jews as well!

Many Jews, either those who observe these traditional dietary practices of Kashrut or those who are aware of them but do not to follow them, often complain that the laws of Kashrut are too difficult and burdensome to observe. After all, once you became aware of the many restrictions and requirements involved in keeping Kosher, many Jews have perhaps rightly protested that keeping Kosher prevents Jews from enjoying a full and satisfying social life with non-Jewish friends or even nonreligious Jewish friends. This is because for those Jews who are fairly strict and conscientious about observing Kashrut, most ordinary non-Kosher restaurants are off-limits as well as dining in the homes of other people who do not keep Kosher. After all, how can you ever fraternize with someone who is not Jewish over a meal if you are serious about observing the details of keeping Kosher? Interestingly enough, some ancient rabbis and scholars argued that this was precisely one of the principal purposes of keeping Kosher—to ensure a certain degree of social cohesiveness within the Jewish community and to guarantee that Jews would be limited in their opportunity to meet and perhaps end up marrying non-Jews. But then again, there is an extensive list of various reasons that rabbis and scholars have proposed for why Jews should keep Kosher that are touched in some of the questions in this chapter.

The majority of questions that I received about Kashrut focused more on how to observe the details of these dietary laws rather than on why. In fact, there is probably more ignorance and misconceptions about Kashrut than any other area of traditional Jewish observance. Even Jews who are generally committed to keeping Kosher are not always familiar with the practical details that might help them observe it. Due to the high volume of questions that I answered dealing with this topic, I ended up posting an article that I entitled "Kashrut Explained" on the Internet in an effort to proactively answer as many questions as possible in advance. Because it is no longer available online, I have included this same article in "Appendix A: Kashrut Explained" at the end of book. In fact, it might be a good idea to read this appendix first before reading the questions and answers of this chapter to help place them in context. The questions and answers in this chapter begin with general questions about Kashrut and then proceed to more detailed questions focusing on specific aspects and components of the dietary laws.

Question number 1: What are the advantages and disadvantages of keeping Kosher?

Answer: Try it and see for yourself! Seriously, since you ask, I'll list a few advantages people have claimed they enjoy by keeping Kosher. But as for the downside, I'll leave that for you to find out if you find any.

First of all, keeping Kosher is a way of imbuing your daily life with holiness and a sense of God's presence. It helps us be aware of God in the most mundane of our daily activities—eating. Plus, when we recite blessings before and after eating, it helps us cultivate a sense of gratitude and humility as human beings. Secondly, keeping Kosher is also a way of being more mindful of how we live life in general. As opposed to never paying attention to what we eat, when we keep Kosher, it demands that we be mindful and aware of how we fulfill our most basic physical appetite. Thirdly, keeping Kosher also instills in us a sense of humility because according to the laws of Kashrut, Jews are not permitted to eat every creature on the planet. Rather, we are limited to certain ones, and this helps us acknowledge the world does not exist solely for our human pleasure and exploitation since we too were created by God along with every other creature on this planet. Therefore, we have certain limits in our lives as human beings, as fellow creations of God.

And finally, keeping Kosher is a way to remind us of our Jewish identity on a daily basis. If you have to spend a few minutes extra shopping for Kosher food or considering what to order at a restaurant in order to make sure that you are keeping Kosher, you are always aware of your Jewish identity and commitment to Jewish life and Jewish practices. These are a few of the advantages of keeping Kosher. I hope you give it a try and see for yourself if it enhances your sense of spirituality and Jewish identity.

Question number 2: I keep Kosher. But recently, one of my friends asked me what is the point of keeping Kosher, and I realized I did not really have an answer. Could you please help me answer my friend's question—both for her and for me—what is the point in keeping Kosher?

Answer: Excellent question! People keep Kosher for lots of different reasons. I have no idea what your reason might be, but here are a number of reasons that various rabbis and scholars have come up with over the centuries to justify and explain why Jews should observe Kashrut:

1. All life belongs to God, and according to the story of Adam and Eve in the Garden of Eden, humans should be vegetarians (see for

yourself in Genesis 1:29-30). Elsewhere in the Hebrew Bible, the prophet Isaiah imagines an ideal future when even the animals will all be vegetarian (see Isaiah 11:6-7, 9). Therefore, keeping Kosher helps us appreciate the sanctity of all life.

2. Kashrut helps define and preserve Jewish identity by preventing Jews from dining with and socializing with non-Jews. Some examples of this are when the prophet Daniel refused to drink the Babylonian King Nebuchadnezzar's wine or eat his food since that would be breaking the laws of Kashrut (Daniel 1:8 and 12). In the time of the Maccabees, a famous hero of the Jews, a woman named Judith, brought her own food to dine with a Greek general so that she wouldn't have to eat non-Kosher food (Judith 12:2). Therefore, Kashrut was a way to prevent Jews and non-Jews from mixing socially and to better preserve Jewish identity.

3. Keeping Kosher helps us develop internal self-discipline. In one story the rabbis taught, "Let not a man say, 'I do not like the flesh of swine.' On the contrary, he should say, 'I like it but I must abstain from eating it seeing that the Torah has forbidden it'" (see the rabbinic Midrash Sifra 11:22). Therefore, keeping Kosher helps us build up our internal self-discipline because we consciously choose not to eat un-Kosher food even if we like it.

4. Keeping Kosher helps us lead holy lives. In the Torah, God says, "I am the Lord your God; sanctify yourselves therefore, and be holy; for I am holy—do not defile yourselves by eating un-Kosher things" (Leviticus 11:44). When we follow the commandments that God gave us in the Torah, we are by definition leading holy lives.

5. Keeping Kosher makes us more ethical and humble people. Some rabbis believe that the specific details of keeping Kosher are actually irrelevant. Rather, the purpose is to limit the consumption of the animal kingdom. Therefore, since we are prohibited from going out and eating any kind of animal in the world, it reminds us of our status as subservient human beings created by God and reminds us to be humble. Just as animals were created by God, so too were all human beings. I hope this

gives you something to think about and gives your friend some answers as to the point of Kashrut!

Question number 3: *Are there any exceptions to keeping Kosher? For example, what if my baby was starving, and the only food I could obtain was pork—isn't the saving of life more important? Also, what if I intentionally ate non-Kosher food? What would I have done in the days of the Temple to atone for this sin? And whatever you might answer me, why would I have had to do anything special to get God to forgive me? Doesn't God forgive us all on Yom Kippur, the Day of Atonement, anyway?*

Answer: Three excellent questions! First of all, you are absolutely correct: saving a life does indeed take precedence over ritual concerns. Therefore, in the situation you described, it is preferable to save a life rather than foolishly adhere to a ritual custom. If the only food you had to feed your starving baby was pork, then saving a life is more important than keeping Kosher. Although I would hope it was pork baby food!

Secondly, if you ate non-Kosher food in the days of the ancient Temple in Jerusalem nearly two thousand years ago, people who committed sins were required to offer special sin sacrifices at the Temple, and the specific animal sacrifice was determined by the severity of the sin. These details are actually spelled out in the book of Leviticus in the Torah. Of course, none of this applies nowadays, but it makes for some interesting reading if you're in the right mood.

And finally, just because Yom Kippur effects expiation for sins between God and human beings, one cannot commit a sin and simply rely on Yom Kippur to take care of it. In fact, the Talmud (Mishnah, Yoma 9:8) specifically says that one cannot use the excuse of Yom Kippur as a kind of premeditated expiation for committing sins, for in that case Yom Kippur has no spiritual effect on that person and their sins. The bottom line in all of this stuff is that if you truly want to live a Jewish life and play by Jewish rules, it helps to be sincere in your desire to play by these voluntary rules and not use them as loopholes to cheat. Thanks for your questions.

Question number 4: I have been studying in Israel, and recently, I have become more religiously observant. I now keep Kosher very strictly, but I am now wondering what to do when I return home to the United States and want to eat in my parents' home because they don't keep Kosher. Should I follow the commandment of keeping Kosher and eat non-Kosher food in their home, or should I follow the commandment to honor my father and mother in their home?

Answer: Good question! While I'm sure more traditional rabbis would give you a different answer, my answer is that the commandment of honoring your father and mother comes first, and this may indeed include eating possibly non-Kosher food in their home; but still try to keep Kosher as much as you can within those parameters.

I recommend this course of action based on personal experience. When I was a young rabbinical student growing more personally observant, one Pesach holiday I went home and drove my parents nuts making the whole house Kosher for Pesach. Oh, the house was Kosher for Pesach, all right; but my relationship with my parents took years to recover for my arrogance and imposition of my personal Halachic (Jewish legal) standards in their home.

Keep Kosher as much as you can in your parents' home; don't eat forbidden foods and request that any dishes your parents cook for you not include un-Kosher food or mixtures of milk and meat. If you want to cook any meals for your family, then by all means you should make the meal with Kosher products. But don't go overboard with insisting on new or separate plates or pots or pans. You may want to eat on paper plates and use plastic utensils, but be sensitive to your parents' feelings about this. However, if you feel that you can do so without insulting your parents, then, of course, you should adhere to Kashrut standards whenever possible. To me, the answer is clear—preserving a loving relationship with your parents come first. No ritual observance should ever interfere with one's family relationships. And recognize that food—eating and cooking—is often symbolic of the acceptance of parental love and nurturing.

Question number 5: *Is it better to keep Kosher in the home and eat non-Kosher food in restaurants than to not keep Kosher at all?*

Answer: Yes, it is better to keep Kosher even part of the time even if it is just in your home and not keep Kosher at restaurants. Keeping Kosher is not an all-or-nothing proposition. Ideally, one should keep Kosher in the home and outside as well. To do otherwise is to make a mockery of the ideals of Kashrut and act in a hypocritical manner. However, we all live in the real world; and as a rabbi, I fully support people taking small half steps in their personal spiritual observance of Jewish traditions. I would prefer Jews to keep Kosher to the best of their abilities. If that means that for some people that they are temporarily keeping Kosher in their homes and eating non-Kosher food outside of the home but they are still nonetheless committed to one day keeping Kashrut completely in the home and out, then that is the best one can hope for in the interim.

Is this an ideal state to be in? No. It should be a state that someone moves through in order to keep complete Kashrut. However, if someone gets stuck in this place, then this is indeed hypocrisy and would make me wonder why he or she is even bothering to keep Kashrut in the first place. I hope I explained my position in an understandable way, and I hope that if you are describing your own personal situation, then I hope that one day you will also begin to keep Kosher even when you eat in restaurants as much as you can.

Question number 6: *Although I keep Kosher, I just got a job working as a waiter in a non-Kosher restaurant. Is it wrong for me to serve people un-Kosher food?*

Answer: You raise an interesting question. There is no problem serving non-Kosher food to non-Jews just as there is no religious obligation for non-Jews to keep the laws of Kashrut. However, when it comes to serving fellow Jews non-Kosher food—even if they don't keep Kosher themselves—some rabbis have indeed objected to Jews potentially serving other Jews non-Kosher food. However, this should not prevent you from earning your living at this job because earning a living takes precedence over these ritual concerns.

Also, it is clear that any Jew going into the non-Kosher restaurant where you work does not care that they will be eating non-Kosher food. Presumably, if they kept Kosher, they wouldn't be going into your restaurant in the first place! It is their decision to eat non-Kosher food, not yours. In fact, none of us have any right to prevent anyone from eating the kind of food that they choose. Although you may feel uncomfortable about being around all of the non-Kosher food you are serving, just remember that you are not the one eating it.

Question number 7: Is eating Kosher meat safer than eating non-Kosher and why?

Answer: Possibly. The reason is because chicken and cattle that are bound for Kosher slaughter cannot—or at least should not—be fed any animal feed that has been supplemented with other animal-derived protein. As awful as it sounds, until the mad cow disease outbreaks a number of years ago, cows and chickens destined for slaughter were routinely fed the leftover animal parts of other slaughtered animals to increase their bulk and weight as quickly as possible with extra protein. Today, most of these practices have been outlawed due to health and safety considerations. Ideally, to be an animal fit for Kosher slaughter, the cow or chicken should be only grass or grain fed. However, although I am not an expert in the Kosher meat industry, I'm sure it is possible that Kosher slaughterhouses might also purchase animals for slaughter from the general cattle and poultry market, in which case, there is no guarantee as to how those animals have been fed and cared for prior to slaughter.

However, what makes the animals Kosher is how they are slaughtered—not what they eat. But in order to be considered fit to be slaughtered in a Kosher slaughterhouse, the animals must be inspected to ensure that there are no deformities or health issues that might invalidate the animal. And even after the slaughter, there is a thorough process of inspecting the slaughtered animal to check for after-the-fact deformities and internal blemishes in the Kosher slaughtering process. Therefore, there may indeed be a slight increase in health and safety of Kosher meat due to this concern with animal feed and the Kosher inspection process.

Question number 8: Is there any information about vegetarianism in the Torah? And what about eating eggs? Are they Kosher or even vegetarian because an egg could grow up to be an animal?

Answer: There is no explicit commandment about vegetarianism in the Torah, but being a vegetarian is an easy way to keep Kosher. In fact, some rabbis think that Kashrut is actually a compromise with keeping a vegetarian diet that is the ideal goal of Kashrut. Some rabbis say this because one of the very first commandments that God gives to Adam in the Garden of Eden states, "God said: See, I give you every seed-bearing plant that is upon all the earth, and every tree that has seed-bearing fruit—*they shall be yours for food*" (Genesis 1:29)! So you see? It appears that God actually intended for all humans to be vegetarian in the beginning!

This ideal diet only changed later on with the story of Noah. After the flood, God said to Noah, "Every creature that lives shall be yours to eat as with the green grasses, I give you all these. You must not, however eat flesh with its life-blood in it" (Genesis 9:3-4). Noah was the first person in the Torah permitted to eat meat, but the first requirement of Kashrut was also specified at that time—no one was to be permitted to eat a slaughtered animal with its blood still in it. The blood must be spilled out or drained before eating the meat. In fact, this is stated explicitly in Deuteronomy 12:16, 24, and 15:23 where it says (referring to slaughtered animals), "Only you must not partake of its blood; you shall pour it out on the ground like water." This is because blood is the representation of life that only God can create and bestow. Therefore, we do not eat the blood of an animal as it is considered a sacred symbol of life that belongs solely to God.

Later on in the Torah, God further limited the kinds of animals that the Israelites could eat, adding further to the basic foundation of Kashrut, or the Jewish dietary laws. In Leviticus 11 and Deuteronomy 14, God designated the kind of animals, birds, and fish that the Israelites could eat and those that were off-limits for consumption. And finally, there was a commandment that appears three times in the Torah that states, "You shall not cook a kid (baby goat) in its mother's milk" (Exodus 23:19, 24:26, and Deuteronomy 14:21). This thrice-repeated commandment was interpreted by the rabbis in the Talmud to mean that Jews should not mix any meat or dairy foods together. Therefore, in Kashrut a meal is either all dairy with no meat products at all or all-meat based with no dairy products at all.

Regarding eggs, the Torah doesn't say anything about them at all except one brief passage in Deuteronomy 22:6 that states that if you want to take the eggs from a bird's nest you find in the wild, you should scare away the mother bird before you steal her eggs. By the way, some rabbis feel that the purpose of this commandment was to spare the feelings of the mother bird so she would not be upset watching you steal her eggs! Regarding other kinds of eggs, some historians and anthropologists suggest that there were no domesticated chickens in the Ancient Near East at the time of the Hebrew Bible. But the rabbis in the Talmud assert that eggs, even though they are the product of an animal, are not considered milk or meat. They are called Pareve that in Yiddish means "neutral." This is because an egg is not really a baby chicken—it is an unfertilized egg that had the potential to be a baby chicken, but the rooster did not fertilize it. Therefore, it is merely an animal product without actually being meat. By the way, fertilized eggs actually have a tiny blood spot in them and are actually un-Kosher. In general, the egg production industry tries to separate unfertilized eggs from potentially fertilized eggs.

Although not a part of the Jewish dietary tradition, some people have extended the concept of vegetarianism to preclude the consumption of any animal product whatsoever. This dietary system is called veganism; and vegans avoid eating any product that came from an animal—including milk, cheese, and eggs. However, this is not part of Kashrut, but you will find people who will claim that eggs should not be considered part of a vegetarian diet either. I hope this answers your questions!

Question number 9*: Where in the Torah does it specifically prohibit eating meat and milk at the same time? The only passage I've ever found about it talked about not eating a baby goat cooked in its own mother's milk. How does this apply to all milk and meat being separate?*

Answer: You are indeed correct: the Torah does not prohibit eating milk and meat at the same time. It only says three times in various verses scattered throughout the Torah, "You shall not cook a kid (baby goat) in its mother's milk" (Exodus 23:19, 24:26, and Deuteronomy 14:21). It was the rabbis of the Talmud based on ancient oral traditions that established this broad, sweeping rule prohibiting the consumption of milk and meat together. It is explained in the Talmud in the volume of Hullin that deals with the laws of keeping Kosher.

Modern Jewish practice is indeed based on the Torah, but the Torah is only the starting point. The rabbis of the Talmud established all of the basic guidelines of modern Judaism. Modern Judaism is actually rabbinic Judaism, not biblical Judaism. For example, you won't find any verse in the Torah saying we should light candles for Shabbat or make Kiddush over wine on Shabbat—that is all rabbinic! Similarly, the law about avoiding mixing milk and meat is derived not from the Torah but the rabbis of the Talmud.

Question number 10: Why is meat Kosher? After all, scientific studies have proved that eating animal flesh is harmful to human health, and doesn't Jewish law state that we should avoid harming our bodies in any way? So shouldn't science take precedence over biblical law?

Answer: As confidently as you state your case, I must say that I cannot completely agree with your claim that science has definitively proved that meat is harmful to human health. While I am not familiar with the vast body of nutritional science and contemporary clinical studies, I'm sure there are indeed various experiments that have indeed concluded that perhaps different kinds of meat in different amounts over long periods of time can be unhealthy for some people depending on their lifestyles. However, human beings have been omnivores since the dawn of our evolution. *Homo sapiens* have been eating meat for over one hundred and thirty thousand years! Perhaps you are referring to problems with infected or tainted beef or even environmental concerns about the waste of energy involved in raising and eating meat?

However, you are indeed correct that Jewish law does enjoin us to guard our health and safety. Yet I do not think this can be applied to the claim that the consumption of all meat is harmful to human health. Modern scientific findings do play an important role in the development of Jewish law, especially when it comes to preserving lives and health. Modern rabbis have often turned to science and medicine when crafting decisions about how to update Jewish laws and customs. But I think you may be overstating the case when you insist that science should always trump Jewish tradition because in general, science often confirms much of the wisdom of the ancient Jewish rituals and practices.

What you might not be aware of is that many rabbis and scholars have claimed that Kashrut is a compromise with being fully vegetarian. However, in the course of the development of the Jewish dietary laws, certain types of animal meat were permitted under certain specific conditions such as ensuring that it was kept completely separate from dairy foods. While it is certainly possible for an observant Kosher Jew to eat a predominantly meat-based diet, the laws of Kashrut have

294 | Rabbi Daniel Kohn

historically served to limit meat consumption for traditional Jews over the centuries. Therefore, perhaps the Jewish tradition already anticipated the dangers of eating a consistently meat-based diet!

Question number 11: I have two questions: What exactly makes the Kosher slaughtering process different from other kinds of meat? And is the Kosher meat cooked or preserved in a different way than non-Kosher meat?

Answer: In order for meat to be Kosher, first of all, only certain kinds of animals can be slaughtered for Kosher meat. Kosher land animals must have split hooves and chewed their cud, which includes cows and sheep. And for birds, they cannot be scavengers or birds of prey; so Kosher fowl includes chickens, ducks, and turkeys. There is indeed a special way to slaughter these animals that is called in Hebrew Shechitah—literally, "slaughter." Shechitah requires the following things to happen for it to be Kosher:

1. The slaughtering must be performed by Shochet, a trained and certified Kosher butcher who has studied and trained in all of the detailed, complex laws of Kosher slaughter.
2. When slaughtering the animal, the trachea and the esophagus of the animal must be cut at the same time in a quick but gentle seesaw-cutting manner so as to kill the animal as quickly and hopefully as painlessly as possible. There are many detailed laws relating to this act of slaughtering such as the prohibitions that a Shochet must not press (chop the neck), pause during the slaughtering process, pierce (stab the neck), tear the flesh of the animal, or cover, meaning to cut so deeply into the neck that the entire width of the knife disappears and is covered by the flesh of the animal.
3. All of the blood of the animal must be drained and buried in dirt, like a kind of burial to respect the blood, which is considered the source of life in the animal. It cannot be collected in any kind of bowl, pit, or other container as that is reminiscent of how ancient pagans gathered blood as offerings to their idols and gods.

4. After slaughter, certain sections of fat from the kidneys and intestines must be removed because they are not considered Kosher as well as the sciatic nerve.

5. An animal cannot be slaughtered in front of other animals or even on the same day as its offspring or parents.

6. To prepare the meat for consumption, all of the blood must be porged, that is, salted and soaked in a salt-water solution to remove as much of the blood as possible.

Kosher meat is not cooked or preserved in any special way that is different from other kinds of meat. It is also not stored in a special way either. There are special Kosher slaughterhouses run by various Kosher meat companies around the country, and all of them package their meat in packaging with special symbols that clearly indicate that the meat is Kosher.

Question number 12: If you keep Kosher, can you wash all of your dishes in the same sink as long as you don't mix up milk and meat dishes?

Answer: As I'm sure you know, the separation of all dairy and meat foods, including all dishes and utensils used exclusively either for dairy or meat foods must also be kept thoroughly separate to maintain the Kashrut of the food and the dishes used to serve Kosher food. Therefore, the answer to your question is no—but of course, this answer depends on how strict a level of Kashrut you observe.

In order to keep dairy and meat food and dishes separate, it is important to wash, dry, and store dairy and meat dishes apart because the food that is washed off one dish can splash and drip on other dishes. Even if you stack the dairy and meat dishes separately in your sink, accidents are likely, and it violates the essence of the separation. Also, your dishwashing sponge can carry meat particles and dirty meat-tainted water on the dairy dishes and the other way around. Even if you use separate sponges for the dairy and meat dishes and utensils, the water splashing from the dairy dishes will splash the meat dishes and vice versa, carrying particles of dairy and meat food on the other dishes. If you wash your meat and milk dishes together, ultimately, all of your meat and milk plates will no longer be Kosher at all!

Dishes from a dairy meal should be washed entirely separately from dishes from a meat meal. Different sponges should be used, and some people even use different drying racks and put different plastic tub inserts into their sinks, one for meat and one for dairy to keep the metal or porcelain sink walls from being affected by the food and from the sink walls from affecting their dishes. Even when dry, they then also store them in separate cabinets and drawers to avoid any mix-ups. The point is to keep your meat and dairy dishes entirely separate all the time, whether clean or dirty, in the sink or on the shelf.

Question number 13: Are ostriches Kosher?

Answer: No. How do we know? Because the Torah in Deuteronomy 14:15 explicitly states that ostriches are considered unclean and therefore not Kosher—no matter how you slaughter it! Although it does beg the question—did the Torah or the ancient Israelites ever have contact with ostriches? Probably not, but this is how the biblical traditions of Kashrut came to be interpreted over the ages, and so no matter what ancient bird may have been referred to in the Torah, nowadays, ostriches are not considered Kosher.

Question number 14: Why are sea creatures that live on the bottom of the sea not Kosher? What difference does it make?

Answer: The Kashrut of sea creatures has nothing whatsoever to do with whether they come from the bottom or top of the sea. Rather, the characteristics of Kosher sea creatures are derived from the Torah, specifically Leviticus 11 and Deuteronomy 14. The verses there speak about a Kosher fish having fins and scales with no other explanation or descriptions. If you want to ask why fins and scales make a sea creature

Kosher, now that is a very good question—and there is absolutely no good answer to that question. This is a question that Bible scholars still struggle with. However, it has nothing to do with where the fish or sea creatures swim or live.

Question number 15: *Why is cheese not Kosher? How come I can't find any cheese with Kosher certification?*

Answer: Actually, there are plenty of cheeses that are Kosher and are marked with Kosher certification symbols. You just have to search for stores that carry Kosher cheeses. The original Kashrut problem with cheese that you may be referring to is that the very process by which the cheese was traditionally created involves the introduction of a meat product, the enzyme called rennet, which is secreted in the stomach of nursing calves and is added to milk that has been curdled and separated into curd (the solid part of milk) and whey (the liquid part). The rennet, along with different kinds of bacteria, creates all different kinds and flavors of cheeses. Therefore, in ancient times, it was impossible to make cheese except by mixing a meat product and milk together; therefore, all cheese used to be un-Kosher.

However, in modern times, Kosher cheese can be made by using rennet substitutes created from vegetables or chemical substitutes so that it is not a forbidden mixture of meat and milk. This is how both Kosher and vegan cheeses are made. People who are strict about their Kashrut will only eat cheese with a Kosher symbol that attests that only vegetarian rennet was used in the cheese-making process.

You should also know that several decades ago, the Conservative movement issued a decision that stated that even non-Kosher certified cheese made in large modern cheese-making facilities is permitted. This decision was based on the principle that even if animal-derived rennet was used to make the cheese, the rennet had undergone so many chemical changes and processing and cleansing so as to be considered a completely new substance entirely divorced from its original animal source. Not all Jews accept this decision, however; so ultimately, the choice is up to you as to how you want to observe Kashrut when it comes to cheese.

Question number 16: Are you permitted to take vitamins if they contain gelatin and glycerin, both of which are derived from animal products?

Answer: You ask a good question because when gelatin and glycerin began to be added to different food products, they were originally derived from the hooves of slaughtered animals, such as cows and horses. Therefore, not only was the gelatin and glycerin from an un-Kosher animal, it might have been added to a dairy-based food, violating the prohibition of mixing milk and meat products.

Although I am not an expert in the food industry, I know that it is possible to use vegetarian substitutes in place of gelatin and glycerin that perform the same role as these food additives. However, some liberal rabbis have issued Jewish legal opinions that state that even animal-based gelatin and glycerin can be considered Kosher because the industrial processes that they have been subjected to in order to be considered safe for human consumption has effectively changed their nature so much as to be completely divorced from their original animal source. In other words, they might have come from an animal originally, but by the time they are added into any product to be consumed by a human, they bear no credible resemblance to their native animal source. Also, in the form they are often used such as in vitamins and food additives, they are not even considered food in and of themselves. That is, no one sits down to an actual meal of gelatin and glycerin; and by the way, Jell-O is different from gelatin! And since they are in vitamins, pills necessary and helpful for human health, they could also be considered permitted due to the principle in the Jewish tradition of Pikuah Nefesh—the saving of a life, which generally trumps all other ritual concerns.

However, please note that more traditional rabbis might not agree that these principles of Kashrut pertain to gelatin and glycerin and might well explain that because of their original animal source, they are always un-Kosher—unless they came from a Kosher animal that was slaughtered in a Kosher way and were used in a meat-based food. When it comes to Kashrut, it all boils down to which Jewish denomination or rabbi or particular interpretation that you want to follow.

Question number 17: I found a kind of yogurt that has a K on the package. But how can it be Kosher if it has gelatin in it?

Answer: Gelatin is not necessarily un-Kosher. It all depends on how strict a level of Kashrut you want to observe. Some Jews will only buy and eat products with a recognizable Kosher certification printed on the packaging whereas others will buy and eat foods that are Kosher by ingredient only; that is, the food item may not have a Kosher certification, but all of the ingredients in it are Kosher. A Kosher certification is called a Heksher, which comes from the Hebrew word "Kosher," meaning "fit" or "acceptable."

The letter *K* by itself is not a recognizable legally guaranteed symbol of Kosher certification because no one can patent or trademark the letter *K*; therefore, it is not considered a trustworthy indication of Kashrut. Any food manufacturer can put a *K* on a food product whether it is Kosher or not. And in fact, there are a number of Kosher food magazines devoted to informing their readership of which food products are legitimately Kosher and those that are not such as some products with only the letter *K* printed on them.

But here is the complicated part: while such food products with only the letter *K* printed on their label may in fact be Kosher, the *K* is not a guarantee by itself. Only foods with trademarked Heksher symbols are officially guaranteed by civil consumer and trademark laws in this country to be Kosher. However, some food producers do not want to bother with the complicated and expensive process of acquiring an official Heksher guaranteeing that the food is truly Kosher. However, they want to inform the public that a food product that they make really is Kosher even if they have not gone to the trouble of officially certifying the Kashrut of the food. Therefore, these companies may indeed simply print the letter *K* on the package. The point is the letter *K* by itself on a food label is not sufficient to guarantee the Kashrut of the food.

You may have noticed that this yogurt you are asking about includes gelatin in the ingredients. Traditionally, gelatin was derived from an animal source like the hooves of horses and added to foods to provide a certain kind of viscosity or physical consistency to food. And perhaps the gelatin listed in the ingredients in this yogurt was indeed from an animal source, in which case it would be a situation of an animal or meat product combined with a dairy food, and as you seem to already know, it is forbidden to mix meat and dairy foods in Kashrut. Therefore, how could the product possibly be Kosher? As I already explained, the letter *K* does not guarantee that the food is Kosher. In addition, to further complicate things, not all gelatin nowadays comes from animal sources and can be derived from plant or nonorganic or even purely chemical sources; therefore, it is not entirely clear this yogurt is a forbidden mixture of dairy and animal foods! Since most food companies have Web sites or toll-free numbers, the best way to deal with this situation is to track down the company that made this yogurt and ask them directly if their yogurt is actually certified Kosher.

Question number 18: *Is lactic acid a dairy product? I have just begun keeping Kosher, and I have been carefully reading the ingredient labels on vegetarian foods if they are not certified as Kosher. Lactic acid was an ingredient that I found on a loaf of bread and wasn't sure if this made the bread dairy.*

Answer: Lactic acid is both a preservative and a flavoring agent derived from cornstarch as well as molasses. As such, it is considered Pareve, meaning "neutral"; and neither milk nor meat and food that contains it does not have to have Kosher certification. However, just to confuse things, lactic acid can also be produced from whey, the liquid elements of milk. Therefore, if you are concerned about serving whatever food contains it with a meat meal, then you should make the effort to find that same food product with a Heksher, or Kosher certification, to indicate that it is dairy. As for your loaf of bread with lactic acid, there is no way to determine whether it was Pareve or dairy without more information. Therefore, if the bread has no Heksher, you should probably assume it is indeed dairy to be on the safe side.

Question number 19: If I stop in a coffee shop and buy a cup of coffee or tea, is it okay if I bring it into a synagogue or someone's home if they are Kosher? I thought all coffee and tea was Kosher.

Answer: According to my understanding, all tea and coffee is Kosher. However, not everyone who keeps Kosher might feel comfortable if you bring in your coffee shop coffee or tea into his or her Kosher home and the same goes for a synagogue. They might feel uncomfortable that it came from a non-Kosher eating establishment even though technically it can be considered okay. Perhaps the machinery was cleaned in a sink with other non-Kosher dishes and utensils, and some of the non-Kosher food came into contact with the tea and coffee machinery. Even if you may be right that the tea or coffee is okay and there is nothing un-Kosher about tea and coffee, it is more important and socially appropriate to adhere to the wishes of your host and the Kashrut policy of the synagogue than to argue about the theoretical Kashrut of tea of coffee. The situation may be more complicated than it might appear.

Question number 20: If a lettuce and tomato salad is prepared using meat utensils and served with a meat meal, is it permissible to serve any leftover salad later on with a dairy meal?

Answer: There are two answers to your questions—yes and no! But the answer you might feel most comfortable with depends on how stringent you are in your observance of Kashrut. Technically, any Pareve, or neutral, food such as lettuce and tomatoes that are prepared with meat utensils and served on meat dishes take on a little bit of the meat flavor imparted to it by the utensils being used to prepare it. Even though the food itself is Pareve, because it has been prepared with meat utensils, it should only be eaten and consumed with other meat foods on meat plates. The assumption is that microscopic or trace amounts of the meat foods that have been absorbed into the meat utensils and dishes have seeped into the vegetables that you prepared, imparting to them a meatlike quality as far as Kashrut is concerned. Therefore, no, you should not serve leftover lettuce and tomatoes prepared with meat utensils on dairy dishes.

However, there is a technical loophole in this scenario that does make it possible to eat a Pareve salad prepared with meat dishes on dairy plates. If the dairy dishes and food that you serve these leftovers on are three steps removed from the original meat utensils used to prepare them, it is actually okay! Let me explain how this works: The original meat utensils used to prepare the vegetables can be considered Klei Rishon, or the first set of food preparation vessels, and they impart some of their trace meat flavor to the Pareve salad. Therefore, when the salad is stored in some kind of storage vessel, the Tupperware or plate on which they have been stored is then considered Klei Sheni, or the secondary vessels, one step removed from the original meat utensils; and these secondary dishes do indeed absorb some of the trace meat flavor from the original meat preparation utensils. Now, when the so-called meat-flavored salad is served on dairy dishes, one might assume that the trace meat flavor would then be transferred on the dairy dishes, which are Klei Shelishi, that is, thrice-removed utensils from the original meat utensils! However, this is not the case.

According to the Halachah, or Jewish law, the ancient rabbis felt that there had to be some kind of natural break in this potentially eternal progression of transferring—in this case—meat flavor on and on and on. Therefore, in the Talmud, the rabbis decreed that there is no further transference of trace meat flavor from Klei Sheni to Klei Shelishi. That is, the transference of meat or dairy status in Pareve stops from the second to the third set of dishes or utensils. The rabbis felt that the amount of trace flavor from either meat or dairy foods would be so diminished when the food was transferred from secondary contact to tertiary contact that there was no further chance of mixing milk and meat food flavors at that point. Therefore, there is no need to worry that the dairy dishes you serve the so-called meat-flavored lettuce and tomatoes on will be made un-Kosher through contact with the salad.

However, the salad is no longer truly Pareve at this point as it is now in the Hezkat, or "presumed status," of being meatlike-flavored food. Therefore, depending on how strict you want to be in your observance of Kashrut, it probably would not be appropriate to eat this salad with dairy food even on those dairy plates, for that could be considered to constitute a prohibited mixture of milk and meat albeit very weak and far removed from the meat source. This is where you would have to decide how strict you would want to be. I know this was a long and detailed answer to your question, but I hope I explained the situation clearly. Enjoy your next salad in peace no matter what set of dishes you choose to enjoy it on!

Question number 21: Why is fish considered Pareve even though fish have blood?

Answer: The fact that fish have blood has nothing to do with why they are considered Pareve, that is, neither milk nor meat. For example, there were some Edot HaMizrach communities, that is, Jews from North Africa and the Middle East, that did not even consider chicken—which certainly has blood—to be meat; and they would eat chicken with dairy meals!

The distinction between dairy and meat foods was of rabbinic origin and is not derived from the Torah. The only mention of the milk or meat status of fish is found in the Mishnah (in Hullin 8:1) where it states, "All meat is forbidden to be cooked (and eaten) with dairy food—except for fish." It is unclear what criteria the rabbis may have used to make this determination of what constitutes meat. However, since the initial distinction between dairy and meat was based on Torah verses prohibiting the cooking of a baby goat in its mother's milk, it can be argued that the rabbis decided fish was to be neutral based on the fact that mother fish do not suckle their young with milk. On the other hand, neither does fowl, so why should Kosher birds be considered meat and not fish? These are excellent questions; and one possible response is that the look, texture, and feel of the meat of fish is qualitatively different than that of fowl which looks, feels, and even tastes more similar to meat derived from land animals. Perhaps it is because fish are not mammals, and neither are birds. Therefore, these questions about the meat status of fish and birds persist. Even the Catholic Church makes a distinction between fish and meat for their religious dietary traditions, but perhaps they were influenced by Kashrut!

Chapter 14

Prayer (Twenty-four Questions)

During the time of the Hebrew Bible, the Israelites interacted with God through animal sacrifices and other offerings of food, drink, or incense. For a short time following the destruction of the First Temple in Jerusalem by the Babylonians in 586 BCE, some scholars think the Jews began to develop a more formal prayer structure. However, the Jews returned to sacrifices and offerings upon the construction of the Second Temple barely a century later. When the Second Temple was destroyed by the Romans in 70 CE, Judaism evolved and officially replaced sacrifices with prayer. The rabbis of the Talmud even justified this substitution using a biblical prooftext, "For I desire Hesed (loving-kindness), not sacrifice" (Hosea 6:6), which they interpreted to mean that God desires prayer, not sacrifices.

The tradition of Jewish prayer evolved slowly beginning with the twice-daily recitation of the Shema, "Hear O Israel, the Lord is our God, the Lord is One" (Deuteronomy 6:4) and then came to include more and more biblical passages, formulaic blessings, creative poetry, and the numerous subsequent additions of additional religious poets, rabbis, and scholars throughout the ages with changes and embellishments for each and every holiday. Even today there are still new prayers and prayer books being written and published.

The Talmudic rabbis themselves recognized long ago a tension between establishing a fixed, unchanging liturgy that might cause us to lose interest in what we are actually saying and the passion, excitement, and enthusiasm that one should ideally bring to uttering spontaneous prayer that we express when consumed with zeal or even fear. Therefore the rabbis encouraged Jews to approach this well-established liturgy as if it were somehow new every time we venture to crack the spine of an old prayer book.

Traditionally, Jewish prayers have been recited in Hebrew. Combined with the massive weight and length of some prayer books, it is not surprising that many people feel uncomfortable, estranged, and even intimidated by Jewish prayer. After all, the services can be long and incomprehensible to a non-Hebrew reader or speaker. Yet synagogues are the primary religious institutions of organized American Jewish life today. It is no wonder that many Jews feel alienated from Judaism today and still have so many questions about Jewish prayer, the primary venue for accessing the Jewish tradition.

The following questions deal with a full gamut of questions related to Jewish prayer from the picayune details of specific prayer services to broader general questions about prayer in general. My hope is that this chapter serves as a primer on Jewish prayer whose questions begin with the broad queries about prayer overall and then focus on questions dealing with specific details of the Jewish liturgy.

Question number 1: *Recently I have felt a strong desire to pray, but I am not sure about how to communicate meaningfully with God. My attempts seemed deficient and are unsatisfying to me. Can you suggest some readings, advice, or methods to help me to be able to pray more meaningfully? Thank you!*

Answer: You are by no means alone or unique in your frustration with prayer. Creating meaningful prayer is one of the hardest tasks that any Jew—or any human being—can engage in. Even for those of us who have been praying in earnest for decades often—if not most of the time—feel profound frustration and encounter many obstacles in trying to establish a spiritual dialogue with God.

My advice is don't give up. The more you practice, the easier it becomes to pray. Pray regularly at home and at synagogue. Buy a Jewish prayer book that you like, one that is easy to hold and read, whether in Hebrew or English. Use it until it finally begins to feel like it is your own. Prayer may feel less alien and more a familiar, comfortable activity the more you do it. Even if you don't get a spiritual lift every time you try to pray, at least the act of trying to pray can become comforting and familiar. Try reading the prayers in English in advance while not praying to gain a better understanding of them. It is very difficult to pray when the words are unfamiliar and unclear—they need to be part of your life so as to take on new meaning each time we approach them. Make the prayers your old friends—comforting and well understood. Perhaps this can help you see through their words to their deeper meanings.

Pray in a group at synagogue or alone at home. Try out different settings that may be more conducive to your prayer—indoors, in a favorite room, or outside in nature. Try to establish a comfortable, peaceful setting. Try to make it as personally significant as possible. Make up your own prayers, not just spontaneously but actually sit down and compose some of your own heartfelt thoughts and ideals. Study the various prayers—they aren't all supplications or requests. They are filled with prayers of thanks and reminders of the ethical ideals we hold sacred. Read the book of Psalms in the Hebrew Bible for examples of ancient prayer.

Try closing your eyes and meditating on different prayerful thoughts that you have. Attend synagogue and learn some of the melodies and songs that accompany different prayers and learn to sing them when you pray alone. Try humming the prayers or even swaying when you sit or stand. It is very traditional to Shuckle or sway back and forth when praying as a means to achieve a kind of semihypnotic state. The ultra-Orthodox Hasidic Jews even encourage people to dance and clap hands during prayer to raise our spirits and achieve a kind of ecstatic state of being during prayer.

Finally, learning to pray easily and meaningfully is like playing a musical instrument. It often takes time to learn the basic notes and scales and oftentimes hours of dull, unsatisfying practice. But in the end, all of that work pays off when you can pick up the instrument and make beautiful music. The same is true with prayer and a Siddur, or "prayer book." If you put in the time and energy and practice, you can make Jewish prayer your own so that someday, sometime when you truly feel like you want to open your heart to God, the prayers you recite—whether in Hebrew or English, whether ancient and traditional or new and original—will roll off your tongue and out of your heart straight into God's ears!

Question number 2: Why do Jews pray facing east? In Russia, I believe they also prayed facing east even though Jerusalem was to the south.

Answer: Jews are indeed supposed to pray in the direction of Jerusalem because that is where the ancient Temple used to stand. This was considered the holiest site in Judaism. However, during the Middle Ages, many Jews migrated and lived in Europe, and the direction of Israel was still generally to the east. Therefore, when Jews moved into Russia later on, they continued that tradition of praying toward the east even though the Russian community was now almost directly north of Israel! They didn't consult a compass although they probably should have. So you are indeed correct—to most Jews in Russia, Jerusalem is south, not east.

Question number 3: Why do we Shuckle when we pray?

Answer: "Shuckling," which is a Yiddish word that means "to shake or rock back and forth when praying," is an ancient time-honored Jewish practice. One traditional reason for Shuckling is that it is the fulfillment of a verse in the Hebrew Bible from the book of Psalms that states, "All of my bones (or limbs) shall say, 'Who is like You, God?'" (Psalm 35:10). Therefore, when we move our entire body, we are using all of our limbs to praise God.

Another reason why Jews may Shuckle is that it is a form of self-hypnosis or a means to get us into a kind of trance. Little kids often sway back and forth as a means of calming themselves, and the same continues to work for us adults as well. It feels good to move, sing, hum, and recite words to ourselves or out loud. Also, it is a way of distracting ourselves from other outside distractions. By fully involving our whole body in praying, we literally put our whole body into prayer, and that helps to further focus our concentration. The ultra-Orthodox Hasidic tradition even claims that when a person Shuckles, their body resembles a flame that is reminiscent of the phrase in Proverbs 20:27, "The soul of man is God's candle." Therefore, when we Shuckle, we are like a divine flame that dances in a breeze.

Question number 4: *When I watch people pray, I have noticed that they perform certain actions during prayers. Like during the Shema, they kiss the Tzitzit [fringes of the Talit, or prayer shawl]; and when they say certain words, they turn from side to side or bow. Where can I learn about these actions?*

Answer: There are indeed a wide variety of different actions during Jewish prayer that I call the choreography of Jewish prayer. Here is a basic breakdown of what to do and when during a regular weekday prayer service. I am not including all of the details of when you are supposed to stand up and sit down because this if far too much information to include here. For all of the details, I encourage you to consult an excellent and very detailed book called *To Pray as a Jew* by Hayim HaLevy Donin. So here are a number of the basic actions to perform during a traditional weekday morning prayer service:

1. When reciting the Borchu, the call to prayer, the tradition is for the leader of the congregation to bend the knees when reciting

the word "Borchu" and then straighten them out again, then bow at the hips on the word "Et" and then stand up fully straight on the word "Adonai." These words literally mean, "Praise God!" The congregation, when responding, bows the knees and then straightens them up and bows the hips, all on the word "Baruch" so that one can stand up fully straight again when reciting the word "Adonai," the name of God.

2. During the prayer Ahavah Rabbah, which means "with great love" and immediately precedes the recitation of the Shema, it is a tradition to gather the four Tzitzit together at the beginning of the line "V'havienu L'shalom," which begins a line that reads, "And bring us together (the Jewish people) in love from the four corners of the world (back to Israel)." Gathering the four fringes is symbolic of God bringing together all of the Jews from the poetic four corners of the earth.

3. When reciting the Shema, there is a tradition to cover the eyes with the hand grasping the Tzitzit to better concentrate on the Shema and the unity of God that bonds all humans, living creatures, and the entire universe together.

4. During the prayer V'ahavta, which is the first paragraph of the Shema and means "you shall love," it is a tradition to take the four gathered Tzitzit and touch the Tefillin (phylacteries) of the arm and kiss the Tzitzit when you mention them in Hebrew at the lines that mention that we, the Jewish people, shall bind these words of the Shema as a sign on our arm; and they shall be a sign between our eyes. These same lines appear in the second paragraph of the Shema as well, and the same actions should be repeated.

5. During the third paragraph of the Shema, it is a tradition to kiss the Tzitzit three times, once each time after mentioning the Hebrew word "Tzitzit" and then a final fourth time when saying the very last line of that paragraph that begins "Adonai Eloheychem Emet," which means the "Lord Your God is truthful."

6. At the beginning of the Amidah, or standing prayer, one takes three steps backward and three steps forward, taking one step

per word of the Hebrew line that reads, "Lord, open my lips and my mouth will speak your praise."

7. One bows at the beginning of the Amidah at the first blessing that begins with the Hebrew words "Baruch Atta Adonai," which is the opening of every blessing in Hebrew and means "Praised are You God." The choreography is that one bows the knees on the word "Baruch" and then straightens them out again, but bows at the hips on the word "Atta" and then stands up fully straight on the word "Adonai." The same procedure is followed with the closing blessing of this first paragraph as well.

8. When the Amidah is repeated out loud during the Kedushah, or sanctification of God's name, one bows to the left and right when reciting a line that refers to the heavenly angels calling one to another, this one to that one. Immediately after that, one then bounces up three times on the balls of the feet, once each time when reciting the words "Kadosh, Kadosh, Kadosh," which mean "Holy, holy, holy (is God's name)." Then, at the next congregational response of "Baruch K'vod," which refers to God's great honor, one bounces up just once.

9. In the weekday Amidah, one gently beats one's breast once when reciting the paragraph asking God for forgiveness. One does this once during the prayer that deals with the theme of forgiveness.

10. When saying the opening words of the paragraph Modim that begins with the words, "We give thanks to You, God" toward the end of the Amidah, one bows forward at the hips only. When reciting the final words of this blessing, one also bows at the last blessing.

11. When reciting the concluding meditation of the Amidah, one takes three steps backward, bows to the left and then the right, and then takes three steps forward while reciting the prayer Oseh Shalom, a prayer for peace.

12. As you are probably familiar with the Aleynu, which comes toward the very end of the service, I'll just quickly mention that one bows at the hips only at the line "V'anachnu Korim," which means "We bend the knees and bow" and then stands up fully

at the words "Lifnei Melech," which means "before the King." You may have noticed that at no point are we ever bowed over when reciting God's name or even mentioning God in a prayer because as human beings, we believe that we have dignity before our Creator and do not need to hold our body in a subservient position when reciting God's name.

13. During the Mourner's Kaddish when reciting the very last line, we take three steps backward, bow to the left and then the right, and then take three steps forward—just like when ending the Amidah.

This is a short, condensed version of all of the choreography during Tefillah. For more details, I encourage you to consult a rabbi and read the book about Jewish prayer that I mentioned above. I just hope that I helped explain the basic moves and helped jump-start your learning process!

Question number 5: What is the significance and symbolism of a Talit? How and why did the Talit develop? How does the Talit relate to other cultures and religions?

Answer: Wow—what a lot of good questions! The Hebrew word "Talit" originally meant a "cloak" and was probably worn by men in ancient times much as a Mexican serape is worn today; it is both a coat and potential bedroll in a pinch. It is similar to the blankets worn by Bedouin Arabs in the Middle East today for protection against the weather, either hot or cold.

The Talit developed religious significance in the time of the Hebrew Bible as is clear from Numbers 15:38-41, which states,

> The Lord spoke to Moses saying, "Instruct the people Israel
> that in every generation they shall put fringes on the corners
> of their garments (Talit) and bind a threat of blue to the fringe
> of each corner. Looking upon it, you will be reminded of all

of the Mitzvot (commandments) of the Lord and fulfill them and not be lead astray by your heart or lead astray by your eyes. Then you will remember and observe all of my Mitzvot and be holy before your God."

Historically, the Talit was an ancient garment worn by men in the Middle East since the beginning of civilization there; but in Judaism, this garment became a ritually significant piece of religious clothing for the common people based on the addition of these special fringes. Today both men and women in liberal synagogues wear the Talit during worship services and only by men in traditional communities. It is worn during morning prayer services during the week and on Shabbat and Jewish holidays during prayer. It is only worn after a child becomes the age of Bar or Bat Mitzvah, after thirteen years old for boys and twelve years old for girls. It is the symbol of Jewish religious adulthood and shows that the child has become obligated to begin observing the Mitzvot of Judaism.

Question number 6: What do Tzitzit mean to you? What are we supposed to think about when we look at them?

Answer: According to the Torah in Numbers 15:37-41, the Tzitzit, or fringes, on a Talit, or prayer shawl, are to serve as a visual reminder of all of the commandments in the Torah. The Torah says, "Looking upon them, you will be reminded of the Mitzvot of Adonai and fulfill them." In other words, it is like the old custom of tying a piece of string around your finger to help you remember something.

The rabbinic tradition has added many layers of symbolism to the Tzitzit. There are seven strands of fringes bound about by an eighth strand. According to Gematria, which is a rabbinic form of symbolic interpretation based on the fact that Hebrew letters also serve as numbers, $7 + 8 = 15$, that when written out in Hebrew letters is the Hebrew word "Yah" comprised of the Hebrew letters Yod and Heh that is one of the names of God and is a shorthand name for the mystical four-Hebrew letter name of God in the Torah.

The eighth Tzitzit strand is bound around the other seven Tzitzit strands in a special order, each bunch of windings separated by a knot. The order and number of these windings is 7, 8, 11, and 13. The rabbis equated particular significance to these numbers. That is because—as we saw above—the Hebrew number 15, when written out in Hebrew letters, is the name Yah, the first two letters of God's name. The number 11, when written out in Hebrew letters, is Veh, the last two letters of God's name. And finally, the number 13, when written out in Hebrew letters, spells out the word "Ehad," which means "one" in Hebrew. Therefore, looking at the strands of the Tzitzit combined in their knots literally spells out in Hebrew "God is one," which is the central message of the Shema, or the central theological declaration in the Torah that affirms the oneness of God.

And the fun doesn't end there! The Hebrew word for "Tzitzit" or in Hebrew letters, Tzadeh-Yod-Tzadeh-Yod-Tav, equals the number 600. If you then add in the 8 strands of the Tzitzit plus the 5 knots on any one corner of the Talit, the total number equals 613, which is the exact number of Mitzvot in the Torah. So as it says in the Torah, "Looking upon them, you shall be reminded of the Mitzvot of Adonai." Pretty cool, isn't it?

Question number 7*: At synagogue, I notice that some men put Talit on in a certain fashion. Is there a proper way for putting on a Talit? If so, what is it?*

Answer: There are many different traditions for how to drape oneself in the Jewish prayer shawl; however, a standard, traditional manner of putting on a Talit follows this particular series of actions stated below:

1. You must be standing to put it on—this is out of respect for the act of putting on the Talit and for the garment itself.
2. You hold the Talit with the Atara, or crown, that is the special strip that goes around your neck facing you straight out before you. Some Atarot (plural) have the Hebrew blessing you are supposed to recite before putting on a Talit embroidered on this

strip. If so, you then read that blessing. The blessing in English is "Praised are you, Lord our God, ruler of the universe, who has sanctified us with Your commandments and commanded us to enwrap ourselves in Tzitzit."

3. You then wrap the Talit around yourself covering your shoulders and back with the fringes of the Talit trailing down in front of you. Some people wrap the Talit around their entire head and recite a special meditation for this moment that is found in traditional prayer books. After this, you can then wrap the Talit around your shoulders and begin your prayers.

Here are some additional points to keep in mind regarding decorum and synagogue etiquette when wearing a Talit:

1. Never enter a bathroom wearing your Talit! Remove it before you enter and put it back on when you exit, but without having to say the blessing again. You can leave it on your seat in the sanctuary, and some synagogues actually have a Talit rack outside of the restrooms to remind congregants to remove their Talit before entering.
2. When you are finished with the worship services, take off your Talit while standing up—never sitting down. This is to show respect for the act and the garment. Also, you never want to drag or trail any part of the Talit on the ground out of respect for the garment.
3. There is no blessing or prayer that we recite when taking a Talit off. We just take it off and fold it up and place it in the special Talit bag, or if you borrowed it from the synagogue, simply hang it back on the rack from where you originally got it.

Question number 8: Is it considered wrong for a Jew to get on their knees to pray in private? Why or why not?

Answer: At an early time in Jewish history, praying on one's knees was probably considered just one of many possible legitimate positions for prayer. After all, the Hebrew Bible describes how many of the famous personalities in the various stories fell to their faces when they encountered God. There is even a story in the Talmud that Rabbi Akiba would begin his prayers in one corner of a room and engage in so many different prostrations that he would end up in another corner of the room by the time he finished! The High Holiday prayer book also records in the Avodah service that in ancient times on Yom Kippur when the high priest would utter the special holy name of God, the people in the Temple courtyard would fall on their faces, prostrating themselves. However, the position of praying on one's knees is probably not a good habit for a Jew to get used to for two reasons:

1. Kneeling is a universal sign of showing subservience, and as Jews, we only bow to God. Look at Mordecai and how he wouldn't bow to Haman in the story of Queen Esther! The only time that Jews traditionally bow is on Yom Kippur during the Aleynu prayer. Throughout the year, whenever we recite that prayer, we only bow at the waist to show that we bow to no earthly rulers, only God. Therefore, kneeling or bowing should only be reserved for those prayers and special occasions so that the act itself remains unique and dramatic.

2. Kneeling has become associated with Christian worship. Therefore, it is not considered particularly Jewish to kneel during prayer. Besides, what's the big deal with kneeling? As Jews, we pray in all kinds of positions—standing; sitting; bowing at the waist; bowing at the knees, prostrating on Yom Kippur; resting our forehead on our arms during Tachanun, or the prayer of entreaty in weekday prayers; and even saying the Shema at night while lying down! There are plenty of traditional authentic Jewish positions for prayer. There is nothing special about kneeling—neither is there anything particularly Jewish about it either.

Question number 9: *Why are we commanded to say one one hundred blessings a day? What is the purpose of blessing in general? How did we arrive at this number?*

Answer: Rabbi Meir the Talmudic rabbi claimed in a somewhat hyperbolic statement that it is the duty of every Jew to recite one hundred blessings a day (Talmud Tractate Menahot 43b). The Midrashic literature of the rabbis claimed that King David originally instituted this tradition of reciting one hundred blessings a day back in the time of the Hebrew Bible (Numbers Rabbah 18:21). However, this is only a tradition and is not considered actual Halachah, or Jewish law. Why one hundred blessings? One hundred is a large symbolically whole and complete number. It is also the sum of 10 x 10, and the number 10 appears numerous times in the Torah, such as the Ten Commandments, the Ten Plagues in Egypt, ten generations from Adam to Noah, and then another ten generations from Noah to Abraham, the first Jew. The purpose of all blessings is to praise God for providing us with creation, for fulfilling certain religious obligations, upon seeing certain sights, and before and after eating. Their goal is to inspire gratitude and spiritual dependence upon God.

Question number 10: *Why are we supposed to kiss the Torah or Siddur* [Jewish prayer book] *when we drop it?*

Answer: There is no official Jewish law that we are supposed to kiss either the Torah or a Siddur when we drop them. However, since kissing is a sign of reverence and love, the custom has developed that whenever we are close enough to kiss the Torah in synagogue on Shabbat or any other day when we take the Torah out of the ark to read it and parade it around the sanctuary, this is an appropriate way to show our love for it. The custom is take a corner of the prayer shawl or Siddur and touch the Torah when it is carried around the sanctuary of the synagogue and then kiss that part of the Talit or Siddur that you used to touch the Torah.

Because the Siddur contains all of the prayers we offer to God and contains God's name in it, while certainly not considered as holy as the Torah, it is nonetheless a holy and important book in the Jewish tradition. Therefore, the custom developed to kiss it only when it happens to fall on the floor after we have picked it back up again. Some people kiss the Siddur whenever they have opened it up to read prayers or immediately after they close it to set it down also as a sign of love and reverence. As you can see, there are few hard and fast customs associated with kissing and the Torah and the Siddur. Therefore, you should feel free to show your love and affection for these sacred ritual objects however you feel comfortable.

Question number 11: *Why do you keep your feet together during the* Amidah [a Hebrew prayer that literally means "standing"]?

Answer: In Isaiah 6, the prophet described a heavenly vision he had of the angels surrounding God's throne. These creatures stood straight with their legs together and sang in unison, "Holy, holy, holy, is the Lord of hosts. The whole earth is filled with God's glory" (Isaiah 6:3). Over time, the practice developed that Jews should emulate this stance and position of the angels in Isaiah's vision. Just as the angels stood perfectly straight with their legs together, so do we when we pray the Amidah—which literally means "standing"—the prayer in which we envision ourselves standing before God's throne. In other words, this is a folkloristic explanation for an ancient Jewish prayer custom. I recommend that you read the book *To Pray as a Jew* by Hayim Donin for a longer explanation of this and other prayer customs.

Question number 12: *Does the Hebrew Bible state anywhere that it is possible to obtain forgiveness from God for our actions through a manner other than animal sacrifice? Is there a biblical answer as to why we no longer need to make animal sacrifices to atone for our sins?*

Answer: In the Torah, there is no other way to achieve forgiveness other than through the ritual of animal sacrifice. However, what you may have noticed—and is indeed confusing—is that there is no explanation in the Hebrew Bible as to why we no longer continue the practice of animal sacrifices today in modern Judaism.

In order to understand this, you have to recognize that Judaism today is not the religion of the Hebrew Bible. It is the religion of the ancient Talmudic rabbis who interpreted the Hebrew Bible when the Temple was destroyed two thousand years ago. Just because it says or does not say something in the Hebrew Bible does not mean that it has any relevance whatsoever to modern Judaism. There are no animal sacrifices today because two thousand years ago, the ancient Temple was destroyed and has never been rebuilt. Judaism evolved two thousand years ago into a religion of prayer, synagogue rituals, and emphasis on righteous, moral behavior. This is why there are no longer any animal sacrifices in modern Judaism today.

To achieve atonement for our sins nowadays, there are two methods. For sins that affect no other human being, we pray for forgiveness on Yom Kippur; and according to the Jewish tradition, God immediately and gladly accepts our repentance. This is called in Hebrew Teshuvah, which means to return in that we depart from our sinful ways and return to the path of righteousness. According to some traditional texts, it involves three stages—first, we must recognize what we have done wrong, then we must regret our actions, and finally, we must resolve never to do these sinful actions again. For sins that affect other people, we must follow these same steps of Teshuvah and add one more, namely, to try to recompense what we did wrong to other people and seek their forgiveness and apologize. According to the Jewish tradition, God cannot forgive us unless we have obtained the forgiveness of those whom we have wronged or injured. Even an animal sacrifice just doesn't cut it in this case!

Question number 13: I am a religious Jew studying in a nonreligious college. But I still enjoy praying three times a day, but I am not sure exactly when I am supposed to begin or end each prayer service. Also, since I am rarely able to find a Minyon every day, sometimes I oversleep and wake up after Shacharit [morning prayer] time. What prayers should I say in compensation?

Answer: How wonderful that you take your Judaism so seriously. Depending on where you are at college, I know how difficult it can be to create and maintain your own religious, spiritual life on your own without community support. I wish you encouragement and strength.

Regarding the times for prayer, there are indeed many details about this very topic in the traditional sources. Shacharit, or the morning prayer service, can be recited very early in the morning, even before the sun rises when it is light enough to see pretty clearly. You can lay Tefillin, or the Jewish prayer phylacteries, and pray the Shacharit service up until around 12:30 p.m. Mincha, the afternoon service, can be recited from 12:30 p.m. until the sunset; and Ma'ariv, the evening service, can be recited anytime during the night, all night after the sun has gone down and it is dark. And if you miss these times, while there is a tradition of different compensatory prayers you could possibly say, the details are complicated and confusing; and trying to explain them would actually detract from the main goal of saying the actual major prayer services at their appropriate times. If you miss a prayer service, then simply say the main prayers of that service right then and there, either the Shema or the Amidah, the central prayer recited while standing. For more detailed information about prayer, I highly recommend two books, *A Guide to Jewish Religious Practice* by Rabbi Isaac Klein and *To Pray as a Jew* by Rabbi Hayim Donin. These will provide you with excellent in-depth explanations about prayer.

Question number 14: *I need help understanding the Yotzer* [a Hebrew prayer meaning "creator"]. *I realize that it is a prayer of thanks, but what are we thanking God for? What is its significance, and why is it important?*

Answer: You ask a most profound question that I think exposes the essential relationship of human beings to God. What do any human beings have to be thankful for? I would answer that the most important thing is our lives! To which our tradition responds that just as much as your individual parents may contribute to your having been born, God was just as much a partner in this process supplying you with life and a soul.

I would also include that we should be thankful for our health and the proper workings of our body. To which our tradition responds with a special prayer. In the beginning of most traditional daily prayer books, there is a prayer that we should say after going to the bathroom that basically thanks God for the proper functioning of our organs. If they didn't work, we wouldn't be able to survive a single moment. We should also be thankful for every new day that we have to live, love, and interact with our friends and family. To which our tradition responds—in the Yotzer section of the daily morning prayers—"God, in God's goodness, creates anew each day, every day."

I guess what it comes down to is your attitude toward life. If you are not grateful for anything in your life, then perhaps by reciting Jewish prayers, and especially the Yotzer, it can help us develop a feeling of gratitude for our lives and the world around us. If we see everything in our lives as a gift and this entire universe into which we are born as a gift—then we truly have a great deal to be thankful for, and the Yotzer expresses our thanks to God for the gift of creation.

Question number 15: Could you please tell me what is the correct way to place a Mezuzah on the door? Thank you?

Answer: The Mezuzah, which literally means "doorposts" in Hebrew, is traditionally placed on the right side of the doorway, which is on your right side when entering in through the doorway, because most people are right-handed. The top should be slightly tipped or angled into the room you are entering and the bottom angled slightly out. That is, it should be placed somewhat diagonally with the top toward the inside of the room or structure you are entering into. It should be around the height of your head or just a little higher.

There is also a special blessing to be recited immediately prior to hammering the nails or affixing the Mezuzah that goes, "Praised are You, Adonai or God, sovereign of the universe, who has sanctified us with Your commandments and commanded us to affix the Mezuzah." This blessing is found in most traditional daily prayer books.

Some people touch the Mezuzah every time they enter or exit a doorway with one and then kiss their hand to show their reverence for the words of the Torah contained inside. The passage of the Torah written on a scroll inside every Mezuzah is a quote from Deuteronomy 4:6-9, which starts with the Shema, "Hear O Israel, the Lord is our God, the Lord is one." It then continues with the rest of the passage from the Torah, "You shall love the Lord your God with all your heart, with all your strength and all your might" and concludes with the verse, "And you shall write these words on the doorposts (Mezuzot) of your house and your gates." Hence, the Mezuzah fulfills this Mitzvah literally—putting these words on our doorways!

Question number 16: What is the prayer we recite three times a day asking God for help in repairing our mistakes?

Answer: I'm not sure there is any specific prayer that is recited three times a day in which we ask God for help in repairing our mistakes. The only major prayer that is actually recited three times a day is called the Amidah, meaning the standing prayer in which there are nineteen petitions addressed to God to help us in a variety of ways.

However, as a matter of theology, Jews do not believe that God can repair anything that human beings have screwed up. In the Jewish tradition, we understand that God will forgive us if we transgress in an area of ritual Jewish practice in which no other human being was affected or hurt. And for these sins that impact only our relationship with God, there is indeed a prayer that is included in the Amidah recited three times a day that goes, "Forgive us, Our Father, for we have sinned; pardon us, our King, for we have transgressed. For You pardon and forgive. Blessed are You, Adonai, who are gracious and ever-forgiving." Perhaps this is what you were thinking about in your question. However, the Jewish tradition is very clear that only human beings can rectify what they have done wrong. And only a human who has been wronged can forgive the person who offended or hurt them—not God.

Question number 17: Is there any significance to the phrase in the traditional Hebrew prayer book in which men say a blessing thanking God for "not having made me a woman"? I am bothered by this blessing and would like your thoughts on it.

Answer: You are indeed correct that in a traditional Siddur or Hebrew prayer book, one of the first blessings a male says in the morning prayer service states, "Praised are you, Lord our God, King of universe who has not made me a woman." The traditional Hebrew prayer book also has an alternate blessing for women to say that thanks God "who has made me according to His will."

This does indeed appear to be a misogynistic statement indicating an inferior status for women in Judaism, and there is some historical truth to this. However, it must be understood in its historical and cultural context. In ancient times, although it may be difficult for some people to acknowledge, women in many Middle Eastern societies were viewed as socially, legally, and certainly economically inferior to men. They were not even accorded equal legal rights in some ancient societies—and even today, certain religions and cultures do not see women as equal to men. It has taken a long time even in modern Western culture for women to achieve equal legal status, and there are still to this day economic inequalities that persist.

The rabbis of the Talmud were also part of this cultural world and accepted many of these ideas. However, many modern scholars—while noting these inequities—also point out that ancient Jewish society was far more egalitarian than surrounding cultures. Jewish women were accorded far more rights and responsibilities than other ancient religions and civilizations. Yet the rabbis at that time, especially the ones who authored many prayers of the traditional Hebrew prayer book, incorporated these views into the prayers and blessings of their day; and many have endured to this day.

Some modern apologists for these ancient chauvinistic blessings try to justify these blessings by noting that in traditional Jewish practice, men are required to observe more of the ritual commandments than women; therefore, men are simply thanking God for the opportunity to perform more of God's laws than women. Others point out that men were given these extra laws to observe because women were either otherwise engaged in raising children and keeping a home, or some even maintain that women were created by God to be more naturally spiritual than men and therefore do not need the structure of these external religious obligations to further spiritualize them.

In modern times, many liberal branches of Judaism have found this blessing to be offensive as well and have either dropped it from their prayer books or substituted it for other blessings to be recited by both men and women, such as thanking God "who has made Me in Your image." This is both biblically correct (see Genesis 1:27) and more gender neutral.

Question number 18: *I'm not Jewish, but I've been studying about Judaism on my own. I recently learned about the Shema prayer and how important it is in Judaism. Could you tell me where I could find it and explain why the Shema prayer is recited? Thanks for your time.*

Answer: The "Shema," which literally means "Hear!" or "Listen up!" is the first word of perhaps the most important prayer in a Jewish prayer book. The full line of the prayer is "Hear O Israel, the Lord is our God, the Lord is one" (Deuteronomy 6:4-9). It is featured rather prominently in all traditional Jewish prayer books. If you can locate one, then use the table of contents to find it. The traditional paragraphs that constitute the Shema are all taken from the Hebrew Bible, specifically the Torah or Five Books of Moses. There are actually three separate passages that constitute the liturgical section known as the Shema; and they are Deuteronomy 6:4-9, 11:13-21 and Numbers 15:37-41. I encourage you to look them up and read what these three short passages have to say and think about why the ancient rabbis thought these three passages out of the whole Torah were so important.

The Shema is recited twice a day in the daily liturgy of Jewish worship because the first paragraph of this prayer section states that Jews are supposed to recite these words of the Shema twice a day, morning and night. It is so important because it emphasizes the unity of God, that is, monotheism and the direct, close relationship that the Jewish people are supposed to have with God. Good luck with your studies!

Question number 19: Could you tell me about Hallel [a section of prayers chanted on certain Jewish holidays]*? Why do we chant it, and what is its origin? Any help would be very appreciated. Thank you and Shalom.*

Answer: Hallel, a section of prayers meaning "praise," is recited on major Jewish holidays as part of the celebration of the day. It consists of a series of Psalms from the Hebrew Bible, specifically Psalms 113 to 118. It is recited on Pesach, Shavuot, Sukkot, Hanukkah, and Rosh Hodesh, the monthly new moon celebration. We recite it because every one of these Psalms begins with the Hebrew word "Halleluyah," which literally means "Praise God!" Its origins are very ancient. Some scholars think that these Psalms were even recited by the priests and Levites at the First Temple in Jerusalem in biblical times nearly three thousand years ago as a distinct liturgical unit associated with animal sacrifices. Because of its connection to celebration, some Jewish communities now also recite Hallel on Israeli Independence Day and the Fourth of July in America to celebrate these new holidays in a religious context.

Question number 20: What are the meanings and root of the Hebrew words "Haftarah" and "Maftir," the readings from the prophets and the last Torah reading on Shabbat? Are there any modern words in Hebrew from this same root?

Answer: The Maftir and Haftarah readings are special passages from the Hebrew Bible chanted every Shabbat in synagogues. These extra readings were probably established nearly two thousand years ago, possibly during the Roman Hadrianic persecutions of the Jews following the defeat of the Bar Kochba revolt in 135 CE during which the Romans prohibited the Jews from reading the Torah. Therefore, the Jews in Israel at that time, to get around this punitive Roman decree, began reading sections of the prophets from the Hebrew Bible on a weekly basis—in place of the weekly Torah readings—and chose readings that were somehow connected thematically to what the real Torah portion should have been; this is the Haftarah. Even when the persecutions ended, Jews returned to reading the weekly Torah portions but also continued to read the Haftarah readings on Shabbat and holidays as a reminder of those hard times.

When Torah readings were ultimately reestablished, the person who was given the honor of chanting the Haftarah was given a special Aliyah, or the ritual honor of being called to the Torah to recite special blessings before and after the chanting of a section of the Torah, at the very end of the weekly Torah reading called the Maftir Aliyah. The reason was so that this person shouldn't feel second best to those who had been called to recite the blessings for Torah reading for the actual weekly Torah reading.

Finally, to answer your question, the root of both of these Hebrew words, "Maftir" and "Haftarah," is rendered by the English letters P, T, R or the Hebrew letters equivalent to these English letters Peh, Tet, Resh; and this root word means "to exempt or fulfill one's obligation." This Maftir Aliyah and the Haftarah prophetic reading were called this in ancient times because the Jewish people felt awful that they were being forbidden to read the weekly Torah portion every Shabbat in synagogue during the period of Roman persecution. Therefore, they hoped that the chanting of the Haftarah—the prophetic substitute for the Torah reading—would serve to exempt the synagogue congregation of their religious obligation to study and chant the weekly Torah portion. The person who was given the honor of chanting this Haftarah was then called the Maftir, meaning "the one who exempts." And yes, this root and other words derived from it are a regular part of daily spoken Modern Hebrew.

Question number 21: *Please tell me why we say Hazak Hazak Venitchazek in synagogue when we complete the reading of a book of the Torah.*

Answer: "Hazak Hazak Venitchazek" is a Hebrew phrase that means, "From strength to strength, may we be strengthened." In other words, we are praying that our reading of the Torah on Shabbat in synagogue will strengthen us and give us strength from God. This line is recited by the congregation during a Shabbat Torah reading service each of the five times we come to the end of one of the five books of the Torah. It is also celebrating the fact that we have made it to this point in our lives to have merited to have heard a complete book in the Torah chanted on Shabbat mornings over the past several months. In other words, it is a traditional way to say, "Yeah! We made it! We finished another one of the five books of the Torah! Now let's do it all over again!"

Question number 22: *From where in the Torah do we learn that you must make Kiddush [the prayer sanctifying a Shabbat or Jewish holiday recited over wine or grape juice]? Can you provide me with a quote? How many parts are there to Kiddush, and what are they?*

Answer: Amazingly enough, there is no place in the Torah where it says we must make Kiddush. The Hebrew Bible does not mention anywhere that it is a commandment for Jews to recite this special blessing over wine on Shabbat or festival evenings. However, it is important to remember that modern Judaism is not identical to the religion described in the Torah. The vast, overwhelming majority of Jews alive today are actually rabbinic Jews, not biblical Jews. And the rabbis of the Talmud who interpreted the Torah and created our modern Judaism interpreted Exodus 20:8, which says, "Remember the Sabbath—to keep it Holy" as referring to Kiddush. In other words, the Talmudic rabbis argued, how do we remember to keep the Shabbat holy? By making Kiddush! This ritual act of making a blessing over wine is the manner by which we remember and make the Shabbat day holy in our lives. The rabbis in the Talmud also noted that in Genesis 2:1-4, it states that God "sanctified the Sabbath day and made it holy." Therefore, whenever we make Kiddush, which literally means "holy" or "sanctification," we are actually emulating God by making the Shabbat day holy to us. It might be a somewhat circular answer; however, this is how many rabbinic and modern traditions have evolved.

There are different parts of Kiddush depending on whether you are reciting it on Friday night or Saturday morning or whether you are reciting Kiddush for a Jewish festival. For Friday night, there are three main parts—an introduction that is actually the quote from Genesis 2:1-4 about God resting on the Shabbat following the six days of creation followed by a second part, the actual blessing over the wine. However, we do not drink it until after we say the third part, another blessing that speaks of God having created the world and resting on the seventh day as well as references to God having brought us out of Egypt. Then we drink the (Kosher) wine or grape juice, and in this way do we remember and make the Shabbat day holy.

Question number 23: I am a congregational leader in my synagogue, and it frustrates me to no end that people in my synagogue seem to shy away from receiving ritual honors in the worship services and avoid participating in even the smallest of ways. What could I say to them to persuade them to be more active?

Answer: What a great question! I am all too aware of the fact that so many Jews inexplicably refuse to accept synagogue honors when offered, so I hope that you will indeed help to change some minds in your community and help people feel less shy and perhaps even create some excitement about participating in the communal prayer services.

First, I would simply present the fact that in the Jewish community's constellation of values, it is considered a great social honor to be recognized with a synagogue honor. In earlier times and in some traditional congregations today, people used to literally bid for these honors, turning synagogue services into temporary auction houses so that they could vie for these small roles and congregational honors! The money raised would be used for the synagogue or charitable purposes. The opportunity to publicly participate in the synagogue service demonstrates one's love of Judaism and sense of commitment to its survival and spiritual health.

Also, people frequently refuse honors due to either ignorance of the ritual or fear of not doing it right or simply not knowing how to do it. Perhaps your synagogue could sponsor a workshop on how to perform such synagogue honors as how to receive an Aliyah to the Torah (say blessings before and after the Torah chanting), do Hagbah and G'lilah that is raising and wrapping the Torah, or even open the ark during the Torah service. Good luck!

Question number 24: *Is it possible to form a Minyon* [minimum number of adult Jews necessary to be present to constitute a traditional prayer quorum] *in a chat room on the Internet? Can a group of ten or more people physically separated, but who have agreed to pray as a specific time, constitute a Minyon?*

Answer: While other rabbis may praise the connective power of the Internet, I believe that a Minyon should constitute a community of people who are physically together in each other's presence. While it is possible to argue about the merits of an online community, it betrays and mocks the commonsense understanding of the Jewish value of community. People being together means being together in each other's bodily presence. As it says in the Mishnah in the tractate of Pirkei Avot, when ten people come together for prayer, the Shechinah, or God's presence, is in their midst. IMHO (that is, in my humble opinion), a chat room Minyon just doesn't cut it. LOL (laugh out loud).

Chapter 15

Death, Funerals, and Mourning
(Thirteen Questions)

Death is perhaps one of the universal topics of theological speculation in every religion because no one knows what will happen to us—our souls, our consciousness, or our sense of self—upon our death. Mortality is a subject that very few people like to discuss openly in public or even in private as it is very frightening and filled with unknowns. However, in the world of religion, musings about death and the concept of some kind of afterlife—called eschatology—are a primary focus of spiritual conjecture.

Whereas other religions have very clearly defined ideas of what happens to us at the end of our lives, the Jewish tradition is less sharply delineated. While there is a tremendous amount of material in the ancient Jewish sources regarding the fate of our souls or spirits upon our demise, there is no one overarching, coherent vision that assimilates all of this material. Religious school students or even candidates for conversion to Judaism are usually not required to study or be familiar with any of this material because it is of secondary importance in the Jewish tradition. This is because the most important aspect of Judaism is an emphasis on holy moral conduct in this world in contrast to an otherworldly emphasis or focus. How Jews behave in the here and now has been historically more important to the Jewish community than what individual Jews believe.

As a result of this, many people—Jews included—are unfamiliar with the traditional sources, mythology, and folklore that the ancient rabbis indulged in when it came to imagining an afterlife. Throughout the ages, Jewish religious leaders and teachers have not shied away from exploring and articulating their own views of what a Jewish afterlife might look like, but this material has been largely sermonic or homiletic in nature with no direct connection or influence on the realm of ritual commandments. Therefore, questions about death and the afterlife remain a popular issue of discussion and inquiry among the Jewish rabbinic world but with little theological consensus. The various questions that I received regarding this otherworldly aspect of the Jewish traditions appear in the following last two chapters on spirituality, Jewish theology, and God.

This chapter focuses on the practical questions dealing with the concrete and emotionally real world of coping with death and dying in the Jewish tradition. Everyone, at some point or other in our lives, has to deal with the reality of the passing of friends and loved ones. And when it comes to death and mourning, the Jewish tradition focuses on how to best fulfill the values of honoring the lives of those who have passed away while attending to the needs of the surviving and grieving family members. Death is real, and grief can be devastating, but mourning should not destroy the fabric of our lives. The traditional Jewish mourning customs enable people to express their pain and suffering in a healthy, supportive context and slowly move them through the various stages of loss and sorrow and gradually help people to reintegrate back into life again. Therefore, the following questions deal with both the reality of death as well as the mythic world of the afterlife. The order of the questions in this chapter follow a chronological order from dealing with those who are dying through the preparation for burial, the funeral, and the mourning customs that follow.

Question number 1: *My mother-in-law is dying of cancer, and my elementary school-aged children are very close to her. Although they know she is dying, I am worried that she will die while they are away at their out-of-state summer camp. My question is, should I bring them home for* *the funeral? Should I even tell them at all or wait until they get home at the end of the summer? Should this be a decision for my husband to make or both of us together or me alone as their mother? Do you think that my children are old enough to make their own choice? Should they even be at the funeral at all? Thank you.*

Answer: You ask very good questions, and I think it is wise that you are seeking some outside guidance in making these decisions. First and foremost, I encourage you to speak to your children before they leave for camp about their grandmother's likely death over the summer. Explain the situation to them in as much detail as you feel comfortable and you think they can handle, for you know them better than anyone. You should tell them the truth and be open and honest. Your husband should be involved as well. Explain your own feelings about the situation so that your children know what you are thinking and considering. You might consider sharing some of the following ideas below with your children but in your own words.

1. Death is a very upsetting part of life, but it is also very natural. And in the case of your mother-in-law, her death will not be unexpected since they already know she is dying of cancer.
2. In order for your children to deal with her dying and death in a healthy and appropriate way, you should encourage them to think about how they want to spend their time with their grandma so they can have some positive lasting memories with her and find a way to say goodbye.
3. Attending a funeral can be a very upsetting but important experience in learning to deal with and accept death. So on the one hand, perhaps you should explain to your children that attending the funeral might be a very sad and possibly scary experience for them but nevertheless an important event in the life of your family and a way to honor the life of their grandma, as well as a chance to say a final farewell. Remind them that you and your husband will be there for them as well.
4. On the other hand, you should also ask your children to consider the fact that leaving summer camp for this experience might be

very sad and a bit overwhelming to combine the two very different experiences.

5. Ask your children what they want to do. Give them plenty of time and explore all of the options as you all talk about it together. Help them process their feelings as well with your guidance.

6. Ask them to think about how they might feel if they did attend the funeral. Would they come in advance of their grandma's death or only after? Would they return to camp afterward? How would they feel in this case? Would a return to camp activities and their friends help them cope with their grandma's death, or would it be too jarring a juxtaposition?

7. Ask them to think about how they might feel if they did not attend the funeral. Would they feel they missed something? How would they feel afterward at the end of the summer if they hadn't attended the funeral?

8. Ask yourself how would you and your husband feel if your children attended or did not attend the funeral? Try to be as honest as possible about your own feelings of whether you would want them there for yourselves as your emotional support.

There are no right or wrong answers here, but you owe it to your children and yourselves to discuss the options honestly and openly. I recommend reading the book *Teaching Your Children about God* by Rabbi David Wolpe. It has an excellent section about dealing with death and children. Also, many Jewish funeral homes have pamphlets about dealing with death with children. None of your decisions will be easy, but I wish you courage and fortitude to do what is best for your family as a whole!

Question number 2: Why do Jews guard their dead at the funeral home while they are being prepared for the funeral? What are you supposed to do?

Answer: You are referring to a practice called Shemirah, or literally "guarding," in the Jewish tradition where upon someone's death, their body is never left alone until the actual funeral and burial. This guarding is purely symbolic and is considered a way to show respect for the life that the person lived and the image of God that the lifeless body still bears.

All that happens is that while the body remains in a cool storage area in the funeral home, volunteers, friends, or family members, usually one at a time, sit outside this room reading from the book Psalms from the Hebrew Bible. It is considered an honor to participate in this Mitzvah; therefore, family friends may organize a number of people to take turns fulfilling this commandment.

This guarding only extends from the moment a person dies until the funeral, rarely more than a day or two. Many friends and family members will often organize themselves into shifts of a few hours so that this burden does not fall on only one person. It is a beautiful and moving way to honor the life of the person who passed.

Question number 3: I was just asked by a friend to officiate at the funeral of one of his family members. I am not a rabbi, but I am fairly involved in my synagogue and familiar with the prayer book. Do you have any suggestions as what prayers or readings I should include other than a eulogy and the Mourner's Kaddish? Thanks for your help.

Answer: What a lovely gesture of respect to you that your friend asked you to conduct the funeral of a family member. As I'm sure you know, you do not need to be a rabbi to officiate at a funeral. So here are several suggestions that you might consider when planning the funeral service.

1. Readings in English or Hebrew from a Hebrew prayer book or the Hebrew Bible. Any selection of creative English readings and Hebrew psalms from the Hebrew Bible may be appropriate. Each family is free to include and read any readings they find relevant and appropriate for the occasion. Please feel free to customize the service as you wish. They don't even have to be

from a Hebrew prayer book or the Hebrew Bible, but that is always a good place to start. Psalm 23 is a good one to start with, the one that begins, "The Lord is my shepherd." Both Psalms 90 and 91 are additional traditional reading at Jewish funerals.

2. The sharing of memories and stories by the family members who might wish to speak. This is the essence of a burial, the sharing of anecdotes and remembrances of the departed as an expression of love and appreciation for their life. I always encourage family members to express their thoughts and feelings as an opportunity to celebrate the life that was and to say goodbye while cherishing the love and memories of the deceased. While I never cajole or force anyone to speak, I tell mourners that it is often better to challenge themselves to find something, anything to say at this time because no matter how inarticulate they might believe they are, they should not let the moment pass without having said something. I do this because I have counseled many people who struggled for years afterward with their guilt that they didn't speak up when the appropriate opportunity was available.

3. The burial. As difficult as it may seem, it is customary for everyone present to participate by shoveling some dirt into the grave after the coffin has been lowered. This is perhaps the most emotionally difficult and intense moment of a burial when the hollow noise of the dirt hitting the lid of the coffin resounds in the grave, and many people often break down in tears at this point. But this is also the moment of recognizing the reality of mortality, and from here on, a healthy grieving and healing process can begin. The more traditional the community, the more of the grave the family and friends fill in. This is because it is part of the Jewish tradition to ensure that we, the members of a family in grief, do not delegate to others, especially the employees of a cemetery, what should be performed by us as a labor of love, respect, and honor.

4. Recitation of El Malei Rachamim. This prayer is traditionally recited on the Yahrzeit, or year anniversary of someone's death. However, it is appropriate to recite it at the burial as well. It can be read in Hebrew or English or both. Essentially, this prayer

(found in nearly all traditional Jewish prayer books) speaks of our hope that the deceased will find rest and peace in the embrace of God.

5. Recitation of Mourner's Kaddish. Everyone present for a funeral may recite the Mourner's Kaddish, a prayer written over a thousand years ago in Aramaic, a language that the Jews spoke then. It actually does not mention death but is rather a prayer praising God's qualities and serves to remind us that the mysteries of life and death are often beyond the understanding of us mere mortals. For more information, I encourage you to contact your local rabbi for consultation and guidance. I'm sure that you will conduct a meaningful service for your friend and his or her family.

Question number 4: I am Catholic and was very close to my Jewish neighbor who just died. At the funeral, I was shocked and disturbed to see the casket lowered into the grave. Is this a traditional Jewish practice or something that the family chose to do on their own? Also, although they did not have a viewing, I was told that the deceased was not dressed in a suit or formal clothing. Why not? Thanks for your help.

Answer: It must indeed have been very confusing and even distressing to be present at a traditional Jewish funeral when you were not familiar with the customs of Jewish burial. And I can only imagine how upsetting it must have been for you to see the casket lowered into the grave if you were not prepared for it. The most important thing to keep in mind when understanding a traditional Jewish funeral is that all of the conventions and practices have evolved in such a way so as to preserve the dignity of the dead and help the family members who mourn confront the reality of mortality and help pave the way for grieving and healing.

Because of this, Jewish dead are prepared for burial by a special volunteer group of Jewish men and women called in Hebrew the Hevra Kadisha or a Holy Society. They wash the body in a respectful fashion, recite special prayers, and dress the body in plain white shrouds. The point being that in death, we are all equal; everyone is dressed the same, rich or poor. In addition, to preserve the dignity of the dead (and the body), there is no open casket or viewing of a body. When someone dies, the close family may see the remains before burial preparation, but the point is to remember the deceased as they were alive and not remember them in death.

In the Jewish tradition, it is considered disrespectful to the dead to embalm them, dress them up, and display them as a lifeless object before other people. We are not permitted to turn the lifeless body into a thing or a mere object. The soul of that person has departed; therefore, to respect their memory—and the remains of their body—we have an obligation to prepare the body for a simple, dignified burial as soon as possible. The soul has returned to God; therefore, we must return the dead body to the earth as soon as possible.

In addition, the body of every human being is created in the image of God. Once the soul departs, the unique spirit of that person is no longer there—dressing someone up and embalming them and putting makeup on them only insults their memory of who they were in life and is a gross attempt to deny the reality of death. Therefore, to respect the image of the divine inherent in every human body, we treat that body with dignity and respect and prepare it for burial as soon as possible.

At the cemetery, the casket is lowered into the grave immediately because it is considered disrespectful to keep the body hanging, suspended above an open grave. There is a tremendous value placed on a speedy burial and returning the body to its origins in the earth after the soul has returned to God. To suspend the body above the grave for our benefit or even the duration of the funeral service is considered mocking the dead. Therefore, a body is lowered immediately into the grave, its final resting place, usually right at the beginning of a traditional Jewish burial service. This is indeed a sad and upsetting sight—but it is the reality of our lives as mortal creatures. Judaism does not delight in hurting people or forcing people to witness painful sights. However, it does not believe in hiding the reality of our mortality. We all die—that is real.

338   Rabbi Daniel Kohn

It is painful for some people to see this and acknowledge it, but hiding from it or trying to deny it is not emotionally or psychologically helpful or healthy.

Also, the Jewish tradition believes that confronting the painful reality of death is a positive and healthy way to begin the grieving and healing process. If we try to run away from the actuality of death, it only delays the grieving and healing process and leads us to expressing our grief in other unhealthy ways. I have conducted many funerals, and despite the pain involved to family members, it has been my experience that it is far healthier to confront the painful reality of death than to deny it. I hope this helps to answer your questions and gives you some insight into the traditional Jewish funeral practices that you observed.

Question number 5: Could you please explain the Kaddish to me and why it is recited? Thanks!

Answer: The Kaddish is a prayer written in Aramaic and probably first began to be said in synagogues in the twelfth century in Europe. It is basically a statement about the greatness and holiness of God. There are five forms of the Kaddish (the word itself means "holy") that appear throughout the Jewish prayer book to punctuate or separate various parts of the weekday, Shabbat, and holiday services.

For instance, the Kaddish DeRabbanan, or the Rabbi's Kaddish, is recited in the morning prayers after studying sections from the Talmud and other rabbinic sources; and the Hatzi Kaddish, or the half Kaddish, is recited at various points of a service as a means to separate one section of prayers from another while the Kaddish Shalem, or the Full Kaddish, is recited at the end of a worship service.

There is another special Kaddish that is recited only at the actual funeral service by the surviving family members. However, the form of the Kaddish that is familiar to most Jews is the Kaddish Yatom or the Orphan's Kaddish, which is also called the Mourner's Kaddish. It is usually recited by Jews who are observing a period of mourning for a family member who has passed away and by people who are commemorating the annual anniversary of a family member's death called the Yarhzeit in Yiddish. It is recited usually at the end of all Jewish worship services. I hope this answers your question.

Question number 6: Why do Jews wash their hands after visiting the cemetery?

Answer: The quick answer is that it is a symbolic way to wash off the ritual impurity of death that is present in a cemetery. But I can't leave you with just this answer; it is too bizarre, and I feel I need to provide some background information for this answer to make sense.

When the ancient Jewish Temple used to stand in Jerusalem almost two thousand years ago where Jews would bring animals to sacrifice to God, there was a vast system of rules and regulations relating to a person's state of ritual cleanness or purity. These terms have absolutely nothing to do with hygienic cleanliness—only ritual states. Only someone who was in a ritually clean or pure state could enter the Temple to offer his sacrifice to God.

How did people become unclean? One primary source of ancient ritual impurity was contact with a dead body, for it was a locus of ritual pollution. If you touched a dead body in ancient times or were even in the same room as a dead body, then you became ritually polluted. Even if you were to take a hot shower, you would still be ritually polluted by the presence of the dead body because it had nothing to do with physical or hygienic cleanliness. What was the significance of this? Because a person had to be ritually pure in order to enter the Temple, make a sacrifice, and do anything connected with Jewish worship in the Temple.

How did a person become ritually pure again? After contact with the dead, a person had to have a Jewish priest, called a Kohen in Hebrew, sprinkle them with a special liquid mixture of water, ashes from a sacrificed burned red calf. Then the person had to immerse himself in a Mikvah, a Jewish ritual bath of natural water, and then they were ritually pure again

A cemetery itself was another source of ritual pollution in ancient times. Anyone who entered a cemetery immediately became ritually polluted because of the mere presence of dead bodies—even below ground. Everyone who entered a cemetery in ancient times had to go through this process to become ritually pure again. However, once the Temple was destroyed, it was not possible to make this special purifying liquid mixture of water and ashes from the special sacrifice because Jews could no longer perform animal sacrifices. Since the year 70 CE, every Jew in the world is now considered to be ritually impure. But since there is no Temple, there actually is no need to ever be ritually pure again. Therefore, for the past two thousand years, there is no such thing as ritual purity or impurity. These concepts still exist in ancient Jewish laws, but the reality that they were designed to deal with disappeared two millennia ago. These ancient states of ritual purity and impurity have no practical use in the Jewish religion in modern times.

However, customs as strong as the Temple rituals die very slowly. For example, as a memory of these ancient states of ritual purity and impurity, Jews still ritually wash their hands before eating Challah on Friday nights on the Sabbath. This is done only as a memory of when people went to the Mikvah in ancient times to become ritually pure. We only do it nowadays as a reminder of what used to be practiced and to spiritually purify ourselves. The same is true for men and women who use the Mikvah today—it is only for spiritual purification.

Finally, to answer your question! Today, some Jews, whenever they visit a cemetery—whether for a funeral or not—still wash their hands upon leaving as a symbolic act of separating between the realms of the living and the dead and to recall the ancient rite of full immersion in a Mikvah to purify oneself after having been in a cemetery. This is a long answer to a short question, but I hope my answer explained the reasons and origin of this custom.

Question number 7: What is the symbolism of placing a rock on a Jewish gravestone? Does it have anything to do with the prayer that is recited at a funeral that begins, "The Rock! His deeds are perfect. Yea, all His ways are just"?

Answer: Jews place rocks on graves as a symbol of remembrance. After all, a rock is a symbol of permanence; and therefore, the rock symbolizes the permanence of the memory of the dead in our hearts. It is not considered a Jewish practice to place flowers on a grave for this very reason—flowers are fragile and impermanent. We want to emphasize not only the permanence of our memories of the dead but also the permanence of God's love. In the burial service, the prayer that you refer to that begins with the words "The Rock" actually is referring to God—this is a traditional appellation for God and not a physical rock. But it was really insightful that you made that connection!

Question number 8: Why do people sit Shiva? And why is it for different numbers of days?

Answer: Shiva is an ancient custom, going back even beyond the time of the Talmud, over three thousand years ago. The word "Shiva" in Hebrew actually means "seven." Jews sit Shiva for seven days because psychologically, this period of time is considered the most intense stretch of mourning, the week immediately following the funeral. For one week, the Jewish tradition encourages people to stay in their homes and mourn in order to express their sadness and enable the community to visit and support those in need.

During the period of Shiva, the mourners are supposed to remain in their homes and sit on low stools close to the floor or on the ground as a sign of humility and mourning. Their friends are then supposed to visit them during these seven days and give them consolation and words of comfort. In addition, since the mourning members of the family are considered to be in a state of shock, others should bring them food and hold worship services in their home so the mourners can recite the Kaddish, a traditional prayer recited by mourners. However, not everyone is able to take off a full seven days from work, and some people condense the seven days of mourning down to three or fewer depending on their circumstances.

After seven days of Shiva, the mourner doesn't completely stop mourning. After the seven days of Shiva, they mourn another somewhat less intense period of mourning called Sheloshim, which means "thirty." That is, after the seven days of Shiva are up, the mourners keep saying Kaddish and do some mourning customs for the next twenty-three days (7 + 23 = 30). At the end of that time, mourning stops. However, when someone mourns the death of a parent, they continue to say Kaddish for the next eleven months to a year. Why do we do this? Because some people claim that these periods of less intense mourning help reintegrate a person back into their regular life while still acknowledging their loss and pain.

Question number 9: Why is it forbidden for a Jew to get a tattoo? And is it true that Jews with tattoos cannot be buried in a Jewish cemetery?

Answer: There are indeed many traditional texts that prohibit Jews from getting tattoos, but like all other Jewish rituals and commandments, everyone is ultimately free to do what they want. Here are a number of quotes from the Torah and other authoritative rabbinic texts that deal with the issue of Jews and tattoos.

1. Leviticus 19:28, "You shall not make gashes in your flesh for the dead or incise any marks on yourselves: I am the Lord." This is a pretty clear quote that forbids the ancient Israelites from marking their skins in a tattoolike fashion.
2. Mishnah Makkot 3:6, "If a man wrote (on his skin) incised-writing . . . he is not guilty (of a sin) unless he writes it and incises it with ink or dye or any material which leaves a lasting mark." This quote from the Talmud contains a more precise description of what is specifically prohibited about tattoos, namely, their permanency in the skin.

3. Rabbi Moses Maimonides, Mishneh Torah, Book of Laws of Idolaters 12:11, "This (practice of tattooing) was a custom among the pagans, who marked themselves for idolatry." Maimonides, who lived nearly a thousand years ago, speculated as to the reason that tattoos were originally forbidden in the Torah. He suspected that they were somehow connected to ancient Canaanite pagan worship. And since the Torah was so antipagan, it is not surprising that anything connected to Canaanite religion would be prohibited.

4. Shulchan Aruch, Yoreh Deah 180:2, "If it (the tattoo) was done in the flesh of another, the one to whom it was done is blameless (of sin)." This law code was published in 1567, and despite the fact that it is five hundred years old, this particular law has some surprisingly contemporary implications. Namely, survivors of the Holocaust who were tattooed are not considered guilty of getting tattoos since it was done against their will.

5. Genesis 1:27, "And God created man in God's image, in the image of God He created him, male and female God created them." Finally, to return to the Torah, perhaps getting a tattoo implies that our bodies are not beautiful or perfect enough and need additional adornment; for after all, we were all created in the image of God.

In summary, tattoos were prohibited beginning with the Torah through the Talmud and up to medieval law codes. Regardless of how you personally may choose to view a tattoo, according to a traditional understanding of Judaism, it is inconsistent with Jewish religious values. Keep in mind that the Nazis tattooed their victims as a way to depersonalize them as human beings. I have heard some people say that because the Nazis forcibly tattooed Jews to humiliate and dehumanize them, Jews should not voluntarily do this to themselves no matter how common tattoos may currently be in popular culture.

Regarding the burial of Jews with tattoos, there is no consensus among the proprietors of Jewish cemeteries and Jewish funeral homes. Some funeral homes and cemeteries may indeed prevent such remains from interment as a form of after-the-fact punishment of the person for having gotten a tattoo. However, no Holocaust survivor with a tattoo has ever been refused burial in a Jewish cemetery. And personally, it does feel a little wrong to punish the mourning family members to refuse them permission to bury their loved one in a Jewish cemetery just because the deceased chose to get a tattoo. However, you should know that this practice of refusing burial to a Jew with a tattoo is not universally practiced and rather rare.

Question number 10: I am embarrassed to admit this, but years after my brother died, I went to a spiritual medium to talk to his spirit as a way of coping with his death. I know that in the Torah it states, "Do not turn to ghosts and do not inquire of familiar spirits, to be defiled by them: I the Lord am your God" [Leviticus 19:31]. If I committed a sin, how can I repent?

Answer: The death of your brother must have been very difficult and painful for you, so much so that you wanted to maintain contact with him after his death. Indeed, the Jewish tradition does not believe any good can come of people trying to maintain some kind of contact with those who have died, if such a thing is at all possible.

Emotionally, it may even serve to impede accepting the pain and grief of death, delaying our healing for some time. I would never want to make anyone feel guilty for something they did after the fact, so I'm not. I hope that consulting a medium brought you peace. However, I would encourage you not to do it again as I do not believe it is an emotionally healthy way to deal with your pain and sadness. Instead, I would encourage you to speak with a mental health professional, perhaps a grief counselor or a rabbi in order to address your legitimate feelings of loss and sorrow.

As far as repenting, that is easy. Just don't do it again! As Jews, we believe that the memories of our loved ones remain alive through us in *our* lives and actions. If you want to keep your brother's memory and values alive, then give money and invest your time and energy into charitable causes that were important to him. Influence the world of the living, not the dead.

Question number 11*: Both my mother and father passed away at different times when I was away on business trips, and I was not able to be with either of them when they passed away. Although it has been years since my parents died, I still feel a void in my life. How can I deal with this lack of closure that I feel?*

Answer: I am so sorry to hear about the very difficult circumstances of the passing of both your parents. The love and presence of a parent can never be replaced or even truly gotten over. As part of the traditional Jewish mourning customs, when a parent dies, a symbolic rip in one's clothing is made directly over one's heart to symbolize how our hearts have been ripped open with the passing of a parent.

One of the most profound and traditional ways to mourn parents in the Jewish tradition is to recite the Mourner's Kaddish for either eleven months in traditional communities or a full year in some liberal Jewish communities. The continuity and routine of this simple ritual act can provide a sense of stability during this time of emotional turmoil. Plus, the human contact with other members of the Jewish community you are part of can also be very comforting and supportive.

While you may never be able to achieve closure for the passing of your parents, if you want to have a more concrete experience, I recommend that you create and arrange a mourning or memorial service for your family and friends close to you. I would urge you to work with whatever rabbi you may be close to in setting something up. It does not have to be elaborate. But it might be an evening service, perhaps after work sometime at which the traditional Ma'ariv (evening) prayer service is recited, and you could recite the Mourner's Kaddish and perhaps even speak to the group for a few minutes, sharing your feelings about the passing of your parents and need to achieve closure. Sometimes articulating your thoughts and sharing your pain in the presence of friends and family can be very healing. If this is not sufficient, I encourage you to seek out a grief counselor who can help you resolve these painful feelings. I wish you a complete and speedy recovery of your emotional and spiritual health.

Question number 12*: I am planning on conducting an unveiling service for my father's headstone next month for close friends and family. Could you share some ideas on what we are supposed to do?*

Answer: The unveiling of a headstone or monument at the grave of a loved one can be a difficult and complicated experience. It has the potential to reawaken painful memories and feelings of loss and grief unresolved from the period of mourning. On the other hand, it can also potentially bring a sense of comfort and closure and, hopefully, even healing. Because there is no single official religious ceremony or ritual accompanying an unveiling, it is an opportunity for a family to create a fitting and appropriate experience tailored to their family's needs.

The establishment of a headstone is an ancient custom whose purpose is to maintain the memory of the departed as well as identify the grave site. According to Jewish law, it permitted to set up a headstone as early as thirty days after the funeral. However, I strongly recommend that the unveiling take place one full year after the funeral, close to the date of the very first Yahrzeit or the anniversary of the date of death. This is because another important function of an unveiling ceremony is to try and achieve a sense of closure on the mourning experience. While it is only natural to experience deep loss and sadness following the death of a loved one, the Jewish tradition gently urges us to mark and define appropriate periods of mourning as we are slowly guided back into our daily lives. The unveiling ceremony marks the last stage in this process, commemorating a full twelve months since the death. Therefore, rather than tearing open fresh wounds of pain and grief, the unveiling ceremony is intended to be a moment of deep reflection and contemplation as well as appreciation for the life that touched the hearts of so many others.

There is no prescribed script for what a headstone should contain. However, it is common to include the Hebrew name of the deceased and dates of birth and death. A Hebrew name consists of their person's first name followed by son or daughter of the Hebrew names of their mother and father. If they were descended from the tribe of Levi or were a Kohen, this information is also typically included in the Hebrew name. Sometimes families have Hebrew letters or phrases inscribed in the stone. The most common Hebrew phrase is one that states, "May his/her soul be bound up in the bond of life."

An unveiling ceremony is not a long service. It can last anywhere from ten minutes to half an hour. Once everyone has arrived, it is appropriate to gather everyone around the gravesite in a U shape or circle and stand together as a group. The ceremony typically consists of some readings in English or Hebrew from the Hebrew Bible. A good selection is Psalm 23 that begins, "The Lord is my shepherd." Next comes the sharing of memories and stories by the family members. This is the essence of an unveiling ceremony, the sharing of anecdotes and remembrances of the departed as an expression of love and appreciation for their life. I encourage family members to express their thoughts and feelings as an opportunity to celebrate the life that was and to achieve a sense of inner closure and healing while cherishing the love and memories of the deceased.

After this usually comes the physical unveiling of the headstone. The headstone is usually covered by a cloth in advance by cemetery personnel that is then removed by members of the family at this point in the service. Again, different prayers and readings may be recited at this point to solemnize the unveiling. This brief service then concludes with recitation of El Malei Rachamim (memorial prayer) in Hebrew or English followed by the Mourner's Kaddish.

It is a Jewish custom to place a small rock or stone on the headstone as a sign of respect. A stone represents the eternal love that God carries for all of us and is symbolic of the enduring influence and memories of the deceased within our hearts. It is also appropriate and considered respectful to place stones on the headstones of other grave sites that you may visit. The Jewish tradition discourages placing flowers on a grave because such money is better spent on Tzedakah (charity) to better perpetuate the ideals of the deceased in this life. Finally, it is customary for family members to enjoy a meal together afterward and so to celebrate the continuity of life.

Question number 13: My mother passed away last year, and I was originally planning on purchasing a memorial plaque in our temple in her honor. However, I feel there must be a better way to honor her memory than have her name engraved on a place on a wall that few people will ever see. Do you have any suggestions on what I might do?

Answer: There is indeed a better way to memorialize your mother—establish a fund in her honor at a charity that was important to her. As you may know, it is a Jewish tradition to give Tzedakah, or charity, in someone's honor and name rather than bring flowers. Flowers look pretty, and then they wither and die within a day or two but won't do anything else. But giving Tzedakah helps people in this world and perpetuates values that were important to the deceased. Let your mother's name and memory be associated with good acts and charitable deeds in this world right now. Help needy people in her name.

Chapter 16

Spirituality and Jewish Theology
(Sixteen Questions)

The behavioral philosophy of Judaism can be summed up in the following pithy maxim: the deed supersedes the creed. That is, deeds—appropriate, correct, moral, Halachic, or Jewish legal behavior—are more important than creed, faith, or what a person believes.

While there is certainly a core body of basic Jewish beliefs such as the existence and unity of God, over the centuries, Judaism evolved as a religion that emphasizes adherence to a wide body of ritual and moral laws rather than a dogmatic insistence upon specific beliefs. The books of the Torah contain the first, original code of 613 laws of the Israelites. The early rabbis of the Talmud further interpreted and added to these laws, and this process continues to the present day. Judaism is a religious system expressed as a legal structure and codified in many different collections of edicts, rulings, and regulations intended to guide a Jew through every stage of life, every day of the week, and throughout the years. In short, Judaism is essentially a vast compendium of laws and practices whose purpose is to provide a format for Jews to live each and every day and hour of their entire lives.

As a result, it should not be surprising that there is little prominence placed on Jewish beliefs. Yet despite the salience of Judaism as a primarily legal tradition, the rabbis of the Talmud and religious leaders during other historical eras of Jewish history did not shy away from expressing and articulating a rich tapestry of spiritual beliefs, ideas, visions, and creative fantasies. These rabbis had no problem communicating their dreams and ideas of what the world might look like after death in a world to come or what role God might play in this final judgment or the function of the Messiah, the nature of our souls, the existence of evil or if there will be a resurrection of the dead or what the heavenly realm of angels and God's celestial throne and retinue might possibly look like.

Yet these rabbis and creative storytellers of the Jewish people did not foist off their visions on anyone else. They did not demand that generations of Jewish students should memorize or accept theological catechisms as part of their religious training. There is no official Jewish credo or succinct statement of beliefs and declarations of faith. Rather, the eschatological or end-of-days visions of these rabbis reveal not so much a snapshot of their beliefs so much as an articulation of the most important values of the Jewish tradition writ at large. In other words, since no one knows what happens to us upon our deaths, the early rabbis used these scenarios much as an artist uses a blank canvas. They wrote upon it what they thought were the most important and enduring of all values in Judaism: justice, God's mercy, the persistence of the soul and the unique, individual personality, and life choices of every person. The stories of an afterlife and the days of the Messiah were not intended to be understood literally but rather, like Aesop's fables, to convey spiritual and moral messages about how we should live our lives now.

As I have written in other places, when answering the numerous e-mail questions about Judaism that I received, I held that it was not my job to tell anyone what they were supposed to believe. That should be up to everyone on their own to decide upon. Rather, I understood that my job as an Internet rabbi was to share the sources and creative thinking of the ancient rabbis to spark our own resourcefulness and to reveal the rich, creative world that the rabbis were not afraid to construct in their own imaginations and inspire in ours. The rabbis never directly stated, "Justice is the most important value to us as Jews." Instead, they fashioned a lengthy eschatological vision in which they imagined all of the peoples of the world parading into God's celestial courtroom before the Holy One, the supreme judge of all humanity, only to be confronted and charged with their numerous sins and cruel actions in history and face punishment for their moral crimes throughout antiquity. For even if the Roman Empire could not be judged and convicted of the murder of hundreds of thousands of Jews and held culpable for horrific persecutions against the Jewish people in historical reality, the rabbis were at least able to have a last laugh by formulating this story and sharing it over and over and over again with their students, generation after generation.

The following questions and answers present a very brief glimpse into the fertile and productive, imaginative minds of the rabbis. Whether you agree or disagree with these answers or the visions and religious beliefs of the rabbis or texts that I quote is not the point. Rather, I hope that these answers will serve as a starting place for everyone to initiate a process of considering and articulating their own theological lens through which to make sense of the world we live in and to learn more about the creative forces and minds that shaped the foundation of rabbinic Judaism nearly two thousand years ago. The questions in this chapter begin with general queries about Jewish beliefs and topics related to this world including Christianity, the Messiah, angels and then delve into the rich world of the Jewish understanding of an afterlife and a world to come and conclude with theological questions about the Holocaust.

Question number 1: What are the five basic beliefs of Judaism?

Answer: I don't know! Did you hear that there were only five? Seriously, there is no such list of the top five beliefs of Judaism. Although I'll bet David Letterman could come up with a list of the top ten! The Jewish tradition in general is not real big on emphasizing people's beliefs. Rather, it is more important how people behave than what they believe.

However, nearly one thousand years ago, Rabbi Moses Maimonides came up with thirteen basic beliefs that he believed were the foundation of the

Jewish religion. However, you should know that many other rabbis at the time quarreled with Rabbi Maimonides about these beliefs—many rejected them altogether. However, the first five of these are the following:

1. God exists.
2. God is one.
3. God is formless, without any body or corporeal existence.
4. God is eternal with no beginning and no end.
5. God alone is to be worshipped by the Jewish people.

It goes on this way, but as you can see, these aren't really the five basic beliefs of Judaism overall. They are statements about belief in God. Every rabbi you ask will most likely give you a different top five set of basic beliefs that are fundamental to Judaism. However, just to fill out this original list, Rabbi Maimonides went on to state that the other basic Jewish beliefs are the following:

6. The words of the biblical prophets are all true.
7. Moses was the greatest prophet.
8. The Torah is true.
9. The Torah is unchangeable; it has never changed and never will be changed.
10. God knows the deeds and thoughts of all human beings.
11. God rewards and punishes people for their behavior.
12. The Messiah will come one day.
13. God will resurrect the dead one day.

Unlike various denominations of Christianity and even Islam, Judaism has no official catechism, that is, an officially or universally acknowledged set of beliefs. Jews do not have to memorize, nor are they required to believe any set of specific beliefs. Jews can still be Jews and believe anything they want. Synagogue membership is not predicated on professing any beliefs. I know this can be confusing, especially for members of religions where adherence to a certain set of beliefs defines membership in that community. But in the Jewish community, righteous and moral behavior is far more important than personal faith.

Question number 2: What does Judaism have to say about Charles Darwin and the theory of evolution? I've been doing some research and haven't been able to find anything.

Answer: Perhaps part of the reason you can't find much is that among the majority of liberal Jews in the world, there is no contradiction between Judaism and the theory of evolution. Most Jews correctly understand that the Hebrew Bible is not a book of science but rather a book of theological truths about God and humanity. Despite the inclusion of the stories of creation in the Hebrew Bible, they are not intended to be historically or scientifically accurate descriptions of the origin of the world. That is a unique and distinctly Christian fundamentalist misunderstanding of the Hebrew Bible and the story of the creation of the world. The Hebrew Bible's stories of creation are intended to emphasize God's role as a creator and God's role as the organizer of an ordered world and universe.

In fact, the whole point of the first chapter of Genesis is that God brought order to chaos. God divided light from darkness, the heavens from the earth, the sea from the land, and organized a hierarchy of creatures and vegetation for food and created human beings as the pinnacle of living creatures. This was never intended to be a chronologically or scientifically accurate description of the creation of the world and all life in it. It is a statement about God's role in the universe and in human history. Even Rashi, one of the greatest early Jewish commentators on the Torah who lived nearly a one thousand years ago, in his very first comment on the first sentence of the Torah notes that it is not pure history or science. Rather, all of the stories of Genesis were intended to provide a brief story of origin of the Jewish people and to explain why they ended up living in the land of Israel and how and why—according to the Torah—they have a legitimate right and place in the Middle East. In other words, Rashi understood the purpose of the book of Genesis to be a political and theological book—not science.

Yet I have to admit that there are still some Jews who—although they would deny it till their dying day—have been influenced by Christian fundamentalists and have also adopted a belief in creationism—that is, the belief that the book of Genesis and creation should be understood as a literal, historically accurate depiction of creation. However, it should be noted that these predominantly ultra-Orthodox Jews have only embraced this belief as part of a larger fearful reaction to the changes they have been witnessing in the Jewish community over the past two centuries. As the world has changed and as Judaism and the Jewish people have adjusted and responded to the challenges of modern life, these fundamentalist Jews have retreated into a position of denial and denunciation of modern Jewish life. These small, insular Jewish communities that espouse a position of creationism are by definition inwardly focused and have little interest in disseminating their ideas about Jewish creationism outside of their own circles, so it is not surprising you find little about this in the general literary world or the Internet. For the most part, the vast majority of Jews have always understood that there is no conflict between science and Judaism. Science tells us about how the world came into existence. Religion tells us why it came into existence or why we think it did. For information on what the majority of liberal Jews believe about creation and evolution, read Darwin and Jay Gould and other evolutionary scientists!

Question number 3: I have been attending services at a traditional synagogue, but I feel like an impostor because I don't have the certainty of Torah min HaShamayim [Torah from Heaven]. Yet when members challenge me that if I don't believe that the Torah is literally the word of God, then why should I bother observing any of the Mitzvot? What should I say to them?

Answer: The word "orthodox" literally means "correct doctrine." In fact, this may sound strange, but the theological strictness of Jewish Orthodoxy is most similar to the Catholic Church that demands that all adherents subscribe to a very particular and specific set of beliefs. So my first answer for you is that anyone who gives you a hard time, ignore him or her! Your spiritual motivations are none of their business, and you are certainly not required to pass any tests about your personal beliefs in order to belong to a synagogue. There are religious institutions where you are strongly encouraged to believe exactly what everyone else does—and they are called cults! No one can—or should—tell you what to believe about Judaism and demand that you believe what they believe if you want to go to that Shul. And if they do insist, then maybe it is time to go Shul shopping and find another synagogue!

So why should you bother observing the Mitzvot of Judaism if you don't believe the Torah is the literal word of God? I'll give you nine different reasons that were articulated by Rabbi David Golinkin who is the head of the Conservative movement's rabbinical seminary in Israel in his short book *Halachah for Our Time: A Conservative Approach to Jewish Law.* All of them are equally legitimate and appropriate motivations for being a Jew and observant. Please feel free to pick and choose among them as to the reasons you observe Jewish law and customs. The first set of arguments as to why we should observe Jewish law are theocentric or God-centered reasons, and they include the following:

1. The Torah is the literal will of God; we should follow it because God said so! However, you already expressed that this reason doesn't really motivate you so you can skip this one.
2. The Torah is the Jewish people's understanding of God's will; it is not the literal word of God, but it is as close as we can get to figuring out what God wants us to do in this world.
3. The Torah is an expression of the Brit, or covenant, between God and the Jewish people; therefore, the Torah represents a special kind of relationship between the Jewish people and God, and the commandments are simply the special way we should live in order to keep this relationship alive.
4. The Torah and the Mitzvot are a means of attaining holiness; all of the commandments are the Jewish way of living a holy, sacred life.

This second set of arguments as to why we should observe Jewish law are ethnocentric or ethnic—and nation-centered reasons, and they include the following:

5. Halachah unites the scattered Jewish people around the world; we should observe Jewish law as a way to maintain the unity of Jewish peoplehood around the world so that all Jews practice essentially the same Jewish laws and rituals.
6. Halachah forms a link between our ancestors and descendants; the same Jewish laws and customs we observe today were also practiced by Rabbi Akiba in the Talmud, Rabbi Moses Maimonides in the Middle Ages, and the Jews who died during the Holocaust. Jewish law connects Jews throughout time.
7. Halachah protects our people from assimilation and intermarriage; observing Jewish laws actually insulates us from social contact with non-Jews and helps to foster intramarriage.

The last set of arguments as to why we should observe Jewish law are anthropocentric or individual-centered reasons, and they include the following:

8. Halachah builds self-discipline and ethically refines people; it is not easy to observe Jewish law, but if we put in the effort, it makes us better people in the long run.
9. The Mitzvot are a joy to keep and observe; we observe Jewish laws and customs because it is fun!

Don't ever let people make you feel like you have to believe in something you don't just because you want to belong to that synagogue. Ignore them or give them a piece of your mind—and tell them to mind their own business. We have enough problems in Iraq and Afghanistan with the Taliban and Al-Qaeda without fellow Jews trying to tell us all what we should or should not believe! Go to whatever synagogue you want to attend where you feel at home and comfortable, and don't ever let anyone make you feel like any synagogue in the world is not and should not be your spiritual home.

Question number 4: *In your opinion, why do some people have such a rough life? My husband has a slow terminal disease, I'm a diabetic, and* *my kids also have significant health problems. What did I do to deserve this? I do my best to be a good person and treat people fairly. What is wrong?*

Answer: I don't think you or your husband or your children did anything wrong to deserve your difficult health conditions. I don't believe that people's lives are the way they are because of some divine plan or in response to someone's sins. While our life choices obviously significantly affect our lives, often we must cope with or suffer from afflictions and tragedies that are far beyond our ability to influence and even comprehend. I am truly sympathetic to your family's health challenges, and I hope that you are able to obtain the health care that you need so that you can all lead as healthy, happy, and meaningful lives as possible.

Many of us suffer from our own internal and external challenges, physical or emotional. The question that we must all answer is how should we respond to these trials? I think that you have already identified the most important way that God provides for us to improve the quality of our own lives by being good people and helping others around us. If we are focused only on our own lives and pursuit of our own happiness all the time, we will most likely end up being miserable a good part of the time. Self-absorption is not only annoying to other people but also an impediment to our own emotional welfare and growth. But if we can learn to be involved in projects and causes larger than ourselves, charitable causes and humanitarian efforts beyond our own immediate interests, then we take solace in the fact that we are helping to improve the state of the world and becoming partners with God in continuing to improve the work of creation by alleviating the pain and suffering of others in the world. We may not be able to get rid of our own grief and anguish, but we can reduce it by changing our perspectives on life and imbuing our lives and actions with meaning and significance.

The point is not to focus on the fact that we are experiencing pain and difficult circumstances in our lives. The point is what do we do about it? Do we wail and bemoan our fate; or do we choose to live good, productive, helpful lives despite it? Which will bring us greater overall happiness and peace? Which do we think God wants from us? It is a choice we must constantly make every day.

Question number 5: *Do Jews believe Satan is a true being like a human or God or just the trials that come to us in life?*

Answer: "Ha-Satan" is a Hebrew word that simply means "the Opponent." In the theology of the rabbis who created Judaism and recorded their ideas in the Talmud two thousand years ago, God was compared to a judge in a courtroom. Different angels played the parts of a prosecutor and defense attorney. According to the rabbis, one day in the future, every nation in the world will be judged by God, and these angelic lawyers will present their cases. In the case of the Jewish people, the eternal special prosecutor of the Jews is called Ha-Satan. He tries to present the deeds of the Jewish people in a bad light before God on an ongoing basis throughout history. Does Ha-Satan or any other angels truly exist? Who knows? And who cares? What is important in Judaism is how we act and behave toward other people. The rabbis of the Talmud may have indeed had wonderful imaginations, for who truly knows anything about God or angels? But in the same Talmud that speaks of angels and Ha-Satan, the rabbis declared that human beings are responsible for their own deeds, whether good or evil, and can blame no one else but themselves for their own actions. And one day there will be an ultimate reckoning of individuals, societies, and entire nations; and then true justice will be meted out so that righteousness will prevail in the universe, whether in this world or some future world to come.

Question number 6: *Why did God create the two impulses—the good impulse and the evil impulse? I have read that the Talmud implies that the evil impulse is somehow involved in the preservation of humanity. How can the evil impulse be a positive force?*

Answer: You are indeed correct. The Jewish tradition holds that God created human beings with two opposing inclinations in our natures, one toward good, the other toward evil. As for why God created the two impulses, who knows? But the fact is that we do seem to have two opposing inclinations in us. You are also right in that the Talmud does state in several places that the evil impulse called the Yetzer HaRah is actually considered good! I prefer to think of it as the selfish impulse rather than an evil impulse. Perhaps the source you read about is the following rabbinic Midrash, or folktale, that states, "Were it not for the Yetzer HaRah, no man would build a house, marry a wife, or beget children" (Bereshit Rabbah 9:7), meaning that all of these productive activities that benefit individuals and society—like marrying, having children, or living productive lives—would not be possible were there not a little bit of pure self-interest involved in these pursuits. Although there are dangers and difficulties in having an evil inclination, according to rabbinic theology, it is necessary for the survival of humanity. For even righteous, heroic, and praiseworthy actions contain some aspect of the Yetzer HaRah as a goal or motivation.

Question number 7: I have been studying about the parallels between Karma in Hinduism and Judaism. As I am sure you know, Karma is a belief that whatever you do in this life will affect your next life. Do we as Jews believe in this? Are there any connections in Judaism to Karma that you know of?

Answer: Although there were many rabbis in the time of the Talmud nearly two thousand years ago who vividly described an afterlife in God's presence for all righteous Jews and Gentiles, the belief in another earthly existence after this present one is not a big part of modern Judaism. There is an esoteric doctrine within certain branches of Kabbalah or Jewish mysticism called Gilgulim, which literally means "circles" or "rolling over." This is basically the idea of reincarnation. If someone sins in this life, then they will come back as an animal or something else but rarely as another human being as a form of spiritual punishment or penance. However, as I mentioned, this is a very cryptic, mystical doctrine that was articulated in Kabbalistic writings in the sixteenth century but is not widely known or greatly embraced by the majority of Jews nowadays.

It is a much more Jewish question to ask how do our actions in this life affect our current life? In the worldview of the Hebrew Bible, the good prosper and the wicked suffer in this world. When that is not the case—which is all too often the reality we all live in—then the traditional Jewish response is that somewhere, somehow, there will be ultimate, universal justice. Somehow, someday the evil people will suffer for their evil actions perhaps even after their deaths in an afterlife, and those who have lived good, righteous lives but suffered in this world will enjoy some kind of recompense or reward. How God goes about achieving that is anyone's guess. So while Karma might focus on another future life, modern Jewish theology focuses on this life and the effort to work for and achieve justice in this world in all of the communities and societies we live in.

Question number 8: Who or what is the Messiah in Judaism? Is the Messiah an individual, a real person who acts as savior to the Jewish people, or does it refer to a Messianic period of time?

Answer: The quick answer to your last question is perhaps both! Belief in an individual Jew who will bring about a series of long-hoped-for, almost-miraculous events to better the world is an ancient part of the Jewish tradition. Both the Hebrew Bible and the Talmud speak about the Messiah a great deal, but there is actually no single, unified understanding of when the Messiah will come and what he will actually do.

By the way, the word "Messiah" is English for the Hebrew word "Mashiach." This word literally means "anointed," that is, chosen or selected by God for some task or mission. The word originally was used to describe the biblical kings of the ancient Jewish Kingdom of Judah and referred to those men who were ritually smeared with scented olive oil on their foreheads as a symbolic act of coronation and consecration as well as elevation to their office.

Despite the fact that every biblical book and individual rabbi had their own unique and separate idea as to what the Messiah must accomplish, a few tasks seem to have been generally accepted in Talmudic times around two thousand years ago. In order to be acknowledged as the Messiah, he—and unfortunately not a she—needed to:

1. be a descendant of King David;
2. achieve political control over the ancestral land of Israel for the Jewish people;
3. end the Diaspora by bringing all Jews from around the world back to Israel, the homeland of the Jewish people;
4. bring about a universal worship of the one God by all of the people of the world;
5. usher in permanent worldwide peace.

Belief in the eventual arrival of the Messiah is deeply rooted in the Jewish tradition; and this hope is included in many daily, Shabbat, and holiday prayers in the Jewish prayer book. However, at the dawn of the modern era, approximately two centuries ago, many liberal Jews felt uncomfortable with these supernatural beliefs and the reality that an actual human might be capable of achieving such miraculous goals. Therefore, the Reform movement in Europe and later in the United States began to reformulate this traditional belief in the Messiah. They declared that they no longer believed in an individual human being who would be the Messiah. Rather, they stated that all Jews and humanity in general were already working toward a Messianic era in which these Messianic goals would be fulfilled collectively. This modified belief in a Messianic era rather than an individual became extremely popular. However, the outbreak of the two world wars along with the Holocaust and the proliferation of nuclear weapons and rise of worldwide terrorism severely eroded many people's belief that humanity was working toward a future Messianic era; and since then, many Jews have once again begun to revert to a traditional albeit vague hope in the coming of an individual who will be the Messiah.

Question number 9: I have a Christian friend who, of course, insists that Jesus was the Messiah. I told him that in Judaism, the Messiah is not supposed to be a deity. My friend has asked me for scriptural references to prove this. Can you help me out here? Thanks!

Answer: You are indeed correct about the Jewish position regarding the Messiah. But you should know that even the Christian church has not held one consistent opinion about the divinity of Jesus. This very subject has been long argued and even fought over even within the Christian church. Believe it or not, Christians have murdered each other and literally gone to battle with their fellow Christians over this very point! So don't get too caught up in a theological debate about which we as Jews have nothing whatsoever to add to.

Also, in general, Jews do not use the Hebrew Bible to justify not recognizing Jesus as the Messiah; he is simply not part of the Jewish tradition just as Buddha, Joseph Smith, Muhammad, and Confucius are not part of the Jewish tradition. They are certainly important figures to their adherents, but there is no official Jewish position about the roles these people played in human religious history. While Christian and Islamic holy texts frequently refer to the Hebrew Bible and derive religious legitimacy from this association, the Jewish tradition was already well established by the time of Jesus and Mohammed. Therefore, Judaism and the Hebrew Bible—as Jews understand it—do not refer to Jesus at all. It is not historically possible.

Having said this, you should know the Hebrew Bible often refers to a vague figure that is sometimes called the Mashiach or Messiah in English. This word literally means "anointed," that is, chosen or selected by God for a special role, like serving as the king of the Israelite tribes. In the latter part of the Hebrew Bible, when the Jewish people were suffering either due to wars, the destruction of the Temple, and exile, the biblical prophets often spoke in glowing terms about this Mashiach, a person who was clearly understood by the ancient Israelites to be a future descendant of King David, who would essentially alleviate all of the problems that the Jewish people were then currently suffering. The clearest example of this is Isaiah 11, which describes a descendant of King David who will put an end to the exile of the Jews in Babylon, bring about universal peace, and even bring about peace in nature whereby even wild animals will become vegetarian and live in peace with their prey, when "the wolf shall dwell with the lamb and the leopard shall lie down with the kid" (Isaiah 11:6).

Despite this hyperbolic, poetic language, these goals—no matter how seemingly unattainable—were understood by the Talmudic rabbis as being accomplishable by a normal, regular human being. The idea that any person could be somehow both human and divine is an utterly alien concept to Jewish thought and anathema to Jewish theology. But don't try arguing these points with your Christian friend. This is because Christianity, from the outset, developed its entire theology predicated on interpreting the Hebrew Bible in just such a way that any reference to a Mashiach was understood to be a reference to Jesus. The entire history of the origins of Christianity and the Christian Bible are completely devoted to explaining and interpreting the Hebrew Bible in just this way. There is no way you can possibly win an argument or convince a devout Christian that their understanding of the Hebrew Bible is inaccurate and could not possibly refer to Jesus. You are going against two thousand years of dedicated Christian biblical scholarship and interpretation. So my advice is sit this argument out with your friend—you won't win, nor will you convince him that he is wrong.

But then again, so what? Why should you care whether his Christian beliefs are based on tendentious, self-referential, erroneous interpretations of the Hebrew Bible or not? Engaging in such an argument will only antagonize your friend, and while this might sound strange coming from a rabbi, I don't think you should try to argue with your friend about the divinity of Jesus because it is insulting to his faith! Why do you want to try and convince him that the most important article of faith in his religion is based on false premises? It would be the same if your friend tried to convince you that the Torah was not meaningful and important to you as a Jew and that Jews should no longer follow anything that is written in it. It does not matter what you—or I—believe about Jesus, nor should it matter what he believes about the Torah. I believe that the best that we can do is learn about and appreciate each other's different faith traditions in the spirit of friendship and shared purpose in seeking holiness in our lives and strive to alleviate the effects of evil and suffering in this world. And if we can even agree on that, that in itself would be quite an accomplishment!

If you would like more specific information about how to more effectively discuss this sensitive topic with your Christian friend, I recommend that you check out the Web site www.jewsforjudaism.org. You should note that the purpose of this Web site is to provide Jews with arguments to make when countering Christian missionaries. So it has a somewhat aggressive, combative tone, but the information is still interesting and worth reading nonetheless. Good luck with your friend, and I hope that whatever the outcome of your discussions, you still can both agree to remain friends!

Question number 10: I recently joined a Messianic Jewish congregation that I love. Why are we not considered Jewish by other Jews? I want to follow the Torah and God! Thank you for your answer.

Answer: Congratulations on your new affiliation with a spiritual group whose worship services speak to your individual spiritual needs. I am heartened when anyone is able to find a spiritual home. However, you are indeed correct in stating that Messianic Jews are not considered Jewish by the rest of the organized Jewish community. You should know that Messianic Jews who were either born Jewish—that is, had a Jewish mother according to traditional Judaism or underwent formal conversion to Judaism involving acceptance by a rabbinic court and immersion in the Mikvah (the original form of baptism)—these people are indeed considered Jews. However, Messianic Judaism as an organized, formal religion is not accepted as a legitimate, authentic form of Judaism.

Your community may indeed insist that you are all authentic, legitimate Jews and your beliefs and ways of worship are Jewish. However, the Jewish community rejected Christianity, including Messianic Judaism, two thousand years ago as being inauthentic, illegitimate expressions of historical Judaism. Belief in Jesus as one's personal savior is where the Jewish community has drawn the line between who is considered a Jew and who is not. You may disagree and argue that it is unfair and try to find individual Jews that may be interested in debating this issue with you. I, however, am not one of them. The form of spiritual worship and beliefs that you have chosen are not considered Jewish and are unlikely ever to be accepted as a legitimate branch of Judaism. I wish you happiness with your new congregation and much spiritual growth in your life as a Christian.

Question number 11: *What role do angels play in Judaism? I know of the Angel of Death, the angel who wrestled with Jacob, and the angel who stopped Abraham from killing Isaac. But I read somewhere that that there are one hundred and fifty angels acknowledged in our religion, and I was wondering about their importance and how they relate to the Christian concept of angels and archangels.*

Answer: The Torah, along with the rest of the Hebrew Bible, frequently mentions angels. The Hebrew word for "angel" is "Malach," that is, a messenger sent by God to earth for a specific task. Angels are indeed mentioned in such stories as Jacob wrestling with the angel (Genesis 32:24), Hagar being saved from death in the desert by an angel (Genesis 16:7), Abraham being stopped from sacrificing Isaac by an angel (Genesis 22:11), the non-Jewish prophet Balaam and his donkey meeting an angel on their way to curse the Israelites (Numbers 22:22-36), and Joshua encountering an armed angel before marching on Jericho (Joshua 5:13) and many others.

While the concept of angels was accepted as normal during the biblical period, it grew in popularity during the period of the Second Temple and immediately afterward. Some scholars claim that this interest in angels originally developed during the Babylonian exile around the sixth century BCE because Mesopotamian culture is filled with semidivine, angelic creatures. It continued to grow over the next several hundred years. Interestingly enough, this period of angelic popularity during the Second

Temple times also coincided with the development of early Christianity and probably played a role in early Christian theology. In fact, the Dead Sea Scrolls, written by a Jewish sect around the first century BCE and sometime after, were highly imaginative in their descriptions of angels and their vast numbers.

Even the rabbis in the Talmud acknowledged the existence of angels. Angels were considered the heavenly functionaries of God: some of whom acted as divine lawyers arguing against or on behalf of the nations of earth, some as messengers conveying the prayers of human beings to God, some as intercessors for humans before God, and some as guardian angels for humans. Chief among the Jewish angels who were accepted directly into Christian angelology were Gabriel, whose name means "the might of God"; Uriel, "the light of God"; Michael,—"who is like God" (from Exodus 15:11); and Rafael, "the healer of God." These angels figure prominently in ancient Jewish folktales and were incorporated directly into Christian theology as the archangels.

Belief in angels grew in medieval times also perhaps due to close Jewish contact with Christian and pagan peoples in Europe and throughout the Near East. Many Kabbalistic texts and medieval folk stories are filled with superstition-laden references to protective amulets and charms to ward off evil spirits and demonic or mischievous angels. In modern Jewish theology, the concept of angels is not widely accepted and plays very little role in modern Jewish beliefs. There are still references to angels in Hebrew prayers, such as the various passages found in many prayer books in the passages associated with the nighttime Shema recited before sleep. Sadly, angels are not as popular in Judaism as they once were, and perhaps our visions of heaven are a little emptier and lonelier as a result!

Question number 12: *What is the Jewish belief and view on hell?*

Answer: There is no word for "hell" in the Jewish tradition. The closest we come is "Sheol" in the Hebrew Bible. The Hebrew word "Sheol" doesn't really have a good translation. It is used occasionally in the Hebrew Bible to describe the netherworld, that is, the abode of the dead. It is an extremely vague concept and basically corresponds to the Greek mythological realm called Hades, the place where dead souls dwell for eternity.

However, the Hebrew Bible doesn't really talk much about an afterlife. There are ambiguous references in the Psalms and prophets about a person's soul going to this place called Sheol, and the Torah often speaks of someone "being gathered unto their fathers" after death (for example, Genesis 25:8). There is also a very strange story in the Hebrew Bible in 1 Samuel 28 that describes how King Saul went to a sorceress who conjured up the spirit of the dead prophet Samuel from Sheol who, by the way, was extremely annoyed at being disturbed! Despite these nebulous references, the Hebrew Bible doesn't really seem interested in the fate of a soul after death.

It is important to remember that in contrast to other Ancient Near Eastern cultures, Sheol was an indistinct concept in the Hebrew Bible, particularly in the prophets and Psalms. While the Hebrew Bible doesn't really describe this place at all, the rabbis of the Talmud spent a lot of time imagining what an afterlife would consist of. Bear in mind, however, that no one is really sure what happens to us after death. Trying to guess is just a matter of different people's opinions. This is why there are many different views about this in the Jewish tradition.

The rabbinic tradition, which consists of those stories and ideas found in the Talmud and Midrashic works, is filled with different opinions about what will happen to people after death. Some rabbis believed that the souls of the righteous are rewarded, and the souls of the wicked are punished. Some rabbis believed that the souls of the righteous study Torah in the afterlife and continue to exist in God's presence. Some other rabbis believed that even the souls of the wicked are not perpetually punished but that after some period of time, they too are allowed to enjoy the rewards of the righteous. The rabbis even came up with a new name for the afterworldly abode of punished souls called Gehinom from which we derive the English word "Gehenna" that is somewhat equivalent to the idea of hell. "Gehinom" is a Hebrew word that means "Hinom's Valley" and is an actual site located in Jerusalem, but it was associated with Canaanite child sacrifice in ancient times and thus considered an especially accursed place. Somehow or other, this valley of Hinom was projected into an otherworldly existence and was sometimes referred to by the Talmudic rabbis as a place where wicked souls were sent to be punished or purged of their sins while living, like the Christian idea of purgatory. It also came to be associated with bodily punishment, which is ironic since it was supposed to be a place of punishment upon the death of our physical bodies. In one particularly poignant passage, the rabbis in the Talmud said, "The Holy One, blessed be God, judges the wicked in Gehinom for twelve months. At first, God afflicts them with itching, after that with fire, at which they cry out, 'Oh, oh!' and then with snow, at which they cry out, 'Woe, woe!'" (Yerushalmi Talmud, Sanhedrin 29b). In another passage, some anonymous rabbi claimed that "ordinary fire is one sixtieth the heat of the fire of Gehinom" (Bavli Talmud, Berachot 57b).

But the point is no one knows what happens to us upon our demise. All attempts to describe any type of existence after our lives are only speculative. Instead, the Jewish tradition largely focuses our lives and attention on this life and this world. Judaism is a religion dedicated to living this life in a holy fashion and helping to alleviate the suffering of others. What happens after our deaths is not a very important issue for our tradition. How you live your life is!

Question number 13: *What is the Jewish view on ghosts and spirits?*

Answer: The Jewish tradition does not really emphasize or deal directly with beliefs in ghosts and spirits in traditional texts. This does not mean that Jews did not believe in such entities. In fact, there is far more information about such popular beliefs regarding demons and angels in the folkloristic Jewish literature of the Midrash. But the Torah and the Talmud only mention such ideas in passing. Although the Ancient Near

East was filled with cultures that believed in the existence and power of demons and spirits, such as the Canaanites and Sumerians, magic and sorcery were explicitly prohibited in the Hebrew Bible (see Exodus 22:17-18 and Deuteronomy 18:10-12).

The few references to spirits in the Hebrew Bible are similar to other cultures' myths—they live in deserts or ruins (see Leviticus 16:10 and Isaiah 13:21), they trouble people's minds (1 Samuel 16:15 and 23), and they deceive people (1 Kings 22:22-23). The only really explicit reference is a great story toward the end of 1 Samuel where King Saul, on the eve of a big battle with the Philistines, breaks his own law forbidding consulting spiritual mediums and calls up the ghost of his long-dead mentor, the prophet Samuel. Samuel's spirit is none too happy about being disturbed in his deathly repose and perhaps nastily remarks that soon enough, Saul will be joining him in the world of the dead! It is a funny, scary, and sad story (see 1 Samuel 28).

In rabbinic literature, the rabbis refer to Shedim (from Deuteronomy 32:17 and Psalm 106:37) that is usually translated as "demons" or "devils" but sounds an awful lot like "shade," another word for "ghost" in English! Some demons have names such as Lilith, a night succubus; Mavet, the angel of death; Azazel, a desert demon; or Asmodeaus, king of the demons. However, most of these myths are rooted in folklore rather than in mainstream rabbinic theology. They were popular beliefs among the common Jewish folk in Talmudic and medieval times that the rabbis were familiar with but didn't want to make a big deal of denying or discussing. For more information, I encourage you to read the definitive book about ghosts and demons in Judaism called *Jewish Magic and Superstition* by Joshua Trachtenberg. You'll learn far more than you ever intended to on this subject!

Question number 14: *How should I respond when someone tells me that the Holocaust happened because the Jewish victims were not practicing Judaism correctly or sincerely and that the Holocaust was a punishment from God?*

Answer: You should respond honestly, directly, and as passionately as possible that they are just flat-out wrong, misguided, and terribly insulting to the memory of not just the six million Jews who died but the additional five million non-Jewish victims of the death camps. First of all, from a simple, objective, and historical perspective, this is simply ridiculous. The Holocaust was the result of a series of interrelated political, social, religious, economic, and racist factors and influences that were present in German history for centuries. To inject a tendentious, prejudiced theological perspective into this discussion is simply irrelevant.

Secondly, it is also untrue because there were millions of fervently, devoutly religious Jews who were murdered by the Nazis along with millions of nonreligious Jews. The Nazis in the Holocaust murdered nearly three million ultra-Orthodox, Hasidic Jews. To claim that these people—or any other Jews for that matter—were not sufficiently religious according to someone's subjective standard of religiosity is unfair and insulting to their memory.

And finally, this point of view is utterly offensive and disgusting. It is also blasphemy for anyone to assert that they alone know how or why God operates in this world. Anyone who asserts such a view is either not cognizant of the terribly bigoted, theologically repulsive nature of such a statement or simply doesn't care. And if they are aware of the implications of this statement but choose to advocate it for their own distorted purposes, then I would highly recommend that you inform the speaker that their views are offensive and inflammatory and state that you will no longer continue to converse with them on this subject, for to even debate the nonexistent merits of such a statement appears to lend legitimacy to such a repugnant sentiment. Anyone who believes this statement is not worth your time to debate.

Question number 15: What does the Torah or the Jewish traditions teach about forgiveness? Can there ever be forgiveness for what happened in the Holocaust? Can there ever be forgiveness for those German soldiers who ran the concentration camps?

Answer: The Jewish tradition encourages us to be generous with forgiveness, but there are limits. Forgiveness is usually limited to social realm and includes such offenses as insults and unintentional wrongdoing against other people or even toward God. Forgiveness for a crime such as rape or murder is a different story altogether for which there is no particular obligation for the victim to forgive the criminal.

In fact, I could argue that the opposite is true. According to the Torah, we should never forget those who have sought to destroy us. In a brief incident following the exodus of the Israelites from Egypt, the Torah describes how the Amalekites, a desert people, attacked the Hebrews as they were marching in the desert from behind at the rear of the column where the women, children, and elderly has fallen back to along the march. The Torah expresses its disgust for such a shameful war tactic that twice the Israelites are commended to wipe out and exterminate the Amalekites (Exodus 17:8-17 and Deuteronomy 5:17-19).

Many Jews react differently to the horror of the Holocaust. Modern scholarship has revealed a tremendous amount of complicity in the crimes of the Holocaust shared by ordinary Germans and the non-Jewish populations of countries the Nazis occupied, making it all the more difficult to differentiate between active and passive civilian collaborators in the monstrous crimes against humanity. Some Jews are willing to let go of the pain and anger. Rabbi Shlomo Carlebach, the late leader and inspiration for many Jews in the Jewish Renewal movement, once said that if he had two souls, he would devote one soul to just hating the Nazis for his entire life. But since he only had one soul, he would prefer to spend his life pursuing love and goodness in the world. But for other Jews, even today—whether survivors or not—they still harbor resentment and mistrust of all Germans however unfair this may seem. So therefore, I would have to say that forgiveness of the Nazis is entirely an individual affair for which the Jewish tradition wisely allows each person to decide for him or herself.

Question number 16: I have always heard that Jews don't believe in cremation for it destroys the soul that is to come to life upon the death of the body. My question is what do Jews believe happened to the souls of those who died in the crematoriums during the Holocaust?

Answer: I believe that you have been misinformed about your concept of traditional Jewish beliefs regarding the soul and cremation. What you stated above may be true of some people, but Judaism is a religion that is not based on beliefs; rather, it emphasizes our actions and behavior in this world. Therefore, it is not entirely accurate to categorically state, "Jews believe X or Y" because there is no official credo of what all Jews do or do not believe. Correct and appropriate actions in this life are what are important to Judaism. Individual or groups of Jews can believe whatever they want, and that doesn't make their opinions official beliefs of Judaism.

However, to address your question, the Jewish tradition does indeed prohibit cremation because the Torah states that all humans were created in the image of God (Genesis 1:27), so to destroy the remains of a human body upon death is considered disrespectful to God. This has nothing to do with the disposition of someone's soul upon his or her death. The body, even lifeless, is still stamped with the image of the God. It is also considered a disgrace to the memory of the person that inhabited that body in life as well as God to burn it and dispose of it like we would dead leaves or trash. Jewish bodies should be buried as it says in the book of Genesis that God told Adam and Eve, "From dust you were created and to dust you shall return" (Genesis 3:19). This verse was interpreted by the ancient rabbis to mean that Jews should bury the bodies of those who have died in the earth to return to the soil from which the first, original human beings were created.

What happens to the souls of people when they die, whether they are cremated or buried? Who knows! I certainly don't, and neither does any other living person. All we have are our personal and religious beliefs. There are all sorts of ideas about this topic described in traditional rabbinic literature that are far too numerous to explore here. I urge you to do some homework on the Internet or a local library for more information (see "Suggested Readings" at the end of this book).

Regarding the cremation of millions of Jewish bodies during the Holocaust, as I mentioned above, there is no official belief about a Jewish afterlife. Some rabbis have expressed a belief that a person's soul, a spark of God that animates us, survives the death of this body and returns to its source in God. If so, then whether a body is burned or buried cannot in any way affect the fate of a person's spirit or soul. What is important in the Jewish tradition is this life, not any future afterlife. Therefore, Judaism emphasizes living a life based on moral values and appropriate behavior while we still live here in this world. And so to honor those who died during the Holocaust, the Israeli government established Yom HaShoah or Holocaust Memorial Day on the twenty-seventh day of the Hebrew month of Nisan (which always falls right after the Jewish holiday of Pesach) to be observed every year for Jewish communities around the world to commemorate the loss of so many innocent victims of the Nazis. As for the fate of their souls, all we can ever do is pray that their spirits are at peace and in communion with God.

Chapter 17

God (Twelve Questions)

Everyone has questions about God. After all, God is at the center of nearly every religious tradition in the world. As the very first monotheistic faith in human history, the Jewish people were the first ones to proclaim the existence and define the nature of this one all-powerful, omnipresent God; and the course of human history has not been the same ever since.

Despite the numerous teachings and clearly articulated beliefs about God there are in the Jewish tradition, it was surprising how many questions people wrote me asking about God. Perhaps this is because God is understood in the Jewish tradition to be beyond the grasp of our basic physical senses and so cannot be easily or directly experienced or comprehended. Therefore, many people turned to whom they assumed would know the answers about God—me, as well as all the other clergy of the myriad faiths in the world. However, the sad truth is that no ministers—even rabbis—have all the answers about God.

The classical Jewish texts are filled with generations of rabbi's beliefs about God, but that is all they are—beliefs. And due to the highly personal, idiosyncratic nature of spiritual encounters with God, one person's experience of the Divine may be merely a hallucination or delusion to another. So when it comes down to it—all we really have are our beliefs. And no one person's beliefs are more authoritative or important than anyone else's—even rabbis. And yet the rabbis of the Jewish tradition, for the last two thousand years up to the present day, have not at all been shy about articulating in fine detail their beliefs about God.

But even beliefs about God can be instructive as they reveal some of the core values and moral principles of a religious tradition. Therefore, the following questions and answers reveal both the profound human desire to draw close to God and also the basic ideals that form the foundation of the entire Jewish tradition.

Question number 1: Where did God come from? In Habakkuk 3:3, it states, "God came from Teman, and the Holy One from mount Paran." What information can you give me concerning Teman? Paran?

Answer: It also states in Deuteronomy 33:2, "The Lord came from Sinai, He shone upon them from Seir; He appeared from Mt. Paran, and approached from Ribeboth-Kodesh." That does not mean that God came from all of those places. The names that you quoted from the book of Habakkuk and which I mentioned from Deuteronomy are simply the ancient names of places in the Middle East. God didn't really come from any of these places as in the sense of origination. God doesn't come from anywhere. According to the Jewish tradition, God always existed and always will exist. God didn't come from anywhere because God was—and is—and will always be here, present and existing. God doesn't even have to go anywhere because God is everywhere. God's presence suffuses and permeates the universe.

The language in Habakkuk and Deuteronomy is poetry that was intended to dramatize God's presence. The purpose of naming the places was to illustrate the vastness of God's presence; it is so big that it encompassed the entire world known in ancient times in the Middle East. Teman is modern-day Yemen, and Paran is what is now modern-day Iraq. The purpose of these biblical quotes is to show that God was not simply the God of Israel and limited to only the land of Israel but that God's presence was everywhere, all over the world that the ancient Israelites were familiar with. As the old child's saying goes, "God is here, God is there, God is really everywhere!"

Question number 2: Do you think G-d cares how we worship him? Does G-d care whether we worship Allah or Christ or even Buddha or Vishnu? It seems to me that G-d should only care whether you are a good person and that you don't harm others while going along your way. What do you think?

Answer: What a great question—thank you for asking it! First of all, I don't even know if God exists. Secondly, if God exists, the Jewish tradition informs me that God is neither male nor female; so I try to avoid referring to God as him or he or even her or she or it! Unfortunately, Hebrew is not a gender-neutral language; and therefore, most accurate translations of the Torah and traditional Jewish prayer books render God as a He and a Him. And so if we do use these pronouns, it is considered more respectful to capitalize these words so that we refer to God as Him and He.

Thirdly, it is interesting that you spell "God" as "G-d." This spelling that you used in your question is actually derived from the Jewish tradition of avoiding using the sacred four-letter Hebrew name of God that is considered so holy that once it is written on a piece of paper, the paper itself is considered as holy as a prayer book or Torah scroll and cannot simply be thrown away but must be disposed of in a special, respectful manner like an actual Torah scroll or Hebrew prayer book. However, since "God" is just the English word for 'God" and not even Hebrew, there is really no need to resort to this Hebrew convention of piety when writing in English.

And by the way, Judaism doesn't really even emphasize personal belief in God as a primary value of the Jewish tradition. God is certainly important in Judaism. In fact, there is an old saying, "A Jew can love God and a Jew can hate God, but a Jew can never ignore God." Therefore, the basic Jewish beliefs about God are that God is one—no other divine beings exist other than God. God is eternal, all-powerful, omniscient, and always present to those who call upon God or seek the Divine presence.

Finally, to answer your question, does God care how we worship God? I don't know. As another old saying goes, "If I knew God, I'd be God!" Many people do indeed believe as you do that despite different names, everyone else's conception of God is ultimately the same no matter what we call that deity. Personally, I don't care what God thinks about anyone worshipping Allah or Buddha or Jesus or Vishnu or whoever. I figure God worries about whatever God wants to worry about. However, the Jewish tradition is much more interested in how you behave as a human being. And in that, I totally agree with you. It doesn't so much matter what you believe about God but rather how you act and if you are a good person in this world.

The problem in this, however, is what defines a good person. Although there may be many overlaps, this is where the many religious traditions of the world differ. Sadly, there are far too many people in this world who believe that the terrorists who flew the planes into the Twin Towers and Pentagon on September 11, 2001, were righteous and even holy people despite the fact—or perhaps because of it—they murdered thousands of people. Every religion defines what characterizes someone as good differently. To Judaism, someone is good or righteous if they observe the laws, rituals, and customs of the Jewish tradition that involves pursuing justice—social, criminal, environmental, and economic justice. This includes preventing bloodshed, giving charity, helping the poor, honoring one's family members, preventing cruelty to animals, treating everyone fairly and in a friendly fashion, protecting the environment, and pursuing peace and lots more. This is far more important than what we might imagine God is worried about!

Question number 3: Can you explain the meaning of the name Adonai?

Answer: Yes, I can. "Adonai" is a Hebrew word that literally means, "My Master" or "My Lord." In fact, in modern Hebrew as it is spoken in Israel today, the word "Adon" simply means "mister" as in, "Excuse me, mister, but does the bus stop here?" It is a regular, ordinary word.

In the Hebrew Bible, God has many different names. One of the most famous consists of four Hebrew letters that in Hebrew are Yod, Heh, Vav, and Hey. It is also referred to as the Tetragrammaton, which is a Greek word meaning a four-lettered name of God. This four-letter Hebrew name of God used to be pronounced in ancient times by the high priest, but its pronunciation has been lost over time. Therefore, instead of trying to sound out those four letters, Jews now say Adonai in place of this four-letter name of God. As a result, Adonai has now become one of the standard, common names for God in Judaism. Another word used for God in the Hebrew Bible is "Elohim," which strangely enough, is actually a plural word meaning "gods"! However, it is used in the Torah only to refer to the monotheistic, single God of the Jewish people.

Now here is an interesting story of the development of one of the names of the Hebrew word for God. When vowel marks were invented for the Hebrew language in the early Middle Ages, some Jews began to apply the vowels for the word "Elohim" to the Tetragrammaton, the four-letter name of God. That is, they used the pronunciation vowel marks from one word and applied them to another different word. They did this so that no one would be tempted to try and pronounce the four-letter Hebrew name of God. But if for some chance they actually did, it would come out completely wrong; and therefore, the secret pronunciation of God's four-letter name would not accidentally be pronounced.

However, Christian biblical scholars in Europe around two or three centuries ago did not know of this substitution of the vowels; and when they tried to actually pronounce the Tetragrammaton, they were unaware that they were using the incorrect vowels derived from another Hebrew name of God! And the result was the word "Jehovah" or "Yahweh" as it is sometimes written. However, both of these names—as is now obvious—are not even close to what the original four-lettered Hebrew name of God sounded like when pronounced by the ancient high priests of the Jewish people in the Temple in Jerusalem over two thousands years ago! So my advice is to stick with Adonai!

Question number 4: How does Judaism refer to God? Someone told me He is neither male nor female. Can you give scripture to prove He is male?

Answer: No, I can't. No one can *prove* anything about God. By definition, belief in God is based on faith, and no rational or universal proof about any of God's qualities or even God's very existence can be proved or disproved despite the best efforts of many medieval scholars. Also, remember that what might be proof to one person may be utterly illogical and ridiculous to someone else.

To answer your question, God is almost universally referred to as He or Him in the Hebrew Bible. This is because Hebrew has no gender-neutral pronouns. In other words, there is no word "it" in Hebrew; nor would we ever use "it" to describe God because God is not a she, God is not a he, nor is God an it like an inanimate object. Rather, God is just God. However, by default, God is referred to and often thought of as male. Consider Exodus 15:3 where God was called in Hebrew a man of war. Even the prophet Hosea symbolically referred to God as a husband, and the people of Israel was considered God's wife (see Hosea 2:18). In addition, in rabbinic literature and traditional Jewish prayers, God is almost always referred to as Our Father in heaven and as a king as opposed to a queen. Liturgically, God is also called Adonai in Hebrew, which literally means "My Lord" in the male gender.

However, there is one appellation for God in rabbinic literature that is actually a feminine word. God is sometimes referred to as the Shechinah, and this signifies the tangible presence of God. It is based on the biblical verse in Exodus 25:8 where God says to the Israelites, "Make Me a sanctuary that I might dwell amongst them." The Hebrew word "to dwell" is the same root as Shechinah and sometimes is used in the Talmud and Midrash to suggest a feminine side of God.

Of course, it should be obvious even from Genesis that God has no gender because in Genesis 1:27 it states, "And God created man in His image, in the image of God He created them—male and female He created them." In other words, both males and females are created in the image of God. Therefore, God cannot have a gender since both males and females are part of the divine image. The concept of God's gender neutrality was derived later on during the medieval period when philosophers, uncomfortable with the anthropomorphic human imagery and concepts used to describe God, reasoned philosophically that God could not have a human form at all since God was all-powerful, all-present, all-wise, and all-knowing. Human form would limit God as a philosophical concept.

However, even in English we still somehow end up referring to God as He. Intellectually, we may understand that God has no body or human form whatsoever; however, linguistically, we still seem to need to refer to God as something with a pronoun. So most often, God is still called Him.

Question number 5: Does God love the Jews? And if God does love us, how would we know?

Answer: According to the Hebrew Bible, God does indeed love the Jewish people as I hope and assume God loves *all* human beings that God created. How do we know? Well, we don't really—how could we possibly know anything about God? Rather, this is what our tradition asserts.

The Hebrew Bible actually is pretty clear about God loving the Israelites as it says in Hosea, "When Israel was a child, I loved him, out of Egypt I called him 'son'" (Hosea 11:1). Some people claim that because the Jewish people have existed for over three thousand years, this is proof of God's love for us. Could be, but I don't know. As Tevye, the milkman in the musical *Fiddler on the Roof*, says, "The way God loves us—we wish God would love somebody else for a while!"

Question number 6: The Torah says to love God—but how is this possible? How do you create love for God who is so remote and unknowable if you don't truly feel this emotion?

Answer: Excellent question! The first paragraph of the Shema (Deuteronomy 4:6) commands us to "love God with all of your heart, all of your soul and all of your might." Some rabbis of the Talmud asked the exact same question as you: how is it possible to command someone to feel an emotion? After all, emotions are affairs of the heart that just can't be turned off or on and especially for God who is, almost by definition as you write, unknowable.

Some scholars point out that what we translate as love actually had a meaning closer to the idea of being loyal or faithful to God and God's commandments. Therefore, perhaps the Torah is not commanding us to feel love but rather to remain steadfast in our loyalty to observing the Mitzvot. Other rabbinic commentators answer that even if this is true—we still cannot always control who or what we love—but we can control our actions. So how do we act or even pretend that we love God? By observing the Mitzvot, or the commandments of the Torah. We observe Shabbat, keep Kosher, pray, belong to a synagogue, give Tzedakah, and continue to study more about Judaism. Even if we cannot conjure up in ourselves some amorphous feeling of love for God, these are traditional actions that are understood to be *acts* of love toward God. Maybe, hopefully, over time the observance of these commandments will lead to a sense of reverence, respect, and possibly even love for God. But if not, we will still have participated in enriching our lives spiritually and improving the quality of life of those around us. It is still a win-win situation.

Question number 7: Does God have essence? Existence? Or both? Are they one and the same for God? How does this work?

Answer: No one really knows what God is like—how can we? Rather, we attribute different characteristics to God. Every religion does this. One of the oldest, most coherent set of characteristics ascribed to God was written by Rabbi Moses Maimonides in the twelfth century. Basically, Maimonides wrote that God is a creator who alone created and creates all things. God is one, unique. God has no body, no form. God is eternal. God alone is to be worshipped. God knows the deeds and thoughts of human beings. God rewards and punishes our actions. In other words, God is omniscient, omnipotent, and eternal. This is the basic Jewish understanding of God according to Maimonides.

Do these attributes really accurately describe God? Who knows? Rather, this is what one rabbi long ago stated are traditional Jewish beliefs. But just because Maimonides wrote this does not mean that you or anyone else or any Jew for that matter has to believe them. Rather, they represent a pretty good description of God as many Jews throughout history have believed in God.

Question number 8: *If God is real, why doesn't He talk to us like He did in the Torah?*

Answer: Good question. We have no idea if God ever really talked to the ancient Israelites either. That is what the Torah tells us, and that is certainly what the ancient Israelites believed and probably a good deal of traditional Jews today. But at some point, most Jews seem to believe that God stopped talking to human beings at least in a way that was acknowledged by the rest of the Jewish community. Perhaps the ancient Israelite prophets were delusional when they claimed that God spoke to them, but back then, everyone seems to have believed them. This was a part of the cultural and religious beliefs of the ancient Israelites in the time of the Hebrew Bible. Nowadays, we tend to think that people who hear God talking to them have mental or emotional problems.

But what if God did in fact talk to people and never stopped? Perhaps God talks to us through our consciences even now. Perhaps God talks to us through the Torah even now. Perhaps God has continued to talk to the Jewish people throughout all of Jewish history and is still talking to us, but maybe we aren't listening anymore. If you are looking for a booming voice coming from the heavens, then I'm afraid you are going to be disappointed. Maybe God never really talked to human beings that way even back then. Maybe God always talked to human beings like it says in the Hebrew Bible, in a "still, small voice" inside of us (see 1 Kings 19:12). If you want to hear God's voice—study the Torah, learn about the Jewish tradition, and follow your conscience. God is real if we indeed believe that—but God is only where we as human beings are willing to see and hear God. According to the Hasidic Kotzker Rebbe, God is wherever we let God into us.

Question number 9: *What happens if you break a promise to God? Is there a way to avoid divine punishment?*

Answer: The Jewish tradition divides promises or vows into two categories—promises that we make to fellow human beings and those we make to God. As for promises that we violate toward other people, the only people that can forgive us are the very ones whom we may have harmed or wronged by not fulfilling our word. But if we violate a promise or an oath that we made to God that affected no one else, then the only way to cope with this situation is to attend the Kol Nidrei worship service on the eve of Yom Kippur. Every year on Yom Kippur, Jews pray to God to forgive them for those promises and vows they have made to God that they were unable to fulfill. And according to the Jewish tradition, if we have done true Teshuvah, or repentance, then God immediately and completely forgives us. This is one of the central theological ideas of the Day of Atonement in Judaism. As for avoiding divine punishment, this is not really a significant component of Jewish theology nowadays. However, I hope this settles what sounds like your guilty conscience!

Question number 10: *Why does everyone talk about God's involvement—or rather, lack of involvement—in the Holocaust; but not much is said about His involvements in such past events as pogroms, expulsions, and the destruction of the Temple in Jerusalem?*

Answer: Good point! I think it is a sad commentary on the lack of Jewish education when people speak about God's involvement or lack thereof in connection with the Holocaust. Many traditional and modern Jewish theologians have rejected the idea of understanding the Holocaust as some form of divine punishment or even an expression of divine will.

Most rational, critical-thinking people accept that despite the enormity of the suffering and violence, the Holocaust was a case of human-created evil and misery. Human beings, namely the Nazis, conceived of it; and human beings, namely the German people and other European sympathizers and collaborators, allowed it to happen and carried it out. This is an inevitable consequence of our having free will.

The question should not be where was God? But rather, where was humanity? And the answer is that human beings created the Holocaust, and ultimately, human beings put an end to the Holocaust. The combined armies of the Allied forces defeated Nazi Germany and put an end to the Holocaust. And the Nuremberg trials afterward ensured justice was carried out on those who committed these crimes against humanity. The tragedy of the Holocaust is indeed immense, overwhelming, and almost incomprehensible. The questions we should be asking—and are asking—are why did humanity allow this to happen in the first place? And why did it take so long for humanity to put an end to it? Not, how could God let this happen? But rather, how could *we* have let it happen?

As to your question about why people don't ask about God's role in previous tragedies in Jewish history—they have! Jewish literature is replete with the cries of poets, rabbis, and ordinary Jews complaining about the lack of cosmic justice in the slaughter of so many innocent Jews throughout history such as in the time of the Hellenistic persecution of Jews that led to the Maccabean war against the Syrian Greeks or the slaughter of Jewish rebels during Roman times or the massacre of innocent Jews during the Crusades or the czarist forces who instigated pogroms against the defenseless Jews of Eastern Europe. Unfortunately, we just happen to be further away in time from those tragedies and less familiar with the literature that poses these theological questions. And the Holocaust, due to its massive scale and horror, has eclipsed our short-term memories of those past events. Also, I think it is a sad commentary on the lack of Jewish education that so many Jews are not even aware of the previous tragedies that you mention.

Question number 11: What are the top three arguments for proving God exists?

Answer: Drum roll, please! Well, I'd have to say that my personal all-time-favorite arguments for the existence of God are the following:

1. Teleological argument. This states that the universe, the physical laws, and all life appear to be intricately patterned and designed. Therefore, if things appear to have a design, there must have been a designer! That is, God.
2. Cosmological argument. This states that the fact that the universe exists at all demonstrates that God must have created it. In other words, the fact that there is something and not nothing shows that it was consciously brought into existence.
3. Intuitive argument. This states that I cannot prove it, but my life and personal experiences lead me to believe in the existence, and sometimes even the tangible presence, of God.

These are just my personal top three arguments. David Letterman and other rabbis might have their own different lineup!

Question number 12: I used to observe Jewish law strictly for many years. But lately, I feel that it is good enough that I am a good person. However, out of habit I continue to keep many Jewish laws. Does God really care whether I observe Shabbat or eat non-Kosher food?

Answer: There is a famous Midrash or rabbinic folktale that states that in fact, God could care less whether we, as Jews, slaughter an animal in a Kosher manner or not! The Midrash states, "What does the Holy One, Praised be God, care whether we slaughter an animal at the throat or the nape of the neck (for to be Kosher, an animal must be slaughtered at the throat to ensure a quick and painless death)? Rather, the purpose of the commandments is to refine the spirit of human beings" (Genesis Rabbah 44:1). In other words, you are right! In some sense, according to this passage, God could care less whether we are observant or not because the value of these activities is not in the actions themselves. Rather, the importance of these Mitzvot, or commandments, is how they affect us in our lives and what kind of people they make us.

Another Midrash puts words into God's mouth to the effect that God would rather we lose faith in God but still keep the Mitzvot! This is because the observance of the Mitzvot will help instill in us through their practice a belief in God. Is this true? I don't know. Behaviorally, it makes sense. In other words, how we behave long-term cannot help but influence how we think and feel and believe.

I am not answering your question directly because how can I? If you feel that there is a value in being observant of Jewish laws and customs, then continue to do so! Or moderate your practice such that it is meaningful to you. But if you find no value in your Jewish practice, then stop. If observance of the Mitzvot is becoming odious and hateful to you, then you are only reinforcing your association of doing Mitzvot with a negative feeling. I personally believe that there is a wide variety of benefits in observing Mitzvot, but I also believe that all of us should moderate and shape our patterns of personal religious observance in such a way that it is meaningful to us. In other words, our religious lives should reflect our highest aspirations, values, and goals as human beings and not an image of any guilt, remorse, or pangs of conscience that may plague us. Although I have no idea what God may want from us in terms of our personal behavior, this is what I would want God to want from us! Good luck!

Conclusion

For the eight years that I served as a volunteer rabbi answering questions about Judaism on the Internet, I felt privileged to briefly share a small slice of life of the people who wrote soliciting advice about every imaginable topic related to Judaism. I was shocked, at times frightened, flattered, and deeply touched by the depth and detail of their intimate, personal lives that they were willing to share with an anonymous Internet rabbi, a stranger to whom they were clearly ascribing a degree of moral authority. They placed their trust in me to care about them and to craft an answer that would address their questions, and I hope I lived up to that trust.

One of the results of spending years studying traditional Jewish texts, history, philosophy, pastoral psychology, law, and liturgy is that you become ever more aware of how much you do not know and how much you will probably never know about the subject you are studying. At the end of my six years of seminary graduate school rabbinical studies, I was keenly aware of how much I did not know about Judaism. And precisely at the moment when I was feeling the most humble and awed by my own ignorance was the moment that I was granted the title of rabbi and people began to turn to me for answers to their questions about Judaism.

To be honest, I had to do a lot of research to answer many of these questions. For some of these questions, I felt sufficiently comfortable enough to respond without opening a book. But many questions sent right back to my books, pouring over classical Hebrew and Aramaic Jewish religious texts and scouring Jewish reference books, indices, and tables of contents, searching for the exact answer to an unusual question. Remember, this was long before Google searches or the Wikipedia Web site either existed or had become so popular, so I had to do this the old-fashioned way—by reading books and relying on my own knowledge of and familiarity with traditional Jewish texts. Because of this, I am grateful for the challenge of having been put in a position to have had to continue my own Jewish professional development and ongoing rabbinical education. Over the course of eight years, I became intimately more familiar with the contents of my own professional Jewish library and always ready to pull a book off a shelf in pursuit of a particular nugget of information that I hoped would be buried within its pages.

I am grateful for the opportunity to have served on the front lines of the Jewish community responding to potentially any question from anyone around the world, Jewish or not, on any topic that even hinted of having a connection with Judaism. Even if the questions that I selected and answered in this book were not the exact same questions that you had, I hope that you enjoyed and benefited from what you found. And if you too have a question about Judaism that still remains unanswered, then I encourage you to contact your rabbi or one close to you because there is no substitute for personal contact with a real live teacher about Judaism. But if you *still* cannot connect to a rabbi in person, then turn to the next best source but still a distant second: the Internet. But still to be on the safe side, don't give up trying to track down a rabbi with whom you can meet and talk to face-to-face. Because as the Jewish tradition teaches, when two people study Torah together, the Divine presence of God dwells between them! May God's sheltering presence be near to you and all God's creatures on this beautiful gift of a world.

Appendix A

Kashrut Explained

Introduction: "Kosher" means "fit" or "acceptable." "Kashrut" refers to the food that is considered fit or acceptable to be eaten by Jews. According to the book of Genesis, vegetarianism is the ideal diet (see Genesis 1:29). However, Kashrut can be understood as a compromise with vegetarianism.

Kashrut in the Torah: According to the Torah (Leviticus 11 and Deuteronomy 14), only certain kinds of animals are considered inherently Kosher. For land animals, any creature that both chews its cud and has split hooves is Kosher. For fish, any creature that has both fins and scales is Kosher; and for birds, only those birds that are not scavengers or birds of prey are Kosher and birds that are specifically identified as non-Kosher, like ostriches. Some additional laws of Kashrut that are also found in the Torah include the prohibition against eating the blood of an animal (Genesis 9:4-5), the prohibition against eating the sciatic nerve of an animal (Genesis 32:33), and it is repeated three times in the Torah (Exodus 23:19, 24:26, and Deuteronomy 14:21) that it is forbidden to cook a baby goat in its own mother's milk.

Development of Kashrut: The rabbis in the Talmud further developed these principles of Kashrut. In order to consume Kosher land animals and birds, it is necessary to slaughter them in a prescribed way, in a manner that has been described as a more humane method than what is practiced commercially. In addition, the prohibition of cooking a baby goat in its own mother's milk is the basis for the complete physical, hygienic separation of all milk and meat products. Therefore, this is the essence of Kashrut:

1. Eating only Kosher land animals, fish, and fowl
2. Special method for slaughtering these animals and fowl
3. The complete separation of all milk and meat products (the Kosher meat from land animals and fowl)

These are the fundamental elements of Kashrut. Every question, problem, or issue about keeping Kosher ultimately revolves around these three basic principles of Kashrut. The most complicated practical aspect of keeping Kosher usually has to do with the last basic element: the complete separation of milk and meat products.

The use of different sets of dishes, as well as pots and pans, developed in order to ensure a greater separation between milk and meat foods. This is also the basis of waiting a certain symbolic amount of time after eating a meat dish and before eating a dairy product. Although there are different traditions, it is common to wait at least three hours after eating a meat meal before eating dairy food so that the two types of food should not even symbolically mix together in our stomachs.

Whether a particular manufactured food product is considered Kosher or not usually has to do with whether any substance or product used in its manufacture was derived from a non-Kosher animal or even a Kosher animal but which was not slaughtered in the prescribed manner or whether there was any mixing of dairy and meat food product in the ingredients.

Categories of Kosher Food: There are three main categories of foods according to Kashrut:

1. Dairy foods—This includes all dairy products from milk produced by a Kosher animal such as cheese, milk, yogurt,

butter, ice cream, and so on. For example, a camel is not Kosher; therefore, no dairy products from camel milk are Kosher.

2. Meat foods—This includes all Kosher land animals and fowl slaughtered in the prescribed manner and their derivative products such as beef, venison, chicken, turkey, hot dogs, hamburgers, meat-derived soup broth, and so on.

3. Pareve foods—This is a Yiddish word meaning "neutral." These are foods that are neither dairy nor meat, such as eggs, fish, tofu, nuts, grains, fruits, and vegetables and most drinks.

In keeping Kosher, it is necessary to keep all dairy and meat foods completely separate. Pareve foods, however, may be mixed in and served with either category of food since these foods are neither milk nor meat.

Buying Kosher Food: In terms of buying Kosher food, there are two general methods practiced by Jews today; the first is called keeping ingredient Kosher, and the second is called keeping Heksher Kosher.

1. Ingredient Kosher—This means that when shopping, you must check the ingredients of every manufactured or processed food product in order to ensure that it does not contain any substance derived from a non-Kosher animal or even from a Kosher animal but which has not been slaughtered in the prescribed manner or has any forbidden mixture of milk and meat together. This basically means that any processed food you buy should not contain any animal product whatsoever unless you are shopping for Kosher meat, in which case you wouldn't have to worry about checking the ingredients.

Herein lies the challenge; for there are many additives, emulsifiers, and preservatives that are derived from animal products and added into food products. But their original organic source is rarely listed, and the ingredient entry is often provided as an unfamiliar chemical term. For example, just to name a few, albumin, which used to be used as a stiffener in baked goods, was derived from animal blood and glycerin, a coagulant derived from the hooves of slaughtered animals,

Kosher or not. Many emulsifiers that are used as preservatives in baked goods are still derived from animal fat. And ambergris, although rarely used nowadays, was used as a flavoring agent in vanilla beverages, ice creams, candy, and baked goods; and it was derived from sperm whale intestines and definitely not Kosher. While more and more food manufacturers are responding to consumers' health concerns and growing interest in vegetarian and even vegan diets and drastically reducing animal-derived food additives for other nonrelated food products, it is helpful to be aware of some of the arcane terms and vocabulary used in today's food labels. An excellent book that is devoted to this subject is called *Is It Kosher? Encyclopedia of Kosher Food Facts and Fallacies* by Rabbi E. Eidlitz (Feldheim Publishers, 1992).

Only dairy foods and milk products may be purchased based on this method of checking the label to ensure there are no un-Kosher ingredients. However, nonprocessed Pareve foods—such as eggs, fresh fish, nuts, fruits, and vegetables—may be purchased without checking the label. And if you want to buy Kosher meat products in a general supermarket, then you must become familiar with keeping Heksher Kosher described next.

2. Heksher Kosher—This means that when food shopping, you must check the package of all products to ensure that they bear a symbol known as a Heksher. Derived from the word "Kosher," a Heksher is a symbol—usually the letter K and a surrounding design or a large letter U surrounded by a circle—that denotes that the product has been processed under the supervision of a specially trained rabbi and is guaranteed by federal law to be strictly Kosher. Depending on the product, the Heksher design will usually indicate whether the product is dairy, meat, or Pareve. For instance, Empire Kosher chicken is clearly meat; but certain foods with a Heksher, like bread or a cake mix, may in fact be Kosher dairy and include various milk products in the mix and therefore should not be mixed or served with meat foods. Other products such as pasta may have a Heksher that denotes that they are Pareve and may be mixed with either dairy or meat foods.

Beware of buying products which only have a plain letter *K* printed on the package as if it were a Heksher because by itself the letter *K* is not a copyrighted symbol, and therefore, any manufacturer can print a *K* on a product whether it is Kosher or not. However, just to make things even more complicated, some food products with only a plain letter *K* are in fact actually Kosher. Perhaps the food manufacturer for some reason chose not to contract with a Heksher certification agency but still wanted to indicate that the food product was Kosher even if not certified by a rabbi. Therefore, just to be sure, it is necessary to write, call, or e-mail the manufacturer and request copies of the certificate of Kashrut for that food item. As mentioned above, foods that are clearly Pareve need no Heksher, such as eggs, fresh fruit, nuts, vegetables, and fresh fish.

The bottom line is that if you want to shop for Hekshered Kosher foods, you might spend another minute or two in the grocery aisle searching for a box or can with a Heksher symbol, but you are guaranteed that the product is definitely Kosher. And given the growth of consumer interest in healthy food products, Kosher foods are seen as healthy food choices by many people, Jews and non-Jews alike. Therefore, more and more major familiar food products are being manufactured with Kosher certification, so it is not so difficult to shop for Heksher Kosher food anymore.

3. The Special Case of Cheese—The question of Kashrut in connection to cheese raises a unique problem. This is because cheese was originally created by adding a curdling agent, an animal enzyme called rennet derived from the lining of the stomachs of calves, into a quantity of milk. Therefore, the very process of creating cheese is a violation of the prohibition separating milk and meat in Kashrut. However, in modern times, manufacturers have found ways to create Kosher cheese by using a chemical substitute for rennet, in which case there is no problem of mixing milk and meat. In fact, certain types of Kosher cheeses are readily available in local supermarkets.

There is also an opinion promulgated by the Conservative movement that states that it is acceptable to eat non-Hekshered cheese because the rennet used in regular commercial cheese factories is so altered from its original animal source that it is not considered meat anymore. As in all aspects of Jewish life, everyone is free to choose how they want to observe Jewish customs and religious rituals; and while some people accept this Jewish religious decision, other Jews do not.

Preparing and Serving Kosher Food: The practice has developed to use separate sets of dishes and utensils as well as pots and pans to prepare and serve the two different categories of Kosher food. It is an ancient Jewish Kosher requirement that dairy foods as well as meat foods and products need their own separate sets of preparation utensils, pots, and pans and dishes in order to maintain a complete separation between the two to ensure that the two never mix. Even if dairy and meat products are inadvertently mixed, the food becomes Treyfe, which is a Yiddish word denoting that the food is not Kosher and therefore inedible for a Jew. Pareve foods may be prepared on either set of dairy or meat dishes; however, some rabbinic authorities are scrupulous in maintaining even a third set of separate preparation utensils for these neutral foods.

The only reason for separate sets of utensils, pots, pans, and dishes is to ensure a complete physical, hygienic separation between dairy and meat products. Glass dishes, however, may be used for both dairy and meat products if they are cleaned thoroughly between use. This is because glass is completely nonporous, and there is no danger that any residual dairy or meat products will come into contact.

Keep in mind that the cleaning and storage of different sets of dishes and preparation utensils also requires separate care. Some Jews use separate dairy and meat plastic kitchen sink tubs to wash their dishes, as well as separate sponges, drying racks, towels, cabinets, and drawers.

Conclusion: Keeping Kosher is a challenge. It involves following several fundamental principles of Kashrut, buying Kosher foods, and preparing these foods according to a few basic principles. Because keeping Kosher is one of the most elemental observances of traditional Jewish life, it is important for everyone to understand the basics of keeping Kosher.

Appendix B

A Guide to the Pesach Seder

Introduction

The two nights of the Pesach Seders are replete with rich symbolism. How the table is set and the Seder plate itself is full of significance. On most holidays and on Shabbat, we set out two Challot in order to remember that when the Israelites wandered in the desert, two portions of manna would fall on Friday, enough to eat on both Friday and Saturday; for none would fall on Shabbat in order that no one might be tempted to go and gather up any manna that might fall on Saturday thereby violating the Shabbat. However, on Pesach we set the table with three Matzahs. We'll discuss this more below.

The Seder plate is filled with different kinds of symbolic foods related to the story of the exodus from Egypt. It is set with Karpas, which is a vegetable hors d'oeuvre, and it is usually parsley or celery. There is also a dish of saltwater to dip the Karpas into and eat. Two commemorative foods that are set out but not eaten contain the Zeroa, or shank bone, representing the Paschal sacrifice and a Betzah, or roasted egg, that represents the Chagigah, or festival offering, that was sacrificed in Temple days. There is also Maror, or bitter herbs of horseradish, and some Seder plates have a space for another kind of Maror called Chazeret, which is usually romaine lettuce. This is so that the horseradish Maror is eaten when it comes the time to eat it by itself, and the romaine lettuce Chazeret is eaten in the Hillel sandwich, which we'll talk more about later. And finally, there is Charoset, a preserve representing bricks and mortar, and is prepared from chopped and pounded fruits, such as apples, nuts, and almonds mixed with cinnamon and wine.

Before we discuss the specific details and features of the Seder, it is important to understand that there is an overall structure and movement of the entire ritual meal. In fact, the word "Seder" itself means "order." Every element of the ritual meals has its own place and significance.

There are exactly fifteen parts of the Seder that in itself is a significant number, for there are also exactly fifteen verses in the song "Dayenu" describing the fifteen stages of redemption that God wrought for the people of Israel when redeeming them from Egypt. There were also fifteen steps in the Temple leading from the lower courtyard into the sanctuary itself, and on these steps would stand the Levites who would sing the fifteen Psalms known as Shir HaMalot or Songs of Ascent sung on the pilgrimage festivals to Jerusalem. Also, according to one count, there were exactly fifteen generations from Abraham, the founder of the Jewish people, till King Solomon, the builder of the First Temple to God. And finally, one of the Hebrew names for God, Yah, composed of the two Hebrew letters Yod and Heh, has the numerical equivalent of 15.

These fifteen parts of the Seder are listed below and are part of every Haggadah. The meaning and explanation of each of these sections follows after that.

a. Kadesh	f. Rachatza	k. Shulchan Orech
b. Urchatz	g. Motzi	l. Tzafun
c. Karpas	h. Matzah	m. Barech
d. Yachatz	i. Maror	n. Hallel
e. Magid	j. Korech	o. Nirtzah

1. Kadesh: The Sanctification of the Wine

1. Wine is the symbol of joy and gladness, for in appropriate amounts it lifts our spirits. Wine is also the symbol of redemption as it says in Psalm 116:13, "The cup of salvation will I raise, and I will call upon the name of God." There are actually four cups of wine to be consumed during the Seder, and these four cups are based upon a verse in Exodus 6:6-7 where God describes the divine plan for redeeming the people of Israel to Moses. God says, "I am the Lord, I will *free* you from the labors of the Egyptians and *deliver* you from their bondage. I will *redeem* you with an outstretched arm and through extraordinary chastisements. And I will *take* you to be My people, and I will be your God."

2. The four cups of wine match and celebrate the four expressions of redemption in these verses from the book of Exodus: free, deliver, redeem, and take. The number 4 is also an important symbolic number and appears again throughout the Seder. Not only are there four cups of wine to match the four terms of redemption, but also there are four questions asked during the Seder, four sons described in the parable later on, and four blessings in the Birkat HaMazon or grace after meals. Also, when Joseph interprets the dream of Pharaoh's former cupbearer while in prison, the dream of Pharaoh's cupbearer mentions the words "cup of wine" four times (Genesis 40:10-13).

3. At a traditional holiday or Shabbat meal, there are ordinarily two cups of wine: the first is used to make Kiddush, or sanctification, and the second cup is used in making the Birkat HaMazon, the grace after meals. The Pesach Seder includes these two of the cups of wine and adds two additional cups. One of these additional cups of wine is used to conclude the first half of the Seder to mark the end of the telling of the story part of the Seder, and the final cup is used to conclude the second half of the Seder when we conclude the recitation of the Hallel, a series of Psalms recited in the synagogue on joyous events and all Jewish holidays. Also, each cup of wine has its own

special blessing. This is because each cup is a separate stage of redemption by itself. One cup by itself is not a fulfillment of God's redemption of the Jewish people by itself. We were redeemed from Egypt in stages, and so too redemption in our time will not happen all at once but in stages according to rabbinic interpretations.

4. While everyone at a Pesach Seder is traditionally required to drink these four cups of wine, there is actually a fifth cup of wine that is poured but not drunk. This fifth cup is the result of a compromise settled on by the rabbis in the Talmud. They argued as to whether there is actually a fifth term of redemption mentioned in the verses of God's promise to rescue the Jewish people. After the initial four terms of redemption of free, deliver, redeem, and take quoted in Exodus 6:6, the passage continues with God saying, "And I will *bring* you to the land that I swore to your ancestors Abraham, Isaac and Jacob." Some rabbis argued that this verse was a continuation of the original divine promise of redemption to the Israelites, and therefore, we should pour and drink a fifth cup of wine. However, other rabbis argued that since it took God forty years to fulfill this promise of bringing the Israelites to the Promised Land, we should not drink the cup of wine in its honor. Ultimately, the rabbis compromised and declared that this fifth cup of wine was to be poured but not drunk. The fate of this cup was left to Elijah the prophet who, according to the Jewish tradition, will come one day to announce the coming of the Messiah at which point he can decide all unresolved matters of Halachah and determine whether we should in fact drink this fifth cup of wine. Therefore, this cup is called Kos Eliyahu or the cup for Elijah, which in popular folklore came to be thought of as a cup of wine poured for Elijah to drink! Rabbi Moses Maimonides wrote in early medieval times that the drinking of this fifth cup is optional, and some modern rabbis have said that we should in fact drink this fifth cup of wine in gratitude for the new State of Israel as a stepping-stone to messianic redemption.

2. Ur-chatz: Washing the Hands

Many of the customs and rituals of the Seder are derived from Greco-Roman customs at banquets. One of these rituals is the cleansing of the diners' hands before eating anything. On Shabbat or a holiday, it is customary to wash the hands and make a blessing before eating bread. However, this washing is done without a blessing because it is only to prepare for eating hors d'ouevres, a green vegetable. In the Jewish legal system, vegetables are considered less important than baked bread. Therefore, this washing before eating a vegetable does not require a blessing.

3. Karpas: Hors d'oeuvres

1. Another Greco-Roman custom that we follow to this day is the eating of some kind of green vegetable as an hors d'oeuvre before the main meal. "Karpas" is a Greek word for "vegetable." The Karpas also has some ritual significance as well. Since Pesach is a spring festival, the greenery represents the coming spring and rebirth of nature. This is symbolic of the birth of the Jewish nation that came into being as a result of the exodus of the Israelites from Egypt. The greenery is also symbolic of the hyssop that was dipped in the blood of the Paschal Lamb to mark the doors of the Israelites in Egypt during the tenth and final plague of the slaying of the firstborn and so is another symbol of redemption.

2. We eat the Karpas, which is dipped in saltwater, symbolizing the tears of our ancestors who were slaves in Egypt in order to arouse the curiosity of the children at the table, to inspire them to ask questions about the Seder so that we may explain the story of the exodus from Egypt.

4. Yachatz: Breaking of the Matzah

1. Usually, there are just two loaves of bread on Shabbat or a holiday, so why are there three Matzahs on the Seder nights?

Two are for the holiday itself and need to remain whole so that we may say the blessing over bread on them while the third Matzah is to be broken in half during the meal before we actually eat it. One-half of this broken Matzah is called the Afikomen and is hidden away and explained below while the remaining half is ultimately eaten as part of the Hillel sandwich when it comes a time to eat the Matzah and other symbolic foods also explained below.

2. Each of the three Matzahs has symbolic meanings, for they represent the three patriarchs of the people of Israel, Abraham, Isaac, and Jacob. They also represent the three strata of ancient Jewish society—Kohanim, or priests; Levites who served as the Temple workers; and ordinary Israelites. These three Matzahs also represent the three occasions when a thanksgiving sacrifice is used to be offered in the Temple in Jerusalem:

   a. Upon being released from prison
   b. Upon recovering from a life-threatening illness
   c. Upon crossing an ocean or desert

   The exodus of the Israelites from Egypt combined all of these together as the Israelites were released from slavery, which is like a prison. They were finally given the opportunity to recover from a life-threatening situation, namely, slavery itself. And they also crossed the Sea of Reeds and a desert after that!

3. The Matzah is also referred to in Deuteronomy 16:3 as Lechem Oni or the bread of poverty or affliction. This is because Matzah was the type of bread that the Israelites made in Egypt when they were slaves. Since their time was not their own to command, they had to make whatever provisions they could in the little time they could find for themselves. Matzah is also flat and lowly, a symbol of humility, servitude, and degradation. So Matzah is considered the bread of slaves. But it is also the bread of freedom, for when the Israelites were redeemed, they had little time to prepare and so were only able to bake Matzah in the little time they had to prepare to leave Egypt.

4. Another explanation of Lechem Oni based on a creative translation is "bread over which we talk," for the Seder nights are to be spent in discussion of the exodus from Egypt when each Jew is obliged to consider themselves as if they themselves had been in Egypt and were redeemed. This discussion involves and takes place around this Lechem Oni or the Matzah. Also, Yachatz involves breaking the middle Matzah but not eating it yet that is intended to arouse the curiosity of the children at the Seder and induce them to ask more questions and provoke further discussion about the story of the exodus.

5. Magid: Telling the Story of the Exodus

1. The Magid is the central part of the Seder as well as the longest, for it contains the repetition of the story of the exodus from Egypt. It begins with the recitation of a paragraph indicating that the Matzah is Lechem Oni, the bread of affliction that also serves as an invitation to anyone who is needy to come and join the Seder.

2. Next come the Four Questions that are usually asked by the youngest person at the Seder. These four questions concern the rituals and customs of the Seder and are framed from a child's perspective that sees the actions but does not comprehend the meaning and significance behind them. The answers that are provided in the Haggadah tell the story of the exodus.

3. There are actually two sets of answers to the Four Questions based on an argument between two rabbis in the Talmud. These two rabbis argued over what should constitute the starting point of the story of our liberation. Does the story of the liberation of the Israelites begin with freedom from physical servitude as slaves in Egypt, and so we need only begin the story with the Israelites as slaves in Egypt? Or does the story of Israelite servitude and liberation go even further back to before the beginning of monotheism? In other words, does the worship of idols constitute a kind of spiritual slavery? The Haggadah actually provides answers to both of these questions but begins with the answer,

"We were slaves to Pharaoh in Egypt." In other words, first we are obliged to discuss our physical bondage and liberation from Egypt. Later on, the Haggadah retells the story of our liberation from a deeper, more spiritual point of view beginning with the words, "In the beginning our ancestors were worshippers of idols" and proceeds to outline the development of the people of Israel coming to worship the One God of heaven and earth.

4. Perhaps one of the most well-known sections of the Magid part of the Seder is the story of the Four Children. These four stereotypical children are called the Wise child, the Wicked child, the Simple child, and the child Who Doesn't Know How to Ask. The origin of these four archetypes of children are actually derived from different passages in the Torah where in reference to Pesach the Torah describes what you should say to your children when they ask you about the exodus from Egypt. However, each of the four times this is mentioned in the Torah the child's question is framed somewhat differently, and the answers given are somewhat changed. These differences were later expanded upon and became the bases of the four types of children. These passages are the following:

a. Deuteronomy 6:20-1—"When your child asks you tomorrow, 'What are the testimonies, the statues and the judgments which the Lord our God commanded you?' Then you shall say to your child, 'We were slaves to Pharaoh in Egypt, and God brought us out of Egypt with a mighty hand.'" This became the basis for the Wise Child.

b. Exodus 12:26-7—"And when your children say to you, 'What is this service to you?' Then you shall say, 'This is the Pesach sacrifice to God, who passed over the houses of the children of Israel in Egypt.'" This became the basis for the Wicked Child because he says *you* and doesn't include himself.

c. Exodus 13:14—"And when your child asks you tomorrow, 'What is this?' You shall say, 'With a mighty hand God brought us out of Egypt, out of the house of slaves.'" This became the basis for the Simple Child.

d. Exodus 13:8—"And you shall tell your child on that day, 'Because of what God did for me when I went out of Egypt.'" This became the basis for the Child Who Doesn't Know How to Ask.

6. The next and longest section within the Magid is a lengthy rabbinic exposition called in Hebrew Tzei U'lmad, or "Go and study." The Haggadah quotes Deuteronomy 26:5-8, which is a very brief encapsulation of the story of the exodus. The Haggadah then provides copious rabbinic commentary on this passage called Midrash. The reason this Midrashic commentary is so long because the rabbis of the Talmud believed that everything in the Torah including every phrase, every word, and even little jots and tittles in the text contained hidden meanings; and therefore, it was left for later generations of rabbis and commentators to uncover and explain all of these cryptic messages.

7. This Midrashic section culminates in the recitation of the Ten Plagues that God sent against Egypt. There is a Midrash that states that when God ultimately drowned the Egyptian army in the Sea of Reeds, the heavenly angels wanted to sing praises before God, but God rebuked them saying, "Silence! Would you sing to Me while my children are drowning?" (Babylonian Talmud, Sanhedrin 39b). This Midrash shows that even though God was delivering the Israelites, God still had feelings of pity and mercy toward the Egyptians whom God was drowning. Based on this sentiment, as each of the Ten Plagues are recited, we dip a finger into our cup of wine and spill out a drop for each of the Ten Plagues on to the rim of our plates to show that our cup of gladness has been diminished because our redemption had to come about through the suffering of others. It is also important to remember not to lick our fingers after we are through with this action as that would contradict the entire symbolic act of spilling out ten drops of wine, for it would seem as if the death of the Egyptians was sweet to us.

8. The next part of the Magid is a quote from the Mishnah of
   Pesachim, the volume in the Talmud that deals with the proper
   way to conduct a Seder. It is a quote by one of the greatest of
   these early rabbis, Rabban Gamliel, that says that a Seder is
   not complete unless three fundamental elements of the Seder
   are mentioned and explained; and these three things are the
   following:

   a. The Paschal Lamb that is used to be sacrificed then eaten
       in Temple times and is a symbol of the fact that God
       passed over the houses of the Israelites during the tenth
       plague of the slaying of the firstborn.
   b. The Matzah that is a symbol of redemption due to the
       speed and haste in which the Israelites were rescued from
       Egypt, not having the time to bake full loaves of bread.
   c. The Maror that in Hebrew means "bitter" for the Egyptians
       embittered the lives of the Israelites through slavery and
       hard work.

9. The Magid section concludes with the recitation of the first
   part of the Hallel, a series of Psalms (113-118) that are sung in
   synagogues on festivals. The second cup of wine is then drunk
   at the conclusion of the Magid section.

6. Rachatzah: Washing the Hands

1. On Shabbat and holidays before the traditional blessing over the
   bread is made, it is a custom to symbolically rinse hands and
   recite a special blessing. This is because in ancient times when
   the Temple still stood, the common Jews were obliged to pay
   certain taxes in order to sustain the Kohanim, the priests, and
   Levites or the Temple workers. A portion of these taxes was paid
   in actual food and produce. Because this food was donated to
   the Temple and thus symbolically dedicated to God, it acquired
   a holy status. Therefore, the priests who ate this food had to
   eat it in a state of ritual purity that meant undergoing a ritual

immersion in a Mikvah. After the destruction of the Temple and
the elimination of animal sacrifices as well as all of the Temple
taxes and priestly duties, the rabbis who created the foundation
for modern Judaism sought to retain as much of the symbolism
of the Temple as possible. Therefore, the rabbis of the Talmud
instituted the ritual of washing hands accompanied by a blessing
so that all Jews would be able to experience, at least symbolically,
the significance of what it must have been like for the Kohanim
to eat Shabbat or holiday food in a similar state of ritual purity.
The washing of the hands takes the place of an actual immersion
in a Mikvah.

2. Because the washing of the hands and recitation of the blessing
is a direct preparation for making the blessing over the bread
and eating it, all of these actions are considered one continuous
ritual. Therefore, it is a custom to not distract ourselves with
talking in between the washing of the hands and blessing and
eating the bread. After washing the hands, people traditionally
remain silent until after eating the bread.

7. Motzi: The Blessing over the Bread

This is the traditional blessing that praises God for bringing forth bread
from the earth.

8. Matzah: The Eating of the Matzah (with a special blessing)

The eating of Matzah is the single-most characteristic element of
celebrating Pesach; therefore, to emphasize our observance, there is
a special blessing before eating the Matzah in addition to the regular
blessing before eating bread. Because participants in the Seder are
supposed to eat the Matzah with gusto and appetite, it is a custom to
refrain from eating Matzah at least several days if not weeks before
the Seder. Some people refrain from eating Matzah a full thirty days in
advance of Pesach.

9. Maror: Eating the Bitter Herbs

The bitter herbs are a symbol of the hardship and bitter servitude that our ancestors experienced as slaves in Egypt. It is traditional to dip the cut-up horseradish into the Charoset, a sweet mixture of apples, nuts, cinnamon, and wine to symbolize the sweetness of redemption but to brush most of it off before we actually eat it so as to fully experience the bitter taste of slavery.

10. Korech: Eating the Hillel Sandwich

1. One of the great early rabbis who lived during Temple times named Hillel made it a practice to combine several elements of Pesach into one act. He used to make a sandwich of the Matzah and the Paschal sacrifice that was offered when the Temple still stood and would be eaten by the family that brought it. We continue his practice, but because the Temple is destroyed and it is not possible to bring a Paschal sacrifice, we make a sandwich instead with the Matzah and Charoset. Charoset is an admixture of chopped and pounded fruits—such as apples, nuts, and almonds—mixed with cinnamon and wine and represents the mortar that the Israelite slaves had to make in Egypt while constructing Pharaoh's building projects.

2. Each of these ingredients used to make the Charoset also have symbolic meaning. Here is the recipe with their explanations:

   a. Red wine—This is symbolic of the blood of Israelites spilled in Egyptian servitude.

   b. Cinnamon—In its raw form, it looks like a stick and is similar to the straw the Israelites used to make bricks.

   c. Apples—This is an obscure reference to the Song of Songs 8:5, which says, "Under the apple tree I roused you. It was there your mother conceived you, there she who bore you conceived you." This refers to a tradition that when Pharaoh ordered baby Israelite boys to be killed at birth, the Israelite women went out into the apple orchards to

408   Rabbi Daniel Kohn

give birth to their children so as to hide them from the Egyptians.

d. Almonds—This is a symbol of redemption because the Hebrew word for "almond" is "Shaked" and is a pun on another similar word in Hebrew meaning "diligent work." The connection is that there is a tradition that ultimate redemption for the Jews and all humanity will only come about through diligent labor on our part to improve the world.

11. Shulchan Orech: The Seder Meal

The most often-asked question at a Seder meal is "When do we eat?" While other Jews may be aware of the lengthy ritual service before the actual meal, it is polite to inform guests and non-Jews who may be attending to actually eat before they come so they don't get too hungry waiting for the meal!

12. Tzafun: Hiding the Afikomen

1. "Afikomen" is not Hebrew but a Greek word probably meaning "dessert." It says in the Talmud that this is to be the last thing eaten at the Seder. It has become a custom for the Seder leader to hide the Afikomen and have the children look for it. Then after it is found, the Seder leader must ransom it back from the finder in order to complete the Seder. Another custom is that the children hide it, and the Seder leader must still ransom it back from the children in order to continue and complete the Seder. In either case, the children get some kind of treat as a reward or ransom.

2. The word "Tzafun" literally means "hidden" and alludes to the fact that the ultimate redemption of the Jewish people is still hidden away and must ultimately one day be brought to light by our work as Jews and human beings by working for justice in this world.

13.   Barech: The Grace after Meals

It is a tradition to recite prayers of thanks to God for the food we have eaten after meals. On Pesach, the Birkat HaMazon includes many special additions specific to Pesach. The third cup of wine is then drunk at the conclusion of these blessings.

14.   Hallel: Psalms of Praise

This is the conclusion of the section of Psalms of praise that were started before the meal began and which are now completed. The fourth and final cup of wine is drunk at the conclusion of this section.

15.   Nirtzah: Concluding Hymn of Seder

"Nirtzah" means "according to Your will" and is the name of the final hymn of the Seder that asks God to accept the performance of our Seder. Its recitation completes the Seder.

Conclusion of Pesach Haggadah Guide

The word "Pesach" means "to skip" or "pass over" because the Angel of Death passed over the Israelites' houses during the final plague of the slaying of the firstborn children. Pesach is also the name of the lamb that was sacrificed in the Temple on this holiday that would then be eaten by the family that brought the offering to the Temple. However, in Hebrew it is possible to break up this word into two separate words, "Peh-Sach," which means "the mouth speaks." Although the Temple no longer exists and Judaism is no longer a sacrificial religion, the Seder ritual is a dramatic ritual reenactment of the exodus from Egypt. Therefore, our words and prayers have come to replace the Paschal sacrifice; our Seder evening ritual is now our offering to God. It is a celebration of language and interpretation. Therefore, during the Seder nights everything spoken of in connection with the exodus from Egypt is considered Peh Sach, the mouth speaking, and our Pesach offering to God on this holiday.

Appendix C

Suggested Readings

This is a short list of excellent resource books on a wide variety of Jewish topics that I have developed and handed out over the years. It is by no means comprehensive; and in fact, in the course of answering many of the questions in this book, I frequently recommended these books as well as others that do not appear below. If you do not find a book here on a topic that interests you or my selection is insufficient to your reading appetite, I highly recommend spending some time doing some research on Amazon.com or Google.com!

Introductions to Judaism

- Diamant, Anita, *Living a Jewish Life*
- Kushner, Harold, *To Life: A Celebration of Jewish Being and Thinking*
- Prager, Dennis, and Telushkin, Joseph, *The Nine Questions People Ask about Judaism*
- Steinberg, Milton, *Basic Judaism*
- Telushkin, Joseph, *Jewish Literacy*

Jewish History

- Eban, Abba, *My People: The Story of the Jews*
- Johnson, Paul, *History of the Jews*
- Seltzer, Robert, *Jewish People, Jewish Thought*

Sacred Text Study

- Cohen, Abraham, *Everyman's Talmud*
- Holtz, Barry, ed., *Back to the Sources*
- *Tanakh: A New Translation*, Jewish Publication Society

Jewish Philosophy

- Dorff, Elliot, *Knowing God*
- Gillman, Neil, *Sacred Fragments*
- Wolpe, David, *The Healer of Shattered Hearts: A Jewish View of God*

"How-to" Books on Jewish Living

- Artson, Bradley Shavit, *It's a Mitzvah!*
- Donin, Isaac, *To Be a Jew*
- Donin, Isaac, *To Pray as a Jew*
- Greenberg, Blu, *How to Run a Traditional Jewish Household*
- Klein, Isaac, *A Guide to Jewish Religious Practice*
- Strassfeld, Michael, *The Jewish Holidays*

Conversion to Judaism

- Diamant, Anita, *Choosing a Jewish Life*
- Epstein, Lawrence, *Conversion to Judaism: A Guidebook*

- Kukoff, Lydia, *Choosing Judaism*
- Lamm, Maurice, *Becoming a Jew*
- Romanoff, Lena, *Your People, My People*
- Kohn, Daniel, *Emerging Jewish: Surviving the Conversion Process with Your Ideals and Relationships Intact*

Internet Resources

- www.MyJewishLearning.com
- www.ConvertingToJudaism.com
- www.Convert.org
- www.Jewish.com
- www.JewFaq.org
- www.BeingJewish.com
- www.interfaithfamily.com

Appendix D

Index of Questions

To help determine whether a particular question appears in any given chapter, I have assembled all of the questions in the order they appear in each chapter. I have also inserted the page number of where this question appears in the book along with the answer.

Chapter 1: Anti-Semitism (Ten Questions)

Question number 1: If the Hebrew Bible says that Jews are the people chosen by God, why are they persecuted so much? And where does that leave other religions such as Catholicism, Islam, etc.? Thank you for your time. (Answer on page 20)

Question number 2: I have heard that in biblical times the Orthodox rabbis practiced a secret form of medicine using herbs and mysterious healing arts, and because of this, it is rumored that these rabbis had a much longer life expectancy than their contemporaries. I hope you can help shed some light on what these traditions were and inform me as to where I may be able to find more information. (Answer on page 22)

Question number 3: What is the Protocols of the Elders of Zion? (Answer on page 22)

Question number 4: *Why do Christians fear or even hate Jews?* (Answer on page 23)

Question number 5: *What is the difference between modern and medieval anti-Semitism?* (Answer on page 24)

Question number 6: *Why do you people insist on taking Palestinian land and murdering the Palestinians? What is happening in Gaza and the West Bank reminds me of what the Nazis used to do to Resistance fighters. What is wrong with you people?* (Answer on page 25)

Question number 7: *I am from Switzerland and I have great respect for Jews and Judaism, that is why I am concerned about the situation in the Middle East. I hope I do not offend you with my question, but I see many similarities between current Israeli governmental policies and the Nazis. The Nazis forcibly settled German colonists in different areas of Europe, saying they needed more "living room." It seems to me that the Israelis are doing the same thing with respect to the Palestinians. Another similarity is with European ghettos and the Palestinian towns and villages that are being blockaded by Israel. I look forward to hearing from you, and I hope that I have not offended you in any way.* (Answer on page 26)

Question number 8: *I recently got in a fight with a friend, and he ended up calling me a Jew. We eventually made up, but I had to ask him if he really was a racist. He apologized and claimed that he does not really hate me because I am Jewish, but I am not sure what to feel or believe anymore. I am still hurt, but am I overreacting?* (Answer on page 28)

Question number 9: *Why aren't the Jewish people considered to be a race? Some friends have claimed that all Jews share certain physical features like big noses and dark hair. I have tried to explain that this is not true and that Judaism is more a culture than a race, and I have pointed to the existence of Ethiopian Jews, Asian Jews, and converts to the faith to prove my point that Jews are not a race, but to no avail. And they continue to tease me that I'm part of the Jewish race. Do you have any suggestions as to how to convince them?* (Answer on page 29)

Question number 10: *I read a Web page the other day that claimed that the Holocaust never happened. At first, I thought this person was an anti-Semite; but then I began to think that if six million Jews died, where is the evidence? Maybe this guy is right! How come I've never seen any ashes, and how come that Anne Frank book got locked away in Israel? Is it a fake?* (Answer on page 32)

Chapter 2: Interfaith Relations (Thirteen Questions)

Question number 1: *Where in the Torah does it talk about interfaith marriages?* (Answer on page 34)

Question number 2: *What are the differences between the Jewish and Christian religions? I am dating a young Jewish man, and I have been growing more interested in the Jewish religion. Can our relationship work out? Is it possible to bring together Judaism and Christianity?* (Answer on page 36)

Question number 3: *I do not understand how intermarriage is causing the Jewish population to decrease. If all non-Jews have to convert to Judaism before they are allowed to marry Jews, then how can the Jewish population be decreasing? Is this not a requirement of all non-Jews who want to marry Jews?* (Answer on page 38)

Question number 4: *How can I convince a young person of how important it is to marry a person from the same faith?* (Answer on page 38)

Question number 5: *I am Christian, and I am deeply in love with a Jewish woman. But she is scared to tell her parents about me and doesn't know what to do because she knows they will strongly disapprove. I don't want to destroy her family, but I don't want to give her up. I didn't realize that Jews think that Christians are so terrible. If we did marry, would her parents cut her off from their family? Would they ever acknowledge our children in any way?* (Answer on page 41)

Question number 6: *I am dating a young man who is not Jewish. We have decided that if we marry and have children, they will be raised Jewish. However, my boyfriend still wants them to be baptized in some way for his mother's sake. I have told him that this essentially would nullify their Jewish identity and they would have to convert back to being Jews! He claims that there are nonreligious ways of performing a Christian baptism. What should we do? Is there any way to rectify this situation?* (Answer on page 42)

Question number 7: *In our multicultural society, it seems that everyone is tolerant and accepting of everyone else. If the values that I choose to raise my children with are the same as someone else who is outside my religion, what is the problem? If I raise my children as Jews and incorporate my values into my family, why should my partner have to be Jewish?* (Answer on page 43)

Question number 8: *My Jewish nephew married a non-Jew, and they have invited me to their son's christening ceremony. And I don't know whether I should attend. You see, my son who is Jewish is also married to a non-Jewish woman; and while they have not yet planned any Christian baby rituals for their young daughter, I am worried that I might communicate the message that it is okay for them to have their baby christened as well. I want my granddaughter to be raised as a Jew, but I also don't want to offend the rest of my family by not attending. What should I do?* (Answer on page 45)

Question number 9: *I am Jewish and love Judaism, but I am seriously dating a Christian man. I feel like we are soul mates. We have talked about getting married and having kids, and he is more than willing to raise our children as Jews and keep Shabbat and everything. I have heard arguments from both sides about whether an interfaith marriage can work, but no one has given me a clear reason that really makes sense to me. I guess my question is what will I face in the future if our relationship works, and why should I even consider not marrying him.* (Answer on page 47)

Question number 10: *I'm Christian, but my serious boyfriend is Jewish and pretty religious. I have wanted to break off our relationship because of our different religions, but he claims that God would not have enabled us to meet or fall in love if He didn't have a plan for us together. But we both understand that if we had children one day, our different religions would be a problem. So should we get married and simply not have kids? And if we do get married, should we have a Jewish wedding or a Christian ceremony?* (Answer on page 49)

Question number 11: *My sister is engaged to a Jewish man, but we are both very religious Roman Catholics. And we are not sure if his family will have a problem with their different religions. Will our families clash, and will his parents forbid the marriage because she is Catholic? Should I urge my sister to convert to Judaism? I would hate for some disagreement to come because of our faiths; and besides, if we all love God, what is the problem?* (Answer on page 50)

Question number 12: *My Christian friend has told me that I will go to hell because I do not believe in Jesus. When I tell her that there is no proof of Jesus's miracles, am I right? I also tell her that it would not be just for God to punish people by going to hell just because they were raised to believe in a different religion. I have asked her to stop talking about this subject with me, but she refuses and accuses me of being afraid. What could I say to make her understand my point of view?* (Answer on page 52)

Question number 13: *I'm not Jewish, but I have attended numerous Jewish ceremonies and services for years. At these, I usually try to say as many of the prayers as I know, but I end up mumbling through the rest. Is this disrespectful? Also, some very traditional religious Jewish friends recently invited me to stay with them over the Sabbath. What should I do? Should I try to observe certain Jewish rules and customs? Can I go with them to their synagogue for worship services? I'm not sure what to do.* (Answer on page 53)

Chapter 3: Conversion and Jewish Identity (Twenty Questions)

Question number 1: I would like to convert to Judaism, but my husband does not want me to and I can understand his position. When we had our children, I insisted on baptizing them although my husband was not religious at all. Now that I am interested in becoming a Jew, he is angry that I spent so much time and effort convincing him to raise our children as Catholic and that I will just be confusing our kids. However, I feel very strongly about becoming a Jew now. What should I do? (Answer on page 57)

Question number 2: If Jews are truly God's chosen people and their offspring throughout the centuries are still God's chosen people today, how can a non-Jew ever truly convert and become a Jew when it seems to me that it is based on genetic heritage? Does becoming a Jew make one chosen, or is it based on blood heritage? (Answer on page 59)

Question number 3: Dear Rabbi, I'm Catholic and my husband is Jewish. We have a three-year-old daughter whom I insisted that we baptize; however, I also want her to learn about Judaism as well. We sort of celebrate Hanukkah and Pesach, but my husband could care less about practicing Judaism. Should I bother trying to teach my daughter about Judaism as well as Catholicism, or should I leave well enough alone and raise my daughter as a Catholic? (Answer on page 60)

Question number 4: I'm fifteen years old and want to convert to Judaism, but I have heard that no rabbi will teach me unless I'm eighteen. I have many Jewish friends, and I found their Bar/Bat Mitzvahs to be the most spiritual events I have ever seen. I don't feel it is fair to deny me the right to convert to Judaism; doesn't the U.S. Constitution grant everyone the freedom of religion? (Answer on page 61)

Question number 5: My fiancé is Jewish and very religious, and even though I am Catholic, I'd still like our future children to be raised as Jews. Is it wrong to convert to Judaism mostly so our children will be

Jewish when they are born? Is it wrong to do it only for the religion of our children? (Answer on page 63)

Question number 6: Is being Jewish more than a religion? If it is just a religion, why is there Hebrew, Jewish food, and Jewish music? Is Judaism a religion or an ethnic group? (Answer on page 65)

Question number 7: A long time ago during a difficult period in my life, I converted to Christianity, but I immediately regretted it and even went to a Mikvah [a ritual Jewish bath for spiritual purification]. But I remember that the church told me that my conversion was irreversible. I want to be Jewish again, and now I feel miserable—is there anything I can do, or is it too late? (Answer on page 66)

Question number 8: My sister and her husband are both Jewish; however, they have never joined a synagogue, sent their children to religious school, or celebrated their Bar and Bat Mitzvahs. They are completely ignorant of Jewish life and customs. I am Jewish, but my wife is not. Yet we belong to a Reform temple, have sent our children to religious school. They can read and write Hebrew, had Bar and Bat Mitzvahs, and continue to celebrate Jewish holidays. According to Halachah [Jewish law], my niece and nephew are Jewish but utterly ignorant of Judaism. Yet according to Halachah, my children are not Jewish, yet they are knowledgeable and observant of Jewish laws and customs. This situation angers me, and so I ask you, whose children should truly be considered Jews? (Answer on page 67)

Question number 9: My mother is Jewish, and my father was Catholic. And although I wasn't raised in any religion, my mother enjoys and still celebrates Christmas with all of the holiday decorations. My husband, who is Jewish, and I are raising our children as Jews; and my mother has agreed to begin celebrating Hanukkah and Pesach with us at her home for her grandchildren. But she still insists that we join her for Christmas. I am afraid this is going to confuse my kids. And I have tried to persuade my mother to stop celebrating Christmas, but she won't. What should I *do? How am I going to explain this situation to my children?* (Answer on page 69)

Question number 10: *Why are people not considered Jewish if their mother wasn't Jewish but their father was? Where is this law written in the Torah? This law doesn't seem very Jewish to me. It sounds like only a man-made law and not from God.* (Answer on page 70)

Question number 11: *What is a secular Jew? How can someone be a Jew without believing in God? I know some Jews who don't believe in God but still celebrate Jewish holidays—but what's to celebrate if you don't believe in God?* (Answer on page 72)

Question number 12: *Our son will be attending a local Catholic high school this year with some of his Jewish friends. Although he is pretty active in our synagogue youth group and has a strong Jewish identity, I'm worried that going to a Catholic high school will somehow undermine his Jewish identity. What are your thoughts?* (Answer on page 74)

Question number 13: *As I have grown older, I have been more attracted to Jewish life such as attending synagogue services regularly and taking adult Jewish education classes. Unfortunately, my husband, who is also Jewish, has no interest in joining me. I love my husband and want to spend time with him, so I feel torn: should I put my husband before my religion? I also want him to join me as a Jewish role model for our college-age children. What should I do?* (Answer on page 76)

Question number 14: *Although my wife's grandmother was born Jewish, she became a Catholic, and my mother-in-law raised my wife in the Catholic Church as well. However, when we got married, my wife reclaimed her Jewish identity by her own choice. Now we are having some problems with my in-laws because they are not respecting our wishes regarding Jewish holidays. For instance, they still insist on giving us Christmas presents on Christmas Day at their home around the Christmas tree and not Hanukkah presents during Hanukkah. I feel like Christmas* *is being forced on me, on my wife, and on our children. Do you have any suggestions as to how to handle my in-laws?* (Answer on page 77)

Question number 15: *My four-year-old daughter is starting to ask questions about Christmas and Santa Claus. She is enthralled by our neighbors' Christmas decorations and wants to put up Hanukkah decorations outside our home. We have no problem with such decorations inside our house, but we do not feel it is appropriate to display public Hanukkah decorations outside our home. We want our daughter to see Jewish holidays as fun and positive—are we being too strict here?* (Answer on page 78)

Question number 16: *My daughter, who is married to a Catholic man, is probably going to convert to Catholicism because she says she wants to be closer to God. I admit that I did not raise her in a very Jewish home; and I tell myself I'm grateful she is happy, healthy, and is a spiritual person. But I still feel heartbroken, and I'm not sure why. Can you help me?* (Answer on page 79)

Question number 17: *Dear Rabbi, my wife and our two-year-old son and I are planning on converting to Judaism together as a family, but not with an Orthodox rabbi. However, I'm concerned that if we ever decide to make Aliyah* [move to Israel to become citizens], *our conversion will not be recognized by the Chief Rabbinate of Israel. I am also troubled that Orthodox Jews will not recognize us as legitimate Jews. What would suggest I do to cope with this problem?* (Answer on page 80)

Question number 18: *Where in the Torah is the term "chosen people" actually used? Is it true that it makes us different and special, but not better?* (Answer on page 83)

Question number 19: *Although I am Jewish, I was not raised in a religious home. I desperately want to learn more about Judaism, but I am worried that because I am already an adult and so ignorant, I would not be accepted in the Jewish community. Is it too late for me to start?*

Could you please help me because I don't know where to begin. (Answer on page 84)

Question number 20: *I was raised as a Christian, but as an adult, I have grown away from my faith and feel attracted to Judaism. I don't know a lot about Judaism, and unfortunately, I don't live very close to any synagogues or rabbis. I would like to teach my children about religion and God but don't know what to tell them. Thank you for your help.* (Answer on page 86)

Chapter 4: Life Cycle Events and Family Issues (Sixteen Questions)

Question number 1: *I am pregnant, and a friend of mine wants to throw me a baby shower. However, my mother is adamant that I should not have one because years ago when she was pregnant before me, she had a baby shower; and then she delivered a stillborn. I don't know what to do. Is it okay in Jewish law to have a baby shower and leave all of the presents at my parents' home and not bring them into the house until the baby is born, or is even having a baby shower bad luck to begin with?* (Answer on page 90)

Question number 2: *What do we need to plan for a home baby-naming ceremony for our daughter who was born last month? Do we need to have a rabbi to perform the blessings, or can we do them ourselves?* (Answer on page 91)

Question number 3: *In all of the Hebrew Bible, there seems to be only one Moses, one David, one Sarah, one Abraham, etc. Was there a religious reason why parents didn't name their children after famous personalities in ancient times as we do today?* (Answer on page 92)

Question number 4: *Can you tell me more about the Jewish practice of circumcision or Brit Milah?* (Answer on page 92)

Question number 5: *Why does it say in the Torah that boys should be circumcised on the eighth day? I have read that the blood-clotting factor is actually above normal eight days after a child has been born. Is this the reason Brit Milah is on the eighth day?* (Answer on page 93)

Question number 6: My sister and her husband don't have children, and I recently learned that they named their new puppy after our grandfather. And this has upset me terribly. I believe only human beings should be named in the honor of a departed loved one. Am I overreacting? (Answer on page 94)

Question number 7: When was the Bar Mitzvah invented? Did it come from the Talmud? (Answer on page 95)

Question number 8: Can I have my Bar Mitzvah at home? I read it can be done without a special ceremony. (Answer on page 96)

Question number 9: Can you explain to me about the concept of the B'sheret or "soul mate"? I've looked everywhere and can't find anything. (Answer on page 97)

Question number 10: Should nonpracticing Jews be allowed to have a religious wedding? (Answer on page 98)

Question number 11: What is the meaning of the word "Aufruf"? (Answer on page 99)

Question number 12: Can you explain the custom of why the bride circles the groom three or seven times at a Jewish wedding? I understand that it is taken from the book of Jeremiah or Hosea, but how did this tradition start? Thanks for your help! (Answer on page 100)

Question number 13: My daughter is getting married next week, and my future in-laws are planning to throw candy at the bride and groom at the end of the ceremony. Can they do this? I thought that this tradition was only for Bar Mitzvahs! (Answer on page 101)

Question number 14: What is the significance of the groom breaking the glass at the end of the wedding ceremony? (Answer on page 101)

Question number 15: A judge married my husband and me, but now we would like to have a Jewish religious wedding. The only problem is that his ex-wife refuses to grant my husband a Get [Jewish divorce document]. What should we do? (Answer on page 102)

Question number 16: My ex-husband will not give me a Get. What options do I have if I ever plan to remarry in the Jewish community? (Answer on page 104)

Chapter 5: Ethical Issues (Thirteen Questions)

Question number 1: What is the basis for determining whether a choice is right or wrong? (Answer on page 106)

Question number 2: I read somewhere that making someone blush is like killing them because the blood rushes to their face for everyone to see, so in a way, you have publicly killed them. Do you know where this passage is from? (Answer on page 107)

Question number 3: What should I do about Jews disrespecting other Jews and disregarding commandments that are written in the Talmud? I just celebrated my Bar Mitzvah, and I take Judaism and the commandments seriously. (Answer on page 108)

Question number 4: How does Judaism treat the issue of the humane treatment of animals? Does Judaism take into account the unique character of a family's relationship with a pet such as a dog or cat? What about our relationship with working animals, such as Seeing Eye or bomb-sniffing dogs? (Answer on page 110)

Question number 5: What is the Jewish view of teen pregnancy and abortion? Also, what current trends in modern society do you find troubling or disturbing from a Jewish perspective? (Answer on page 111)

Question number 6: Are there any references in the Jewish tradition to self-defense, and when is it appropriate to resort to it? (Answer on page 112)

Question number 7: The other day, a friend and I beat up some skinheads at our school that had attacked one of my friends who is also Jewish. Afterward, I felt awful that I had sunk to their level. I was trying to stand up for my friend and fight against racism, but now I am confused. Is what I did wrong? (Answer on page 113)

Question number 8: Where do you draw the line for compassion regarding an abuser and their victim? Must we always forgive a criminal? I have been a victim of domestic violence for many years and have only recently gained the courage to get on with my life. Should I still try to find compassion toward my abuser? (Answer on page 115)

Question number 9: As a police officer, I sometimes participate in elaborate sting operations intended to fool people and lure them into committing a crime that they might or might not have committed if we were not arranging this sting operation. My problem is that I feel guilty about being part of the entrapment because I am not God to judge these people. Is it wrong for me to be part of this? Should I help catch these potential criminals? Am I part of God's plan for making the world more just? (Answer on page 116)

Question number 10: Why doesn't the United States just assassinate evil leaders of other countries, like the president of Iran or North Korea, to alleviate the suffering of the people in those countries? What is the Jewish perspective on this issue? (Answer on page 117)

Question number 11: Does Israel have the right to destroy the home of a Palestinian who is involved in an act of terror? This only deepens hatred

Rabbi Daniel Kohn

of Israel among the surviving family members. Amnesty International has charged Israel with illegally detaining Palestinians in their prisons and using torture. How can I maintain the feeling that Israel is a wonderful place and central to my religion and still acknowledge the horrible nature of the acts I have mentioned? Of course, I grieve and feel anger when Jews are attacked just because they are Jews. But Palestinians are people too. What does the Jewish tradition have to say about my emotional conflict? (Answer on page 118)

Question number 12: *What is the general Jewish view on war and peace?* (Answer on page 119)

Question number 13: *What are some important biblical passages dealing with Shalom (peace)? What is the significance of peace in the Jewish tradition?* (Answer on page 120)

Chapter 6: Questions from Kids and Teens (Sixteen Questions)

Question number 1: *Hi, I am nine years old, and I have a question for you. Why did God talk to Adam and Eve, Moses, and lots of other people but not to us?* (Answer on page 123)

Question number 2: *Where does God live?* (Answer on page 124)

Question number 3: *Hello, Rabbi. I am twelve years old and Jewish, but I'm not sure that God exists. I really want to believe in God, but I find it difficult sometimes. I still say the prayers, attend synagogue on the holidays, and celebrate the various holidays. My question is can you prove that God exists for me? And does my questioning the existence of God make me a bad Jew, or not even Jewish?* (Answer on page 125)

Question number 4: *What should I say to my teenage son who, after years of sending him to Hebrew school, says there is no God?* (Answer on page 126)

Question number 5: Dear Rabbi, I am nineteen years old, and although I celebrated my Bat Mitzvah and continue to observe Jewish holidays, lately I have been questioning the existence of God. I don't understand how God can exist when there are innocent people dying every day and wicked people prospering. Also, everyone claims his or her religion is the only true one; how can we be sure Judaism is the only true religion? (Answer on page 128)

Question number 6: Although I am fifteen years old and Christian, I have spent the last two years of my life trying to find answers about God because I feel I need some help. I have read the holy books of other religions. And recently, I have begun to study about Judaism, and I really enjoy what I am learning. Christianity no longer satisfies the thirst I have for God. So I am turning to you, Rabbi, to counsel me in this matter. How do I properly ask God to help me? I am crying out to God, and I have no strength left. Please help me in any way that you can. (Answer on page 129)

Question number 7: My brother has believed in God all of his life. But recently, he has been asking a lot of questions, and I don't think he believes in God anymore. He says that since there is no proof that God exists, the Torah may all be just myths. How can I help him? I still want him to believe in God because if he doesn't, I am scared that God will punish him. Please help! (Answer on page 131)

Question number 8: Hi, Rabbi! I am fourteen years old, and I don't know a lot about Judaism. I never had my Bat Mitzvah because I can't read Hebrew because I quit my temple's Hebrew school, and I still feel bad about that. But I would like to become more involved in my religion now, but I am the only Jewish kid in my high school. So I would appreciate some advice. Thanks for your answer! (Answer on page 132)

Question number 9: There is a kid in my class who's Jewish, and everyone hates him, what should I do? (Answer on page 133)

Question number 10: As a religious schoolteacher in a temple, what should I teach my nine-year-old students about Tisha B'Av [Jewish fast day commemorating the destruction of the Temple in Jerusalem]? (Answer on page 135)

Question number 11: *Help me, Rabbi! My teacher gave us a question to answer that I don't understand. I am only twelve years old, and I can't figure this out. Here is the question: "All things are mortal but the Jews; all other forces pass, but he remains. What is the secret of his immortality?" Thank you for your help.* (Answer on page 136)

Question number 12: *I heard a story that one time at a Jewish day school, a thirteen-year-old boy was fooling around and gave his girlfriend a ring and recited the traditional wedding formula as he did it. When the families found out, they had to get a Get [Jewish divorce document] since the two kids were considered officially married. Could this story be true? And if so, shouldn't it be a little more difficult to get married than that?* (Answer on page 137)

Question number 13: *Dear Rabbi, I am trying to eat only Kosher food, but it is difficult since I am living with Christian parents. I try to pick out Kosher foods when I go shopping with my mom, but sometimes I have no idea if the ingredients are Kosher. My parents won't let me get two sets of dishes, and although my parents are trying to help me, I'm not sure what to do. Do you have any suggestions on how I can maintain a Kosher lifestyle until I finish high school?* (Answer on page 137)

Question number 14: *I am thirteen years old, and I have experienced many difficulties in my life. And I was wondering, what should I do when people tease me about being Jewish?* (Answer on page 138)

Question number 15: *Although I feel grown-up, why should it matter so much to my parents that I only date Jewish guys? After all, I'm only fifteen years old! There are so few Jews in my school that there is practically no one to date. Thanks for your help.* (Answer on page 139)

Question number 16: *I am in the ninth grade, and it has gotten progressively more difficult for me to accept Judaism. Why should I* *believe the Torah, a three-thousand-year-old book, instead of scientific facts today? I don't like putting my faith into something unless I'm sure that it is valid. How can I blindly put my faith in something without any verification? Doesn't this kind of faith lead to extremism and terrorism?* (Answer on page 140)

Chapter 7: Sex (Eleven Questions)

Question number 1*: Please help me, Rabbi. I'm a young Jewish man who is having trouble finding Jewish girls to date because I live in an area with few other Jewish families. I desperately want to masturbate, but I don't want to have sex until I'm married. How can I fulfill my sexual urges without having premarital sex?* (Answer on page 143)

Question number 2*: I am in a very serious relationship with my girlfriend, and she wants to have sex and do other things like oral sex. Is this something we are allowed to do in Judaism? We are not married, and I'm not sure what to do.* (Answer on page 145)

Question number 3*: I am a female college student, and next semester I'm planning on renting an apartment with my best friend who is a man. We would be living together as roommates and not as a boy and girlfriend. In fact, we are not even interested in each other sexually. The problem is my dad; he is dead set against my plans and says it is against Jewish law for a man and woman to live together unless they're married. Since my dad is helping me with my college expenses, I need his consent. That's why I'm writing to you. Is my dad right? Would I really be breaking Jewish law?* (Answer on page 146)

Question number 4*: Dear Rabbi, I am in love with two young men, and while I have not had sex with either of them yet, one of them is starting to become upset that we have not being seeing each other as often as he would like. I know I have to choose between them eventually, but how do I know whom to choose?* (Answer on page 148)

Question number 5: Is it okay to have sex with more than one girl at a time as long as you like them both? (Answer on page 149)

Question number 6: Does the Torah prohibit fornication between two consenting adult lovers? (Answer on page 149)

Question number 7: Dear Rabbi, I am upset because recently a Christian friend told me that I am sinning because I am in a relationship with a woman and we are not married. I have heard that sex outside of marriage is not forbidden in Judaism. Do you know more about this? Can you give me some quotes from the Hebrew Bible or elsewhere about this? Thank you. (Answer on page 151)

Question number 8: I am going to be married soon, and while I'm not the most traditional young Jewish woman, I'm interested in learning more about the custom of going to a Mikvah [Jewish ritual bath] before my wedding. Can you tell me more about this specifically why I should go and what to do there? Thank you. (Answer on page 152)

Question number 9: Since the Sabbath is a day of rest, doesn't that mean sex should be forbidden since it is technically "work" for procreation? Wouldn't it be considered a violation of the Sabbath to have sex on such a holy time? (Answer on page 155)

Question number 10: What is the historical Jewish position on the issue of sexual harassment? (Answer on page 156)

Question number 11: I am doing research in ancient religious texts and was wondering if you can tell me if there were any ancient customs or laws against women cutting their hair in the Hebrew Bible. For example, was there any particular Jewish rule that required women to have either short or long hair? And did the custom of women covering or veiling their heads or faces have anything to do with hair? (Answer on page 157)

Chapter 8: The Hebrew Bible and Torah Study (Twenty-five Questions)

Question number 1: *Was the Torah written by God or by several people?* (Answer on page 159)

Question number 2: *I have only just learned about the documentary hypothesis regarding the authorship of the Torah that claims that there were a number of different ancient versions of the Torah that were written by different people and all combined together. What is the value of this hypothesis, and is it accepted in the academic world?* (Answer on page 161)

Question number 3: *Archeologists studying prehistoric man seem to suggest that human beings lived on the earth before Adam and Eve. How can we counter their arguments?* (Answer on page 162)

Question number 4: *When God said, "Let Us create man in Our image," who was God talking to?* (Answer on page 163)

Question number 5: *A friend recently asked me about the significance of the snake in Judaism. He claimed that the snake represents evil in Christianity. Does the snake have any significance in the Jewish religion? Also, what is the Jewish view of Eve's sin of eating the forbidden fruit?* (Answer on page 164)

Question number 6: *I'm not clear on the Cain and Abel story in chapter 4 of Genesis. What exactly did Cain do to anger God? As I understand it, both Cain and Abel gave what they could from what they produced or herded as a gift to God. In addition to this, why, after Cain slew Abel, did the Lord protect him from the wrath of others—especially if the Lord was already upset with him? The entire Genesis story makes sense up until this point to me. Any assistance you could offer would greatly be appreciated.* (Answer on page 166)

Question number 7: *How old was Isaac when Abraham almost sacrificed him?* (Answer on page 166)

Question number 8: *When did the exodus of the Israelites from Egypt take place? And who was the Egyptian Pharaoh who was in power at the time of the exodus?* (Answer on page 167)

Question number 9: *Why does the number 40 keep coming up in Jewish history, such as forty days of rain in the story of Noah and the flood or forty years of wandering in the desert?* (Answer on page 168)

Question number 10: *I am troubled by the law in the Torah that commands "an eye for an eye" (Exodus 21:24). Where is this law discussed in the Talmud?* (Answer on page 168)

Question number 11: *Could you please explain the origin of the Kohanim, or ancient Jewish priests, and their duties? Also, why are they not allowed to enter cemeteries, and why do they get special honors bestowed upon them in synagogue services?* (Answer on page 169)

Question number 12: *How does Leviticus 7:8-9 apply to modern life today?* (Answer on page 170)

Question number 13: *When does the Jubilee year spoken of in the Torah begin and end, and is there anything special we are supposed to do during this year? What is the year of Jubilee all about, and when was the last one?* (Answer on page 173)

Question number 14: *What are the symbols for each of the tribes of Israel? Can you describe them to me?* (Answer on page 174)

Question number 15: *What happened to the Ark of the Covenant? I've read that the Ethiopians took the Ark to their own country during the reign of King Manasseh. Does the Hebrew Bible offer any information about this?* (Answer on page 175)

Question number 16: *What is the verse from Isaiah 53:5 referring to? It states, "But he was wounded because of our transgressions, he was crushed because of our iniquities: the chastisement of our welfare was upon him, and with his stripes we were healed." Is this referring to Jesus Christ? If not, who else?* (Answer on page 175)

Question number 17: *Who is the author of Kohelet, that is, the book of Ecclesiastes? Why do they think it is King Solomon? If it wasn't him, then who was it?* (Answer on page 177)

Question number 18: *In Proverbs 1:8, it differentiates between the "instruction of the father" and the "law of the mother." Are there different traditions unique to each of the parents in Judaism?* (Answer on page 178)

Question number 19: *What is the Jewish understanding of reward and punishment as described in Daniel 12?* (Answer on page 178)

Question number 20: *Were the books of Tobit, Judith, and Maccabees and Wisdom of Solomon ever part of the Hebrew Bible?* (Answer on page 179)

Question number 21: *When were the Books of the Maccabees translated from Greek back into Hebrew?* (Answer on page 180)

Question number 22: *How important is the Book of Enoch, and how accurate or true do you think it is?* (Answer on page 181)

Question number 23: *I am trying to find information on the Dead Sea Scrolls. What is the Jewish view of the doctrines described in the Dead Sea Scrolls? Are they accepted?* (Answer on page 182)

Question number 24: *What is the Septuagint?* (Answer on page 183)

Question number 25: *I know the Temple in Jerusalem was destroyed a long time ago, but will there ever be another Jewish temple built there? And if so, who will serve as the priests and Levites there? How will they know if they are descended from the tribe of Levi?* (Answer on page 183)

Chapter 9: Jewish History and Denominations of Judaism
(Twenty-five Questions)

Question number 1: *Any idea why we read Hebrew from right to left?* (Answer on page 187)

Question number 2: *I have always believed that Judaism was the oldest religion in the world, but someone recently told me it is Hinduism. Is that right?* (Answer on page 188)

Question number 3: *When was the first Talit made and worn, and who made it? I know the Torah describes the fringes, or Tzitzit, but when did the Talit itself begin to be used and by whom?* (Answer on page 189)

Question number 4: *How was the synagogue first started?* (Answer on page 189)

Question number 5: *The word "Jew," as I understand it, literally means "someone from the tribe of Judah." Are all Jews today descended from the tribe of Judah? Or do we even remember what tribes we're from?* (Answer on page 190)

Question number 6: *I saw a show on TV about the ten lost tribes of Israel. Some people think that some of the tribes went to South America because Spanish conquerors that first met with the native tribes claimed that they had greeted them with Hebrew prayers. Also, some of the Aztec or Mayan temples are apparently similar to ancient Israelite architecture. Is it probable or even possible that some of the lost tribes could have found their way across the Atlantic to settle there?* (Answer on page 191)

Question number 7: What is Hellenism, and how did it influence Jewish thought? (Answer on page 192)

Question number 8: What was King Herod really like? I have read that the Jews he ruled hated him since he was a puppet of Rome and killed many of his own family members as well as rabbis. Was he truly evil or just an opportunist? (Answer on page 193)

Question number 9: Who really killed Jesus Christ? Was it the Jews or the Romans? Why don't Jews believe Jesus is the son of God? (Answer on page 194)

Question number 10: I have read that ancient historians such as Josephus, Tacitus, and Pliny have all affirmed the historical existence of Jesus; yet you have claimed in previous answers that there are no sources outside of the Christian Bible referring to Jesus, which do not seem to be correct. Would you care to comment? (Answer on page 197)

Question number 11: What is Kiddush HaShem? (Answer on page 198)

Question number 12: Why were the Jews pestered so badly by the crusaders if they were innocent? (Answer on page 199)

Question number 13: Who are the Marranos, and are they Sephardic Jews? (Answer on page 200)

Question number 14: I heard that there was once a Jewish pope, is that really true? (Answer on page 201)

Question number 15: What is a Golem? Is this a fictional character that has been handed down and is specific to Jewish culture in Europe? (Answer on page 202)

Question number 16: What can you tell me about the life and mind of Shabbatai Tzvi? (Answer on page 203)

Question number 17: Was there ever a Jewish mob? (Answer on page 204)

Question number 18: What is the Jewish position in regard to brotherhood and our growing multicultural society? (Answer on page 204)

Question number 19: What does Judaism teach about African-Americans and interracial marriages? (Answer on page 204)

Question number 20: Where did Jewish law come from, and what are the main denominations of American Judaism? (Answer on page 205)

Question number 21: How is the Conservative movement different from the Orthodox movement in terms of observance of Shabbat? (Answer on page 208)

Question number 22: Why do some Orthodox rabbis think that Conservative Jews are not Jews? I am a Conservative Jew, and I am very concerned. (Answer on page 208)

Question number 23: Where do Orthodox laws and customs come from? Are they in the Hebrew Bible? (Answer on page 210)

Question number 24: Why does the Reform movement not celebrate the second day of Rosh HaShanah? I also heard that a Kipah [head covering] is not always worn in a Reform temple. If so, why? (Answer on page 211)

Question number 25: What can you tell me about Messianic Judaism? I don't know much about it, but I am confused; how can they even call it Judaism? (Answer on page 213)

Chapter 10: Jewish Law and Mysticism (Twelve Questions)

Question number 1: What is the origin of the Hebrew phrase, "Kol Yisroel Arey'vim Zeh B'zeh," and what does it mean? Who said it, and under what circumstances? (Answer on page 218)

Question number 2: Can you tell me the location of the passage, "If you save a life, you save the world"? (Answer on page 218)

Question number 3: I was taught that you were not supposed to shoot someone even if it would save your life. If someone said, "Shoot this one person, or I will shoot these ten people," what are you supposed to do? (Answer on page 219)

Question number 4: I have read that if a Jewish court kills one man in seventy years it is a bloodthirsty court. Can you explain what this means? (Answer on page 219)

Question number 5: What does the Jewish religion think of abortion? (Answer on page 220)

Question number 6: Why is fishing permitted while other types of hunting are banned? (Answer on page 221)

Question number 7: I recently learned that baptism is not a Christian invention. John the Baptist, as a Jew, was acting in the long tradition of Jewish practice. It seems that ritual cleansing, as well as baptism for converts to Judaism, was part of Jewish practice for centuries. Is there some equivalent rite today within Judaism? (Answer on page 222)

Question number 8: In the Torah Numbers 15:37-41, it says to use a blue or purple thread on each corner of the Tzitzit, or the fringes on a Jewish prayer shawl. However, nowhere does it state what shade of blue or where or what animal to get this dye from. In my research on the Internet, it says that the formula for the blue dye has been lost and that white is okay. How can it be okay when God said to use blue? (Answer on page 223)

Question number 9: What is the role of women in the Jewish faith? (Answer on page 224)

Question number 10: I once heard a rabbi tell a story about the seven righteous men who held up the world. Could you tell me where to find it? Thank you very much. (Answer on page 226)

Question number 11: *What is Kabbalah?* (Answer on page 227)

Question number 12: *Why is Kabbalah so popular now? Is it considered a cult? Are there any cults in Judaism?* (Answer on page 228)

Chapter 11: Shabbat, Jewish Festivals, and the Hebrew Calendar (Twenty-four Questions)

Question number 1: *Why is the lunar calendar used for festivals and the High Holidays whereas it is the solar calendar that we use for weekly Sabbaths? Was the choice of Saturday for Shabbat made by the rabbis, or did it come from the Torah?* (Answer on page 232)

Question number 2: *What year is it in the Jewish calendar? My understanding is that the Jewish calendar began in 3761 BCE. How was that date determined, and what does that make the current year of 2007? I would appreciate your help.* (Answer on page 233)

Question number 3: *Could you tell me the importance of Shabbat for a Jew?* (Answer on page 234)

Question number 4: *What does Exodus 31:13 mean when it says that the Shabbat is a sign between God and the Jewish people? Can you explain this?* (Answer on page 235)

Question number 5: *Why are the Jewish people commanded to sacrifice more animals as offerings to God on Rosh Hodesh than on Shabbat? I thought Shabbat was considered to be the most important day in the Jewish calendar of holidays.* (Answer on page 236)

Question number 6: *Why are we not supposed to touch or handle money on Shabbat? Who made this a rule?* (Answer on page 237)

Question number 7: I am moving into my first apartment and living on my own for the first time ever. This might sound funny, but growing up, it was always my mother who lit the Shabbat candles on Friday nights. One time I tried to light the candles, but my grandmother told me that lighting the Shabbat candles is a "woman's job." My father then told me that if no women are present to light the candles, I am exempt from having to light Shabbat candles. My question is should I light candles myself in my apartment on Friday nights because no women will be present, or am I really exempt from having to light Shabbat candles as a single man living on my own? (Answer on page 239)

Question number 8: Why is the Challah bread loaves that we eat on Friday nights braided? (Answer on page 240)

Question number 9: What's the best way to blow a Shofar? (Answer on page 240)

Question number 10: Can you please give me a brief history on the Shofar and why, when, and how it is used? I'm especially interested in the different calls and patterns of the sounds. Thank you. (Answer on page 240)

Question number 11: What are the prohibitions and restrictions for Yom Kippur? (Answer on page 241)

Question number 12: What is the practice of fasting, and why is it practiced? (Answer on page 245)

Question number 13: This is a question about Yom Kippur. I am currently breast-feeding my son and would like to know what are the rules about fasting for a nursing mother. On the one hand, it's only one day; but on the other hand, my son will not get proper nutrition for that day. I can give him a bottle, but it is rather inconvenient to prepare that much breast milk in advance. What is your opinion? (Answer on page 247)

Question number 14: *What does Kol Nidrei mean? And why is it chanted three times?* (Answer on page 248)

Question number 15: *What does Hoshanah Rabbah mean, and what is it about?* (Answer on page 250)

Question number 16: *Are you only allowed to get only one present on Hanukkah every night, or is it as many presents as your parents give you each night?* (Answer on page 251)

Question number 17: *During this Christmas season, I have several Jewish friends, and I'd like to give them a holiday gift. I am not Jewish, so I would appreciate any advice about what would be appropriate and tasteful to let them know that they are special to me.* (Answer on page 251)

Question number 18: *I recently read an interesting story about the legend of Hanukkah. It had something to do with Judah Maccabee fighting the Greeks and capturing the sacred Temple in Jerusalem and finding only a single flagon of holy olive oil used to light the Menorah. When did this happen? Did the Menorah have seven branches or nine like modern Hanukkah Menorahs? And did the light in the Menorah last for eight days straight? I am confused by this story and would appreciate an accurate version. Thank you.* (Answer on page 252)

Question number 19: *I recently learned that the miracle of the oil in the Hanukkah story was made up a long time ago. If this is so, why do we even bother to light the candles and say a blessing that implies that God had something to do with this made-up event? Also, the blessing over the candle lighting implies that God gave us the commandment to kindle the lights of Hanukkah. I can appreciate the miracle of the spiritual and military victory of the holiday without the farce of lighting the candles. I have been disturbed about this for some time. Please help me understand. I want to believe again in the miracle of the Hanukkah story!* (Answer on page 254)

Question number 20: *Is it okay to use a Hanukkiyah on a night other than Hanukkah?* (Answer on page 256)

Question number 21: I have often wondered why, if the Jewish people received the Torah on Mt. Sinai on the holiday of Shavuot, we complete the reading of the Torah and begin reading it again on the holiday of Simchat Torah, which comes after the holiday of Sukkot four months later. (Answer on page 257)

Question number 22: What is the Halachah regarding working on the holiday of Shavuot? Are there Shabbat-like restrictions? (Answer on page 258)

Question number 23: My daughter is planning a wedding next year sometime in the spring. I recall learning once that there is a period of time in the spring in which Jewish weddings should not be scheduled. When is this period of time, and what is it all about? (Answer on page 259)

Question number 24: I recently read in a guide to synagogue customs that the fifteenth day of Av is listed as a partial Jewish holiday. I can find no reference to that date. What is this holiday? (Answer on page 260)

Chapter 12: Pesach (Fourteen Questions)

Question number 1: What criterion determines when Pesach occurs from year to year? (Answer on page 263)

Question number 2: I am confused—do we celebrate Pesach for seven or eight days? (Answer on page 264)

Question number 3: Why do we burn Hametz before Pesach begins, and what is its purpose? (Answer on page 265)

Question number 4: Why do we have two Seders during Pesach? Is one more important than the other? (Answer on page 266)

Question number 5: *The Pesach Haggadah says that when Pesach falls on a Saturday night, the final blessing of Havdalah* [the ceremony on Saturday night marking the end of the Sabbath] *should be recited at the beginning of a Seder on Saturday evening. Yet there is no mention of the Havdalah or the remainder of the ceremony. My family loves celebrating the Havdalah ritual using the special braided candle on Saturday nights! Even though the Haggadah instructions don't mention this candle, may we still light a Havdalah candle before lighting candles for the Saturday night Seder and conduct the entire Havdalah ritual?* (Answer on page 268)

Question number 6: *What is the significance of lettuce on the Seder plate? Why is it that all Seder plates do not have lettuce?* (Answer on page 270)

Question number 7: *Since Matzah is made of wheat flour and water, why is wheat among the non-Kosher foods for Pesach? Also, if the Matzah is Kosher for Pesach, why couldn't I bake more Matzah during Pesach with wheat flour? Why is the wheat flour forbidden during Pesach?* (Answer on page 271)

Question number 8: *Why do we use only wine or grape juice for the Kiddush and the Four Cups on Pesach? Why not another kind of alcohol?* (Answer on page 272)

Question number 9: *My adult children have become vegetarians and do not even eat eggs. Cooking for Pesach is difficult enough, but having to avoid eggs makes it nearly impossible. It seems that all Pesach foods and recipes include eggs! Are there Pesach noodles that don't have eggs? Where could I find them?* (Answer on page 274)

Question number 10: *Why don't we eat lamb at the Pesach Seder if it is a Torah commandment and not a rabbinic interpretation?* (Answer on page 275)

Question number 11: Why is it that we can use peanut oil on Pesach but not peanut butter? And why are legumes prohibited on Pesach? (Answer on page 276)

Question number 12: I have heard that it is permitted in Jewish law to eat non-Kosher-for-Pesach food, that is, food with Hametz at the very end of Pesach and then put them away for the next Pesach. Is that right? If so, does that mean that I can use any of my dishes and utensils that I have used throughout the year on Pesach as long as I haven't used them for a full year? And what about using dairy dishes and utensils for meat food and vice versa if I haven't used them for a year? Does not using a set of dishes for a whole year make them Kosher for other kinds of food? (Answer on page 277)

Question number 13: Could you please explain the background of Elijah the prophet? Why is Elijah not in the Hebrew Bible in the section with other prophets? He certainly is of significance to the Jewish people! And regarding those other prophets in the Hebrew Bible, could you please provide me with time frames for them? What I don't understand is if Elijah was part of the Pesach story, why isn't he mentioned anywhere in the Torah? (Answer on page 279)

Question number 14: Why do we read Shir HaShirim on Shabbat Pesach? (Answer on page 281)

Chapter 13: Kashrut: Jewish Dietary Laws (Twenty-one Questions)

Question number 1: What are the advantages and disadvantages of keeping Kosher? (Answer on page 283)

Question number 2: I keep Kosher. But recently, one of my friends asked me what is the point of keeping Kosher, and I realized I did not really have an answer. Could you please help me answer my friend's question—both *for her and for me—what is the point in keeping Kosher?* (Answer on page 284)

Question number 3: *Are there any exceptions to keeping Kosher? For example, what if my baby was starving and the only food I could obtain was pork—isn't the saving of life more important? Also, what if I intentionally ate non-Kosher food? What would I have done in the days of the Temple to atone for this sin? And whatever you might answer me, why would I have had to do anything special to get God to forgive me? Doesn't God forgive us all on Yom Kippur, the Day of Atonement, anyway?* (Answer on page 286)

Question number 4: *I have been studying in Israel, and recently I have become more religiously observant. I now keep Kosher very strictly, but I am now wondering what to do when I return home to the United States and want to eat in my parents' home because they don't keep Kosher. Should I follow the commandment of keeping Kosher and eat non-Kosher food in their home, or should I follow the commandment to honor my father and mother in their home?* (Answer on page 287)

Question number 5: *Is it better to keep Kosher in the home and eat non-Kosher food in restaurants than to not keep Kosher at all?* (Answer on page 288)

Question number 6: *Although I keep Kosher, I just got a job working as a waiter in a non-Kosher restaurant. Is it wrong for me to serve people un-Kosher food?* (Answer on page 289)

Question number 7: *Is eating Kosher meat safer than eating non-Kosher and why?* (Answer on page 289)

Question number 8: *Is there any information about vegetarianism in the Torah? And what about eating eggs? Are they Kosher or even vegetarian because an egg could grow up to be an animal?* (Answer on page 290)

Question number 9: Where in the Torah does it specifically prohibit eating meat and milk at the same time? The only passage I've ever found about it talked about not eating a baby goat cooked in its own mother's milk. How does this apply to all milk and meat being separate? (Answer on page 292)

Question number 10: Why is meat Kosher? After all, scientific studies have proved that eating animal flesh is harmful to human health, and doesn't Jewish law state that we should avoid harming our bodies in any way? So shouldn't science take precedence over biblical law? (Answer on page 293)

Question number 11: I have two questions: What exactly makes the Kosher slaughtering process different from other kinds of meat? And is the Kosher meat cooked or preserved in a different way than non-Kosher meat? (Answer on page 294)

Question number 12: If you keep Kosher, can you wash all of your dishes in the same sink as long as you don't mix up milk and meat dishes? (Answer on page 295)

Question number 13: Are ostriches Kosher? (Answer on page 296)

Question number 14: Why are sea creatures that live on the bottom of the sea not Kosher? What difference does it make? (Answer on page 296)

Question number 15: Why is cheese not Kosher? How come I can't find any cheese with Kosher certification? (Answer on page 297)

Question number 16: Are you permitted to take vitamins if they contain gelatin and glycerin, both of which are derived from animal products? (Answer on page 298)

Question number 17: I found a kind of yogurt that has a K on the package. But how can it be Kosher if it has gelatin in it? (Answer on page 299)

Question number 18: Is lactic acid a dairy product? I have just begun keeping Kosher, and I have been carefully reading the ingredient labels *on vegetarian foods if they are not certified as Kosher. Lactic acid was an ingredient that I found on a loaf of bread and wasn't sure if this made the bread dairy.* (Answer on page 300)

Question number 19: *If I stop in a coffee shop and buy a cup of coffee or tea, is it okay if I bring it into a synagogue or someone's home if they are Kosher? I thought all coffee and tea was Kosher.* (Answer on page 301)

Question number 20: *If a lettuce and tomato salad is prepared using meat utensils and served with a meat meal, is it permissible to serve any leftover salad later on with a dairy meal?* (Answer on page 301)

Question number 21: *Why is fish considered Pareve even though fish have blood?* (Answer on page 303)

Chapter 14: Prayer (Twenty-four Questions)

Question number 1: *Recently I have felt a strong desire to pray, but I am not sure about how to communicate meaningfully with God. My attempts seemed deficient and are unsatisfying to me. Can you suggest some readings, advice, or methods to help me to be able to pray more meaningfully? Thank you!* (Answer on page 306)

Question number 2: *Why do Jews pray facing east? In Russia, I believe they also prayed facing east even though Jerusalem was to the south.* (Answer on page 308)

Question number 3: *Why do we Shuckle when we pray?* (Answer on page 308)

Question number 4: *When I watch people pray, I have noticed that they perform certain actions during prayers. Like during the Shema, they kiss the Tzitzit* [fringes of the Talit, or prayer shawl]; *and when they say* *certain words, they turn from side to side or bow. Where can I learn about these actions?* (Answer on page 309)

Question number 5: *What is the significance and symbolism of a Talit? How and why did the Talit develop? How does the Talit relate to other cultures and religions?* (Answer on page 312)

Question number 6: *What do Tzitzit mean to you? What are we supposed to think about when we look at them?* (Answer on page 313)

Question number 7: *At synagogue, I notice that some men put Talit on in a certain fashion. Is there a proper way for putting on a Talit? If so, what is it?* (Answer on page 314)

Question number 8: *Is it considered wrong for a Jew to get on their knees to pray in private? Why or why not?* (Answer on page 315)

Question number 9: *Why are we commanded to say one one hundred blessings a day? What is the purpose of blessing in general? How did we arrive at this number?* (Answer on page 317)

Question number 10: *Why are we supposed to kiss the Torah or Siddur* [Jewish prayer book] *when we drop it?* (Answer on page 317)

Question number 11: *Why do you keep your feet together during the Amidah* [a Hebrew prayer that literally means "standing"]*?* (Answer on page 318)

Question number 12: *Does the Hebrew Bible state anywhere that it is possible to obtain forgiveness from God for our actions through a manner other than animal sacrifice? Is there a biblical answer as to why we no longer need to make animal sacrifices to atone for our sins?* (Answer on page 318)

Question number 13: *I am a religious Jew studying in a nonreligious college. But I still enjoy praying three times a day, but I am not sure exactly* when I am supposed to begin or end each prayer service. Also, since I am rarely able to find a Minyon every day, sometimes I oversleep and wake up after Shacharit [morning prayer] time. What prayers should I say in compensation? (Answer on page 319)

Question number 14: I need help understanding the Yotzer [a Hebrew prayer meaning "creator"]. I realize that it is a prayer of thanks, but what are we thanking God for? What is its significance, and why is it important? (Answer on page 320)

Question number 15: Could you please tell me what is the correct way to place a Mezuzah on the door? Thank you. (Answer on page 321)

Question number 16: What is the prayer we recite three times a day asking God for help in repairing our mistakes? (Answer on page 322)

Question number 17: Is there any significance to the phrase in the traditional Hebrew prayer book in which men say a blessing thanking God for "not having made me a woman"? I am bothered by this blessing and would like your thoughts on it. (Answer on page 323)

Question number 18: I'm not Jewish, but I've been studying about Judaism on my own. I recently learned about the Shema prayer and how important it is in Judaism. Could you tell me where I could find it and explain why the Shema prayer is recited? Thanks for your time. (Answer on page 324)

Question number 19: Could you tell me about Hallel [a section of prayers chanted on certain Jewish holidays]? Why do we chant it, and what is its origin? Any help would be very appreciated. Thank you and Shalom. (Answer on page 325)

Question number 20: What are the meanings and root of the Hebrew words "Haftarah" and "Maftir," the readings from the prophets and the last Torah reading on Shabbat? Are there any modern words in Hebrew from this same root? (Answer on page 325)

Question number 21: *Please tell me why we say Hazak Hazak Venitchazek in synagogue when we complete the reading of a book of the Torah.* (Answer on page 327)

Question number 22: *From where in the Torah do we learn that you must make Kiddush* [the prayer sanctifying a Shabbat or Jewish holiday recited over wine or grape juice]*? Can you provide me with a quote? How many parts are there to Kiddush, and what are they?* (Answer on page 327)

Question number 23: *I am a congregational leader in my synagogue, and it frustrates me to no end that people in my synagogue seem to shy away from receiving ritual honors in the worship services and avoid participating in even the smallest of ways. What could I say to them to persuade them to be more active?* (Answer on page 328)

Question number 24: *Is it possible to form a Minyon* [minimum number of adult Jews necessary to be present to constitute a traditional prayer quorum] *in a chat room on the Internet? Can a group of ten or more people physically separated, but who have agreed to pray as a specific time, constitute a Minyon?* (Answer on page 329)

Chapter 15: Death, Funerals, and Mourning (Thirteen Questions)

Question number 1: *My mother-in-law is dying of cancer, and my elementary school-aged children are very close to her. Although they know she is dying, I am worried that she will die while they are away at their out-of-state summer camp. My question is, should I bring them home for the funeral? Should I even tell them at all or wait until they get home at the end of the summer? Should this be a decision for my husband to make or both of us together or me alone as their mother? Do you think that my children are old enough to make their own choice? Should they even be at the funeral at all? Thank you.* (Answer on page 332)

Question number 2: *Why do Jews guard their dead at the funeral home while they are being prepared for the funeral? What are you supposed to do?* (Answer on page 333)

Question number 3: *I was just asked by a friend to officiate at the funeral of one of his family members. I am not a rabbi, but I am fairly involved in my synagogue and familiar with the prayer book. Do you have any suggestions as what prayers or readings I should include other than a eulogy and the Mourner's Kaddish? Thanks for your help.* (Answer on page 334)

Question number 4: *I am Catholic and was very close to my Jewish neighbor who just died. At the funeral, I was shocked and disturbed to see the casket lowered into the grave. Is this a traditional Jewish practice or something that the family chose to do on their own? Also, although they did not have a viewing, I was told that the deceased was not dressed in a suit or formal clothing. Why not? Thanks for your help.* (Answer on page 336)

Question number 5: *Could you please explain the Kaddish to me and why it is recited? Thanks!* (Answer on page 338)

Question number 6: *Why do Jews wash their hands after visiting the cemetery?* (Answer on page 339)

Question number 7: *What is the symbolism of placing a rock on a Jewish gravestone? Does it have anything to do with the prayer that is recited at a funeral that begins, "The Rock! His deeds are perfect. Yea, all His ways are just"?* (Answer on page 341)

Question number 8: *Why do people sit Shiva? And why is it for different numbers of days?* (Answer on page 341)

Question number 9: *Why is it forbidden for a Jew to get a tattoo? And is it true that Jews with tattoos cannot be buried in a Jewish cemetery?* (Answer on page 342)

Question number 10: *I am embarrassed to admit this, but years after my brother died, I went to a spiritual medium to talk to his spirit as a way of coping with his death. I know that in the Torah it states, "Do not turn to ghosts and do not inquire of familiar spirits, to be defiled by them: I the Lord am your God"* [Leviticus 19:31]. *If I committed a sin, how can I repent?* (Answer on page 344)

Question number 11: *Both my mother and father passed away at different times when I was away on business trips, and I was not able to be with either of them when they passed away. Although it has been years since my parents died, I still feel a void in my life. How can I deal with this lack of closure that I feel?* (Answer on page 345)

Question number 12: *I am planning on conducting an unveiling service for my father's headstone next month for close friends and family. Could you share some ideas on what we are supposed to do?* (Answer on page 346)

Question number 13: *My mother passed away last year, and I was originally planning on purchasing a memorial plaque in our temple in her honor. However, I feel there must be a better way to honor her memory than have her name engraved on a place on a wall that few people will ever see. Do you have any suggestions on what I might do?* (Answer on page 348)

Chapter 16: Spirituality and Jewish Theology (Sixteen Questions)

Question number 1: *What are the five basic beliefs of Judaism?* (Answer on page 351)

Question number 2: *What does Judaism have to say about Charles Darwin and the theory of evolution? I've been doing some research and haven't been able to find anything.* (Answer on page 353)

452 | Rabbi Daniel Kohn

Question number 3: *I have been attending services at a traditional synagogue, but I feel like an impostor because I don't have the certainty of Torah min HaShamayim* [Torah from Heaven]. *Yet when members challenge me that if I don't believe the Torah is literally the word of God, then why should I bother observing any of the Mitzvot? What should I say to them?* (Answer on page 354)

Question number 4: *In your opinion, why do some people have such a rough life? My husband has a slow terminal disease, I'm a diabetic, and my kids also have significant health problems. What did I do to deserve this? I do my best to be a good person and treat people fairly. What is wrong?* (Answer on page 357)

Question number 5: *Do Jews believe Satan is a true being like a human or God or just the trials that come to us in life?* (Answer on page 358)

Question number 6: *Why did God create the two impulses—the good impulse and the evil impulse? I have read that the Talmud implies that the evil impulse is somehow involved in the preservation of humanity. How can the evil impulse be a positive force?* (Answer on page 358)

Question number 7: *I have been studying about the parallels between Karma in Hinduism and Judaism. As I am sure you know, Karma is a belief that whatever you do in this life will affect your next life. Do we as Jews believe in this? Are there any connections in Judaism to Karma that you know of?* (Answer on page 359)

Question number 8: *Who or what is the Messiah in Judaism? Is the Messiah an individual, a real person who acts as savior to the Jewish people, or does it refer to a Messianic period of time?* (Answer on page 360)

Question number 9: *I have a Christian friend who, of course, insists that Jesus was the Messiah. I told him that in Judaism, the Messiah is not supposed to be a deity. My friend has asked me for scriptural references to prove this. Can you help me out here? Thanks!* (Answer on page 362)

Question number 10: *I recently joined a Messianic Jewish congregation that I love. Why are we not considered Jewish by other Jews? I want to follow the Torah and God! Thank you for your answer.* (Answer on page 364)

Question number 11: *What role do angels play in Judaism? I know of the Angel of Death, the angel who wrestled with Jacob, and the angel who stopped Abraham from killing Isaac. But I read somewhere that that there are one hundred and fifty angels acknowledged in our religion, and I was wondering about their importance and how they relate to the Christian concept of angels and archangels.* (Answer on page 365)

Question number 12: *What is the Jewish belief and view on hell?* (Answer on page 367)

Question number 13: *What is the Jewish view on ghosts and spirits?* (Answer on page 368)

Question number 14: *How should I respond when someone tells me that the Holocaust happened because the Jewish victims were not practicing Judaism correctly or sincerely and that the Holocaust was a punishment from God?* (Answer on page 370)

Question number 15: *What does the Torah or the Jewish traditions teach about forgiveness? Can there ever be forgiveness for what happened in the Holocaust? Can there ever be forgiveness for those German soldiers who ran the concentration camps?* (Answer on page 371)

Question number 16: *I have always heard that Jews don't believe in cremation for it destroys the soul that is to come to life upon the death of the body. My question is what do Jews believe happened to the souls of those who died in the crematoriums during the Holocaust?* (Answer on page 372)

Chapter 17: God (Twelve Questions)

Question number 1: Where did God come from? In Habakkuk 3:3, it states, "God came from Teman, and the Holy One from mount Paran." What information can you give me concerning Teman? Paran? (Answer on page 375)

Question number 2: Do you think G-d cares how we worship him? Does G-d care whether we worship Allah or Christ or even Buddha or Vishnu? It seems to me that G-d should only care whether you are a good person and that you don't harm others while going along your way. What do you think? (Answer on page 376)

Question number 3: Can you explain the meaning of the name Adonai? (Answer on page 377)

Question number 4: How does Judaism refer to God? Someone told me He is neither male nor female. Can you give scripture to prove He is male? (Answer on page 379)

Question number 5: Does God love the Jews? And if God does love us, how would we know? (Answer on page 380)

Question number 6: The Torah says to love God—but how is this possible? How do you create love for God who is so remote and unknowable if you don't truly feel this emotion? (Answer on page 381)

Question number 7: Does God have essence? Existence? Or both? Are they one and the same for God? How does this work? (Answer on page 381)

Question number 8: If God is real, why doesn't He talk to us like He did in the Torah? (Answer on page 382)

Question number 9: What happens if you break a promise to God? Is there a way to avoid divine punishment? (Answer on page 383)

Question number 10: Why does everyone talk about God's involvement—or rather, lack of involvement—in the Holocaust; but not much is said about His involvements in such past events as pogroms, expulsions, and the destruction of the Temple in Jerusalem? (Answer on page 384)

Question number 11: What are the top three arguments for proving God exists? (Answer on page 385)

Question number 12: I used to observe Jewish law strictly for many years. But lately, I feel that it is good enough that I am a good person. However, out of habit I continue to keep many Jewish laws. Does God really care whether I observe Shabbat or eat non-Kosher food? (Answer on page 385)

Glossary of Hebrew Words and Concepts

Most of the Hebrew words and concepts I use are explained in location throughout the book in the context of responding to individual e-mail questions. However, I removed multiple repetitious explanations so that it would not be too tedious to read the same descriptions over and over again. Therefore, I have relegated many of these clarifications to this glossary. These words and concepts represent a core Hebrew vocabulary of Jewish intellectual and historical discourse. These brief explanations are intended only for reference. Longer, more detailed explanations are located all over the book in the specific answers where I use them. If you cannot find my longer descriptions and this glossary leaves you wanting, I encourage you to turn to Google or Wikipedia.

Adon, Adonai—Hebrew for "Lord." The traditional appellation for God in the Hebrew Bible and in Hebrew prayers.

Aleynu—Hebrew for "It is incumbent upon us." The first word and title of one of the most significant concluding prayers of traditional Jewish worship services. The full sentence reads, "It is incumbent upon us to praise the Lord of all."

Aliyah (to Israel, to the Torah)—Hebrew for "to ascend." In a liturgical context, it refers to a synagogue honor where a congregant is called up to the reading table to make a blessing before and after the chanting of the Torah. In a political context, it refers to act of immigrating to the land of Israel.

Amidah—Hebrew for "standing." It is the name of a central prayer in the Jewish liturgy recited while standing.

Ark of the Covenant—An ancient portable chest described in the Hebrew Bible as the repository of the Torah and other holy objects.

Ashkenazic—The word "Ashkenaz" was the ancient Hebrew name for Europe. Therefore, Jews from Europe or descended from Jews who lived there are referred to as Ashkenazic Jews.

Atara, Atarot—Hebrew for "crown." In a liturgical context, it refers to an embroidered strip sewn into the collar of a Jewish prayer shawl (see Talit below).

Aufruf—Yiddish for "Get up!" It is the name of a traditional honor and minor advance celebration accorded to a bride and groom the Shabbat before their wedding in a synagogue.

Bar/Bat Mitzvah—Hebrew for "son/daughter of commandments." A ritual celebration for Jewish girls at the age of twelve and for boys at the age of thirteen to demonstrate their entrance into Jewish adulthood and their ritual obligations to observe the traditional Jewish commandments.

Baruch—Hebrew for "blessed." The first word of all traditional Hebrew blessings that continues, "Blessed are You, Lord our God."

Beit Din—Hebrew for "house of judgment." The name of a traditional rabbinic court consisting of at least three rabbis.

Birkat HaMazon—Hebrew for "blessing after food." This is the name of a set of prayers recited after a meal where bread was eaten.

Borchu—Hebrew for "Bless!" It is the first word of a prayer toward the beginning of worship services that invites the participants to begin the prayer service.

Brit Bat—Hebrew for "covenant of a daughter." A relatively modern ritual to welcome and initiate Jewish baby girls into the Jewish people similar to a Brit Milah.

Brit Milah—Hebrew for "covenant of circumcision." Jewish baby boys are ritually circumcised on the eighth day after birth.

B'sha'ah Tovah—Hebrew for "at a propitious time." The traditional greeting for a Jewish woman during her pregnancy that essentially means "May you give birth at the right time" in terms of the health of the baby.

B'sheret—Yiddish for "destiny." Usually used in the context of seeking and finding one's destined soul mate.

Chai—Hebrew for "life."

Challah—Hebrew for "bread." Refers to braided loaves of bread traditionally served on Shabbat and Jewish holidays.

Chazeret—Hebrew for "bitter herb." Refers to an alternate kind of bitter vegetable eaten during the Pesach Seder as a symbol of the bitterness of slavery that the Israelites experienced during their years of bondage in Egypt.

Chuppah—Hebrew for "canopy." Refers to the wedding canopy held over the bride and groom's head at a traditional Jewish wedding.

Derech Eretz—Hebrew for "way of the land." It is an idiom that is used to refer to proper or respectful manners and behavior.

Dina D'Malchuta Dina—Aramaic for "The law of the kingdom is the law." A principle from the Talmud quoted in many places to refer to the principle that no matter where a Jew lives, they are obliged to follow the laws of that country or kingdom.

Duchaning—An English word derived from the Yiddish word "Duchan," which means "stage" or "platform." This refers to the ceremony in some traditional synagogues when Kohahim, or descendants of the ancient priests, ascend to the stage in front of the synagogue to bless the congregation.

Edot HaMizrah—Hebrew for "Eastern tribes." Refers to Jews descended from North African or Middle Eastern countries.

Ehad—Hebrew for "One."

El Malei Rachamim—Hebrew for "God, full of compassion." It is the opening line and name of a prayer traditionally recited in the memory of the departed.

Elohim—Hebrew for "God."

Etrog—Hebrew for "citron." A species of fruit related to a lemon that is used to celebrate the Jewish holiday of Sukkot.

Gemara—Aramaic for "learning." Another name for the Talmud; a sixty-three-volume set of books containing the once-oral legal traditions of the ancient rabbis nearly two thousand years ago.

Get—Aramaic word for a divorce document that a man presents to his wife upon the dissolution of their marriage permitting her to remarry.

Get Zikui—A special kind of divorce document in which a rabbinic court presents a divorce document to a woman without her ex-husband's consent usually because he has proved to be recalcitrant or malicious.

Gilgul, Gilgulim—Hebrew for "cycle" or "cycles." Used in Jewish mysticism to refer to a Jewish understanding of reincarnation.

Gilui Arayot—Hebrew for "revealing nakedness." Refers to forbidden incestuous sexual relationships as described in the Torah, Leviticus chapter 18.

G'lilah—Hebrew for "wrapping." This is the name of a traditional synagogue honor where someone helps to roll and tie up the Torah scroll after it has been read during a worship service.

Golem—Hebrew for "raw material." The name of a mythical creature, a human being with superhuman strength brought to life through mystical means.

Haftarah—Hebrew for "exemption." Refers to selections in the Hebrew Bible usually from the prophets or Writings that are read on Shabbat and Jewish holidays after the Torah reading.

Hagbah—Hebrew for "raising." This is the name of a traditional synagogue honor where someone helps to lift and raise up the Torah scroll after it has been read during a worship service.

Haggadah—Hebrew for "telling." Refers to the pamphlet of prayers, blessings, and narratives that is recited on the eve of the Pesach Seders describing the exodus of the Israelites from Egypt.

Halachah, Halachic—Hebrew for "to go." Refers to Jewish law and called this because it is the way that a traditional religious Jew goes through life.

Hallel—Hebrew for "praise." Refers to Psalms 113 to 118 that are recited as a unit on Jewish holidays in worship services.

Halleluyah—Hebrew for "Praise God."

Hametz—Hebrew for "leaven." Refers to food with wheat, barley, rye, oats, and spelt with yeast that leavens the food. All foods made with these grains in addition to yeast are forbidden during the Jewish festival of Pesach.

HaMotzi—Hebrew for "the One who brings forth." This refers to the blessing recited before eating bread. The full blessing reads, "Praised are You, Lord our God, ruler of the universe, who brings forth bread from the ground."

Hanukkah—Hebrew for "dedication." The name for the eight-day festival commemorating the liberation of the ancient Temple in Jerusalem by the Maccabees in 163 BCE.

Hanukkiyah—The name of the nine-branched candelabra that is lit during the festival of Hanukkah.

Ha-Satan—Hebrew for "the adversary." Refers to the title of an angel that in rabbinic theology was the heavenly prosecutor of the Jewish people. This word evolved in Christianity into the name Satan.

Hasidim—Hebrew for "pious ones." Refers to various sects of Jews throughout Jewish history who adhered to rigorous standards of Jewish worship and observance of traditional Jewish laws.

Hatafat Dam Brit—Hebrew for "drawing blood of the covenant." Refers to a ritual that is performed on a male who is already circumcised when he converts to Judaism. It is a symbolic Brit Milah and entrance ritual into the Jewish people.

Havdalah—Hebrew for "separation." Refers to a short ritual and series of blessings performed on Saturday night after dark to bid farewell to the peace of Shabbat and welcoming a return to the regular workweek.

Heksher—Hebrew for "Kosher certified." Refers to various symbols printed on food labels attesting that the food has been guaranteed Kosher by a Jewish religious certifying agency.

Hesed—Hebrew for "kindness."

Hevra Kadisha—Aramaic for "Holy Society." Refers to a group of Jews, both men and women, who perform certain cleansing rituals to prepare the bodies of the departed for traditional Jewish burial.

Hezkat—Hebrew for "under the status of." A term that is used in the Jewish dietary laws of Kashrut to refer to whether a dish or utensil has been used with either dairy or meat foods.

Hol HaMoed—Hebrew for "weekdays of the holiday." Refers to the intermediate days of the Jewish holidays of Sukkot and Pesach that are partly ordinary workdays and partly semiholiday days in the middle of these two multiday Jewish holidays.

Hoshanah Rabbah—Hebrew for the "the great Hoshanah." This is the name of the seventh and final day of Sukkot when special rituals are performed while praying for rain.

Hoshanot—Hebrew for "save us" prayers. These are the names of specific prayers recited each day of the Jewish holiday of Sukkot that call upon God to "save us" by sending rain to sustain crops.

Kabbalah—Hebrew for "that which is received." Refers to Jewish mysticism or special knowledge that has been passed down from generation to generation.

Kaddish—Hebrew for "holy." This is a noun and the name of specific prayers that appear in various formats in traditional Jewish worship services.

Kadosh—Hebrew for "holy." This is an adjective.

Karaites—An English word derived from a Hebrew word that means "the scripture readers." It is the name of an offshoot of Judaism from the ninth century. These Jews rejected rabbinic Judaism and followed only what they read in the scriptures of the Hebrew Bible.

Kasher—Hebrew for "to make Kosher." Refers to various cleansing practices to prepare dishes and utensils to be used in a Kosher kitchen.

Kashrut—Hebrew for "Kosher laws." Refers to the entire corpus of laws and rituals surrounding the dietary practices of traditional Judaism.

Kedushah—Hebrew for "holy." Refers to a specific prayer in traditional Jewish worship services.

Ketubah—Hebrew for "written document." Refers specifically to a Jewish wedding contract.

Kiddush—Hebrew for "sanctification." Refers to the special blessings recited over wine or grape juice on the eve and afternoons of Shabbat and Jewish holidays.

Kiddush HaShem—Hebrew for "sanctification of the name." This is the Hebrew term for Jewish martyrdom.

Kipah, Yarmulke—Hebrew for "head covering." This is the name of the skullcap worn by traditional Jewish males. In Yiddish, it is called a Yarmulke.

Kitniyot—Hebrew for "legumes." In Jewish dietary laws, it refers to a category of foods eaten by some ethnic Jewish groups during the Jewish holiday of Pesach and not by others.

Klei Rishon, Sheni, Shelishi—Hebrew for "first, second, third vessel." In the Jewish system of dietary laws, it refers to any series of plates or dishes that food is placed on in succession.

Kohen, Kohanim—Hebrew for "priest" and "priests." Refers to the ancient biblical caste that officiated at animal sacrifices.

Kol Nidrei—Aramaic for "all vows." Refers to a solemn set of prayer and the evening worship services on the eve of the Jewish holiday of Yom Kippur.

Kosher—Hebrew for "fit" or "acceptable." Refers to food that is deemed acceptable to be eaten by religious observant Jews.

Ladino—The name of a Jewish dialect that is a combination of Hebrew and Spanish. It evolved and was spoken by Jews who lived for centuries in Spain.

Lag B'Omer—Hebrew for "the thirty-third day of the sheaves." This is the name of a minor holiday that falls in the forty-nine-day period connecting the Jewish holidays of Pesach and Shavuot.

Lamed-vavnik—Hebrew for "one of the thirty-six." Refers to an ancient Jewish tradition that in any given generation, there only thirty-six truly, thoroughly righteous people.

Lashon HaRah—Hebrew for "evil tongue." Refers to the traditional Jewish laws governing and limiting malicious speech about others.

Levite—An English word derived from the Hebrew word "Levi." This refers to a member of the ancient tribe of the Levites who were entrusted with certain tasks to maintain the ritual of animal sacrifice.

Lulav—Hebrew for "palm branch." This is one of the four traditional plant species used to celebrate the Jewish holiday of Sukkot. It also refers to an aggregate of palm, willow, and myrtle branches all bound together and waved at certain points in Jewish prayer during Sukkot celebrations.

Ma'ariv—Hebrew for "evening." Refers to the daily evening Jewish prayer service.

Maccabees—The English name of the ancient family of warrior priests who fought a war against the Syrian Greeks to preserve the right for Jews to practice traditional Judaism.

Maftir—Hebrew for "the one who exempts." Refers to someone given the ritual synagogue honor of reading selections in the Hebrew Bible usually from the Prophets or Writings that are read on Shabbat and Jewish holidays after the Torah reading.

Malach—Hebrew for "messenger." This is the traditional Hebrew title of an angel in Judaism.

Maror—Hebrew for "bitter." Refers to a bitter vegetable, usually horseradish, that is eaten during the Pesach Seder as a symbol of the bitterness of slavery that the Israelites experienced during their years of bondage in Egypt.

Mashiach—Hebrew for "the anointed one." This is the Hebrew word for "the Messiah."

Matzah, Matzot—Hebrew word for the unleavened bread that is eaten during the eight-day Jewish holiday of Pesach and is a symbol of both Egyptian slavery and freedom.

Mazal Tov—Hebrew for "a good constellation." This is the traditional celebratory phrase offered when someone experiences good fortune or a joyous life cycle event. It essential means "congratulations."

Menorah—Hebrew for "candelabra." Refers to the ancient seven-branched lampstand that was lit each night in the ancient Temple. It is also erroneously used to refer to a Hanukkiyah, the nine-branched candelabra used to celebrate Hanukkah.

Mezuzah—Hebrew for "doorpost." Refers to a small decorative covering protecting a small sheet of parchment with a selection from the Torah written on it that is affixed to the sides of doorways in a traditional Jewish home.

Midrash—Hebrew for "explanation." Refers to creative, imaginative stories and folktales told by the rabbis in ancient times to fill in gaps in the biblical narrative or add interesting details.

Mikvah—Hebrew name for the ritual bath of waters from natural sources described in the Hebrew Bible and used up to this day for ritually cleansing immersions for both men and women.

Mincha—Hebrew for "meal offering." This is the name of the daily afternoon worship service.

Minyon—Hebrew for "counting" or "quorum." Refers to the minimum number of ten adult Jews (males in traditional Jewish communities) necessary to be present before reciting certain prayers.

Mishnah—Hebrew for "repetition." This is the name of the first classical book of rabbinic legal thought composed nearly two thousand years ago. It forms the core of modern rabbinic legal interpretation.

Mishneh Torah—Hebrew for "Second Torah." This is the name of a series of volumes on Jewish law written by Rabbi Moses Maimonides nearly one thousand years ago.

Mitzvah—Hebrew for "commandment." Erroneously and frequently mistranslated as "good deed."

Modim—Hebrew for "We thank." Name of a particular prayer in a section called the Amidah.

Mohel—Hebrew for "circumcisor." The title of someone trained in the medical ritual of religious circumcision.

Musaf—Hebrew for "addition." Refers to a section of prayers that are added to daily worship services only on the Shabbat and Jewish holidays.

Musar—Hebrew for "that which is passed along." This is the name of a large body of Jewish ethical and moral literature and laws that were written and sparked a social movement in Jewish life over two hundred years ago.

Pareve—Yiddish for "neutral." Used to describe certain foods that are neither dairy nor meat in the Jewish dietary system of Kashrut.

Pesach—Hebrew for the Jewish holiday of "Pesach."

Pikuah Nefesh—Hebrew for "saving a life."

Rosh HaShanah—Hebrew for "head of the year." The Jewish High Holiday that celebrates a new calendar year.

Rosh Hodesh—Hebrew for "head of the month." Refers to the monthly semiholiday that celebrates the beginning of new moon and new Jewish month in the Jewish lunar calendar.

Sandek—Hebrew for "companion of child." Refers to someone given the honor of holding a baby boy during the ritual circumcision. In Yiddish, this person is referred to as the Kvatter and is similar to a godfather.

Sanhedrin—A Hebrew word derived from Greek that means "council." It refers to the ancient rabbinic court of seventy-one rabbis that governed Jewish life over two thousand years ago.

Seder—Hebrew for "order." This refers to the Pesach ritual and meal on the eve of the holiday.

Sefirat HaOmer—Hebrew for "counting the sheaves." This refers to the forty-nine-day period connecting the Jewish holidays of Pesach and Shavuot.

Sephardic—An English word derived from the Hebrew name for Spain. It refers to Jews who originally came from Spain.

Shabbat—Hebrew for "rest." This is the name for the seventh day of the week, or Saturday, the traditional day of rest in the Jewish calendar.

Shacharit—Hebrew for "dawn." This is the name of the daily morning Jewish worship service.

Shalom—Hebrew for "peace." It is also used as a greeting for hello and goodbye.

Shavuot—Hebrew for "weeks." This is the name of the first Jewish harvest festival in the early summer.

Shechitah—Hebrew for "slaughter." This refers to the specific Kosher method of slaughtering an animal so that it is ritually fit to be eaten by religious Jews.

Shedim—Hebrew for "spirits." Used to refer to mischievous demons in Jewish mysticism and popular folklore.

Shehecheyanu—Hebrew for "who has kept us alive." This is the name of a traditionally blessing recited on Jewish festivals and at major life cycle celebrations. The full text of the blessing reads, "Praised are You, Lord our God, ruler of the universe, who has kept us in life, sustained us, and brought us to this day."

Sheloshim—Hebrew for "thirty." Refers to a special period of mourning that lasts for thirty days following a funeral.

Shema—Hebrew for "Hear!" The first line of the most central declaration of Jewish beliefs in the liturgy. The full verse from Deuteronomy 6:4 reads, "Hear O Israel, the Lord is our God, the Lord is one."

Shemini Atzeret—Hebrew for "eighth day of gathering." This is the name of a Jewish holiday that falls on the eighth day following the first day of the Jewish festival of Sukkot.

Shemirah—Hebrew for "guarding." Refers to the honor and duty of remaining with the body of the departed from their death until burial so as not to leave the remains alone, neglected, or ignored.

Sheol—Hebrew for "the pit." Used in the Hebrew Bible to refer to the underworld and is similar to the Greek mythological term Hades, the abode of the dead.

Shevarim—Hebrew for "Brokayen." This is the name of a particular call or sound of the Shofar, or ram's horn, on Rosh HaShanah. It is a series of three short blasts on the Shofar.

Shir HaShirim—Hebrew for "the Song of Songs." This is the name of a book of love poetry in the Hebrew Bible.

Shiva—Hebrew for "seven." Refers to a special period of mourning that lasts for seven days following a funeral.

Shochet—Hebrew for "slaughterer" or "butcher." Someone who is trained and receives special Jewish licensing to perform the special method of Kosher slaughter.

Shofar—Hebrew for "horn." Usually made from the horn of a ram or an antelope and sounded on Rosh HaShanah, the Jewish New Year.

Shuckle—Yiddish derivation from a Hebrew word meaning "throw." Refers to the practice of swaying or rocking during Jewish prayer.

Shul—Yiddish for "school." Refers to a synagogue where religious school was held.

Shulchan Aruch—Hebrew for "a set table." This is the name of one of the most authoritative works of Jewish law written in 1567.

Siddur—Hebrew for "order." This is the generic name of a Jewish prayer book.

Simchat Torah—Hebrew for "rejoicing of the Torah." This is the name of a Jewish holiday in which the yearly liturgical cycle of reading the Torah is completed and resumes again with much celebration.

Sukkah—Hebrew for "shelter" or "hut." A temporary structure with a roof made of branches and leaves that is constructed for the Jewish holiday of Sukkot. Its primary purpose is to eat meals in it.

Sukkot—Hebrew for "booths" or "huts." The name of the Jewish holiday that celebrates the final harvest before the rainy season begins in fall.

Taharat HaMishpachah—Hebrew for "purity of the family." This is a euphemism for a series of laws and practices related to rituals associated with the menstrual cycle of a woman and the pattern of sexual relations with her husband.

Talit—Hebrew for "cloak." Refers to the ritual prayer shawl worn by adults over the age of twelve for girls and thirteen for boys. It is worn only by men in traditional Jewish communities.

Talmud—Hebrew for "learning." This is the name of a sixty-three-volume set of books containing the once-oral legal traditions of the ancient rabbis nearly two thousand years ago. Also called by its Aramaic name, the Gemara.

Tanach—A Hebrew word that refers to the Hebrew Bible. It has no meaning and is merely the acrostic of the initial letters of the three names of the internal divisions of the Hebrew Bible.

Techelet—Hebrew for "purple." Refers to a special color and dye concocted in ancient times to dye the fringes of the Talit or prayer shawl.

Tefillah—Hebrew for "prayer."

Tefillin—Hebrew for "phylacteries." These are leather boxes and straps containing parchment with certain sections of the Torah written on them. They are worn by men and boys over the age of thirteen in traditional Jewish communities every weekday during the daily morning prayer service.

Tekiah—Hebrew for "blast." This is the name of a particular call or sound of the Shofar, or ram's horn, on Rosh HaShanah. It is one blast on the Shofar.

Tekiah Gedolah—Hebrew for "the long blast." This is the name of a particular call or sound of the Shofar, or ram's horn, on Rosh HaShanah. It is one blast on the Shofar that is held as long as possible.

Teruah—Hebrew for "tremble." This is the name of a particular call or sound of the Shofar, or ram's horn, on Rosh HaShanah. It is a series of at least nine staccato blasts on the Shofar.

Teshuvah—Hebrew for "return." Refers to the spiritual process of repentance that is traditionally practiced prior to and during the Jewish High Holiday prayer season in the fall.

Tisha B'Av—Hebrew for "the ninth day of Av." This is the date that both the ancient First and Second Temple in Jerusalem were destroyed. The First Temple was destroyed by the Babylonians in 586 BCE, and the Second Temple was destroyed by the Romans in 70 CE.

Torah—Hebrew for "teaching." Refers to the scroll or book containing the Five Books of Moses.

Treyfe—A Yiddish word derived from a Hebrew word meaning "torn." It generically refers to any kind of food that is not Kosher.

Tzadikim—Hebrew for "righteous ones."

Tzar Ba'alei Hayyim—Hebrew for "pain of a living creature." This refers to a value in Judaism to avoid harming or causing pain to any living creature.

Tzedakah—Hebrew for "justice." Refers to the practice of giving charity.

Tzitzit—Hebrew for "fringes." Refers to the special tassels affixed to the corners of a Talit, the Jewish prayer shawl.

Tzniut—Hebrew for "modesty." Refers to practices governing appropriate, chaste behavior between the sexes.

V'Ahavta—Hebrew for "and you shall love." This is the first word following the Shema and refers to an entire paragraph recited in the liturgy detailing the obligations of Jews to love God.

Yahrzeit—Yiddish for "year time." Refers to the anniversary of the date of the passing of a loved one.

Yetzer HaRah—Hebrew for "the evil inclination."

Yiddish—The name of a Jewish dialect that is a combination of Hebrew and medieval German. It evolved and was spoken by Jews who lived for centuries in Germany.

Yod, Heh, Vav, Hey—The four Hebrew letters comprising the holy and mystical name of God that is used in the Torah but never pronounced as written. It is read as Adonai.

Yom Kippur—Hebrew for "day of atonement." The Jewish High Holiday on which Jews fast and pray for divine atonement for their sins.

Yom Tov—Hebrew for "a good, festive day." This is the generic name for certain Jewish holidays.

Yotzer—Hebrew for "creator." Refers to a prayer in the morning liturgy.

Zemirot—Hebrew for "songs." Refers specifically to Jewish song sung on and about Shabbat.

Index

Made in United States
North Haven, CT
11 May 2024

52404413R00259